Letter & Spirit 2 (2006)

The Authority of Mystery:
The Word of God and the People of God

Letter & Spirit 2 (2006): 3–6

CONTRIBUTORS

∾: Avery Cardinal Dulles, S. J. :∾

Cardinal Dulles is the Laurence J. McGinley Professor of Religion and Society at Fordham University, a position he has held since 1988. Cardinal Dulles served on the faculty of The Catholic University of America from 1974 to 1988. He has been a visiting professor at numerous institutions, including The Gregorian University (Rome), Campion Hall (Oxford University), the University of Notre Dame, the Catholic University at Leuven, and Yale University. The author of over 750 articles on theological topics, Cardinal Dulles has published twenty-two books including: *Models of the Church* (1974), *The Craft of Theology: From Symbol to System* (1992), *The Assurance of Things Hoped For: A Theology of Christian Faith* (1994), *The Splendor of Faith: The Theological Vision of Pope John Paul II* (1999; revised in 2003 for the twenty-fifth anniversary of the papal election), and *The History of Apologetics* (1971; rev. ed., 2005). The fiftieth anniversary edition of his book, *A Testimonial to Grace*, the account of his conversion to Catholicism, was published in 1996, with a new afterword. Past president of both the Catholic Theological Society of America and the American Theological Society, Cardinal Dulles has also served on the International Theological Commission. He was created a Cardinal of the Catholic Church in Rome on February 21, 2001 by Pope John Paul II, the first American-born theologian who is not a bishop to receive this honor.

∾: Mary Healy :∾

Mary Healy is adjunct professor of Scripture at the Institute for Pastoral Theology at Ave Maria University in Naples, Florida, and at the Notre Dame Graduate School of Christendom College in Alexandria, Virginia. She earned a doctorate in biblical theology at the Gregorian University in Rome. She is the author of *Men and Women Are from Eden: A Study Guide to John Paul II's Theology of the Body* (Servant Books, 2005), and co-editor of *Behind the Text: History and Biblical Interpretation* (Zondervan, 2003) and *Out of Egypt: Biblical Theology and Biblical Interpretation* (Zondervan, 2004).

∾: John C. Cavadini :∾

John Cavadini is the chair of the theology department at the University of Notre Dame and director of the university's Institute for Church Life. He is a scholar of patristic and early medieval theology, with special interests in the theology of Augustine and in the history of biblical exegesis. He is the author of two books, *Miracles in Christian and Jewish Antiquity: Imagining the Truth* (University of Notre Dame, 1999); and *The Last Christology of the West: Adoptionism in Spain and Gaul, 785–820*, (University of Pennsylvania, 1993). He is the editor of *Gregory the Great: A Symposium* (University of Notre Dame, 1996), and associate editor of *Augustine Through the Ages: An Encyclopedia* (Eerdmans, 1999). His articles have appeared in such journals as *Theological Studies, Religious Studies Review, Traditio, Augustinian Studies*, and *American Benedictine Review.*

❧ David Fagerberg ☙

David Fagerberg is associate professor of theology at the University of Notre Dame. Working in the areas of liturgical and sacramental theology, his writings have explored how the Church's *lex credendi* (law of belief) is grounded in the Church's *lex orandi* (law of prayer). His books include: *What is Liturgical Theology?* (Pueblo, 1992), *The Size of Chesterton's Catholicism* (University of Notre Dame, 1998), and *Theologia Prima: What is Liturgical Theology?* (Hillenbrand, 2003). His articles have appeared in such journals as *Worship, America, New Blackfriars, Pro Ecclesia, Diakonia, Touchstone*, and *Antiphon*. He serves on the editorial board of the *Chesterton Review*, and is a contributing editor to *Gilbert! A Magazine of Chesterton.*

❧ Brant Pitre ☙

Brant Pitre is the Donum Dei Professor of Word and Sacrament at Our Lady of Holy Cross College in New Orleans, Louisiana. He received his Ph.D. in Theology from the University of Notre Dame, where he specialized in the study of the New Testament and ancient Judaism and graduated with highest honors. He is the author of *Jesus, the Tribulation, and the End of the Exile*, which focuses on the eschatology of Jesus as the key to the origin of the doctrine of the atonement (Baker Academic, 2005).

❧ Scott W. Hahn ☙

Scott Hahn, founder of the St. Paul Center for Biblical Theology, holds the Pope Benedict XVI Chair of Biblical Theology and Liturgical Proclamation at St. Vincent Seminary in Latrobe, Pennsylvania, and is professor of Scripture and theology at Franciscan University of Steubenville, Ohio. He has held the Pio Cardinal Laghi Chair for Visiting Professors in Scripture and Theology at the Pontifical College Josephinum in Columbus, Ohio, and has served as adjunct faculty at the Pontifical University of the Holy Cross and the Pontifical University, Regina Apostolorum, both in Rome. Hahn is the general editor of the *Ignatius Study Bible* and is author or editor of more than 20 books, including *Letter and Spirit: From Written Text to Living Word in the Liturgy* (Doubleday, 2005);

Understanding the Scriptures (Midwest Theological Forum, 2005), and *The Lamb's Supper: The Mass as Heaven on Earth* (Doubleday, 1999).

~: James Swetnam, S. J. :~

James Swetnam entered the Missouri Province of the Society of Jesus in 1945 and was ordained a priest in 1958. He holds degrees in classical languages, philosophy, theology and Scripture. His doctoral degree is from the University of Oxford. Since 1962 he has been a scholar of the Pontifical Biblical Institute in Rome, where he has held numerous posts, including vice rector and dean of the biblical faculty. He has also served in an editorial capacity for several academic journals, including: *Orientalia, Analecta Orientalia,* and *Biblica.* His area of specialization is the Epistle to the Hebrews. Swetnam is the author of *Jesus and Isaac: A Study of the Epistle to the Hebrews in the Light of the Aqedah* (Analecta Biblica, 1981) and *An Introduction to the Study of New Testament Greek* (Pontifical Biblical Institute, 1992).

~: Pablo T. Gadenz :~

Pablo Gadenz is a priest of the Diocese of Trenton, New Jersey, ordained in 1996. A graduate of Princeton University and Columbia University, he prepared for the priesthood at Franciscan University of Steubenville and St. Charles Borromeo Seminary, Philadelphia. He received his Licentiate in Sacred Scripture (S.S.L.) from the Pontifical Biblical Institute in 2005, and is currently a doctoral candidate in biblical theology (S.T.D.) at the Pontifical Gregorian University. His doctoral dissertation will focus on Pauline ecclesiology in Romans 9–11.

~: Guigo II :~

Guigo II (d. 1188) was a Carthusian monk and prior and a spiritual writer. His *Scala Claustralium,* which we publish here in a new translation, was in the past attributed to St. Augustine and St. Bernard, and influenced generations of spiritual writers, most notably St. John of the Cross.

~: Jeremy Holmes :~

Jeremy Holmes is assistant professor of theology at Ave Maria University in Naples, Florida. He earned a master's degree in theology from the International Theological Institute in Gaming, Austria in 2001, and is currently finishing his doctoral dissertation in theology with a specialization in New Testament at Marquette University in Milwaukee, Wisconsin. He has published articles in *Nova et Vetera, The Downside Review, Homiletic and Pastoral Review,* and elsewhere.

❧ Hans Urs von Balthasar ☙

Hans Urs von Balthasar (1905–1988) was one of the great Catholic theologians of the twentieth century. The centerpiece of Balthasar's theological project was a trilogy of multi-volume works: *The Glory of the Lord: A Theological Aesthetics* (7 vols.); *Theo-Drama: Theological Dramatic Theory* (3 vols.); and *Theo-Logic: Theological Theory* (3 vols.). He is also the author of *Explorations in Theology* (4 vols.). He was one of the co-founders of the Catholic journal *Communio*. In 1988, he was appointed by Pope John Paul II to be a Cardinal of the Church, but two days before his elevation, while preparing to celebrate morning Mass, he died. His "The Word, Scripture, and Tradition," is reprinted here with permission of Ignatius Press.

❧ Jean Cardinal Daniélou, S. J. ☙

Jean Cardinal Daniélou, S. J. (1905–1974) was a theologian and patristics scholar who became a key figure in the theological renewal movement known as the *Ressourcement.*

His classic work is the groundbreaking, *The Bible and the Liturgy* (1956). Among his dozens of books are: *Holy Pagans of the Old Testament* (1957); *The Dove and the Darkness in Ancient Byzantine Mysticism* (1957); *The Lord of History: Reflections on the Inner Meaning of History* (1958); *The Presence of God* (1958); *From Shadows to Reality: Studies in the Biblical Typology of the Fathers* (1960); *Primitive Christian Symbols* (1964); and *The Theology of Jewish Christianity* (1964).

❧ Christoph Cardinal Schönborn, O. P. ☙

Cardinal Schönborn (b. 1945), is archbishop of Vienna, and a dogmatic theologian. From 1987–1992, he served as general editor of *The Catechism of the Catholic Church*, the first comprehensive statement of Catholic belief and practice to be published in more than 450 years. He is the author of several books, including: *God's Human Face: The Christ Icon* (Ignatius, 1994); *From Death to Life: The Christian Journey* (Ignatius, 1995); and *Loving the Church: Spiritual Exercises Preached in the Presence of Pope John Paul II* (Ignatius, 1998). "The Kingdom of God and the Heavenly-Earthly Church" is reprinted here with permission of Ignatius Press.

Letter & Spirit 2 (2006): 7–16

INTRODUCTION

The authority of mystery is a phrase used by Pope Benedict XVI to describe the power of the divine liturgy.[1] For us, it is also a good way to understand the broader relationship between the Word of God and the people of God, the Church. The Church is born under the authority of mystery. It bears witness to the mystery of the incarnation, the mystery of the Word of God made flesh. This Word, Jesus Christ, discloses the face of the Father and the mystery of his will, the plan of the mystery hidden for all ages.[2]

The mystery of God is his loving plan of salvation—to share his life with his people by means of a new covenant, making them divine sons and daughters in his Church, the kingdom of God. This mystery forms the content of the canon of sacred Scripture. The Bible narrates the slow unfolding of the mystery in history, culminating in the paschal mystery—the passion, death, and resurrection of Christ. This mystery is remembered and celebrated through scriptural words and signs in the Church's liturgy. And this mystery is the source and purpose of the sacred *mysteries*—the sacraments of the Church, by which God establishes and renews his covenant with each believer.

Understood in this light, there is an indivisible unity between the Word of God and the people of God. The Word—made flesh in Christ and spoken in the human language of Scripture—cannot be known or understood apart from the Church. All the interlocking organs of the Church's tradition—apostolic succession, the canon, the rule of faith, the teaching office, the divine liturgy and sacraments—serve the Church's mission of protecting and proclaiming the Word.

Beginning as long ago as the Reformation and the Enlightenment, this original understanding ceased to be normative. Indeed, the separation, if not the outright opposition of Word and Church, is a philosophical presupposition of the modern age. This has resulted in no end of trouble. Cut off from the Church, there is no necessary relationship between Christ and the words we read in the Bible or hear in the liturgy. What Christ really said—if he really said anything at all—and what his words might mean for us today, are subjects of endless debates and theorizing, carried out in pulpits, classrooms, and academic journals.

This is why biblical interpretation is such a flashpoint in our time. How to read the Bible is, at bottom, a question about the identity of Jesus. Is he Jesus of Nazareth only, or is he also the Christ, the Son of the living God? Did he have a divine mission to reveal the mystery of God, or was he only a man like others?

---

1 Joseph Cardinal Ratzinger, *A New Song for the Lord: Faith in Christ and Liturgy Today*, trans. Martha M. Matesich (New York: Crossroad Herder, 1997 [German ed.: 1995]), 32.

2 Compare Eph. 1:9; 3:9; Col. 1:26.

Does he remain among us in sacrament and liturgy? Is he the way, the truth, and the life, the same yesterday, today, and forever?

The modern crisis of christological belief, rooted in the crisis of biblical interpretation, has been the keen concern of Pope Benedict, even long before his now-famous Erasmus Lecture of 1988.[3] It is telling—and unprecedented—that he spoke at length about biblical interpretation in the most symbolic of his papal inaugural statements, his homily upon assuming the chair of the Bishop of Rome.[4]

The life's work of the former Joseph Cardinal Ratzinger casts a long shadow over this issue of *Letter & Spirit*. This is not out of any superficial fealty to the new pontiff; it is, rather, in recognition that his scholarship represents some of the deepest and finest thinking available on this, the most fundamental of the issues facing the Church today.

Dei Verbum *and the "Hermeneutics of Continuity"*

In "Vatican II and the Interpretation of Sacred Scripture," **Cardinal Avery Dulles, S. J.**, begins with a long and pointed quote from Benedict, concerning the misrepresentations of *Dei Verbum*, the Second Vatican Council's document on divine revelation. In the post-conciliar period, prominent voices claimed that *Dei Verbum*, in sharp departure from Church tradition, had exalted historical-critical methods as the privileged means for studying and interpreting the sacred page. Such claims, of course, mark a serious distortion, as Cardinal Dulles demonstrates in his careful, illuminating rereading of the document.

The Council actually taught that Scripture must be understood in light of its unique nature, as both a human document and the inspired Word of God. This led the Council to posit three "norms" (which the *Catechism* would later call "criteria") for interpretation—the unity of Scripture, the tradition of the Church, and the analogy of faith, that is, the consistency of the scriptural witness with the Church's dogmas, doctrines, and liturgy. In this, the Council was in faithful conformity to the traditional teaching and practice of the Church. As Cardinal Dulles points out, *Dei Verbum* affirms and clarifies the essential unity of Scripture and the Church's tradition, especially its magisterium.

Although Cardinal Dulles does not here allude to his earlier work, we see his article as part of his larger contribution to the dialogue on Vatican II's reception and implementation. Cardinal Dulles advances in these pages a reading of *Dei Verbum* according to a "hermeneutic of continuity," that presumes the "diachronic solidarity of the Council with the whole Catholic tradition."[5] He focuses attention

---

3   Joseph Cardinal Ratzinger, *Biblical Interpretation in Crisis: On the Question of the Foundations and Approaches of Exegesis Today*, The 1988 Erasmus Lecture (Rockford, IL: Rockford Institute, 1988).

4   Pope Benedict XVI, Homily, Mass of Possession of the Chair of the Bishop of Rome (May 7, 2005), in *L'Osservatore Romano*, Weekly Edition in English (May 11, 2005), 3.

5   Avery Cardinal Dulles, "Vatican II: Myth and Reality," *America* 188 (February 24, 2003). This

on the copious references the Council fathers make to the teachings of the popes, the Church fathers, and earlier Church councils. As he has argued elsewhere, appealing to Cardinal John Henry Newman's *Essay on the Development of Christian Doctrine* (1854), those who abandon a hermeneutic of continuity "usually end up by abandoning the supernatural claims of Christianity—a phenomenon that is no less common today than it was in Newman's day."[6]

We would assert that this is precisely what happened in the post-conciliar period. Those who interpreted *Dei Verbum* as being in "discontinuity" with the great tradition of the Church, wound up abandoning the supernatural claims the Church makes for Scripture; as a result, the Bible was reduced to the status of an ancient literary text. Cardinal Dulles' essay restores the understanding of *Dei Verbum* in light of the Church's constant tradition. And on the grounds of that tradition, he seeks to unite theologians and scholars in the service of the Church's mission—of opening up the Word of God, so that the people of God might be "more responsive to the voice of the Holy Spirit and more faithful to the Lord."

Mary Healy is also interested in the reception of *Dei Verbum*, especially its stipulation that Scripture must be "read and interpreted according to the same Spirit by whom it was written." Her article, "Inspiration and Incarnation: The Christological Analogy and the Hermeneutics of Faith," highlights an important legacy of the patristic interpretive tradition, as it is developed in *Dei Verbum*.

The "christological analogy" is the comparison drawn—by Church fathers such as Chrysostom, Origen, and Ignatius—between the incarnation of Christ as "true God and true man," and the Scriptures as God's Word spoken in human language. In Christ, God came among us like a man in all things except sin; in Scripture he gives us his word in language that is like our own in all things except for error. As the incarnation marked a loving "condescension" of God in order to reveal himself, so too the giving of Scripture is an act of loving solicitude.

Writing in the late patristic era, Archbishop Rabanus Maurus of Mainz expressed this analogy beautifully: "As in these last times the Word of God, clothed with flesh taken from the Virgin Mary, has come forth into this world, though there is one element in him that is visible and another that is hidden, even so, when the Word of God is set before men by prophet or legislator, it is set forth in befitting garments, the letter being visible like the flesh of Christ, while the spiritual meaning is hidden within, like his divinity."[7]

---

too, is a critical concern of Pope Benedict, who has spoken of the need for a correct "hermeneutic" with which to read the Council's documents, contrasting a "hermeneutic of discontinuity and rupture" with a "'hermeneutic of reform,' of renewal in continuity." See his Address to the Roman Curia Offering them his Christmas Greetings (December 22, 2005), at www.vatican.va/ holy_father/benedict_xvi/ speeches/2005 /december/documents/hf ben_xvi_spe_20051222_ roman-curia_en.html.

6   Dulles, "Vatican II: Substantive Teaching," *America* 188 (March 31, 2003).

7   Quoted in J. H. Crehan, "The Analogy Between *Verbum Dei Incarnatum* and *Verbum Dei*

This analogy, as Healy points out, is taught by Pope Pius XII and taken up in similar language by *Dei Verbum*. With appeals to papal teachings, Thomas Aquinas, and the *Catechism*, Healy unpacks the analogy's interpretive implications for exegetes and theologians. She brings to light a crucial and often overlooked dimension of the Church's teaching—the "sacramentality" of Scripture, its power not only to signify the words and events of salvation history, but also to make these saving events real and present in our lives.

A *"Scriptural Catechesis"*

John C. Cavadini, in "The Use of Scripture in the Catechism of the Catholic Church," takes up the question of Vatican II's pastoral and catechetical realization. He compares the *Roman Catechism*, issued after the Council of Trent (1545–1563), with the current *Catechism*, the first to be published since Trent, and expressly "prepared following the Second Vatican Ecumenical Council."[8] He sees considerable development since Trent, reflecting Vatican II's integration of historical and literary scholarship with a recovery of the "scriptural rhetoric of the fathers."

Cavadini acknowledges that his particular subject is also of great importance to Pope Benedict, whom he quotes as saying, "there has never been until now a catechism so thoroughly formed by the Bible." Cavadini's attentive reading of the *Catechism's* christological catechesis provides rich confirmation of this. The *Catechism* itself interprets Scripture according to *Dei Verbum's* three norms—the unity of Scripture, the tradition of the Church, and the rule of faith. And Cavadini finds ample evidence that the *Catechism* quietly deploys the findings of historical and literary research to clarify teachings and to advance its "evangelical" goals.

Scripture is not simply used as a "proof-text" for Catholic dogmas and doctrines, Cavadini argues; rather, Scripture forms the very substance of the teaching. What we have in the *Catechism* is "a *scriptural catechesis*, a catechesis carried out not simply with the support of the words of Scripture, but *in* the words of Scripture . . . so that it almost becomes a kind of glossed scriptural proclamation."

Cavadini notes the ease with which the *Catechism* weaves "scriptural tapestries" and the natural "interplay between the threads drawn from Scripture and threads drawn from traditional sources—the creeds, the writings of the fathers, and the teachings of the Church councils."

In its scriptural catechesis and its weaving of Scripture and tradition, the *Catechism* recovers the ancient mystagogical methods of the Church fathers; these methods were likewise shaped by the letter and spirit of sacred Scripture. The

---

Scriptum in the Fathers," *Journal of Theological Studies*, New Series 6 (1955), 87–90, at 87.

8   See Pope John Paul II, *Fidei Depositum*, Apostolic Constitution on the Publication of *The Catechism of the Catholic Church*, Prepared Following the Second Vatican Ecumenical Council (October 11, 1992), in *The Catechism of the Catholic Church*, 2d. ed. (Vatican City: Libreria Editrice Vaticana, 1997), 1–6. The *Catechism* is dated, symbolically, on "the thirtieth anniversary of the Second Vatican Ecumenical Council."

Catechism, then, is a model for what Cavadini calls a "critically aware scriptural catechesis," that draws its content from the Word of God, as it is transmitted in Scripture, the liturgy, and the teachings of the Church.

The Liturgical Mystery and the Mystery of God

David Fagerberg taps into the rich treasures of eastern Catholicism and Orthodoxy to show how Scripture, liturgy, and theology are inseparably united in the task of revealing the mystery of God and transacting the "deification" of the believer.

His "Theologia Prima: The Liturgical Mystery and the Mystery of God" reminds us that Scripture was never meant to be understood solely as a narrative history of God's dealings with humanity. As the Word of God, it is meant to be read in the Spirit, as a divine solicitation, an invitation for the hearer of the Word to enter into that history and to be filled with the divine life that reveals itself through that history.

This is the intention, also, of the divine liturgy. Fagerberg argues that, through the sacraments, everything in God's creation, "is destined for liturgical fulfillment." In the Church's divine liturgy, the trinitarian mystery of God is made present in our midst in the communion of heaven and earth. Speaking in the language of the saints and mystics, Fagerberg wants us to see liturgy as "our trysting place with God," the site where the believer embraces "God, our divine lover." Theology, too, he argues, is at the service of the mystery of God. It is intended to be conceived as a spiritual science, nourished by prayer, in which the grammar learned in the Scriptures and the liturgy comes to reshape our souls in the image of Christ.

In his contribution, "The Lord's Prayer and the New Exodus," **Brant Pitre** offers an important new interpretation of this prayer, which is the centerpiece of Christian identity and devotion, and has been called the summary of the Gospel.

It has long been observed that Christian prayer is scriptural prayer. That means that, especially through the psalms and the prayer Jesus taught his disciples, we respond to the Word of God using the very words of God given in Scripture. Pitre shows us how the Lord's Prayer, itself, is composed of an intricate layer of biblical quotes and allusions to the events and promises of Old Testament salvation history. Building on the exegetical intuitions of such scholars as Raymond Brown and N. T. Wright, Pitre argues that Jesus is teaching his followers to pray for "the fulfillment of *all* God's covenant promises to Israel and the world."

He explores the deep Old Testament language and imagery underlying nearly every word and phrase in Jesus' prayer. He demonstrates that the prayer reflects a "typological" understanding of Scripture—the belief, found already in the Old Testament, that God's actions in the future will parallel and echo his actions in the past. Specifically, Jesus is appealing to the prophets' hopes for a "new Exodus"—a restoration of Israel from exile, and a reestablishment of the kingdom of David. This new Exodus would follow the same pattern as the original Exodus of the Israelites from Egypt. In this important article, Pitre has prepared the way for a profound spiritual exegesis of the Lord's Prayer, one that would establish the Exodus as a paradigm and pattern for the spiritual life of the believer.

The Full Flowering of Biblical Renewal

This issue of *Letter & Spirit* comes full circle in the contribution of **Scott W. Hahn**, "The Authority of Mystery: The Biblical Theology of Benedict XVI." This is the first major study of Benedict's thought since he assumed his papal office and it is the first to emphasize how the content and method of Scripture determines the content and method of Benedict's theology.

"There is no other Catholic theologian in the last century, if ever, whose theology is as highly developed and integrated in explicitly biblical terms," Hahn concludes. "We would be hard pressed to find another thinker who has so allowed sacred Scripture to shape and direct his theologizing." Hahn argues that Benedict's command of the biblical texts, the patristic interpretive tradition, and the findings of historical and literary scholarship, represents the full flowering of the Catholic biblical renewal promoted by the popes and culminating in *Dei Verbum*.

We are also proud to present in this issue two fine exegetical studies. **James Swetnam, S. J.**, argues that the final chapter of Hebrews can only be understood fully in light of the early Christian liturgy. He demonstrates a close connection between the "sacrifice of praise" (Heb. 13:15) and the ancient Israelites' *todah* sacrifice, which offered thanks to God for saving the believer from some life-threatening circumstance. Swetnam also detects a liturgical pattern in this chapter that is remarkably similar to the canon or Eucharistic Prayer found in the Latin Rite Mass. Swetnam's study deepens our understanding of the Jewish roots of the Eucharist and, at the same time, has important implications for further study of the structure and development of Christian liturgy. **Pablo Gadenz** offers a detailed literary analysis of Romans 9:24–29, a complex and difficult passage that has ramifications for understanding the New Testament teaching on the salvation of Israel and the nations. Gadenz sheds new light on this critical text by examining Paul's use of Jewish exegetical techniques, and his nuanced appeal to Old Testament prophetic texts.

"A New Spiritual Springtime"

In our *Tradition & Traditions* section, we retrieve four seminal works that we feel can help contribute to the restoration and renewal of the ancient way of reading the

Bible from "the heart of the Church." This renewal is one of the primary purposes of this journal.

Pope Benedict has asserted that a return to the ancient practice of *lectio divina* would bring to the Church "a new spiritual springtime."[9] With this in mind, we specially commissioned, for this volume, the first new scholarly translation in twenty-five years of the *Scala Claustralium* by **Guigo II** (d. 1188), the classic text on *lectio divina*.

Lectio divina is the prayerful study of Scripture that brings about an intimate dialogue between the reader and the divine Word that speaks in its pages; or, as Guigio says, *lectio divina* aims to have the reader feed on the bread of the Word, to "taste the joys of eternal sweetness." In this excellent new translation, **Jeremy Holmes** highlights the rich biblical substratum of Guigo's language and argument. *Lectio divina* is shown to be a means of entering into Christ's thoughts and sentiments, as they are communicated in the words of sacred Scripture.[10]

Hans Urs von Balthasar (1905–1988) provides a deep, penetrating meditation on the relation of Scripture and tradition.[11] Scripture is the written Word that testifies to the Word made flesh. Balthasar sees that "Scripture is itself tradition," a gift of the Bridegroom to his bride, the Church. Christ comes among us as the "compendium of all the Scriptures," and he delivers himself, as Eucharist and Scripture, to the Church until the end of the age. By these means of the Church's living tradition, Christ remains "present in the Church as the one, ever active, unchanging life."

The contribution from **Jean Cardinal Daniélou, S. J.** (1905–1974) is perhaps the finest treatment of the relationship between biblical salvation history and the sacramental liturgy.[12] Through a detailed study of the patristic legacy, especially the use of typology in ancient mystagogical, or baptismal instructions, Cardinal Daniélou shows how the sacraments continue and actualize, in the era of the Church, God's saving acts recorded in the Old and New Testaments. As a result,

---

9   Address to the Participants in the International Congress Organized to Commemorate the Fortieth Anniversary of the Dogmatic Constitution on Divine Revelation "Dei Verbum" (September 16, 2005), in *L'Osservatore Romano*, Weekly Edition in English (September 21, 2005), 7.

10 Pope Benedict XVI, Reflection on the Opening of the Eleventh Ordinary General Assembly of the Synod of Bishops (October, 3, 2005), in *L'Osservatore Romano*, Weekly Edition in English (October 12, 2005), 7.

11 The selection published in this volume is excerpted from Balthasar, *The Word Made Flesh*, Explorations in Theology 1 (San Francisco: Ignatius, 1989 [first German edition, 1960]), 11-26. Used by permission of Ignatius Press.

12 This text, which dates to the 1950s, is widely available on the internet and elsewhere. However, for this issue, we have corrected several errors in the original text and added several explanatory footnotes to increase its value to contemporary students of Scripture and the liturgy.

the Church's "liturgy is the mistress of exegesis," because in the liturgy the true purpose and meaning of the Scriptures is brought to light and made actual in the lives of believers.

Finally, **Christoph Cardinal Schönborn, O.P.** (b. 1945) retrieves the patristic notion of the relation between the Church and the biblical kingdom of God.[13] This essay is a classic rereading of *Lumen Gentium*, Vatican II's constitution on the Church, in which Cardinal Schönborn retracts positions he once held. He demonstrates that the Council, in continuity with the Church fathers, believed "the pilgrim Church is nothing other than the 'kingdom of heaven' that Christ has established on earth."

This understanding of the Church as the kingdom of God was another casualty of the "hermeneutic of discontinuity." As Cardinal Schönborn shows, distortions of the Council's teaching resulted in the secularization and politicization of Jesus' message about the kingdom. As such, Cardinal Schönborn's study makes an important contribution, not only to ecclesiology, but to christology and eschatology, as well.

Awe, Obedience, and the Antichrist

The contributions to this volume of *Letter & Spirit* testify to the authority of mystery that lies at the heart of the relationship between the Bible and the Church, the Word of God and the people of God.

This relationship is glimpsed in the beautiful painting on our cover, made in the 1430s by the Blessed Fra Angelico, the great early-Renaissance painter.[14] He depicts St. Peter preaching the Word in a crowded marketplace, while the disciple Mark, in the lower left, faithfully writes it down. In the San Marco Convent in Florence, Italy, this painting is found at the base of an altarpiece adorning the Linaiuoli tabernacle. The main image in the altarpiece is of the Virgin presenting the infant Jesus, who stands in her lap in a gesture of blessing. Alongside the image of Peter and Mark in the altarpiece are two further paintings—one of the Magi adoring the infant Jesus, and the other portraying Mark's martyrdom.

Taken together, in this altarpiece we see the Church born under the authority of mystery. The apostles considered themselves servants of the Word, entrusted by Christ himself with a "divine office . . . to make the Word of God fully known, the mystery hidden for ages and generations" (Col. 1:25–26). They were ministers

---

13   The selection published in this volume is excerpted from Schönborn, *From Death to Life: The Christian Journey*, trans. Brian McNeil, (San Francisco: Ignatius, 1995 [1988]), 65–98. Used by permission of Ignatius Press.

14   "Saint Peter Dictating the Gospel of Saint Mark," from the predella of the Linaiuoli altarpiece, 1433–1435. Photo Credit: Nicolo Orsi Battaglini / Art Resource, NY. Used by permission.

of the Word of truth, the gospel of salvation, and stewards of the mysteries, the sacraments.

As we see in Acts and the New Testament epistles, the apostles spoke and wrote under the influence of God, with words taught by the Spirit. They proclaimed the mystery of the incarnation—of the virgin birth of the Word made flesh. He was the newborn king of the Jews, whom the Magi discovered prophesied in the Scriptures of God's chosen people. The apostles proclaimed Christ to be the fulfillment of those Scriptures, and they wrote that all might believe and have life in him; that like the Magi, every knee might bow to his name and every tongue confess that he is Lord.

The apostles protected the Word from false interpretations, again under the guidance of the Spirit. And by the true Word they proclaimed, the sick were healed, the dead raised, and lives transformed. Those in the marketplace and the synagogue who accepted the Word—not as the word of men but as what it really is, the Word of God—received new life in the sacraments. As Peter said to the newly baptized, "You have been born anew . . . through the living and abiding Word of God" (1 Pet. 2:23). This was the reason the Word was made flesh and dwelt among us. This was the reason the Word of Scripture was given to us by servants like Peter, Mark, and Paul—all of whom shed their blood to hand this Word on to us.

The Word continues to abide in the Church, which remains his servant, under the authority of mystery. That the mystery of God has authority, implies that the Church must be obedient to the Word and allow the Word to direct and shape its life. Obedience to the Word, in turn, must characterize the attitude of the scholar and the student of the sacred page, as it must every believer. The contributions to this volume would suggest that authentic understanding and interpretation only emerges in discipleship—through giving oneself in trusting obedience to the Word and the mystery the Word unveils. "We have to enter into a relationship of awe and obedience toward the Bible," Pope Benedict has written.[15] The crisis in biblical interpretation, and the resulting crisis of faith in Christ, comes because many scholars and teachers have lost this sense of awe and obedience.

Benedict sometimes points ironically to a prophetic story by Vladimir Soloviev about the coming of the Antichrist. In the tale, the Antichrist's work in theology and exegesis earns him an honorary doctorate from the renowned University of Tübingen.[16] It is sobering, too, to recall that one of the devil's temptations of Christ, turns on the devil's interpretation of a messianic psalm.[17]

---

15 *A New Song for the Lord*, 50.

16 See, for instance, Joseph Ratzinger, *On the Way to Jesus Christ*, trans. Michael Miller (San Francisco: Ignatius, 2005 [German ed.: 2004]), 91–92.

17 See Matt. 4:5–7.

The separation of the Word of God from the people of God results, almost as a matter of course, in the denial that Jesus is the Christ, whose coming is the object and hope of the Scriptures. Benedict suggests that this may be the original New Testament meaning of the term, noting that John "calls those who deny that Jesus is the Christ, *antichrists* . . . to be against Jesus as the Christ, to deny him the predicate 'Christ.'"[18]

The crisis in biblical interpretation manifests itself today as a crisis in the image and identity of Jesus Christ. It is, then, a crisis of truth—the truth about history and the destiny of each individual. Thus, it becomes urgent to restore the authority of mystery, the indissoluble unity of the Word of God and the people of God. We hope that this volume, in which we take up the intellectual and spiritual project of Pope Benedict, might make some small contribution to the cause.

---

18   *A New Song for the Lord*, 30. See 1 John 2:18,22; 4:3.

Letter & Spirit 2 (2006): 17–26

Vatican II on the Interpretation of Scripture

~: Avery Cardinal Dulles, S.J. :~

Fordham University

In the Catholic understanding, the Bible is not self-sufficient. It does not determine its own contents, vouch for its own inspiration, or interpret itself. The Bible is God's gift to the Church, which is its custodian and authoritative interpreter. The Councils of Trent and Vatican I clearly made these points. In summary fashion Vatican II declared that tradition, Scripture, and the magisterium "are so linked and joined together that one cannot stand without the others" (*Dei Verbum* 10). In other words, nothing is believed on the authority of tradition alone, Scripture alone, or the magisterium alone.

Vatican II dealt with Scripture most explicitly in the third chapter of its Constitution on Divine Revelation, *Dei Verbum*, especially in section 12. *Dei Verbum* 12, which lays down the principles for the Catholic interpretation of Scripture, is of great importance but has often been misunderstood. In 1988, then Cardinal Joseph Ratzinger wrote:

> I am personally persuaded that a careful reading of the *entire* text of *Dei Verbum* can yield the essential elements for a synthesis between historical method and theological hermeneutics, but this connection is not easily comprehensible. For this reason the post-conciliar reception has practically dismissed the theological parts of its statements as a concession to the past and has taken the text simply as an unqualified official confirmation of the historical-critical method. One may reckon such a one-sided reception of the Council in the profit column of the ledger insofar as the confessional differences between Catholic and Protestant exegesis virtually disappeared after the Council. The debit aspect of this event consists in the fact that by now the breach between exegesis and dogma in the Catholic realm has become total and that even for Catholics Scripture has become a word from the past, which every individual tries to transport into the present in his own way, without being able to put all too much trust in the raft on which he sets himself. Faith then sinks into a kind of philosophy of life that the individual seeks to distill from the Bible as best he can. Dogma, no longer able to rest on the ground of Scripture, loses its solidity. The Bible,

which has cut itself loose from dogma, has become a document
of the past and itself belongs to the past.[1]

Misleading Translations

The idea that the Council exalted historical-critical exegesis as the supreme norm
of faith would be a serious misinterpretation but, as we shall see, this mistake is
supported by some of the most popular translations of the text.

The first paragraph of *Dei Verbum* 12 makes a crucial distinction between
two types of exegesis, which are discussed separately in the subsequent paragraphs.
The interpreter, it states, must seek to discover what the sacred writers really meant
and what it pleased God to manifest by their words. In Latin: *"attente investigare
debet, quid hagiographi reapse significare intenderint et eorum verbis manifestare Deo
placuerit."*

Several of the English translations are misleading. The translation edited
by Austin Flannery[2] reads: The interpreter . . . "should carefully search out the
meaning which the sacred writers really had in mind, *that meaning* which God has
thought well to manifest through the medium of their words." This translation
drops out the word "et" ("and") in the Latin original and substitutes "that meaning,"
implying that God cannot manifest anything more than what the sacred writers
had in mind.

The translation edited by Norman Tanner is even more misleading.[3] It reads:
The interpreter must "carefully investigate what meaning the biblical writers had in
mind; *that will also be* what God chose to manifest by means of their words." The
words "that will also be" have no counterpart in the Latin text.

The translation edited by Walter Abbott and Joseph Gallagher[4] renders the
Latin correctly: "The interpreter . . . should carefully investigate what meaning
the sacred writers really intended and what God chose to manifest through their
words" (*Dei Verbum* 12). That sentence taken alone, however, does not settle the
question whether or not the two meanings are identical.

The history of the text shows that an earlier draft of the initial sentence had
mentioned only the meaning intended by the inspired writer and that the second
clause was added in order to make provision for a genuinely theological exegesis.

---

1   Joseph Ratzinger, ed., *Schriftauslegung im Widerstreit*. Quaestiones Disputatae 117 (Freiburg:
     Herder, 1989), 20–21. This passage is lacking in the English version of Ratzinger's essay in
     Richard John Neuhaus, ed., *Biblical Interpretation in Crisis* (Grand Rapids, MI: Eerdmans,
     1989).

2   Austin P. Flannery, ed., *Documents of Vatican II* (Grand Rapids, MI: Eerdmans, 1975).

3   Norman P. Tanner, ed., *Decrees of the Ecumenical Councils*, 2 vols. (Washington, DC:
     Georgetown University, 1990).

4   Walter M. Abbott, Joseph Gallagher, eds., *The Documents of Vatican II With Notes and
     Comments by Catholic, Protestant, and Orthodox Authorities* (New York: Guild Press, 1966).

Both forms, or stages, of exegesis are necessary. The *Relatio* (official explanation), dated July 3, 1964, states that a merely rational hermeneutic is insufficient.[5] The *Relationes* of July 3 and November 20, 1964 both state that the Council does not wish to settle the disputed question of the *"sensus plenior."*[6] But as we shall see, the teaching of *Dei Verbum* 12 is not easy to reconcile with the idea that Scripture has no meaning beyond what the sacred writers intended to communicate.

The opening sentence just discussed introduces the next two paragraphs—the second and third of *Dei Verbum* 12. Paragraph 2 deals with what the biblical writers intended, whereas paragraph 3, beginning with *Sed* ("but" or "moreover") deals with further divinely intended meanings.[7] The Council here builds on the distinction made in Pius XII's biblical encyclical *Divino Afflante Spiritu* between "the 'literal meaning' of the words intended and expressed by the sacred writer" and further spiritual meanings "intended and ordained by God."[8]

Historical and Literary Study

Before going into the secondary meanings, we may briefly examine what the Council has to say about the first level. Literary and historical study, as understood in *Divino Afflante Spiritu* and *Dei Verbum*, aims to disclose what the sacred writers wanted to say and did say. Presupposing sufficient study of the languages and historical circumstances, technical exegesis requires various kinds of criticism: *textual criticism* to determine the best reading, *source criticism* to determine literary dependency on earlier texts, *literary criticism* to ascertain the rhetorical and stylistic devices, *form criticism* to determine the literary form and the life-situation in which

---

5   *Acta synodalia sacrosancti concilii oecumenici Vaticani II* (Vatican City: Libreria Editrice Vaticana, 1970-1980), Series III, vol. 3, 69–109, at 92. (Henceforth this work will be abbreviated AS III/3, or similarly.)

6   AS III/3, 93 and IV/1, 359.

7   Here again, the Abbott edition is superior to the Flannery and Tanner editions. Abbott, following the Latin text officially promulgated on November 18, 1965, divides §12 into three paragraphs. For some reason, the other two translations divide the second paragraph into two, thus obscuring the structure of the text. See the official version in AS IV/6, 579–609, at 602–3.

8   Pope Pius XII, *Divino Afflante Spiritu*, Encyclical Letter Promoting Biblical Studies, 16, in *The Scripture Documents: An Anthology of Official Catholic Teachings*, ed. Dean P. Béchard, S.J. (Collegville, MN: Liturgical Press, 2002), 115–139, at 126: "For what was said and done in the Old Testament was ordained and disposed by God with such consummate wisdom, that things in the past prefigured in a spiritual way those that were to come under the new dispensation of grace. Wherefore, the exegete, just as he must search out and expound the 'literal' meaning of the words intended and expressed by the sacred writer, so also must he do likewise for the spiritual sense, provided it is clearly intended by God. For God alone could have known this spiritual meaning and have revealed it to us. Now our divine Savior himself points out to us and teaches us this same sense in the holy Gospel. The apostles also, following the example of the Master, profess it in their spoken and written words."

the text was composed, and *redaction criticism* to determine how the final author or redactor has recast the materials to suit his own pastoral and literary concerns.[9]

Dei Verbum 12, following *Divino Afflante Spiritu*, attaches great importance to literary criticism and form criticism. "Attention must be paid," it declares, "to the customary and characteristic styles of perceiving, speaking, and narrating that prevailed at the time." For an application of these principles one may consult *Dei Verbum* 19. Discussing the historicity of the Gospels, the Council here points out that the original reports of the "words and deeds of Jesus" underwent developments at the stage of oral transmission because the message was reformulated to address the varying situations of the churches. Then the sacred writers, composing the four Gospels, made further adaptations in view of their literary and theological perspectives.

To be correctly understood, *Dei Verbum* 19 should be read in light of the Pontifical Biblical Commission's 1964 instruction on the historical truth of the Gospels,[10] which is referenced in a footnote. This instruction treated the three stages of the Gospel tradition more amply. While holding that all four Gospels are genuinely historical, the Council alerts us to the fact that they are not, and are not intended to be, verbatim reports or descriptions such as might come from an audiovisual tape. The Gospels are proclamatory documents, written from faith to faith. The Council's broad understanding of historicity thus obviates fundamentalist oversimplification.

In its treatment of the first level of meaning the Council gives great freedom to exegetes to follow the rules of their craft. It does not indicate that they are to treat the inspired text differently than if it were a profane text. But in its final paragraph, *Dei Verbum* 12 takes up what may be called theological or spiritual exegesis. To bring the meaning of the sacred text correctly to light, exegetes must, it states, take into account that the Bible is the inspired Word of God.[11]

---

9   These and similar modes of criticism are explained in standard introductions, e.g., Joseph A. Fitzmyer, *Scripture, the Soul of Theology* (New York: Paulist, 1994), 19–24. For applications of such methods to the New Testament see Raymond F. Collins, *Introduction to the New Testament* (New York: Doubleday, 1983). Both these authors, however, neglect the teaching of *Dei Verbum* 12 on the spiritual meanings of Scripture.

10   Pontifical Biblical Commission, *Sancta Mater Ecclesia*, Instruction on the Historical Truth of the Gospels (April 21, 1964), in *The Scripture Documents*, 227–235.

11   Meanings that go beyond what the sacred writer might have grasped are sometimes called "more than literal," the term used by Raymond Brown in the *New Jerome Biblical Commentary*. See Raymond E. Brown and Sandra M. Schneiders, "Hermeneutics," in *New Jerome Biblical Commentary*, ed. Raymond E. Brown, Joseph A. Fitzmyer and Roland E. Murphy, 2 vols. (Englewood Cliffs, NJ: Prentice Hall, 1990), 1146–65, at 1153. But Brown's terminology is not universally accepted because it seems to suggest that *Dei Verbum* is here departing from the meaning of the words (the literal meaning). Classical theology, represented by Thomas Aquinas, held that since God was the author of Holy Scripture, and since God understood much more by the words than the sacred writer, the literal words of Scripture could also convey more than one "spiritual" sense, although these additional spiritual senses were based upon and presupposed

Reading in the Spirit

This third paragraph of *Dei Verbum* 11 begins by remarking that since the biblical text is inspired, as previously stated in *Dei Verbum* 11, it must be read in the same Spirit by whom it was written. To enter into the meaning of the inspired text, one must rely on the Holy Spirit and on faith, which is a gift of the Spirit. The text does not at this point go into meanings that the Spirit may manifest to individual readers for their spiritual profit, a topic that will be touched upon in chapter 6 of *Dei Verbum*.[12] Many of the Church fathers, including Origen, Jerome, and Gregory the Great, taught that there must be a spiritual affinity between the interpreter and the text. Medieval monasticism built up a rich tradition of *lectio divina*, a practice that is still fruitfully pursued in our day under the name of spiritual exegesis. In chapter 3, however, the constitution is concerned with objective meanings, which are intended for all readers and for the Church at large. The concern is not with free charismatic exegesis, but with a theological style of interpretation that is, in its own way, scientific.

Dei Verbum 12 proposes three norms: the unity of Scripture, the tradition of the Church, and analogy of faith. Each of the three requires some comment. In speaking of the unity of Scripture, *Dei Verbum* treats the Bible in its entirety as a single book, inspired by God. It is God's Word inasmuch as God has made himself its author by way of inspiration. Because inspiration affects all the authors as a group, it is not a merely individual phenomenon. It guarantees that the Bible, taken as a whole, provides a solid foundation on which the Church may found her beliefs, her moral system, and her life of worship.[13]

In its treatment of inspiration and inerrancy, *Dei Verbum* 11 had manifested the Council's recognition of the human input of the sacred writers, with all their personal and cultural limitations. Vatican II speaks freely, not only of God as the "author" of Scripture, but also of the human authors as "true authors."[14] In its treat-

---

the literal sense. "The author of Holy Scripture is God, in whose power it is to signify his meaning, not by words only (as man also can do) but also by things themselves. . . . Therefore the first signification whereby words signify things belongs to the first sense, the historical or literal. That signification whereby things signified by words have themselves also a signification is called the spiritual sense, which is based on the literal, and presupposes it." *Summa Theologica*, Pt. I, Q. 1, Art. 10 (New York: Benzinger Brothers, 1947). Some modern exegetes prefer to speak instead of a secondary literal meaning or a "fuller meaning" (*sensus plenior*). See Paul Synave and Pierre Benoit, *Prophecy and Inspiration* (New York: Desclee, 1961), 149–51.

12 Chapter 6 of *Dei Verbum* refers at several points to the spiritual profit that individual readers may derive from a prayerful reading of Holy Scripture.

13 To speak of the unity of Scripture is to invoke what has often been called canonical criticism—a method that has been fruitfully practiced and persuasively advocated by Brevard S. Childs of Yale University, among others. See Childs' *Introduction to the Old Testament as Scripture* (Philadelphia: Fortress Press, 1979).

14 "Therefore, since everything asserted by the inspired authors or sacred writers should be regarded as asserted by the Holy Spirit, it follows that we must acknowledge the books of Scripture as teaching firmly, faithfully, and without error the truth that God wished to be recorded in

ment of inerrancy in *Dei Verbum* 11, the Council refrained from stating explicitly that every declarative sentence in the Bible is true. It says instead that the books of Scripture (in the plural) teach firmly and without error the truth that God wanted to commit to them for the sake of our salvation.

The unity of the Bible, founded upon its divine inspiration, is of decisive importance for a Christian reading of the Old Testament. In chapter 4, the Council states that the books of the Old Testament "acquire and show forth their full meaning (*significationem completam*) in the New Testament . . . and in turn shed light on it and explain it" (*Dei Verbum* 16). The passage from prophecy to fulfillment and from type to antitype is a staple of classical Christian exegesis.[15]

With reference to the second norm for theological exegesis, our text declares: "The living tradition of the Church must be taken into account" (*Dei Verbum* 12). Earlier on, in *Dei Verbum* 8, the Council had stated that tradition is necessary for the full canon to be known and for the sacred writings to be more profoundly understood. Then in *Dei Verbum* 10, as we have seen, it affirmed that Scripture and tradition together constitute one sacred deposit. It is incorrect, therefore, to speak as though Scripture alone, examined with the tools of historical-critical scholarship, could adequately deliver the Word of God. *Dei Verbum* insists on the necessity of the "living tradition," and of the magisterium as its locus, for discerning the divinely intended meaning. An example would be the Catholic practice of attributing the words of Jesus to Peter as addressed likewise to the successors of Peter, the popes (Matt. 16:18–19).

The third criterion is called in Latin "*analogia fidei.*" The Abbott edition translates this term rather felicitously as "the harmony that exists between elements of the faith." We know *a priori* that God could not inspire a meaning that was contrary to the truth embodied in the dogmas of the Church. The dogmas serve as negative norms for excluding misinterpretations. More than this, they throw positive light on what the Holy Spirit was intimating in various biblical texts. The dogma of the Immaculate Conception, for example, permits a deeper understanding of the expression "full of grace" (translating the rare Greek word, *kécharitôménê*) applied to Mary by the angel at the Annunciation.

The regressive movement from the developed dogma to the biblical source is an approved method, sanctioned by Pius XII in *Humani Generis*.[16] But in that encyclical, the Pope cautioned that theology becomes sterile if it neglects to renew

---

the sacred writings for the sake of our salvation." *Dei Verbum* 11. *Dei Verbum* thus seems to attribute inerrancy to the Bible as a whole, more than to individual passages, which must then be read in the context of the whole.

15 See Manlio Simonetti, *Biblical Interpretation in the Early Church: An Historical Introduction to Patristic Exegesis* (London: T & T Clark, 1994); Henri de Lubac, *Scripture in the Tradition* (New York: Crossroad, 2000).

16 Pope Pius XII, *Humani Generis*, Encyclical Letter on Certain False Opinions Threatening to Undermine the Foundations of Catholic Faith, 21, in *The Scripture Documents*, 140–146.

itself from the sacred sources of Scripture and tradition. Thus Alois Cardinal Grillmeier correctly remarks in his commentary on *Dei Verbum*:

> There is here a reciprocal relationship: the living tradition of the Church helps us through its growing understanding of faith to a deeper understanding of Scripture. An ever renewed rereading of Scripture, however, must become the soul of theology and of the whole of tradition, so that everything can be led back to the unified fullness of the beginning, where everything was still "together."[17]

The 'Living Tradition' and Theological Interpretation

The authors of *Dei Verbum* may not have wished to settle the disputed question of the *sensus plenior*, or the fuller literal meaning. But the paragraph on theological interpretation clearly favors some such sense. It would be hard to believe that the Old Testament authors could have grasped all the deeper signification of their words, as those would later be disclosed by the New Testament writers, Catholic tradition, and Catholic dogma—sources to which these inspired authors had no access.

The paragraph on theological interpretation concludes with the statement: "All that has been said about the way of interpreting Scripture is subject finally to the judgment of the Church, which carries out the commission and ministry of guarding and interpreting the word of God" (*Dei Verbum*, 12). The magisterium does not enter only at the end of the process, but is involved at every stage. Speaking of the relation between exegetes and the magisterium, *Dei Verbum* 23 teaches that "Catholic exegetes . . . using appropriate means, should devote their energies, under the watchful care of the sacred magisterium, to an exploration and exposition of the divine writings."

The magisterium is intimately involved in each of the three phases of theological exegesis. It plays an essential role in drawing up and defining the canon of Scripture, and thus in establishing the Bible as a unit. Tradition, as described in chapter 2, is inseparable from the magisterium, because it develops under the vigilance of the pastors and "through the preaching of those who have received through episcopal succession the sure gift of truth" ("*charisma veritatis certum*"—*Dei Verbum*, 8). The analogy of faith, finally, depends on the magisterium which alone has authority to proclaim articles of faith and dogmas.

Dei Verbum 10 states that only the magisterium, speaking in the name of Jesus Christ, can give an "authentic" interpretation. The Latin word "*authentica*" in

---

17 Alois Grillmeier, "The Divine Inspiration and the Interpretation of Sacred Scripture," in *Commentary on the Documents of Vatican II*, ed. Herbert Vorgrimler, 5 vols. (New York: Herder and Herder, 1969), 3:199–246, at 245.

this context does not mean genuine but authoritative, that is to say, issued by persons having a mandate to teach in the name of the Lord. Authentic interpretations of this kind are rather rare, but they have considerable weight, especially when they are infallible.

Doctrinal definitions are normally based on a convergent use of many biblical texts, prayerfully read in the tradition of the worshiping Church under the light of the Holy Spirit. There are relatively few cases in which the Church has defined the meaning of particular texts, as the Council of Trent, for example, did in its decree on original sin and in its canons on the institution of various sacraments. Even in these cases, as Raymond Brown points out, the Church "was not settling a historical question about what was in the mind of the author when he wrote the text, but a religious question about the implications of Scripture for the life of the faithful."[18] The theological meaning is a true meaning of the text, and cannot be dismissed as "eisegesis," as if the Church were reading something into the text that was not really there.

A difficulty against the teaching of *Dei Verbum* and earlier councils on the authority of the magisterium is that some interpretations of Scripture have, in the course of time, proven to be unsound. One might think in this connection of some arguments used to condemn Galileo's heliocentrism, or certain aspects of the earlier decrees of the Pontifical Biblical Commission.

In the Galileo case, we can now see that the original papal commission failed to make necessary distinctions between the "salutary meaning" of Scripture and scientific assumptions derived by interpreters of the sacred writers.[19] The Vatican's Congregation for the Doctrine of the Faith, in its Instruction, *Donum Veritatis* ("On the Ecclesial Vocation of the Theologian"), conceded that some pastoral decisions ("prudential judgments") by the magisterium "might not be free from all deficiencies."[20] At his press conference presenting this instruction, then

---

18 Brown and Schneiders, "Hermeneutics," 1163.

19 In various papers and addresses dealing with the Galileo case, Pope John Paul II pointed out the gradual process by which the Church learned to distinguish between matters of faith and the scientific systems of a given age. See, for instance, "A Papal Address on the Church and Science," *Origins* 13 (June 2, 1983): 49–52.

20 Congregation for the Doctrine of the Faith, *Donum Veritatis*, Instruction on the Ecclesial Vocation of the Theologian (May 24, 1990), 24, in *L'Osservatore Romano*, Weekly Edition in English (July 2, 1990), 1. The document, however, adds this cautionary note: "Bishops and their advisors have not always taken into immediate consideration every aspect or the entire complexity of a question. But it would be contrary to the truth, if, proceeding from some particular cases, one were to conclude that the Church's magisterium can be habitually mistaken in its prudential judgments, or that it does not enjoy divine assistance in the integral exercise of its mission . . . [S]ome judgments of the magisterium could be justified at the time in which they were made, because while the pronouncements contained true assertions and others which were not sure, both types were inextricably connected. Only time has permitted discernment and, after deeper study, the attainment of true doctrinal progress."

Congregation prefect Cardinal Ratzinger referred specifically to some decisions of the Biblical Commission:

> As warning calls against rash and superficial accommodations, they remain perfectly legitimate: no less a personage than J. B. Metz, for example, has remarked that the anti-Modernist decisions of the Church performed the great service of saving her from foundering in the bourgeois-liberal world. Nevertheless, with respect to particular aspects of their content, they were superseded after having fulfilled their pastoral function in the situation of the time.[21]

Insofar as they dealt with technical, non-doctrinal matters, such as the dating and composition of particular books, the decrees were not truly infallible judgments, requiring interior assent.[22] The vigilance of the Catholic magisterium at the time helped to protect the faithful against the conclusions of radical historical-critical exegesis. Tensions, however, still can and do arise, particularly in cases when technical exegetes and hierarchical officials go beyond their specific spheres of competence and responsibility.

The same is true of the relationship between critical exegesis and theological exegesis. Although tensions sometimes arise, the normal relationship, foreseen in *Dei Verbum*, is one of cooperation. Biblical scholars who are trained in historical-critical methods are perhaps best equipped to establish what the words meant to the inspired authors and their contemporaries. But canonical criticism, tradition-criticism, and dogmatic exegesis, all of which take account of the sacred character of the text, are needed to confirm, qualify, or enrich the findings of historical-critical scholarship so that the Church may be effectively guided by the Word of God.

The hierarchical magisterium, in its authentic pronouncements, does not speak as an independent authority but as an organ of the living tradition, informed by the inspired biblical texts. Its voice is not a foreign one, because it is by nature a servant of the Word of God. Thanks to the charisms given through episcopal ordination and appointment to office, the hierarchy can speak with deeper insight, but it will be best able to do so if it takes advantage of the prior work of biblical scholars, one of whose functions is to prepare for the judgment of the magisterium.

---

21   For the text of the Cardinal's press conference, see Joseph Cardinal Ratzinger, *The Nature and Mission of Theology* (San Francisco: Ignatius, 1995), 101–107. For a fuller discussion of the matter see Ratzinger's address on the hundredth anniversary of the Pontifical Biblical Commission, "100 Years: The Magisterium and Exegesis," *Theology Digest* 51 (Spring 2004): 3–8.

22   In Ratzinger's words, they were "a signal for pastoral prudence, a sort of provisional policy. Their kernel remains valid, but the particulars determined by circumstances can stand in need of correction." *Nature and Mission of Theology*, 106.

As Pope Benedict XVI has stated, the work of scholars is a considerable help in understanding the living process in which the Scriptures developed,

> Yet science alone cannot provide us with a definitive and binding interpretation.... A greater mandate is necessary for this, which cannot derive from human abilities alone. The voice of the living Church is essential for this, of the Church entrusted until the end of time to Peter and the college of the apostles.[23]

Scripture scholars, theologians, and pastors should not go their separate ways, ignoring or fearing one another. Catholic exegetes should be skilled in theological as well as in philological interpretation. Dogmatic theologians and pastors should be familiar with the findings of technical exegesis.

When biblical scholars, theologians, and pastoral leaders work in harmony, the Church as a whole advances in its penetration of the Word of God. The mutual openness and cooperation of all who are concerned with the meaning of the Bible can help the entire people of God to be more responsive to the voice of the Holy Spirit and more faithful to its Lord.

---

23   Pope Benedict XVI, Homily at Mass of Possession of the Chair of the Bishop of Rome (May 7, 2005), in *Origins* 35 (May 26, 2005): 26–28, at 28.

Letter & Spirit 2 (2006): 27–41

Inspiration and Incarnation:
The Christological Analogy and the Hermeneutics of Faith

❧ Mary Healy ❧

Ave Maria University

> *Holy Scripture, in its way of speaking, transcends all other sciences*
> *because in one and the same statement while it narrates an event it*
> *sets forth the mystery.*—St. Gregory the Great[1]

The Second Vatican Council stipulated as a principle for authentic biblical inter-pretation that "holy Scripture must be read and interpreted according to the same Spirit by whom it was written."[2] This axiom, originally formulated by St. Jerome, has been a constant in the Catholic tradition.[3] But what exactly does it mean? What implications does it have for biblical exegesis today? And in what sense can this ancient notion of "interpretation in the Spirit" guide contemporary biblical scholars seeking to employ the most rigorously objective, critical methodologies?

The lack of clarity or consensus regarding the meaning of the conciliar state-ment is illustrated by the widely divergent English translations. The edition avail-able on the Vatican website, for example, reads: "holy Scripture must be read and interpreted in the sacred spirit [sic] in which it was written."[4] Another standard edition of the Council's documents is even more imprecise: "sacred Scripture must be read and interpreted with its divine authorship in mind."[5] The *Catechism of the*

---

1 *Morals on the Book of Job*, 20, 1, quoted in Thomas Aquinas, *Summa Theologiae*, Pt. I, Q. 1, Art. 10 (New York: Benzinger Brothers, 1947).

2 Second Vatican Council, *Dei Verbum*, Dogmatic Constitution on Divine Revelation, (November 18, 1965), 12, in *The Documents of Vatican II*, ed. Walter M. Abbott (Piscataway, NJ: New Century, 1966), 120. The Latin text reads: "*Sacra Scriptura eodem Spiritu quo scripta est etiam legenda et interpretanda sit.*" This extremely important phrase was inserted in the document only at the end of the last session of the Council. See Ignace de la Potterie, "Il Concilio Vaticano II e la Bibbia," in *L'esegesi cristiana oggi*, eds. de la Potterie, et al. (Casale Monferrato: Piemme, 1991), 19–42.

3 *Dei Verbum* cites Pope Benedict XV, *Spiritus Paraclitus*, Encyclical Letter Commemorating the Fifteenth Centenary of the Death of St. Jerome (September 15, 1920), in *Enchiridion Biblicum: Documenti della Chiesa sulla Sacra Scrittura* [Documents of the Church Concerning Sacred Scripture] 2d. ed., ed. A. Filippi and E. Lora (Bologna: Dehoniane, 1993), 469; Jerome, *Commentary on Galatians* 5, 19–20, in *Patrologiae Cursus Completus. Series Latina*, ed. J.P. Migne (Paris: Garnier and J.P. Migne, 1844–1864), 26, 417A. Hereafter abbreviated *PL*.

4 See www.vatican.va/archive/hist_councils/ii_vatican_council/documents/vat-ii_const_ 19651118_ dei-verbum_en.html.

5 Austin Flannery, ed. *Vatican Council II: The Conciliar and Post Conciliar Documents*, rev. ed. (Northport, NY: Costello, 1988).

Catholic Church's quotation of the text reads, "holy Scripture must be read and interpreted in the light of the same Spirit by whom it was written."[6] Oddly enough, the most important document issued by the Pontifical Biblical Commission since the Council, *Interpretation of the Bible in the Church* (1993), never mentions this injunction from *Dei Verbum* 12.[7]

Despite the confusion and lack of attention, I would contend that "interpretation in the Spirit" expresses a principle of capital importance that, if properly applied, will help extricate biblical scholarship from the crisis in which it finds itself today.[8] My aim in this article is to reflect on the principle of "interpretation in the Spirit" and show how it points the way toward a renewed biblical hermeneutic for the twenty-first century.

God's "Condescension" and the Sacramentality of Scripture

Dei Verbum itself immediately provides three criteria for interpreting Scripture in the Spirit, which have been spelled out in slightly more detail in the *Catechism*. It specifies that attention must be paid, first, to the content and unity of the whole of Scripture (the canon); second, to the living tradition of the Church; and third, to the harmony that exists between elements of the faith (the analogy of faith). These criteria, though necessary, are not necessarily sufficient, and they do not yet give us a substantive description of what it means to interpret in the Spirit.

To find the theological premise that grounds the principle of interpretation in the Spirit, we must look in the immediately subsequent paragraph of *Dei Verbum*. There, in describing the divine condescension by which God deigns to speak to us in humanly understandable words, the Council fathers drew an analogy with Christ's incarnation:

> In Sacred Scripture, therefore, while the truth and holiness of God always remains intact, the marvelous "condescension" of eternal wisdom is clearly shown, "that we may learn the gentle kindness of God, which words cannot express, and how far he has gone in adapting his language with thoughtful concern for

---

6   *Catechism of the Catholic Church*, 2d. ed. (Vatican City: Libreria Editrice Vaticana, 1997), no. 111.

7   Pontifical Biblical Commission, *Interpretation of the Bible in the Church* (September 21, 1993), in *The Scripture Documents: An Anthology of Official Catholic Teachings*, ed. Dean P. Béchard, S.J. (Collegeville, MN: Liturgical Press, 2002), 244–315. The document does, however, allude to it in a reference to *Dei Verbum* 23 (*Interpretation*, III.B.3) and obliquely in its section on philosophical hermeneutics (II.A.2).

8   For an incisive diagnosis of this crisis, see Joseph Cardinal Ratzinger, "Biblical Interpretation in Crisis: On the Question of the Foundations and Approaches of Exegesis Today," in *Biblical Interpretation in Crisis: The Ratzinger Conference on the Bible and the Church*, ed. Richard J. Neuhaus (Grand Rapids, MI: Eerdmans, 1989), 1–23.

our weak human nature."[9] For the words of God expressed in human language have been made like human discourse, just as the Word of the eternal Father, when he took to himself the flesh of human weakness, was in every way made like men.[10]

This analogy, comparing Scripture to the incarnation of Christ, hails from the earliest centuries of the Church. *Dei Verbum* itself is quoting St. John Chrysostom. Origen made a similar comparison: "Just as this spoken word cannot according to its own nature be touched or seen, but when written in a book and, so to speak, become bodily, then indeed is seen and touched, so too is it with the fleshless and bodiless Word of God; according to its divinity it is neither seen nor written, but when it becomes flesh, it is seen and written."[11] Even earlier, Ignatius of Antioch said, "We must go to Scripture as to the flesh of Christ."[12] The basic meaning of the analogy is clear: as Christ is fully human, like us in all things but sin, so Scripture is fully human, composed by human agents within the limitations of their historical, cultural and linguistic contexts and exercising the full powers of their intelligence and freedom. At the same time, as Christ is fully divine, so Scripture is truly the Word of God and expresses the revelation of God in all its fullness.

But this christological analogy is not merely a felicitous and enlightening comparison. It is making a theological assertion the significance of which is often overlooked—namely, that Scripture itself is a sacrament. That is, Scripture is a visible sign that both signifies *and makes present* the invisible divine mystery. This sacramentality of Scripture—like that of the seven sacraments of the Catholic Church, properly speaking—is founded on the sacramentality of Christ's human nature, which is eternally joined to the Word of God and thus makes that Word visible, audible, and tangible in time and space. As the *Catechism* expresses it, "His humanity appeared as 'sacrament,' that is, the sign and instrument, of his divinity and of the salvation he brings: what was visible in his earthly life leads to the

---

9   The quotation is from St. John Chrysostom, *Commentary on Genesis* 3, 8 (Homily 17, 1), in *Patrologiae Cursus Completus. Series Graeca*, ed. J.P. Migne (Paris: Garnier and J.P. Migne, 1957–1866), 53, 134. Hereafter abbreviated *PG*.

10   *Dei Verbum*, 13. Pope Pius XII referred to the same analogy in his *Divino Afflante Spiritu*, Encyclical Letter Promoting Biblical Studies, 37 in *The Scripture Documents*, 115–139; see also Pope John Paul II, "On the Interpretation of the Bible in the Church," Address to the Pontifical Biblical Commission (April 23, 1993), in *The Scripture Documents*, 170–180.

11   *Commentary on Matthew* (PG 17, 289AB). See also Augustine, *City of God*, XVII, 6.2, in *A Select Library of the Nicene and Post-Nicene Fathers of the Christian Church. First Series*, vol. 1, ed. Philip Schaff (New York: Christian Literature Publishing, 1866–90); Chrysostom, *Homilies on the Gospel of John*, at 1:18 (PG 59, col. 97 sq.).

12   *Letter to the Philadelphians*, 4, 1, in *The Ante–Nicene Fathers*, vol. 1, ed. Alexander Roberts and James Donaldson (Buffalo: Christian Literature Publishing, 1885–1887), 79–85.

invisible mystery of his divine sonship and redemptive mission."[13] Scripture, and especially the Gospels, extends this sacramentality of Christ's humanity throughout the whole age of the Church by unveiling Christ's identity and mission in such a way so that we are not merely told about him, but *brought into contact with him.*

How does Scripture do this? Let us consider first the New Testament. As some recent authors have emphasized, the New Testament, and particularly the Gospels, were written with the conviction that Jesus Christ is risen from the dead, and therefore all that he lived and taught on earth has been transfigured into a new mode of existence which becomes a source of grace for all who believe in him.[14] The evangelists narrate each event in the earthly life of Jesus in such a way as to proclaim that this historically contingent event is *still present* because its protagonist is alive, and that the reader can come into contact with him by accessing the unique grace and power revealed in this event. In other words, the New Testament authors relate Christ's earthly words and deeds in a manner that is "transparent" to the post-resurrection Church and the present activity of the risen Lord, so as to enable the reader to see how the living Jesus is accessible to us, here and now.

For example, in the account of the healing of the blind man, Mark mentions that after receiving his sight, the blind man followed Jesus "on the way" (Mark 10:52). Since "the way" was the earliest term for Christianity (Acts 9:2; 24:14), this subtle allusion helps the reader recognize that he or she too has been set on the path of discipleship by being healed of (spiritual) blindness by Jesus. The Gospel account is written so as to uncover the true depths of this event that took place in Jericho 2,000 years ago. It is a sign drawing the reader into an *experience* of the risen Lord's power to open the eyes of the blind, a power still at work for those who cry out to him in faith. The pattern of Jesus' action is somehow replicated in our own present-day experience, such that we are mysteriously drawn into ontological participation in the event.

A similar movement is discernible in the story of the healing of the paralytic lowered through the roof (Mark 2:1–12; Matt. 9:2–8; Luke 5:18–26). All three Synoptics recount Jesus' declaration of his power to forgive in such a way that it may readily be interpreted as a parenthetical remark to the reader: "But that *you* may know that the Son of man has authority on earth to forgive sins, he said to the paralytic."[15] They thus portray the experience of forgiveness in someone who was

---

13 *Catechism*, no. 515.

14 Francis Martin, "St. Matthew's Spiritual Understanding of the Healing of the Centurion's Boy," *Communio* 25 (1998), 160–77. See also Ignace de la Potterie, "Interpretation of Holy Scripture in the Spirit in Which It Was Written," in ed. René Latourelle, *Vatican II: Assessment and Perspectives*, vol. 1 (New York: Paulist, 1988), 220–66; Luke Timothy Johnson, *Living Jesus: Learning the Heart of the Gospel* (San Francisco: Harper San Francisco, 2000).

15 This reading does not preclude others, and it may well be that the evangelists deliberately left the syntax ambiguous (there being no punctuation in the Greek). See Mark 7:19; 13:37 for other examples of such asides to the reader.

also physically healed by Jesus, in a manner that helps the reader recognize that such forgiveness is *now* available to all those who are led to him in faith.[16] In the words of St. Leo the Great, "All those things which the Son of God both did and taught for the reconciliation of the world, we not only know in the account of things now past, but we also experience in the power of works which are present."[17]

For the evangelists to narrate in this way is not to disregard history, or "what actually happened," but to consciously interpret history in a way that is open to the invisible mystery revealed through it. This is why the events in Jesus' earthly life have traditionally been called "mysteries" (which is simply the Greek equivalent of "sacraments")—they have an interior depth and power to which we are led by the manner in which Scripture recounts those events.[18] As the Gospel is proclaimed, especially in the liturgy, and as the hearer contemplates these mysteries in faith, "what was visible in [Christ's] earthly life" *still today* "leads to the invisible mystery of his divine sonship and redemptive mission."

"The Heart of Christ" and Scripture's Spiritual Sense

The sacramental quality of the Gospels also applies, though in a more hidden and indirect way, to the entire Bible. From the beginning, the Church has held that Jesus Christ is the definitive revelation and fulfillment of all that is contained in the Hebrew Scriptures—that the Old Testament as well as the New leads us into the mystery of the Son of God made man. This conviction, according to the New Testament, was rooted in the interpretive practice of Jesus himself. "Today this Scripture is fulfilled in your hearing," he said to the Jews gathered in the synagogue at Nazareth, after reading from the prophet Isaiah (Luke 4:21). Luke frames Jesus' entire public ministry within this context of scriptural fulfillment by noting at the end of the Gospel that on the road to Emmaus, "beginning with Moses and all the prophets, he interpreted to them in all the Scriptures the things concerning himself" (Luke 24:27–28). Luke thereby indicates that "all of Jesus' preaching is an interpretive program about all the Scriptures,"[19] in which the things done

---

16 For further examples, see Francis Martin, "Historical Criticism and New Testament Teaching on the Imitation of Christ," *Anthropotes* 6 (1990): 261–87.

17 Pope St. Leo the Great, *On the Passion*, 12, quoted in Martin, "St. Matthew's Spiritual Understanding," 163.

18 Compare the *Catechism*, 512–521. After stating that "Christ enables us *to live in him* all that he himself lived, and *he lives it in us*," the *Catechism* goes on to quote St. John Eudes: "We must continue to accomplish in ourselves the stages of Jesus' life and his mysteries and often to beg him to perfect and realize them in us and in his whole Church .... For it is the plan of the Son of God to make us and the whole Church partake in his mysteries and to extend them to and continue them in us and in his whole Church. This is his plan for fulfilling his mysteries in us."

19 See Denis Farkasfalvy, "The Pontifical Biblical Commission's Document on Jews and Christians and Their Scriptures: An Attempt at an Evaluation," *Communio* 29 (2002), 715–37, at 721.

and taught in the past are now understood in a new light as "fulfilled," that is, definitively realized in their deepest meaning, by Christ.

The fulfillment motif is even more pronounced in Matthew, who regularly draws attention to specific biblical prophecies fulfilled by Christ and indicates through typological correspondences how Christ mysteriously recapitulates in himself the history of the chosen people.[20] The theme is equally prominent in the Gospel of John, where Jesus indicts the Jewish authorities for their failure to recognize that even the Pentateuch points to him: "You search the Scriptures, because you think that in them you have eternal life; but it is they that bear witness to me . . . . If you believed Moses, you would believe me, for he wrote of me" (John 5:39, 46). The fact that this pronouncement is in the form of a reproach implies that these erudite students of the law should have understood that the law was pointing to Christ, and that, therefore, a christological meaning is objectively present, though hidden, in the words and deeds of God as recounted in the Old Testament, and is available (at least incipiently) to those whose hearts are open to it.

As Schnackenburg observes, "For the evangelist, it is not only that individual sayings of Scripture are fulfilled in Jesus (John 12:38; 13:18; 15:25; 17:12; 19:24, 36), but the whole of Scripture is directed towards him and speaks of him (12:41). The word of Scripture and his own word form a unity (2:22), and in the light of his glorification the Scripture finally discloses its hidden meaning (12:16; 20:9)."[21] The letters of Paul and the apostolic preaching recorded in Acts provide further evidence that for the early Church, the gospel kerygma was inseparable from, and found its essential credentials in, the validity of the claim that Jesus confers on the Hebrew Scriptures their ultimate, God-given meaning and intelligibility (see Acts 3:18; 1 Cor. 15:3–5). And conversely, the coming of Christ is only intelligible against the background of its preparation in the Old Testament.

Reflecting on the New Testament witness, the fathers of the Church elaborated the principle that because God is the Author of history, every event recounted in Scripture is a mystery whose inner depths reveal something of God and his gracious dealings with humanity. And because the center and culminating point of those dealings is the new covenant established through the incarnation and paschal sacrifice of God's Son, there is a christological sense in all parts of the Bible. In the famous words of Hugh of St. Victor, "All Sacred Scripture is but one book, and this one book is Christ, because all divine Scripture speaks of Christ, and all divine Scripture is fulfilled in Christ."[22] Every event narrated in the Old Testament, as well as every prophecy and poem and prayer, is also a revelation of

20 Cf. Matt. 1:22; 2:15, 17, 23; 4:14; 5:17; 8:17; 12:17; 13:35; 21:4; 26:54, 56; 27:9.

21 Rudolf Schnackenburg, *The Gospel According to St. John*, vol. 2 (New York: Seabury, 1980), 125.

22 Hugh of St. Victor, *De arca Noe*, 2, 8, in *PL* 176, 642, quoted in *Catechism*, no. 134.

Christ the incarnate Word, capable of "leading us into the mystery" of his divine sonship and salvific mission when it is read in light of the gospel.

The notion of a hidden christological meaning that pervades the Bible, which was held unanimously by Christian tradition until the last few centuries, is what was traditionally called the "spiritual sense" of Scripture.[23] Strictly speaking, the spiritual sense refers to the Old Testament's foreshadowing of the New, since in the New the reality of Christ and the new covenant is no longer hidden but patent. But the term is sometimes used more broadly. As noted above, both the Old Testament and the New have a "spiritual sense" understood as a capacity to lead us into the invisible mystery of Christ. The difference, of course, is that the christological significance of Old Testament passages cannot be attributed to the conscious intent of the human authors.

It is important to define the spiritual sense properly, since it is frequently confused with other phenomena that occur in text reception and interpretation, especially in the ancient world. The New Testament's spiritual interpretation of the Old is sometimes described by biblical scholars, for instance, as an instance of pesher exegesis like that practiced by the ancient rabbis, in which earlier texts are quoted or paraphrased in new contexts that alter their meaning.[24] So, for instance, when the fourth Gospel quotes Zechariah at the crucifixion scene, "They shall look on him whom they have pierced" (John 19:37), he is applying a method similar to that of the Essenes at Qumran when they reinterpreted Habakkuk as a cryptically encoded allegory referring to the founder of their own community.[25] Or the spiritual sense is described as an "added" sense—added, that is, by the interpreter.[26] Even the Pontifical Biblical Commission falls into this confusion when it speaks of the New Testament's "retrospective re-readings" of the Old Testament,[27] as Abbot Denis Farkasfalvy, himself a member of the commission, has pointed out.[28] To speak of a retrospective re-reading is to imply (even if inadvertently) that this interpretation is not based on something inherent in the text. The term "sensus plenior,"

---

23 Farkasfalvy, "The Pontifical Biblical Commission's Document."

24 Cf. Richard N. Longenecker, *Biblical Exegesis in the Apostolic Period* (Grand Rapids, MI: Eerdmans, 1999), esp. 26–27, 54–58.

25 *Habakkuk Commentary*, 7.1–6 in *The Midrash Pesher of Habakkuk*, trans. William H. Brownlee, Society of Biblical Literature Monograph Series 24 (Missoula, MO: Scholars Press, 1979).

26 Joseph Fitzmyer, "Problems of the Literal and Spiritual Senses of Scripture," *Louvain Studies* 20 (1995), 134–146.

27 Pontifical Biblical Commission, *The Jewish People and Their Sacred Scriptures in the Christian Bible* (Boston: Pauline Books and Media, 2003), 21. The document goes so far as to assert that, "Although the Christian reader is aware that the internal dynamism of the Old Testament finds its goal in Jesus, this is a retrospective perception whose point of departure is not in the text as such, but in the events of the New Testament proclaimed by the apostolic preaching."

28 Farkasfalvy, "The Pontifical Biblical Commission's Document," 729.

coined by recent exegetes, can also tend to perpetuate this misunderstanding by reducing the spiritual sense to a "fuller" literal sense.[29]

Why are these descriptions inadequate? Perhaps no one has done more to retrieve a correct understanding and appreciation of the ancient doctrine of the spiritual sense than Henri de Lubac.[30] As de Lubac has demonstrated, the spiritual sense, correctly understood, is not a property of texts but of history. The spiritual sense does not refer to a literary relationship but an ontological relationship. It is founded on the unity of the two covenants within the divine economy of salvation: by God's infinite wisdom and foreknowledge, all the events, persons and institutions in the old covenant prefigure, prepare for, and point to the new. Thus the spiritual sense is not an additional meaning retrospectively superimposed on the texts in the light of new events, but something that was *already hidden* in those things written about in the texts. As de Lubac expressed it:

> [T]he very facts have an inner significance; although in time, they are yet pregnant with an eternal value . . . the reality which is typified [typologically prefigured] in the Old—and even the New—Testament is not merely spiritual, it is incarnate; it is not merely spiritual but historical as well. For the Word was made flesh and set up his tabernacle among us. The spiritual meaning, then, is to be found on all sides, not only or more especially in a book but first and foremost *in reality itself.*[31]

This view is in full accord with Aquinas' classical definition of the literal and spiritual senses of Scripture,[32] which, significantly, has been taken up virtually unmodified by the *Catechism* (see no. 117), though it was not mentioned in *Dei Verbum*. According to Aquinas, the literal meaning is that which is signified by the words of Scripture; the spiritual meaning is what is in turn signified by the *things or events* conveyed by the words. For instance, the word "temple" in its literal sense denotes the Jewish house of worship in Jerusalem; the Temple itself (the historically existing house of worship, not merely texts about the Temple) spiritually signifies the Church. God's deliverance of his people through the crossing of

---

29 See Henri de Lubac, *Scripture in the Tradition*, trans. Luke O'Neill (New York: Crossroad, 2000), 150. This volume is a compendium of texts from de Lubac's *Histoire et Esprit* and *Exégèse médiévale*, earlier published in English as *Sources of Revelation* (New York: Herder and Herder, 1968).

30 For helpful assessments of de Lubac's contribution in this area, see Marcellino D'Ambrosio, "The Spiritual Sense in de Lubac's Hermeneutics of Tradition, *Letter & Spirit* 1 (2005), 147–57; Susan K. Wood, *Spiritual Exegesis and the Church in the Theology of Henri de Lubac* (Grand Rapids, MI: Eerdmans, 1998).

31 Henri de Lubac, *Catholicism*, trans. Lancelot Sheppard and Elizabeth Englund (San Francisco: Ignatius, 1988), 168, citing Maximus the Confessor.

32 Thomas Aquinas, *Summa Theologiae*, Pt. I, Q. 1, Art. 10.

the Red Sea, not merely the narrative of the crossing of the Red Sea in Exodus, spiritually prefigures baptism.[33] Rightly understood, therefore, the spiritual sense is a property unique to sacred Scripture, as having a divine Author who is also the Author of all history. The Old Testament's radical christological orientation "was not imposed from without, like a label, by Christian apologetics: 'It is within [the Old Testament] and penetrates all its parts.' If we represent salvation history by a line, Christ is at its end, middle, and every point in between."[34]

Readers will recognize that the Exodus example raises a problem: that of the historicity of the events narrated in the Bible, especially in the Old Testament. To what degree did the Israelites' actual departure from Egypt differ from the stylized account of it handed down through centuries of oral tradition and preserved in the final redaction of the book of Exodus? Generations of biblical exegetes have debated this question without resolution; indeed complete resolution is impossible given our distance from the event and the meagerness of the historical record. However, this problem need not jeopardize the inquiry into the literal or spiritual senses. As philosophical hermeneutics has shown, it is an illusion to think we can attain a raw, "objective" factuality independent of human testimony.[35] Our primary (in some cases, only) access to biblical events is through the biblical narrative; thus the literal sense of the narrative (on which the spiritual is based) is not "what really happened" but the historical referent precisely *as mediated to us by the canonical text*. In the words of *Dei Verbum*: "[God's] plan of revelation is realized by deeds and words having in inner unity; the deeds wrought by God in the history of salvation manifest and confirm the teaching and realities signified by the words, while the words proclaim the deeds and clarify the mystery contained in them."[36]

Although the history of the chosen people was already objectively pregnant with this mysterious christological significance, that is not to say that this significance could have been discerned beforehand. The marvelous preparations and hidden rays of anticipation can only be appreciated in retrospect, when they are all woven together in transcendent fulfillment. In that sense, the incarnation and the act of love in which Christ died effects "a real change in Scripture, which the ancients compare to the eucharistic consecration. They love to see Scripture as a loaf of bread in Christ's hands: 'The Lord Jesus took the loaves of Scripture in his hands. . . .' In his very act of offering himself to the Father in sacrifice, the bread is consecrated and changed into him."[37] As the *Catechism* (see no. 112) puts it, quoting

---

33 See Mary Healy, "Behind, in Front of . . . or Through the Text? The Christological Analogy and the Lost World of Biblical Truth," in *"Behind" the Text: History and Biblical Interpretation* (Grand Rapids, MI: Eerdmans / Carlisle, UK: Paternoster, 2003), 181–195.

34 Mariano Magrassi, *Praying the Bible: An Introduction to Lectio Divina*, trans. Edward Hagman (Collegeville, MN: Liturgical Press, 1998), 16, quoting Hoskyns.

35 See Iain Provan, "Knowing and Believing: Faith in the Past," in *"Behind" the Text*, 229–66.

36 *Dei Verbum*, 2.

37 Magrassi, *Praying the Bible*, 52, quoting Rupert, *Commentary on John*, VI (PL 169, 443d).

St. Thomas, "The phrase 'heart of Christ' can refer to Sacred Scripture, which makes known his heart, closed before the Passion, as the Scripture was obscure. But the Scripture has been opened since the Passion; since those who from then on have understood it, consider and discern in what way the prophecies must be interpreted."

Who could have ever imagined, for instance, that the Ark of the Covenant before which David danced for joy prefigured an infinitely more intimate dwelling place for God among his people, Mary the Ark of the New Covenant in whose womb his very flesh was enclosed, and before whom John the Baptist leaped for joy before his birth? Who could have fathomed that Eve's creation from the rib of the sleeping Adam would foreshadow the Bride of the New Adam, the Church, born from his pierced side in the sleep of death? Who could have guessed that Joseph's betrayal by his brothers, which ultimately led to his saving them from famine as prime minister of Egypt, would anticipate Christ's rejection by his own "brothers," which led to his saving them from eternal death through his gift of the bread of life? These examples, found already in the New Testament's use of the Old Testament and then developed in the writings of the Church fathers, could be multiplied indefinitely.

The Mysticism of Exegesis

At this point we can return to the question of "interpretation in the Spirit," since it is clear that the spiritual depths with which Scripture is laden can only have been imparted to it by the Holy Spirit. The christological analogy has a further implication: as Christ became incarnate in the womb of the Virgin through the Holy Spirit, so the Word of God becomes "incarnate" on the sacred page through the Holy Spirit. The Spirit's work of inspiration is not merely a one-time event; for the fathers, "inspiration is not just something that acted once on the sacred writers, resulting in the inspired texts. It is an ongoing and ever-present influence at work within the Books themselves, which are and remain inspired. . . . They remain filled with the Spirit of God and are constantly and 'miraculously made fruitful by him.'"[38] Here we could draw an analogy with creation: in the biblical view, creation is not an act that once accomplished, is over, but is rather God's continuous act of holding the universe in existence by his creative power.[39]

Dei Verbum implicitly grounds its directive regarding "interpretation in the Spirit" in this doctrine of inspiration by the Spirit. In the immediately preceding section, the document quotes the classic biblical text on inspiration, 2 Timothy 3:16–17: "All Scripture is inspired by God [literally, God-breathed] and profitable for teaching, for reproof, for correction, and for training in righteousness, that the man of God may be complete, equipped for every good work" (*Dei Verbum*, 2). The

---

38 Magrassi, *Praying the Bible*, 27.

39 Magrassi, *Praying the Bible*, 28.

implication is that the same Holy Spirit who inspired the writing of Scripture and thus imparted its sacramental quality, must equally inspire the interpretation of what was written, just as, if a message is written in code, the code is also required in order to read it. As Gregory the Great expressed it, "Just as the Spirit of life touches the mind of the prophet, he also touches the mind of the reader."[40] Scripture is a divine act of communication, and an act of communication is not complete until it has been received and understood according to the intent of the speaker.[41]

This logical connection between inspiration and interpretation is asserted explicitly in another Pauline passage, where the apostle tells the Corinthians that "no one comprehends the divine realities except the Spirit of God. Now we have received. . . . the Spirit from God, that we might understand what has been given us by God. And we impart this in words not taught by human wisdom but taught by the Spirit, interpreting spiritual realities to those who are spiritual" (1 Cor. 2:11–13). Unlike the understanding of earthly realities, which is acquired through sense experience or reason, understanding of the depths of God and his hidden counsels surpasses the natural capacities of the mind and can only be acquired through the Spirit. Although the mystery is mediated through human communication (both oral proclamation and written scripture), the Holy Spirit must preside over the entire process of communication from beginning to end. "Already in Pauline theology, inspiration and interpretation are regarded as correlatives—that is, the principles and the method used in exegesis depend on what one thinks about the way God influenced the origins of the text."[42] This is why Paul insists that to perceive the christological sense of the Old Testament requires an act of conversion and of yielding to the Spirit: "Whenever Moses is read, a veil lies over their hearts, but whenever a person turns to the Lord the veil is removed. Now the Lord is the Spirit" (2 Cor. 3:15–16).

The Gospels, in a different way, also allude to an understanding that can only be conferred by God, that penetrates beyond the surface of things (and especially of the Scriptures) to the divine mystery concealed in them.[43] Luke, in particular,

---

40 *Commentary on Ezekiel*, Hom. VII, I, 9–16 (*PL* 76, 844–48).

41 For thought-provoking analysis of the implications of interpreting Scripture as a divine speech-act, see Kevin J. Vanhoozer, "From Speech Acts to Scripture Acts: The Covenant of Discourse and the Discourse of Covenant," in eds. Craig Bartholomew, et al., *After Pentecost: Language and Biblical Interpretation* (Carlisle, UK: Paternoster / Grand Rapids, MI: Zondervan, 2001), 1–49.

42 Farkasfalvy, "The Pontifical Biblical Commission's Document," 718.

43 The evangelists, each in his own characteristic manner, portray Jesus as repeatedly prompting his disciples to become aware of a deeper level of reality, and expressing surprise at their incomprehension of it. Mark in particular develops the theme of the disciples' spiritual obtuseness in regard to parables and enigmatic sayings (4:13; 7:18; 8:17–21), the meaning of human realities such as death (5:39), Jesus' gestures as revelatory of his person (6:52), and the understanding of God's plan for a crucified and risen Messiah (8:33; 9:10, 32; 10:38). The motif is also present in Matthew (15:16; 16:9–12, 23; 20:22) and Luke (9:45; 18:34; 24:25–27). John too emphasizes the spiritual dullness of Jesus' interlocutors (8:27; 12:16; 13:7; 20:9) and the

emphasizes that such spiritual understanding occurs by a divine work of "opening their minds," as Jesus did for the disciples on the road to Emmaus (Luke 24:45). For John, to impart such understanding is the specific role of the Spirit: "the Spirit of truth, who proceeds from the Father. . .will bear witness to me" (John 15:26; compare John 12:16; 14:25–26; 16:12–15; 20:9; 2 Pet. 1:20–21).

Thus for the New Testament, the power of Scripture to bring us into contact with the living Christ is dependent on an ongoing work of the Spirit, bringing to light its deepest meaning and bearing witness to its truth in the mind of the believer. The conclusion that inescapably follows is that exegesis can never be completely reduced to the application of correct methods to the text. There is necessarily a subjective, personal involvement of the interpreter as a recipient of the divine act of communication. This is why de Lubac insists, following the patristic and medieval tradition, that biblical interpretation is inseparable from the spiritual life, or indeed from mysticism, understood as the personal appropriation of the mystery of Christ revealed in Scripture.[44]

> The Christian mystery is not something to be curiously con-
> templated like a pure object of science, but is something which
> must be interiorized and lived. It finds its own fullness in being
> fulfilled within souls. . . . Still more fundamentally, the entire
> process of spiritual understanding is, in its principal, identical to
> the process of conversion. It is its luminous aspect.[45]

For this reason de Lubac argues that biblical exegesis can never be a purely objective science.[46] "Exegesis is not technique; it is mysticism."[47] Biblical interpretation cannot be complete unless it takes into account "the connection between spiritual understanding and the personal conversion and life of the Christian . . . . the relationship between 'New Testament' and 'New Man,' between newness of understanding and newness of spirit."[48]

Christological Heresies and the Future of Exegesis

If this is the case, must we give up on the possibility of objectivity in the field of biblical exegesis? Does "interpretation in the Spirit" dissolve the distinction between exegesis and "eisegesis" (reading into a text), and open the door to a

---

Lord's distress over it (3:10; 14:9), and develops the theme of the deeper, spiritual meaning of earthly realities such as the temple (3:21), birth (3:4), water (4:15), bread (6:34), to awaken (11:11), to wash (13:9), and to depart (7:35; 13:36).

44   See William F. Murphy, "Henri de Lubac's Mystical Tropology," *Communio* 27 (2000), 171.

45   De Lubac, *Scripture in the Tradition*, 21.

46   De Lubac, *Scripture in the Tradition*, 23. See also D'Ambrosio, "Spiritual Sense," 152–54.

47   Magrassi, *Praying the Bible*, 52.

48   De Lubac, *Scripture in the Tradition*, 144.

profusion of subjective and fanciful interpretations whose only limit is the piety of the exegete? Are there no longer any controls to distinguish between valid and invalid interpretations? The christological analogy helps point the way out of the quandary. As in Christ's hypostatic union, the two "natures" of Scripture are not in tension or juxtaposition but in indissoluble unity; we cannot pick apart a verse or chapter and decide which part is "divine" and which is "human." However, there is an order to the two with regard to our knowing. Just as we cannot come to know the triune God except through the humanity of Christ, so we cannot approach the divine or revelatory meaning of the Bible except through its human meaning. The spiritual meaning shines precisely *through* the literal, as the divinity of Christ radiates through his humanity. This is the basis for the traditional insistence on the priority of the literal sense as the foundation for the spiritual.[49]

Just as there are imbalanced christologies, so there can be forms of scriptural interpretation which fail to hold the two dimensions of the biblical word in full integrity and unity. One of these might be called a "Monophysite" type of exegesis. Like the ancient heresy which denied Christ's human nature, this kind of approach downplays or ignores the human factors that went into the composition of the biblical text. It accords the biblical words an absolute value, independent of the conditions of human language and culture.[50] In its extreme form, it envisions the human authors as sacred secretaries who simply transcribed as the Holy Spirit dictated—in other words, not as *authors* in any authentic sense. In a more mild form, it blithely disregards the literal sense of the text and thus gives rise to spiritual interpretations which range from the subjective and arbitrary to the self-serving and even frivolous. As critics often point out, there are examples of such fanciful readings among certain writings of the fathers.

The other one-sided form of exegesis, more typical of modern scholarship, might be called "Nestorian."[51] Similar to the heresy that denied the unity of Christ's two natures in one person, this approach, while not necessarily denying the divine dimension of Scripture, so isolates it from the human that it is reduced to a post-exegetical addendum. Such an approach intentionally and methodologically considers the text as a purely human reality, and superimposes the divine only as a second operation *after* the crucial interpretive judgments have already been made. Questions regarding the genesis of the text and the concerns of the authors or redactors are asked and answered within a purely human framework, ignoring or abstracting from the fact that God himself is speaking through the biblical word.[52] The danger is that horizontal explanations are then constructed for what

---

49 *Catechism*, no. 116; *Summa Theologica*, Pt. I, Q.1, Art. 10, Resp. 1.

50 See Pope John Paul II, "On the Interpretation of the Bible in the Church," 8.

51 This use of the term "Nestorian" as applied to exegesis seems to have originated with Louis Bouyer, "Où en est le mouvement biblique?" *Bible et vie chrétienne* 13 (1956), 7–21.

52 It is important to note that, as philosophical hermeneutics has shown, all interpretation

actually has only a vertical explanation. The result is often a reductive interpretation, which leaves ordinary believers uneasy and confused about the compatibility of the exegetical conclusions with Christian faith, and doubtful about the divine realities being conveyed in the text.

At times, this kind of exegesis can tend toward a kind of fideism in which Church doctrine is affirmed even while the supposedly objective exegetical results are tending in the opposite direction. In its extreme form (exemplified by the Jesus Seminar[53]), it results in a secular explanation of the text, irreconcilable with other biblical assertions and with the unity of the biblical testimony as a whole. It is important to note that this kind of exegesis is not incapable of producing valid insights. But its failure to come to grips with the sacramentality of Scripture—that is, Scripture's power to lead us into the divine mystery—leaves it vulnerable to the risk of error and distortion, and renders it ultimately defective as a means of access to the word.

How, then, is the humanness of Scripture to be granted its legitimate autonomy without draining the word of its divine power? What is needed is a "Chalcedonian" form of exegesis, which, like the creedal formulation that resolved the christological heresies of the early Church, does full justice to the human and the divine aspects of Scripture in their integral unity. Such an exegesis would take seriously the human authorial processes and rigorously investigate the relevant manuscripts, languages, literary genres, historical contexts, cultural settings, and so on—but as open *from the beginning* to the Word's own dynamic movement toward the interior and the vertical.[54] The logical priority of the human dimension is at the service of the teleological priority of the divine: interpretation is for the sake of the knowledge of God in Christ.

Pope John Paul II articulated this balance well when he exhorted the

---

depends upon, and is conditioned by, fundamental presuppositions. The relevant question is whether that pre-understanding is informed by Christian faith or not. For a detailed discussion of this development see Anthony Thiselton, *The Two Horizons: New Testament Hermeneutics and Philosophical Description with Special Reference to Heidegger, Bultmann, Gadamer, and Wittgenstein* (Grand Rapids, MI: Eerdmans, 1980). For a brief summary, see R.L. Maddox, "Contemporary Hermeneutic Philosophy and Theological Studies," *Religious Studies* 21 (1985), 517–29. For an illuminating example of how the interpreter's presuppositions influence even such apparently neutral and technical levels of exegesis as textual criticism and lexicography, see Al Wolters, "Confessional Criticism and the Night Visions of Zechariah," in *Renewing Biblical Interpretation*, eds. Craig Bartholomew, et al. (Carlisle, UK: Paternoster; Grand Rapids, MI: Zondervan, 2000), 90–117.

53   For a representative text of the Jesus Seminar, see Robert W. Funk, Roy W. Hoover, and the Jesus Seminar, *The Five Gospels: The Search for the Authentic Words of Jesus: New Translation and Commentary* (New York: Macmillan, 1993).

54   Peter Stuhlmacher argues for a "Hermeneutics of Consent to the biblical texts," which is marked by "a willingness to open ourselves anew to the claim of tradition, of the present, and of transcendence." *Historical Criticism and Theological Interpretation* (Philadelphia: Fortress, 1977), 83, 85.

members of the Pontifical Biblical Commission: "The Church of Christ takes the realism of the incarnation seriously, and this is why she attaches great importance to the 'historico-critical' study of the Bible. . . . Nevertheless, this study is not enough. . .it is obviously necessary that the exegete himself perceive the divine word in the texts. He can do this only if his intellectual work is sustained by a vigorous spiritual life."[55] The interpenetration of critical methods and faith is an instance of the broader interrelationship of reason and faith:

> [In the biblical text] Faith intervenes not to abolish reason's au-
> tonomy nor to reduce its scope for action, but solely to bring the
> human being to understand that in these events it is the God of
> Israel who acts. Thus the world and the events of history cannot
> be understood in depth without professing faith in the God who
> is at work in them. . . . There is thus no reason for competition of
> any kind between reason and faith: each contains the other, and
> each has its own scope for action.[56]

A deeper appreciation of the christological analogy and the implications of the doctrine of biblical inspiration for exegesis can lead us to a new springtime of Scripture study in the Church. If Catholic biblical scholarship follows the wise counsel of *Dei Verbum*, it will avail itself of all the rich resources of critical methods, but will, at the same time, lead the faithful to feed on that life-giving bread, to eat and drink Christ the Word made flesh. I would like to conclude by quoting a friend and distinguished biblical scholar, Craig Bartholomew:

> The subject of Scripture is Christ, and an adequate hermeneutic
> looks for and finds him again and again in the Bible. Scripture
> is that field in which is hid Christ, the great treasure, and any
> hermeneutic which does not make its goal to dig up that treasure
> is misdirected. God has, through the events that underlie the
> Bible, 'led his people to the feet of Someone.' Biblical interpreta-
> tion should have as its goal those same feet![57]

---

55 Pope John Paul II, "On the Interpretation of the Bible in the Church," 7, 9.

56 Pope John Paul II, *Fides et Ratio*, Encyclical Letter on the Relationship of Faith and Reason (September 14, 1998), 16–17, in *The Encyclicals of John Paul II*, ed. J. Michael Miller, C.S.B. (Huntington, IN: Our Sunday Visitor, 2001), 849–913.

57 "Protestants and Catholics Together," (Paper delivered at the Seventh Annual Seminar of the Scripture and Hermeneutics Project, Rome, June 24, 2005).

Letter & Spirit 2 (2006): 43–54

The Use of Scripture
in the Catechism of the Catholic Church

∼: John C. Cavadini :∼

University of Notre Dame

What is the role of Scripture in the *Catechism of the Catholic Church?* [1] However we answer that question, one thing is certain: the *Catechism* cites scriptural texts with profusion. The *Roman Catechism*, the only previous official *Catechism* of the magisterium of the Church, does cite Scripture frequently and often to a beautiful rhetorical effect. [2] However, compared with the *Roman Catechism*, the *Catechism of the Catholic Church* seems almost littered with scriptural sentences, phrases, words, and allusions, found on almost every page. How can we characterize the use to which this rich scriptural apparatus is put? A secondary question might be, what is the relationship between the use of Scripture in the *Catechism* and historical-critical exegesis? Do the fruits of historical-critical exegesis show up in the *Catechism* in any meaningful way?

As is well known, the *Catechism* has been criticized for its use of Scripture as descending to critically uninformed proof-texting, with passages abstracted from their original contexts in the text of Scripture and in the circumstances in which they were written. It is implied that this use of Scripture is a return to pre-critical methods of scriptural citation more characteristic of a certain kind of dogmatic apologetics from an era before the Second Vatican Council. [3] With these criti-

---

1   This paper was presented in an earlier form at a conference held at the University of Notre Dame, June 13–15, 2005, to celebrate the fortieth anniversary of the Second Vatican Council's Dogmatic Constitution on Divine Revelation, *Dei Verbum*. The conference was co-sponsored by the United States Catholic Bishops' Committee on Doctrine and the University of Notre Dame's Institute for Church Life and Department of Theology. I wish to acknowledge their support, and that of the Lilly Endowment, who funded this conference. I would also like to thank Nancy Cavadini, Brian Daley, Scott Hahn, Cyril O'Regan, Michael Signer, and Matt Zyniewicz, who commented on earlier versions of this paper (of course, the errors in it are irremediably my own).

2   See for example Pt. 1, art. 12, §12–13 (cited henceforth in the following form: *Roman Catechism* 1.12.12–13), on the goods to be enjoyed by the blessed. It is also known as the "Catechism of Trent" because it was produced in the aftermath of the Church's Council of Trent (1545–1563). All citations and translations are taken from *The Roman Catechism*, trans. and annot. Robert I. Bradley, S.J. and Eugene Kevane (Boston: St. Paul Editions, 1985).

3   These criticisms are taken up briefly by Pope Benedict XVI, then Cardinal Joseph Ratzinger. See "The Catechism's Use of Scripture," in *On the Way to Jesus Christ*, trans. Michael J. Miller (San Francisco: Ignatius, 2005), 146–53, and "The Biblical Realism of the New *Catechism's* Christological Catechesis," in *Gospel, Catechesis, Catechism: Sidelights on the Catechism of the Catholic Church* (San Francisco: Ignatius, 1997), 63–69, though I believe the glancing criticism

cisms in mind, but without conceding them as the terms of inquiry, I would like to meditate upon the presentation of Scripture in the *Catechism*.

To begin, it is interesting to return to the comparison of the *Catechism* with the *Roman Catechism*. The latter, as has been already noted, uses Scripture with some frequency, but for the most part these uses are in the genre of appeal to authority—citations or allusions to Scripture used to corroborate or verify doctrinal statements made in a different voice, the authorial voice of the text of the catechism. For example, in a passage introducing the incarnation:

> [T]he same Person, remaining God as he was from eternity, became man (see John 1:14), what he was not before. That this is the meaning of these words is clear from the profession of the holy Council of Constantinople, which says, *who for us men, and for our salvation, came down from heaven, and became incarnate by the Holy Spirit of the Virgin Mary, and was made Man.* The same truth we also find explained by St. John the Evangelist, who took in from the bosom of the Savior himself the knowledge of this profound mystery. When he had declared the nature of the divine Word as follows, *"In the beginning was the Word, and the Word was with God, and the Word was God,* he concludes, *the Word became flesh and dwelt among us* (John 1:1, 14)."[4]

The article continues in this fashion, ending in a short reflection on the usefulness of preaching on the incarnation. After citing Luke 2:6–7 to show the poverty and humility of the Incarnate Word, the *Roman Catechism* adds, "Could the Evangelist have described under more humble terms the majesty and glory that filled the heavens and the earth? He does not say, 'there was no room in the inn,' but there was no room for *him*, who says *the world is mine and the fullness thereof* [Ps. 49:12]. As another Evangelist has expressed it: *He came unto his own and his own received him not* [John 1:11]."[5] This beautiful meditation explicitly takes the form of a reflection on Luke 2:6–7 as a passage from Scripture ("Could the Evangelist have described . . . ") supplemented by other passages from Scripture; but the whole meditation is used to verify from Scripture the incarnation of the "majesty and glory that filled the heavens and the earth."[6]

---

of John Meier is misplaced here. I would like to thank Scott Hahn for drawing my attention to these articles.

4   *Roman Catechism*, 1.3.1.

5   *Roman Catechism*, 1.3.11.

6   I hasten to add that I do not want to overdraw the contrast. The Scripture passage is used in this example not only to verify and corroborate, but to enrich and amplify the doctrinal statement such that one could preach on it more effectively. The scriptural meditation adds to the power of the doctrinal expression. The wonder and awe of the incarnation become more visible and accessible than they were just from the statement of the doctrine. The Catechism of

The Catechism's Scriptural Catechesis

Turning now to the *Catechism*, we can examine passages on a similar point of doctrine. At the beginning of the discussion of Christ, preceding and introducing discussions of the articles from the Creed, "And In Jesus Christ, His Only Son, Our Lord" and "He Was Conceived by the Power of the Holy Spirit, and Born of the Virgin Mary," we find:

> 422. *But when the time had fully come, God sent forth his Son, born of a woman, born under the law, to redeem those who were under the law, so that we might receive adoption as sons* (Gal. 4:4–5). This is *the gospel of Jesus Christ, the Son of God* (Mark 1:1): God has visited his people. He has fulfilled the promise he made to Abraham and his descendants. He acted far beyond all expectation—he has sent his own *beloved Son* (Mark 1:11; compare Luke 1:55, 68).

> 423. We believe and confess that Jesus of Nazareth, born a Jew of a daughter of Israel at Bethlehem at the time of King Herod the Great and the emperor Caesar Augustus . . . is the eternal Son of God made man. He *came from God* (John 13:3), *descended from heaven* (John 3:13; 6:33), and *came in the flesh* (1 John 4:2). For *the Word became flesh and dwelt among us, full of grace and truth; we have beheld his glory, glory as of the only Son from the Father* . . . .*And from his fullness have we all received, grace upon grace* (John 1:14, 16).

> 424. Moved by the grace of the Holy Spirit and drawn by the Father, we believe in Jesus and confess, *You are the Christ, the Son of the living God* (Matt. 16:16). On the *rock* of this faith confessed by Peter, Christ built his Church (see Matt. 16:18; Pope St. Leo I, Sermon 4, 3; 51, 1; 62, 2; 83, 3).[7]

Trent, oriented toward the preaching of the Word and attuned to the emphases of the humanist rhetorical culture, is more alert to the rhetorical power latent in the scriptural texts, beyond their usefulness as so-called proof texts, than many later catechetical summaries of the faith. Still, Scripture is used much less frequently than in the *Catechism*. There is retained a much greater sense that Scripture is something being "employed" or "used" in an essentially separate endeavor of doctrinal exposition. By contrast, in the words of Ratzinger, the *Catechism* is "shaped from one end to the other by the Bible. As far as I know, there has never been until now a catechism so thoroughly formed by the Bible." *Gospel, Catechesis, Catechism*, 61.

7   *The Catechism of the Catholic Church*, 2d. ed. (Vatican City: Libreria Editrice Vaticana, 1997). nos. 422-424. Cited henceforth in the following form: *Catechism*, nos. 422-424.

In these passages, we find Scripture not only cited but actually woven into the text of the *Catechism*. Thus, Galatians 4:4–5 is not a citation supporting a point made in the authorial voice of the text of Section 422, but instead *is* the text of 422. The *Catechism* lets Scripture make its central point rather than taking Scripture as a corroboration of points made in non-scriptural language. The "this" that begins the next sentence has Galatians 4:4–5 as its antecedent, and Mark 1:1 is used to make the point that what Galatians 4:4-5 proclaims is what Mark calls "the Gospel of Jesus Christ, the Son of God." The subsequent explanatory text could in no way stand alone without these scriptural texts. In fact, the subsequent text has as its aim to bring out the surprise—"far beyond all expectation"—implied in the phrase from Mark 1:11, "beloved Son."

The next section, 423, goes on to specify even more fully the terms of the surprising lengths to which God has gone, stating that Jesus of Nazareth, a fully historical figure, is "the eternal Son of God made man." The rest of the section is expressed entirely in scriptural phrases and sentences woven together into one cohesive catechetical statement thematized by the doctrinal statement about "the eternal Son of God made man." The next section places the confession of Peter from Matthew 16:16 on the lips of the reader as his or her own, finishing with a use of the scriptural word "rock," characteristic of the preached exegesis of Pope St. Leo the Great.

I think it would be fair to style this as a *scriptural catechesis*, a catechesis carried out not simply with the support of the words of Scripture but *in* the words of Scripture. It is a catechetical narrative that *relies* on the words of Scripture to speak its main points, so that it almost becomes a kind of glossed scriptural proclamation rather than a scripturally corroborated dogmatic statement.

We find this strategy employed again and again in the *Catechism*. One could say that Scripture breathes freely in the *Catechism*, or that Scripture's spirit is allowed to fill the text and determine its form, to carry its own moment and challenge, enlivening the catechesis with its ever-present appeal to the imagination. In another sequence on the incarnation (*Catechism*, nos. 461–463), the text begins with John 1:14 and uses this Scripture to specify the content of the dogmatic word "incarnation":

> Taking up St. John's expression, 'the Word became flesh,' the
> Church calls 'incarnation' the fact that the Son of God assumed
> a human nature in order to accomplish our salvation in it.[8]

This way of putting it, far from using the scriptural text as a proof-text for an independent dogmatic assertion, places the traditional dogmatic word, "incarnation," in tandem with the scriptural text. It appears as an *interpretation* of the scriptural assertion. It serves to specify the meaning of the scriptural text for the

---

8   *Catechism*, no. 461.

purposes of catechesis, but it does not exhaust its meaning. The inspired text has an overplus of meaning, which can never be fully specified in non-scriptural language. By allowing the text to stand on its own, the *Catechism* makes just this point. The scriptural text is not just a "proof" of the doctrinal statement, but rather its context, keeping the doctrinal statement from closing in on itself as though it could ever fully express the lofty mystery it states. And yet we must have a normative way of stating the mystery lest the overplus of Scripture become a kind of indeterminate ambiguity that cannot ever be summarized and handed on. After lengthy citations from Philippians 2:5–8 and Hebrews 10:5–7, the whole sequence ends with a citation of 1 Timothy 3:16 ("He was manifested in the flesh . . . ") as a statement of the mystery under consideration, not as the scriptural proof of an independently stated doctrine.

Perhaps one of the most stunning examples of this scriptural catechesis is the sequence on the redeeming love of Jesus in the passion as it manifests and reveals the loving Trinitarian communion between Father and Son (*Catechism*, nos. 606–609).[9] The passage is woven from texts from John, 1 John, Hebrews, Isaiah,

---

9   606. The Son of God, who came down "from heaven, not to do [his] own will, but the will of him who sent [him]" (John 6:38), said on coming into the world, "Lo, I have come to do your will, O God." "And by that will we have been sanctified through the offering of the body of Jesus Christ once for all" (Heb. 10:5–10). From the first moment of his incarnation the Son embraces the Father's plan of divine salvation in his redemptive mission: "My food is to do the will of him who sent me, and to accomplish his work" (John 4:34). The sacrifice of Jesus "for the sins of the whole world" (1 John 2:2) expresses his loving communion with the Father. "The Father loves me, because I lay down my life," said the Lord, "[for] I do as the Father has commanded me, so that the world may know that I love the Father" (John 10:17; 14:31).

607. The desire to embrace his Father's plan of redeeming love inspired Jesus' whole life (see Luke 12:50; 22:15; Matt. 16:21–23), for his redemptive passion was the very reason for his incarnation. And so he asked, "And what shall I say? 'Father, save me from this hour'? No, for this purpose I have come to this hour" (John 12:27). And again, "Shall I not drink the cup which the Father has given me?" (John 18:11). From the cross, just before "It is finished," he said, "I thirst" (John 19:30; 19:28).

608. After agreeing to baptize him along with the sinners, John the Baptist looked at Jesus and pointed him out as the "Lamb of God, who takes away the sin of the world" (John 1:29; Luke 3:21; Matt. 3:14–15; John 1:36). By doing so, he reveals that Jesus is at the same time the suffering Servant who silently allows himself to be led to the slaughter and who bears the sin of the multitudes, and also the Paschal Lamb, the symbol of Israel's redemption at the first Passover (Isa. 53:7, 12; Jer. 11:19; Exod. 12:3–14; John 19:36; 1 Cor. 5:7). Christ's whole life expresses his mission: "to serve, and to give his life as a ransom for many" (Mark 10:45).

609. By embracing in his human heart the Father's love for men, Jesus "loved them to the end," for "greater love has no man than this, that a man lay down his life for his friends" (John 13:1; 15:13). In suffering and death his humanity became the free and perfect instrument of his divine love which desires the salvation of men (Heb. 2:10, 17–18; 4:15; 5:7–9). Indeed, out of love for his Father and for men, whom the Father wants to save, Jesus freely accepted his passion and death: "No one takes [my life] from me, but I lay it down of my own accord" (John 10:18). Hence the sovereign freedom of God's Son as he went out to his death (see John 18:4–6; Matt. 26:53).

and the synoptic Gospels. Reading this sequence, one cannot help feeling moved by the unexpected beauty of the truth of God's love in Christ as it is proclaimed here in pervasively scriptural language. It serves to engender understanding of the importance of the doctrine, previously expounded, of the two natures in one person, clarifying why it is important to specify our belief in just this way. At the very same time it opens our mind to the principle that doctrine is not an end in itself, or, as the *Catechism* itself expresses it, that "[w]e do not believe in formulas, but in those realities they express, which faith allows us to touch" (*Catechism*, no. 170).

The "Rule of Faith" and the Context of Scriptural Interpretation

One could argue that, even if these scriptural texts are not being used as proof-texts in the narrow sense of the word, they are still being taken out of their context in the particular biblical books from which they come. The question of what is the context for a scriptural passage, however, is complex, as the Second Vatican Council's constitution on divine revelation, *Dei Verbum*, makes clear. On the one hand, in a passage both cited and paraphrased by the *Catechism*, "Rightly to understand what the sacred authors wanted to affirm in their work, due attention must be paid both to the customary and characteristic patterns of perception, speech, and narrative which prevailed in their time, and to the conventions which people then observed in their dealings with one another."[10] That is, one must pay attention to historical and literary context.

On the other hand, *Dei Verbum* continues, "since sacred Scripture must be read and interpreted with its divine authorship in mind, no less attention must be devoted to the content and unity of the whole of Scripture, taking into account the tradition of the entire Church and the analogy of faith, if we are to derive their true meaning from the sacred texts."[11] As the inspired Word of God, the context for any passage of Scripture is the whole of Scripture within the living tradition of the whole Church. In the scriptural rhetoric of the *Catechism*, Scripture is contextualized by what the fathers of the Church called the "rule of faith"—the living confession of the Church's faith which summarized and thematized, as it were, Scripture, even as its content found inspired expression in sacred Scripture.

The scriptural tapestries that are woven in the *Catechism* juxtapose texts that, in their very juxtaposition, interpret each other, enrich each other,[12] and call

---

10   Second Vatican Council, *Dei Verbum*, Dogmatic Constitution on Divine Revelation (November 18, 1965), 12, in *Vatican Council II: The Conciliar and Post Conciliar Documents*, ed. Austin Flannery, O.P. (Northport, NY: Costello, 1986); see also *Catechism*, nos. 109–110.

11   *Dei Verbum*, 12; see *Catechism*, nos. 111–114.

12   On this idea, I feel indebted to the excellent point made by Robert Wilken in oral comments at a conference called "Handing on the Faith," held at Boston College in September 2004. His point, if I can paraphrase it, was that some so-called proof-texting actually represents creative juxtapositions of scriptural texts with other Scripture or with new material, and is meant to invite the imagination to make connections unimagined before. I would add that this is not a license to juxtapose any text with any other text, but that there is perhaps a lost art here,

forth new meaning from each other, as they are contextualized by the rule of faith, the tradition of the Church, which is also a stream of transmission for revelation. The interplay between the threads drawn from Scripture and threads drawn from traditional sources—the creeds, the writings of the fathers, and the teachings of the Church councils—is the interplay between Scripture and tradition which, in the words of *Dei Verbum*, "come together in some fashion to form one thing and move towards the same goal."[13]

The role of the magisterium as "servant" to the Word of God[14] is present in the *Catechism* as the authorial voice, arranging and organizing the texts from Scripture and tradition. It serves them both by allowing the interplay which precludes the formulas of tradition from closing in on themselves as though they were fully equivalent substitutes for the mysteries they express, while also precluding the "overplus" of meaning in the scriptural passages from appearing as an indeterminacy of meaning. In other words, the key to the usage of Scripture in the *Catechism* is the dogmatic constitution, *Dei Verbum*, as its words are cited in the early sections of the *Catechism* itself.

Historico-Critical Scholarship and the Catechism

But what about the literary and historical context of the texts used in this way? Are they forgotten? Are the fruits of historico-critical scholarship evident in the text of the *Catechism*? Staying with the treatment of Jesus and the incarnation, with regard to the Gospels themselves, the *Catechism* is aware that these are not biographies in the contemporary sense: "Almost nothing is said about his hidden life at Nazareth, and even a great part of his public life is not recounted. What is written in the Gospels was set down there *so that you may believe that Jesus is the Christ, the Son of God, and that believing you may have life in his name*" (*Catechism*, no. 514). The evangelists wrote in order to share faith in Jesus with others. According to the *Catechism*, "they could see and make others see the traces of his mystery in all his earthly life," and they portrayed Jesus in such a way that his humanity appears clearly as "'sacrament,' that is, the sign and instrument, of his divinity and of the salvation he brings" (*Catechism*, no. 515). Following this evangelical impulse, the *Catechism* claims that the Creed's "articles of faith concerning his incarnation and passover . . . shed light on the *whole* of his earthly life" (*Catechism*, no. 512). In this way, the whole method of scriptural catechesis according to the rule of faith is seen to arise in part from an awareness

---

a patristic practice which can be done well or poorly, in response to the Spirit of the text or against it. I believe the *Catechism* is trying to recover or to recall this lost art. Wilken also made the larger point that it is important to let scriptural words and images retain some primacy in "handing on the faith," and his way of putting this helped me to read the *Catechism* in a new light.

13   *Dei Verbum*, 9; *Catechism*, no. 80.

14   *Dei Verbum*, 10; *Catechism*, no. 86.

of the literary genre of the Gospels produced by work in contextualizing historical scholarship. Going through the incidents of Christ's life, the *Catechism* attempts, not a biography of Jesus, but to further the proclamation of the mystery of Christ taken up by the Gospels and summarized by the Creed.[15]

In the treatment of Christ's life, we notice one of the most salient points of development from the *Roman Catechism*—the *Catechism's* treatment of Jesus as a Jew and its consideration of first-century Judaism in general. Surely one of the most enduring fruits of historico-critical examination of the Bible is a deeper awareness of the "Jewishness" of Jesus and of what it meant to be a Jew in the sectarian environment of the first centuries before and after the birth of Christ. We have already seen the emphatic identification of "Jesus of Nazareth, born a Jew of a daughter of Israel," and, precisely as such, as the "eternal Son of God made man" (*Catechism*, no. 423).

The *Catechism* acknowledges that the word "Messiah" would not have been heard fully univocally at the time of Jesus. This means, among other things, removing the stereotype that all Jews would have thought of the Messiah as an "essentially political" figure. The fact that it would be understood in this way by "some of his contemporaries" explains the reserve with which Jesus accepted this title, as well as his efforts to revise this expectation, or, in the *Catechism's* words, to "unveil the authentic content of his messianic kingship" (*Catechism*, nos. 439–440).

The same is true for the phrase "Son of God." The *Catechism* acknowledges that this title, in and of itself, would not have been heard by contemporaries as a statement of the divinity of Jesus in any way: "When the promised Messiah-King is called 'son of God,' it does not necessarily imply that he was more than human, according to the literal meaning of [certain Old Testament] texts. Those who called Jesus 'son of God,' as the Messiah of Israel, perhaps meant nothing more than this" (*Catechism*, no. 441).[16]

The *Catechism* goes on to argue that this is not the case for Simon Peter's confession, that he recognizes "the transcendent character of the Messiah's divine sonship" (*Catechism*, no. 442). But it does not use language taken from the doctrinal formulations of four and five centuries later. It also recognizes that Peter's faith at the time of his confession could not have been what it would be after the resurrection, when "the apostles can confess: *We have beheld his glory, glory as of the only Son from the Father, full of grace and truth*" (*Catechism*, no. 445, citing John

---

15   "The *Catechism* trusts the biblical word. It holds the Christ of the Gospels to be the real Jesus . . . .We rediscover as if for the first time how great the figure of Jesus is, how it transcends all human measures and precisely thus meets us in true humanity. Acquaintance with this figure evokes joy: this is evangelization." Ratzinger, *Gospel, Catechesis, Catechism*, 64, 68–69.

16   Ratzinger notes, in general, that "the *Catechism* quietly incorporates the truly solid results of modern exegesis," and he gives as an example the historically informed use of christological titles, drawing attention especially to *Catechism*, nos. 109–19. Ratzinger, *Gospel, Catechesis, Catechism*, 65.

1:14). Even here, the confession is left in scriptural terms—with all of their richness, resonance and, in some ways, indeterminacy.

The *Catechism* does not say that after the resurrection "the apostles can confess that 'the same Christ, Lord and only-begotten Son, is to be acknowledged in two natures without confusion, change, division or separation,'" though it will go on later to cite this formula of the Council of Chalcedon as constitutive of the Church's faith (*Catechism*, no. 467). The point is, the *Catechism* recognizes a legitimate trajectory of doctrinal development, and it does not repeat some of the patristic characterizations of what Peter believed, which frequently put a two-nature, one-person confession on his lips.

Turning to some of the events in Jesus' life as recorded by the evangelists, the *Catechism* comments on the coming of the Magi: "Their coming means that pagans can discover Jesus and worship him as Son of God and Savior of the world only by turning toward the Jews and receiving from them the messianic promise as contained in the Old Testament."[17] Jesus does not save as someone who renounced his own religion, Judaism, to found another one, Christianity, or who in any way saves apart from his status as a Jew. Nor does Jesus reject Judaism as a dry, literalistic legalism devoid of spiritual content.

In this regard, the *Catechism's* treatment of the Pharisees is of particular interest. The *Catechism* points out that Jesus endorses "some of the teachings imparted by this religious elite of God's people" (*Catechism*, no. 575). More strikingly, it notes that the "principle of integral observance of the Law not only in letter but in spirit was dear to the Pharisees."[18] Not only are the Pharisees not demonized, but their spiritual view of the Law is presented as the context out of which Jesus' integral understanding of the Law and its fulfillment could have developed, even if his conflict with them over "certain human traditions" and over his own status as acting with authority appropriate only to God is real enough (*Catechism*, nos. 581–82). And, although the *Catechism* certainly accepts the traditional presentation of the prophets as foreshadowing and predicting the Messiah as Jesus Christ, it also understands that the actual fulfillment of the promises, when it came in Jesus, was "so surprising a fulfillment" that it "allows one to understand" the Sanhedrin's "misunderstanding of Jesus" as "tragic" (*Catechism*, no. 591).

The religious authorities are not presented as unanimous in their assessment of Jesus (*Catechism*, nos. 595–96); nor are the "Jews" as a people, in Jesus' time or thereafter, ever assigned responsibility for Jesus' death. The crowd's cry, "His blood be upon us and on our children" (Matt. 27:25), is specifically disclaimed as justification for extending responsibility for Jesus' death to Jews of different

---

17 *Catechism*, no. 528, cited by Joseph Cardinal Ratzinger in *Many Religions—One Covenant: Israel, the Church, and the World* (San Francisco: Ignatius, 1999), 25.

18 *Catechism*, no. 579, also pointed out by Ratzinger as a passage which resists simplifying Jesus' conflictual history as one of "an ostensibly prophetic attack on hardened legalism." *Many Religions—One Covenant*, 31–32.

times and places, and the disclaimer is explained on the basis of a historico-critical observation—this is simply a "formula for ratifying a judicial sentence" (*Catechism*, no. 597). As the *Catechism* observes, all sinners were the authors of Christ's passion, and even as it quotes the *Roman Catechism* to show that this is a constant teaching, it also shows the distance that doctrinal development, much of it on the basis of historical scholarship, has taken.

The *Roman Catechism* states that our crime is greater than the Jews, who *would not have crucified the Lord of glory* if they had known who he was,[19] but the *Catechism* never uses any language that would suggest that the crucifixion is the "crime of the Jews."[20] And, if the Gospel of John talks about the "Jews" in a negative way, this, the *Catechism* points out, is not usually meant as a reference to the "ordinary People of God" but to the "religious authorities for whom the words and deeds of Jesus constituted a sign of contradiction" (*Catechism*, no. 575). Jesus' positive relationship to and respect for the Temple at Jerusalem is also highlighted (*Catechism*, nos. 583–86).

In all of these ways, we find that the *Catechism* has reaped and affirmed the enormous benefits of the literary and historical contextualizing scholarship of the last decades of Catholic biblical study, without at the same time reducing the scope of what counts as "scriptural" to a context any less wide than that proclaimed on the basis of the rule of faith. One could style this a critically aware scriptural catechesis, using the results of critical scholarship to help strain out anachronisms and clarify theological views in order to make the proclamation of the Word made flesh ever more persuasive and attractive in our own time.

The Scriptural Rhetoric of the Fathers

What is the model for this scriptural catechesis of the Word of God? The frequency of patristic citations in the text of the *Catechism* should be a clue here. Patristic homilies often employ scriptural texts, woven together in a tissue of citation and allusion, not simply to corroborate points made in non-scriptural language but to carry the points themselves. Augustine's homilies on the Creed are an excellent example of this technique, and, in particular, his treatment of the incarnation (Sermons 212–214); but the scriptural rhetoric of the fathers is too familiar a practice to belabor here. Further, one of the distinctive characteristics of the Second Vatican Council was its departure from the dialectic, conciliar style favored by Trent and subsequent Church councils, in favor of the rhetorical style of the fathers. John O'Malley has recently commented on this change in style:

> That style did not, of course, spring out of nowhere. In Germany

---

19   *Roman Catechism*, 1.4.11, cited at *Catechism*, no. 598 (cited incorrectly as 1.5.11).

20   Note also how, by contrast with the *Catechism*, the *Roman Catechism* presents the messianic expectations of the Jews as homogenous and political: "But the kingdom of Christ is not what the Jews expected, an earthly one, but a spiritual and eternal kingdom" (1.6.5).

and Belgium but especially in France, theologians had for several decades been trying to find alternatives to the rigidity of the dominant style, and a number of them turned to the Fathers in what they called a *ressourcement*, a "return to the sources." As it turns out, the documents of the council often read like a commentary or homily by one of the Fathers—or by Erasmus. A greater contrast with the style of the discourse of the Council of Trent would be difficult to find.[21]

Commenting further on this style, he notes:

> The documents published by the council manifest many of the characteristics of epideictic rhetoric, for they want to raise appreciation for the issues at stake and to celebrate them. They abound in metaphor and analogies.[22]

We could add to O'Malley's observation that the texts of Vatican II, just as the texts of the fathers, abound in scriptural vocabulary and phraseology, and their metaphors and analogies are often drawn from scriptural images. Consider, for example, paragraph 17 of *Dei Verbum*. This is the paragraph that most closely parallels the sections of the *Catechism* on the incarnation and I have chosen it for the purposes of comparison:

> The Word of God, which to *everyone who has faith* contains *God's saving power* (Rom. 1:16), is set forth and marvelously displays its power in the writings of the New Testament. For *when the time had fully come* (Gal. 4:4), *the Word became flesh and dwelt among us, full of grace and truth* (John 1:14). Christ established on earth the kingdom of God, revealed his Father and himself by deeds and words and by his death, resurrection and glorious ascension, as well as by sending the Holy Spirit, completed his work. *Lifted up from the earth* he *draws all people to* himself (John 12:32), for he alone *has the words of eternal life* (John 6:68). This *mystery was not made known to other generations as it has now been revealed to his holy apostles and prophets by the Holy Spirit*

---

21 John O'Malley, *Four Cultures of the West* (Cambridge, MA: Harvard University, 2004), 175. Though, as I have already implied above, I think this contrast can be overstated when it comes to the *Roman Catechism*, concerned as it is, above all, with forming preachers. In some ways one can think of the *Catechism*'s use of Scripture as developing a practice that responds even more fully to the intention of the *Roman Catechism*, because it provides an opportunity for preachers to preach on doctrine *while* preaching on Scripture, and *vice versa*. Because of its use of Scripture, the *Catechism* obviates the false dichotomy of wondering whether to preach on Scripture or to preach catechetically.

22 *Four Cultures of the West*, 176.

(see Eph. 3:4–6), that they might preach the Gospel, foster faith
in Jesus Christ the Lord, and bring together the Church. The
writings of the New Testament stand as a perpetual and divine
witness to these realities.[23]

The use of the Bible in this passage is exactly analogous to its use in the
Catechism—not so much to corroborate points but to fully inform the vocabulary
and imagery of the main text itself, thus appealing to the imagination and seeking
in this way to persuade readers of the truth of the teachings presented.

From this perspective, far from being a throwback to a pre-conciliar use of
the scriptural text, the *Catechism*'s use of Scripture cannot be understood apart
from the Second Vatican Council's adoption of what we could call the scriptural
rhetoric of the fathers. The *Catechism*, as did the Council in general, very clearly
states the basic and necessary doctrines of the Catholic faith. But it does so with
the help of a language drawn heavily from Scripture—pressing into service the
richness and beauty of scriptural language in an attempt to make those doctrines
appeal to the imagination and ideals, to the "joys and hopes," of people in the
modern world, believers and seekers alike.[24]

---

23 *Dei Verbum*, 17. See also, the first chapter of *Lumen Gentium*, Dogmatic Constitution on the
Church (November 21, 1964), 1–8, in *Vatican Council II*. Here we have another particularly
compelling example of this technique as it seeks not only to define, but also to impart, an
understanding of the Church in scriptural image, analogy, and metaphor.

24 The phrase "joys and hopes" is an allusion to the first line of the Second Vatican Council's
Constitution on the Church in the modern world, *Gaudium et Spes* (December 7, 1965), in
Vatican Council II, 903. Also, see section 3 of Pope John Paul II's Apostolic Constitution
Fidei Depositum, printed as the dedicatory letter to the *Catechism*, which mentions as among
the *Catechism*'s intended audience all the Church's pastors and faithful, as well as separated
Christians and indeed "every individual . . . who wants to know what the Catholic Church
believes." *Catechism of the Catholic Church*, 6. We could indeed think of these individuals as
including the "accedentes," seekers who have not enrolled as catechumens, but who are interested
enough to come to a catechetical lecture (or, in this case, pick up a catechetical text). It could also
include all people of good will with deeper questionings about human life to whom *Gaudium et
Spes* is addressed. *Gaudium et Spes*, 10.

Letter & Spirit 2 (2006): 55–67

Theologia Prima:
The Liturgical Mystery and the Mystery of God

~: David W. Fagerberg :~

University of Notre Dame

The great tradition of the Church understands liturgy, Scripture, and theology in a way that is somewhat different from the way they are commonly understood today. I think it behooves us to figure out what that difference is. Toward that end, I would like here to think about the relationship of these three things within a larger context. How does the mystery of God encountered in the *liturgy* affect our understanding of *theology* and *Scripture?*

Entering this world of discourse requires of us a conversion of mind. As is well known, the Greek word for conversion was *metanoia*, coming from *meta*, meaning beyond or after, and *nous*, which is not so much "reason" as what Metropolitan Hierotheos calls "the eye of the heart."[1] If we want to see liturgy, Scripture, and theology differently, we must see them with a *meta-nous*, and that will change our rational understanding of them. The thesis I would like to explore here is this: in order to see each one of them more clearly, we must see them all together. To see each one correctly, we must see all of them as connected and bound to one another holistically. Our task is not so much to replace the curricula of liturgy, Scripture, and theology with a new content (like opening three shoe boxes to replace shoes with sandals). Our task is to let the connection between liturgy, Scripture and theology be a path to a thickened understanding of each of them. That is what we have ceased doing because we no longer see these three in the light of the singular mystery of God.

Casting around for some metaphors to make my point, I have come up with two. The first one comes, as do so many of my mental images, from G. K. Chesterton. In *The Autobiography* he writes that he always understood there to be some truth in pagan philosophical systems, but says he became a Catholic because he believes these truths are also contained *and better coordinated* in Catholicism. "That almost any other theology or philosophy contains a truth, I do not at all deny. . . . [But] I have only found one creed that could not be satisfied with a truth, but only with the Truth, which is made of a million such truths and yet is one. . . . Flowers grow best in a garden, and even grow biggest in a garden; and in the

---

1   Metropolitan Hierotheos, *Orthodoxy Psychotherapy: The Science of the Fathers* (Levadia: Birth of the Theotokos Monastery, 1994), and *St. Gregory Palamas as a Hagiorite* (Levadia: Birth of the Theotokos Monastery, 1997).

wilderness they wither and die."[2] Scriptural exegetes have some truths; liturgiologists also keep some truths in their back pocket; theologians keep their truths tidy in various systematic pigeon holes; but whatever truths they have will grow biggest when they are coordinated in the garden of Truth.

Chesterton remembers thinking it odd, even before his conversion, to remove one part of the Christian faith, namely Scripture, and isolate it from the rest, as if a part can be played off against the whole. It is absurd to take the Bible out of the Church, or to use the Bible to condemn the great tradition of the Church. He makes his point by condensing the sixteenth century exaltation of the Bible to a single episode of a single afternoon.

> The ordinary sensible skeptic or pagan is standing in the street . . . and he sees a procession go by of the priests of some strange cult, carrying their object of worship under a canopy, some of them wearing high head-dresses and carrying symbolical staffs, others carrying scrolls and sacred records, others carrying sacred images and lighted candles before them, others sacred relics in caskets or cases, and so on. I can understand the spectator saying, "This is all hocus-pocus"; I can even understand him, in moments of irritation, breaking up the procession, throwing down the images, tearing up the scrolls, dancing on the priests and anything else that might express that general view. I can understand his saying, "Your croziers are bosh, your candles are bosh, your statues and scrolls and relics and all the rest of it are bosh." But in what conceivable frame of mind does he rush in to select one particular scroll of the scriptures of this one particular group (a scroll which had always belonged to them and been a part of their hocus-pocus, if it was hocus-pocus); why in the world should the man in the street say that one particular scroll was *not* bosh, but was the one and only truth by which all the other things were to be condemned? Why should it not be as superstitious to worship the scrolls as the statues, of that one particular procession?[3]

Ever since this brawl in the streets of the sixteenth century, it is as if Protestants and Catholics have thought they must scuffle over the remaining debris. They have sounded like children choosing up teams for a game of kickball: "We'll take Scripture, faith, and grace." "Then we get the pope, Mary, and the other

2   G. K. Chesterton, *The Autobiography*, vol. 16 of *The Collected Works of G. K. Chesterton* (San Francisco: Ignatius, 1988), 328–329.

3   G. K. Chesterton, *The Catholic Church and Conversion*, vol. 3 of *The Collected Works of G. K. Chesterton* (San Francisco: Ignatius, 1990), 73.

five sacraments." There is a problem with allowing these fault lines to continue. It just may be that a particular scroll only blooms if it remains securely rooted in the whole Scripture; and the whole Scripture may only be intelligible if read as the marching orders for a liturgical procession; and the theology that comes from this liturgical life is about participation in the life of God. Liturgy, Scripture, and theology must be seen in light of the mystery of God.

I submit to the reader a second metaphor. This one entails some risk, because it comes from a world of science I have not dealt with since high school. As I remember it, when one hydrogen atom is bonded to another hydrogen atom, and those are bonded to an oxygen atom, the end molecule is substantially different from the atoms. The three atoms are gasses; the molecule H_2O is a liquid. To produce the liquid, one doesn't change one of the atoms to look like a different box on the Periodical Table of the Elements. Instead, one brings these three atoms into conjunction with each other to make a compound. Let the three atoms lose contact with each other and there won't be a liquid any more, only gasses. Let liturgy, Scripture, and theology lose contact with one another, and instead of something refreshing you have something rather gaseous. This sometimes happens in the academy, where associating Scripture study with the mystery of God is assumed to corrupt the objectivity of the examiner; and liturgy is disassociated from the mystery of God and turned into a history of sacramentaries or a phenomenology of rite; and theology puts the mystery of God under a slide for our controlled examination.

Gathering my metaphors together, I can say that I would like to replant our scattered truths about liturgy, Scripture, and theology in a single garden of Truth. I would like to pick up the scattered pieces of our stumbled liturgical procession and return the scroll of Scripture to the arms of liturgical theologians. I would like to first consider liturgy, Scripture, and theology on their atomic level, and then make some comments on the molecular level about their relationship to the mystery of God.

One Liturgy, On Earth and in Heaven

There are not two liturgies, one on earth and one in heaven. There is one liturgy, on earth and in heaven. The liturgy of the Church is the heavenly liturgy as it is practiced on earth, and it is crucial to restore this eschatological dimension to our practice of liturgy. In the liturgy we do what the angels do, namely, lose ourselves in a joy that erupts in praise. St. John Chrysostom said joy issues when the lover receives the beloved. In that case, the liturgy issues when the Church receives her beloved. The liturgy is our trysting place with God. According to the dictionary, a tryst is "an agreement, as between lovers, to meet at a certain time and place." Exactly! God, our Divine Lover, has agreed to meet us on holy ground for communion, and from that encounter with the Father through the risen Christ, the Holy Spirit creates "theologian souls."[4]

In order to identify this reality, we call the liturgy "sacramental." Paul Evdokimov speaks of sacraments as "an action of 'punching holes' in the closed world by powerful explosions from the Beyond." By the sacraments we are taught "that everything is destined for a liturgical fulfillment."[5] So the Divine Liturgy, the liturgy of the hours, the sacraments, and sacramentals, and our personal liturgies of devotion, piety, and ministry to charity, are all points at which the reign of God presses through the partition that sin has constructed. The kingdom of God approaches us in liturgy in a way that is material, communal, and ritualistic, which is why the Church is a sacramental, political, and social entity.

"To swim" is a verb and "swimmer" is the noun. "To run" is a verb and "runner" is the noun. "Liturgy" is a verb and "Christian" is the noun. Liturgy is the activity of Christians, and Christians become what they do. My teacher, Aidan Kavanagh, also used to say "I don't go to Mass because I'm Catholic, I'm Catholic because I go to Mass."

Imagine liturgy in the Church as blood is in the body. Or, better still, imagine liturgy in the Church as soul is in the body—what the scholastics meant by *anima forma corporis*. Etienne Gilson clarifies the meaning of the term "forma." For St. Thomas Aquinas, he writes, "the soul does not first make a body move, it first makes it a body. A corpse is not a body. The soul makes it exist as a body."[6] Applied to our case, the liturgy is the form of the Church. The liturgy makes the assembly exist as the body of Christ. An assembly by itself is not a body. The liturgy does not first make an assembly move, it first makes it the body of Christ. The Eucharist makes the Church, as Henri de Lubac has reminded this generation.

Leitourgia originally meant a work done by a few on behalf of the many. "It denoted a work (*ergon*) undertaken on behalf of the people (*laos*). Public projects undertaken by an individual for the good of the community in such areas as education, entertainment or defense would be *leitourgia*."[7] Christ undertook a work on behalf of the vital interests of the clan to which he chose to belong—the family of Adam and Eve—and his liturgy continues in the activity of his body. We are the body of Christ because this activity continues in us. By baptismal grace, we

---

4   Archimandrite Vasileios, *Hymn of Entry: Liturgy and Life in the Orthodox Church* (Crestwood, NY: St. Vladimir's Seminary, 1984), 23.

5   Paul Evdokimov, *Art of the Icon: A Theology of Beauty* (Redondo Beach, CA: Oakwood, 1990), 117.

6   Etienne Gilson, *The Christian Philosophy of St . Thomas Aquinas* (Notre Dame: University of Notre Dame, 1956), 187.

7   Lawrence Madden, "Liturgy," *The New Dictionary of Sacramental Worship*, ed. Peter Fink (Collegeville, MN: Liturgical Press, 1990), 740.

are incorporated into the sacred humanity of Christ, his Spirit is poured into our bodies, and we are made one of a new race. Baptism makes a new people called into existence for the very purpose of continuing the work of Christ. *Leitourgia* is Christ's work become ours.

Liturgy is not, then, a performance of *our* religion. Liturgy is the religion of Christ—the religion he enacted in the flesh before the Father—perpetuated. The religion that Jesus did in his humanity, he left to his Church to continue performing. We join Jesus in his liturgy to the Father and on behalf of the many. That would be why Pope Pius XII defined liturgy this way: "The sacred liturgy is . . . the public worship which our Redeemer as head of the Church renders to the Father, as well as the worship which the community of the faithful renders to its founder, and through him to the heavenly Father. It is, in short, the worship rendered by the Mystical Body of Christ in the entirety of its head and members."[8] It is not a thing that Jesus left to his Church, but himself. And he is, himself, the mediator of the Father's grace to us, and the mediator of our thanksgiving to the Father, all in the Holy Spirit. Liturgy is best understood as a relationship. Liturgy is participating in the relationship of love that flows between the persons of the Trinity.

Scripture, an Invitation to Enter Sacred History

I therefore consider Christ to be the premier liturgist, and baby liturgists are born in the baptismal font when they are grafted into his life. The entire economy of salvation, as it is recorded in Scripture, has had as its purpose to produce liturgists. Obviously this only makes sense with a thickened definition of "liturgist" because what need has the world for more cantors and thurifers? But if liturgy is, as defined above, the extension of the Father's love to the world through the body the Holy Spirit has knitted together in the waters of the font, then we can say the entire economy of salvation recorded in Scripture exists to bring mankind into liturgy.

This makes the Bible something more than a book of religious propositions. The Bible is neither a catechism nor a morals manual. It is a record of the self-disclosure of God, made in history because we are historical beings. Furthermore, it is an invitation to step into that history. The revelation of God is not in the words of the book, the revelation of God is in the history recorded by the inspired words of the book. When we approach the Scriptures, we search for a person, not for a proposition. Luther said the Bible is the manger in which the Christ-child is laid, and we should never confuse the straw with the baby.

Augustine famously said, "In the Old Testament the New lies hid; in the New Testament the meaning of the Old becomes clear."[9] Marcion tried to take a

---

8   Pope Pius XII, *Mediator Dei*, Encyclical Letter on the Sacred Liturgy (November 20, 1947), 20, in *Mediator Dei* (Mahwah, NJ: Paulist, 1948).

9   Augustine's "old saying" is quoted in *The Catechism of the Catholic Church*, 2d. ed. (Vatican City: Libreria Editrice Vaticana, 1997), no. 129.

hatchet to this reciprocal correlation and divide the New Covenant from the first Covenant. If he had succeeded, we would not have been able to understand either covenant, because we cannot understand Christ apart from the Old Testament covenant, or what the Old Testament was driving at without seeing Jesus as its omega point.

It is crucial that Christians discover the relationship of the Church to the Old Testament. Remember that the top row of the Orthodox iconostasis contains icons of the "Church of the Old Testament." Charles Journet said "The Church made its appearance in time before Christ did. The frontier of the Church passes through each one of those who call themselves her members."[10] The Church may have been born at Pentecost to become a public, visible thing, but its moment of conception was earlier.[11] Israel is the womb for the human race and the Church of the Old Testament is the Church *in utero*.

"Typology" is the name for this connection between the testaments. Jean Daniélou calls typology "the science of the similitudes between the two testaments."[12] When the yellow paint of Scripture meets the blue paint of Jesus, the green paint that results is called typology. Typology is the mystical art of finding Christ foreshadowed in the Hebrew Scriptures, and finding the Scriptures illuminated by the eschatological outpouring of the Spirit.

Since Jesus himself understood his identity in light of the Old Testament, what would it mean to us when he called himself the "bread of life" if we did not know Exodus 12? Or the "lamb of God," without Exodus 16? How could we understand sacrifice without the book of Leviticus, or the Son of Man without Isaiah and Daniel? Typology sees Christ in the light of Scripture and reads the spiritual meaning of the letter in light of the mystery made flesh. This is what the apostles did. The apostles' preaching is nothing but this. And when the apostolic faith was written down, it composed the New Testament.

So the New Testament is neither an addendum to nor a replacement of the Scriptures; there are not two Bibles. The New Testament is apostolic witness to the hour when the Word of God spoken in the Old Testament became flesh. The authority of the New Testament derives from the apostles' authority. They are the twelve pillars of the Church's Scripture and her tradition. The Church is Israel renewed (which is a better way of saying "a new Israel"). In the words of Alexander Golitzin, "The Church is nothing more nor less than Israel in the

---

10   Charles Journet, *The Church of the Word Incarnate* (New York: Sheed and Ward, 1955), xxvii.

11   "Doubtless, the Holy Spirit was already at work in the world before Christ was glorified. Yet on the day of Pentecost, He came down upon the disciples to remain with them forever (cf. John 14:16). The Church was publicly displayed to the multitude . . . " Second Vatican Council, *Ad Gentes*, Decree on the Church's Missionary Activity (December 7, 1965), 4, in Austin Flannery, ed. *Vatican Council II: The Conciliar and Post Conciliar Documents*, rev. ed. (Northport, NY: Costello, 1988), 816–817.

12   Jean Daniélou, *The Bible and the Liturgy* (Notre Dame: University of Notre Dame, 1956), 4.

altered circumstances of the Messiah's death, resurrection, and the eschatological outpouring of his Spirit."[13] The Old Testament and the New Testament are like the two cherubim facing each other, sitting atop the ark of the covenant, God's throne, looking at the Lord seated between them.[14]

Pope Benedict XVI says, "apostolic succession is essentially the living presence of the Word in the person of the witnesses."[15] And that is the same reason why Karl Rahner insists on understanding the apostolic succession as a living experience. "It is not only propositions about their experience that the apostles bequeath, but their Spirit, the Holy Spirit of God, the very reality, then, of what they have experienced in Christ. Their own experience is preserved and present together with their Word."[16]

The First Letter of John provides a definition of apostolic tradition when it defines the aim of the apostles. "We declare to you what we have seen and heard so that you also may have fellowship with us; and truly our fellowship is with the Father and with his Son Jesus Christ" (1 John 1:3). The twelve pass on what they have seen and heard, not so we can know what they saw and know what they heard, but so that we too may participate in the Son. If the witness recorded in the New Testament does not lead to the spiritual fellowship the apostles had with the Father through his Son Jesus Christ, then we are misreading the whole Scripture. It becomes dead letter. It is not theological. It is not read liturgically.

The content of Christian tradition is proclaimed by the Church in the liturgy as the rule of faith. Such a tacit knowledge of the Church's rule of faith is called by Andrew Louth our participation in tradition, and it emerges, he writes, from the silence of prayer. "Prayer is seen in the fathers to be, as it were, the amniotic fluid in which our knowledge of God takes form."[17] Liturgical prayer is the mother of theology.

---

13   Alexander Golitzin, "Scriptural Images of the Church: An Eastern Orthodox Reflection" (Unpublished paper, 2001), available at http://www.marquette.edu/maqom/church.

14   The thought is from a homily by St. Gregory the Great: "In the two angels [who appeared in Christ's tomb] we can recognize the two Testaments. . . . They have come together where the Lord's body is, because, by announcing in convergent fashion that the Lord took flesh, died, and rose again, the two Testaments are as it were seated, the Old at his head and the New at his feet. That is why the two cherubim who protect the mercy seat face each other. . . . Cherub indeed means fullness of knowledge. . . . When the Old Testament foretells what the New Testament declares accomplished in the Lord, they face each other like the two cherubim, their gaze fixed on the mercy seat, because they are looking at the Lord between them and they . . . are recounting in harmony the mystery of his loving purpose." Quoted in Olivier Clement, *The Roots of Christian Mysticism* (New York: New City, 1996), 98.

15   Joseph Ratzinger, "Primacy, Episcopate, and Apostolic Succession," in Karl Rahner and Joseph Ratzinger, *The Episcopate and the Primacy* (New York: Herder & Herder, 1962), 54.

16   Karl Rahner, "The Development of Dogma," in *Theological Investigations*, 10 vols. (New York: Seabury, 1974), 10:68.

17   Andrew Louth, *Discerning the Mystery: An Essay on the Nature of Theology* (Oxford: Clarendon, 1983), 65.

Theology, the Science of the Scriptures

The western Church, straight up to Thomas Aquinas, called theology "the science of the Scriptures." Theology is not necessarily constructed by a lone Ph.D. in an office lined with academic books because academic theology is only one species in the genus of theology. The kind of theology meant here consists of the ability to find Christ in the Scriptures, and to read the ecclesiological, moral, and eschatological meanings contained in the letter (these were the three "spiritual meanings" in tradition, called the typological, tropological, and anagogical). According to Yves Congar, the medieval Church understood theology to be "an extension of faith, which is a certain communication and a certain sharing of God's knowledge." Theology includes "the construction of God in us, or rather the construction of Christ in us."[18]

Theology's more relevant practitioner is Mrs. Murphy who has been capacitated by the mystery of God in the liturgy to see the world in the light of Mount Tabor. She may not be able to say something about other theologians, but she can do something more important: she can say something theological about everything else in the world. The person who has been capacitated by liturgy to read the Scriptures in the light of Christ sees all things with the eye of the dove, which is how St. Gregory Nyssa spoke of "spiritual sight": it is seeing by means of the Holy Spirit. Becoming a theologian is therefore the calling and the responsibility of every baptized Christian.

The content of Christian tradition is tracked in the pages of Scripture. Being a tracker means knowing how to read trails; being a theologian means knowing how to read Scripture. And who are we tracking? The *Logos*. And where does he lead us? To *Theos*, to God the Father. And by what power can we do this? Not our own; the Holy Spirit must illuminate the process. Thomas Spidlik's work on spirituality notes that the Church fathers "understood the practice of theology only as a personal communion with *Theos*, the Father, through the *Logos*, Christ, in the Holy Spirit—an experience lived in a state of prayer."[19] That is why prayer is the amniotic fluid for theological knowledge.

Being a theologian means being able to use the grammar learned in liturgy to speak about God. Even more, it means speaking of God. Yet even more, it means speaking with God. That is why Evagrius of Pontus calls prayer theology: "If you are a theologian you truly pray. If you truly pray you are a theologian."[14] And before there were universities with theology faculties, it was possible to learn and to use this theological grammar. *Theologia* stood at the end of a process of asceticism that conformed a life to Christ. The starting point of theology was not the library card catalogue, but the Eucharist, the grammar of faith learned in the *lex orandi* ("law of prayer") of liturgical life.

18   Yves Congar, *A History of Theology* (New York: Doubleday, 1968), 261.

19   Thomas Spidlik, *The Spirituality of the Christian East* (Kalamazoo: Cistercian, 1986), 1.

For the fathers, theology meant a knowledge of God which comes from an illumination of the soul by the Holy Spirit, and this is the very substance of the soul's deification. Theology is not only knowledge about God, it is the supernatural communication of God's very life. Irenaeus called the Son and the Holy Spirit the two hands of the Father. What does the Father want to do with his two outstretched hands? I picture God, who once formed man by crouching over the clay of the earth and sculpting it into a human form (see Gen. 2:7), now wanting to finish his handiwork. The Father reaches out through the Son and the Holy Spirit to bring us to completion. The image grows further into the likeness of God. Within this context, theology is less the fruit of a graduate program at university, and more the fruit of a rightly-ordered existence. Theology is as much a practice as a cognition.

The Mystery of God's Will

Now we want to find some water. We must turn from the atomic level to do molecular theology. We want to find out what bonds these atomic elements of the Church. How are liturgy, Scripture, and theology unified, and what prevents them from drifting apart? We want to avoid loss of harmony lest we lose the mystery itself. Why is there a salvation history recorded in Scripture, and a Church which performs liturgy, and theologians formed for Mount Tabor?

The *Catechism of the Catholic Church* suggests the following reason for the inauguration of the economy of salvation: "Disfigured by sin and death, man remains 'in the image of God,' in the image of the Son, but is deprived 'of the glory of God,' of his 'likeness.' The promise made to Abraham inaugurates the economy of salvation, at the culmination of which the Son himself will assume that 'image' and restore it in the Father's 'likeness' by giving it again its glory, the Spirit who is 'the giver of life.'"[20] Man and woman, the image of God, are to grow into the likeness of God, and this is the reason for all of salvation history, this is our liturgical life, and this is theology in motion. But what is the mysterious charge that bonds these three together?

Let me suggest an answer by means of an imaginary illustration. Suppose with me that you had a friend to whom you lent a copy of the Bible. He was curious about the Christian Bible, so you invited him to examine one. A week or so later you ask "What did you think of it?" and suppose he soberly answers, "It is a great book. I've never seen such sturdy binding, and I thought the typography elegant, and the paper is certainly top quality." If your friend said something like that, I should suppose that he was not attending to the book as a Bible, but attending to the book as a book. Maybe he was a bookbinder by profession; maybe he sold paper and ink and covers for books; maybe he was a Bible collector and knew all about

---

rare Bibles. Whatever the case, he would not be attending to the Bible as a believer, but as a bibliophile.

> Suppose with me further that the Bible was lent to another person who, after careful examination, looked up with a furrowed brow and pointed out a chronological discrepancy in Second Kings, or an error about the Hittites which more recent archeology has now corrected. That person would be attending to the Bible as a historian. Or suppose a reader mused about Abraham's conflicted mind during his trip up Mount Moriah with Isaac, or opined about whether it was sexual insecurity which caused Solomon to aspire to a greater harem than the King of the Euphrates had; then we would think this person was attending to the book as a psychiatrist. A scientist could attend to the cosmological descriptions in Genesis, a sociologist to the kinship structure of Israel's patriarchal era, a Hellenist to the parallels between Jesus and a wandering cynic, a comparative religionist to the subtle similarities between Israel's temple cult and Hindu sacrifice—in any of a hundred ways a person could attend to the book in a different way from what we might have expected.[21]

Now we can see the question I want to ask: to what would one have to be attending in order to experience the Bible as Scripture? This same question should have two other echoes. To what would one have to be attending in order to experience the ritual as liturgy, and the words as theology? How do we approach liturgy, Scripture, and theology in order to receive them from God?

In each case, I submit, we have to attend to the mystery of God. And we experience the mystery of God as our deification, our growth in holiness, our increased union with God. What we have been talking about throughout is the Church as she manifests herself in liturgy, Scripture, and theology. The Church is the mystery of God coming to fruition. Paul unpacks it this way in Ephesians 3.

> With all wisdom and insight [God] has made known to us the mystery of his will, according to his good pleasure that he set forth in Christ, as a plan for the fullness of time, to gather up all things in him. . . . He has abolished the law with its commandments and ordinances, that he might create in himself one new humanity in place of the two. . . . In former generations this mystery was not made known to humankind, as it has now been revealed to his holy apostles and prophets by the Spirit:

---

21   David Fagerberg, "On the Reform of Liturgists," *Antiphon*, 5 (June 2000), 5–7.

that is, the Gentiles have become fellow heirs, members of the same body, and sharers in the promise in Christ Jesus through the gospel.[22]

The mystery is the Father's will. The mystery is the Father's will to join humankind into the perichoresis, the dynamic interpenetration and mutual reciprocity that flows between himself and the Son and the Holy Spirit. The mystery is Christ, who enacts that will. And the Church is where Christ (the mystery of God) and the Holy Spirit (the breath of God) are accomplishing God's will. All this the Church has included in its understanding of "tradition." Louis Bouyer identifies four strands of meaning in the way the Church has used the term: First of all, tradition is the rule of faith, the synthetic statement of what every Christian and the whole Church, at all times must believe. It is also the Scripture, the Old Testament first of all, but also what the apostles had expressed, together with the Gospel of Christ which he himself proclaimed. It is further the organized and organic life of the Church in her hierarchical structure and her liturgical structure. Finally, tradition is the incarnate life of charity, the life of the Spirit, the Spirit of God which is the Body of Christ.[23]

Jean Daniélou's lovely little book on the angels cites St. John Chrysostom when the latter describes the angels' reaction when the mystery was revealed to heaven, that is, when the incarnated one ascended into heaven. Chrysostom writes:

> St. Paul speaks here [in Ephesians 3] of a mystery, because not even the angels knew it. The angels only knew that the Lord had chosen His people as His portion (Deut. 32:8) . . . That is why we need not be surprised that they did not know this [mystery], since, properly speaking, it is the gospel. God had said he would save his people Israel, but had said nothing about the nations. The angels knew that the nations were called, but could not imagine that they would be called to the same end and would be seated upon the throne of God.[24]

The same thought was expressed in the west by St. Paschasius who likened Jesus to a needle, whose eye was pierced by his passion, but who now "draws all after him, so repairing the tunic rent by Adam, stitching together the two peoples of

---

22   Eph. 1:8–9; 2:15; 3:5–6.

23   Louis Bouyer, *The Church of God* (Chicago: Franciscan Herald, 1982), 10–11. See also, Jean Danielou, *God and the Ways of Knowing* (New York: Meridian Books, 1967), esp. chapter 5.

24   Jean Daniélou, *The Angels and Their Mission* (Westminster: Newman, 1957), 33.

Jew and Gentile, making them one for always."[25] To Chrysostom, this completely explains the behavior of the angels at the Ascension.

Do you want to know how they rejoiced in the Ascension? Listen to the account in the Bible, "They rise and descend continuously." That is the behavior of those who want to contemplate a very special sight. They want to see the unheard-of spectacle of man appearing in heaven. That is why the angels are constantly showing themselves: when He is born, when He dies, when He rises into heaven.[26]

The angels were startled by the mystery because the mystery is, in Bouyer's words, "the secret plan of salvation which only God can reveal and which he reveals by carrying it out."[27] They rose up on tiptoes to see such a thing. Christ, our brother, brings human nature into heaven where we who cling to his ascension by faith, having clung to his death and resurrection by faith, can join the divine dance of love. The angels didn't want to miss it.

Jean Daniélou summarily says: "The Christian faith has only one object, the mystery of Christ dead and risen. But this unique mystery subsists under different modes: it is prefigured in the Old Testament, it is accomplished historically in the earthly life of Christ, it is contained in mystery in the sacraments, it is lived mystically in souls, it is accomplished socially in the Church, it is consummated eschatologically in the heavenly kingdom."[28]

The Auto-graph of God

If you will understand my use of the term, I could propose that there is a difference between the way liturgy, Scripture, and theology are commonly understood today, and the way they are understood by the great tradition. The great tradition saw them as more *mystical* than we do. By "mystical" I do not mean baffling, bewildering, confusing. In the Christian tradition, *mysterion* means the Father's love for humankind revealed in and shared by Christ, and for something to be more mystical would mean something is drawn deeper into full, active, and conscious participation in salvation history.

If *Scripture* is read mystically, it will bring us before the mystery of God. That, claims Louth, was the real reason for typology or allegory, though few introductions to typology written today give this impression. "The traditional doctrine of the multiple senses of Scripture, with its use of allegory, is essentially an attempt to respond to the *mira profunditas* of Scripture, seen as the indispensable witness

---

25 Quoted in Henri de Lubac, *Catholicism: Christ and the Common Destiny of Man* (San Francisco: Ignatius, 1988), 35.

26 Daniélou, *Angels*, 35.

27 Louis Bouyer, *The Christian Mystery: From Pagan Myth to Christian Mysticism* (Edinburgh T & T Clark, 1990), 133.

28 Jean Daniélou, quoted in Robert Taft, "Toward a Theology of the Christian Feast," *Beyond East and West* (Rome: Pontifical Oriental Institute, 1997), 29.

to the mystery of Christ. This is the heart of the use of allegory."[29] Bouyer adds that the mystical cannot be had outside the liturgy because "the mystical is the experience of what the Scriptures reveal to us in the Spirit who has given them to us and of what this Spirit communicates to us in the sacraments, in the Eucharist first and foremost."[30]

If *liturgy* is celebrated mystically, it will bring us before the mystery of God. "In the beginning was the *Logos*," John's Gospel tells us, "and he pitched his tent among us." The *Logos* is the Word in the sense of reason, principle, standard, or logic. He is the wisdom of the Father, the Father's thought. By the *Logos* the cosmos was made, and by the *Logos* all things hold together, from electrons to galaxies. The *Logos* is the reason of things, and the reason for things—their *telos*, their end, that toward which providence aims. What we have every eighth day, then, is a liturgy of the *Logos* and a liturgy of the Eucharist. Mystical liturgy would be a way into God's *Logos*, who is the mystery that invites the sons of Adam and daughters of Eve home to the Father's covenantal love.

If *theology* were to become more mystical, then we would understand it not as a rational science by us, but as the Father's *Logos* shared with us. Blessed Columba Marmion asked, "What in fact is faith?" And he answered, "It is a mysterious participation in the knowledge that God has of himself. God knows himself as Father, Son, and Holy Spirit."[31] When we acknowledge Christ as divine, then our confession is an echo of the very knowledge that God has of himself.

The Church fathers thought of theology as knowledge of the Trinity. But this is more than information. Theology is the art of life—spiritual life, to be exact. Becoming a theologian-soul means being further conformed to the God-man. We are to become an image of Christ, who was the image of the Father. We are to become an icon of the icon of God. To say that this process takes place all by grace is only to say that God is writing each of us as an image of his Son by his own hand. We are the Father's auto-graph: Christ the mystery is inscribed in us by the Holy Spirit.

---

29   Louth, *Discerning the Mystery*, 112.

30   Bouyer, *The Christian Mystery*, 183.

31   Columba Marmion, *Christ in His Mysteries* (St. Louis: B. Herder, 1931), 237.

Letter & Spirit 2 (2006): 69–96

THE LORD'S PRAYER AND THE NEW EXODUS

∾: Brant Pitre :∾

Our Lady of Holy Cross College, New Orleans

For almost two thousand years, Christians have recited the words of the Lord's Prayer, the only one that Jesus is recorded as having taught his disciples (Matt. 6:9–13; Luke 11:2–4). In the second century, Tertullian declared it to be "truly the summary of the whole gospel," and, much later, St. Thomas Aquinas deemed it "the most perfect of prayers."[1]

But what does the prayer actually mean? More specifically, what did *Jesus himself* mean when he taught it to his disciples? And how would they, as first century Jews, have understood its language and imagery? These are important questions, and modern commentators have spilled an enormous amount of ink in the attempt to understand the prayer in its first-century context.[2] Despite the widespread agreement that the Lord's Prayer reflects the heart of Jesus' message, questions still remain regarding exactly what the prayer reveals about how Jesus understood himself, his mission, and the coming of the kingdom of God.

Several years ago, N. T. Wright published a brief but thought-provoking article in which he argued that the Lord's Prayer should be understood as a prayer for the "new Exodus."[3] Throughout the Old Testament, the prophets had expressed the hope that God would once again redeem the people of Israel in much the same

---

1   Tertullian, *On Prayer*, 1 in *Patrologiae Cursus Completus. Series Latina*, ed. J.P. Migne (Paris: Garnier and J.P. Migne, 1844–1864), 1, 1155; Thomas Aquinas, *Summa Theologica* [Summary of Theology], Pt. II-II, Q. 83, art. 9, cited in *Catechism of the Catholic Church*, 2d. ed. (Vatican City: Libreria Editrice Vaticana, 1997), nos. 2761, 2763.

2   The secondary literature on the Lord's Prayer is vast indeed. For our purposes here, some of the more notable treatments include: James D. G. Dunn, *Jesus Remembered* (Grand Rapids, MI: Eerdmans, 2003), 226–28, 409–411, 546–55, 589–91; N. T. Wright, "The Lord's Prayer as a Paradigm for Christian Prayer," in *Into God's Presence: Prayer in the New Testament*, ed. Richard N. Longenecker (Grand Rapids, MI: Eerdmans, 2001), 132–54; Gerd Theissen and Annette Merz, *The Historical Jesus: A Comprehensive Guide*, trans. John Bowden. (Minneapolis: Fortress, 1998), 261–64; Jürgen Becker, *Jesus of Nazareth*, trans. James E. Crouch (New York and Berlin: Walter de Gruyter, 1998), 265–71; N. T. Wright, *Jesus and the Victory of God* (Minneapolis: Fortress, 1996), 292–94; John P. Meier, *A Marginal Jew: Rethinking the Historical Jesus*, 3 vols. (New York: Doubleday, 1991, 1994, 2001), 2:291–302; W. D. Davies and Dale C. Allison, Jr., *A Critical and Exegetical Commentary on the Gospel According to Saint Matthew*, 3 vols. (Edinburgh: T. & T. Clark, 1988, 1991, 1997), 1:590–615; G. R. Beasley-Murray, *Jesus and the Kingdom of God* (Grand Rapids, MI: Eerdmans, 1986), 147–57; Joseph A. Fitzmyer, *The Gospel According to Luke*, 2 vols. (New York: Doubleday, 1983, 1985), 2:896–909; Joachim Jeremias, *New Testament Theology*, (New York: Scribner, 1971), 193–203; and *The Prayers of Jesus* (Naperville, IL: A. R. Allenson, 1967), 82–107; Raymond E. Brown, "The Pater Noster as an Eschatological Prayer," in *New Testament Essays* (New York: Doubleday, 1968), 275–320.

3   See Wright, "The Lord's Prayer," 132–54.

way that he had done in the Exodus from Egypt. In this new Exodus, God would release his people from slavery to sin and death, put an end to their exile from the promised land, and gather them, along with the Gentiles, into a restored kingdom and a new Jerusalem.[4] According to Wright, the ancient Jewish hope for a new Exodus is the key to unlocking the meaning of the Lord's Prayer:

> The events of Israel's Exodus from Egypt, the people's wilderness wandering, and their entry into the promised land were of enormous importance in the self-understanding and symbolism of all subsequent generations of Israelites, including Jews of the Second Temple period. . . . When YHWH restored the fortunes of Israel, it would be like a new Exodus—a new and greater liberation from an enslavement greater than that in Egypt. . . . And the Lord's Prayer can best be seen in this light as well—that is, as the prayer of the new wilderness wandering people. . . . This can be seen more particularly as we look at each of the clauses of the Lord's Prayer from a new Exodus perspective.[5]

---

4   For primary texts, see, e.g., Isaiah 40–66; Jeremiah 3, 16, 23, 30–31; Ezekiel 20, 36–37; Hosea 2, 11; Micah 4, 7; Zechariah 9–10; Sirach 36. For secondary literature, see Dale C. Allison, Jr., "Q's New Exodus and the Historical Jesus," in *The Sayings Source Q and the Historical Jesus*, Bibliotheca Ephemeridum theologicarum Lovaniensium 158, ed. A. Lindemann (Leuven: Leuven University, 2001), 395–428; Andrew C. Brunson, *Psalm 118 in the Gospel of John: An Intertextual Study on the New Exodus Pattern in the Theology of John*, Journal for the Study of the New Testament Supplement Series 229 (Sheffield: Sheffield Academic, 2002); F. Ninow, *Indicators of Typology within the Old Testament: The Exodus Motif* (New York: Peter Lang, 2001); David W. Pao, *Acts and the Isaianic New Exodus* Wissenschaftliche Untersuchungen zum Neuen Testament 2:130 (Tübingen: Mohr Siebeck, 2000; repr. Grand Rapids, MI: Baker Academic, 2002); Sylvia C. Keesmaat, *Paul and His Story: (Re)–interpreting the Exodus Tradition*, Journal for the Study of the New Testament Supplement Series 181 (Sheffield: Sheffield Academic, 1999); Rikki E. Watts, *Isaiah's New Exodus in Mark*, Wissenschaftliche Untersuchungen zum Neuen Testament 2:88 (Tübingen: Mohr Siebeck, 1997; repr. Grand Rapids, MI: Baker Academic, 2000); Joel Marcus, *Mark 1-8: A New Translation with Introduction and Commentary*, The Anchor Bible 27a (New York: Doubleday, 2000), 388–89, 483–85; W. D. Davies, "Paul and the New Exodus," in *The Quest for Context and Meaning: Studies in Biblical Intertextuality in Honor of James A. Sanders*, eds. Craig A. Evans and Shemaryahu Talmon (Leiden: Brill, 1997), 443–63; Dale C. Allison, Jr., *The New Moses: A Matthean Typology* (Minneapolis: Fortress, 1993); T. F. Glasson, *Moses in the Fourth Gospel*, Studies in Biblical Theology 40 (London: S.C.M., 1963); J. Manek, "The New Exodus in the Books of Luke," *Novum Testamentum* 2 (1958): 8–23. See also Jean Danielou, *From Shadows to Reality: Studies in the Biblical Typology of the Fathers* (Westminster: Newman, 1960), 153–228.

5   See Wright, "The Lord's Prayer," 139–140. The close reader will note that I have left out the problematic elements of Wright's hypothesis by which he ties the new Exodus of the Old Testament prophets to his concept of "the end of Exile"—that is, deliverance from pagan rule and the return of YHWH to Zion. As I have argued elsewhere, although I agree with Wright's emphasis on the importance of the exile, I have some fundamental disagreements with his understanding of the concept. For a full discussion, see Brant Pitre, *Jesus, the Tribulation, and the End of the Exile: Restoration Eschatology and the Origin of the Atonement*, Wissenschaftliche

Although Wright's proposal has not yet received a great deal of scholarly attention, I believe that he has uncovered a fundamental insight into the meaning of the Lord's Prayer in its first-century Jewish context, an insight that is worthy of further exploration.[6]

In this essay, I will attempt to show that Wright's suggestion is correct and that the ancient Jewish hope for a new Exodus is, in fact, a very important key to understanding what Jesus himself meant when he taught the Lord's Prayer to his disciples. Moreover, I will attempt to strengthen Wright's proposal by examining the Old Testament and ancient Jewish background of the Lord's Prayer in greater depth.

As we will see, each line of the prayer is rooted in the language and imagery of the Scriptures of Israel and in the prophetic hope for a new Exodus. When this Old Testament background is adequately taken into account, the Lord's Prayer does, in fact, appear to be a prayer for the new Exodus and all that it entails: the coming of the Messiah, the release of God's scattered people from exile, and the ingathering of the Israel and the Gentiles to the promised land of a new Jerusalem. To borrow a felicitous phrase from Wright himself, the Lord's Prayer reveals what can be called a "typological eschatology," in which the events of the first Exodus establish a prototype for how God will save his people in the end-times.[7]

I will operate with several basic presuppositions. First, while I recognize that the brief and powerful petitions of the Lord's Prayer are inherently open to a multitude of interpretations, my primary goal here is to try, insofar as is possible, to ascertain what Jesus himself meant when he taught the prayer to his disciples. Along these lines, I will assume, following most scholars, that the Lord's Prayer is historically authentic to Jesus.[8] Second, because Matthew and Luke's Gospels preserve slightly different versions of the prayer, I will focus my attention on the opening address and the five petitions that they have in common. I do this primarily for reasons of space, but also because most scholars recognize that these elements originated with Jesus. Third and finally, I will argue that the key to unlocking the original meaning of the Lord's Prayer can be found by closely examining the Old Testament context of the language and imagery used by Jesus in each petition. As we will see, when this is done, in remarkable fashion, each of its petitions can be tied to the ancient Jewish hope for the coming of the Messiah and the ingathering of Israel and the Gentiles in a new Exodus.

Untersuchungen zum Neuen Testament 2:204 (Tübingen: Mohr-Siebeck; Grand Rapids, MI: Baker Academic, 2005), 31–40.

6   I have already drawn on Wright's insights in *Jesus the Tribulation, and the End of the Exile*, 132–59. In this article, I will expand on these initial arguments.

7   Wright, "The Lord's Prayer," 146.

8   I address the scholarly debate on questions of historicity in detail in Pitre, *Jesus, the Tribulation, and the End of the Exile*, 154–58. As I show there, most scholars conclude that the elements of the prayer common to Matthew and Luke are authentic.

"Our Father"

The first aspect of the Lord's Prayer that evokes both the Exodus from Egypt and the new Exodus is the opening address to God as "Our Father" (πάτερ ἡμῶν) or "Father" (πάτερ) (Matt. 6:9; Luke 11:1). Although at first glance the practice of addressing God as "Father" in prayer may seem unremarkable, when we turn to the Old Testament, it is by no means common. Although on several occasions God is depicted as, or compared to, a father, *he is almost never addressed as "Father" in a prayer*—except in a few key instances.[9] When these are examined we find that both the image of God as father and the practice of addressing God as "Father" in prayer are tied with remarkable consistency to *the Exodus from Egypt* and the prophetic hope for a *new Exodus.*

As Wright points out, God's command to Pharaoh to release the Israelites was directly based on his paternal relationship to Israel: "Thus says the Lord: Israel is my first-born son, and I say to you, 'Let my son go that he may worship me'; if you refuse to let him go, behold, I will slay your first-born son" (Exod. 4:22–23). Moreover, we find the same link present in the book of Hosea, when God refers to the past Exodus in terms of his paternal relationship to Israel: "When Israel was a child, I loved him, and out of Egypt I called my son" (Hos. 11:1). Finally, the first explicit use of the Hebrew word "father" (אב) for God in the Old Testament comes from the famous "Song of Moses," which is, of course, a recollection of God's past act of deliverance in the Exodus from Egypt (see Deut. 32:9–14). In light of such texts, Wright concludes:

> Calling God "Father" not only evokes all kinds of associations of family life and intimacy; more importantly, it speaks to all subsequent generations of God as *the God of the Exodus*, the God who rescues Israel primarily because Israel is God's first-born son. The title "Father" says as much about Israel, and about the events through which God will liberate Israel, as it does about God.[10]

We can go much further than Wright, however, for this connection between the fatherhood of God and the Exodus is not only present in passages that refer

---

9   Most frequently, Israel is referred to as the sons or children of God, without God explicitly being called "father" (Deut. 14:1; Hos. 11:1–3; Wis. 5:5). In a few cases, God is explicitly called a "father": either with reference to him as creator (Deut. 32:6; Mal. 2:10), or by way of analogy (Ps. 103:13), or as a protector of orphans (Ps. 68:5), or with regard to his special relationship with the king of Israel under the Davidic covenant (2 Sam. 7:14; Ps. 89:27). Apart from the examples we will discuss below, the only cases of God being addressed as "Father" in prayer in the Old Testament come from the books of Sirach and Wisdom, where God is called "Father" on a few occasions (see Wis. 14:3; Sir. 23:1, 4; 51:10). For a concise discussion of references, see Fitzmyer, *The Gospel according to Luke,* 2: 902–903; Davies and Allison, *Saint Matthew,* 1:600–602. See further Jeremias, *The Prayers of Jesus,* 11–29.

10   Wright, "The Lord's Prayer," 140.

to the first Exodus. It is even more explicit in prophetic texts concerned with the new Exodus.

There are at least three key passages from the Old Testament that utilize the terminology of God as "Father" precisely in the context of describing the eschatological events that will accompany the new Exodus. Although these texts are somewhat lengthy, it is important that they be cited here as fully as possible so that the context of their use of "father" terminology is clear. The first two are from the prophetic books of Isaiah and Jeremiah, and the third is from the closing chapters of the book of Tobit:

> *Then [the Lord] remembered the days of old, of Moses his servant.*
> *Where is he who brought up out of the sea the shepherds of his*
>   *flock?*
> *Where is he who put in the midst of them his holy Spirit,*
> *who caused his glorious arm to go at the right hand of Moses,*
> *who divided the waters before them to make for himself an everlast-*
>   *ing name, who led them through the depths? . . .*
> So you did lead your people, to make for yourself a glorious
>   name.
> *Look down from heaven and see,* from your holy and glorious
>   habitation.
> Where are your zeal and your might?
> The yearning of your heart and your compassion are withheld
>   from me.
> *For you are our Father,* though Abraham does not know us
> and Israel does not acknowledge us;
> *you, O Lord, are our Father,*
> our Redeemer from of old is your name.
> O Lord, why do you make us err from your ways
> and harden our heart, so that we fear you not?
> *Return for the sake of your servants the tribes of your heritage.*
>   (Isa. 63:10–17)[11]

> *In those days, says the Lord, they shall no more say, "The ark of the*
> *covenant of the Lord." It shall not come to mind, or be remembered,*
> *or missed; it shall not be made again.* At that time Jerusalem
> shall be called the throne of the Lord, and *all the Gentiles shall*
> *gather to it,* to the presence of the Lord in Jerusalem, and they

11   Unless otherwise noted, all translations of Scripture used herein are from the Revised Standard Version, Catholic Edition (RSVCE), eds. Bernard Orchard and R.C. Fuller (London: Thomas Nelson and Sons, 1966).

shall no more follow their own evil heart. *In those days the house of Judah shall join the house of Israel, and together they shall come from the land of the north to the land that I gave your fathers for a heritage.*

"I thought how I would set you among my sons,
and give you a pleasant land,
a heritage most beauteous of all nations.
And I thought you would call me "My Father,"
and would not turn from following me." (Jer. 3:16–19)

Blessed is God who lives for ever, and blessed is his kingdom . . .
Acknowledge him before the Gentiles, O sons of Israel;
for he has scattered us among them.
Makes his greatness known there, and exalt him in the presence of all the living;
because he is our Lord and God, *he is our Father* for ever.
He will afflict us for our iniquities; and again he will show mercy,
and will gather us from all the nations among whom you have been
scattered.
If you turn to him with all your heart and with all your soul,
to do what is true before him, then he will turn to you
and will not hide his face from you. . . . (Tob. 13:1–6)

Although a great deal could be said about each one of these texts, for our purposes here, we must confine ourselves to making three basic observations. First, each bears strong *linguistic parallels* with the Lord's Prayer. The most important in this regard is Isaiah, who actually addresses God as "our Father" (אבינו; πατὴρ ἡμῶν) (Isa. 63:16; 64:8)[12]—the same expression we find in the Lord's Prayer: "our Father" (πάτερ ἡμῶν) (Matt. 6:9).[13] Similarly, Jeremiah declares that when God gathers Israel and the Gentiles to the restored Jerusalem, they will "call" God "my Father" (אבי; πατέρα) (Jer. 3:19).[14] This too parallels the shorter version of the Lord's Prayer, which simply addresses God as "Father" (πάτερ) (Luke 11:2). Finally,

---

12   Unless otherwise noted, all Hebrew quotations of the Old Testament cited herein reflect the Masoretic Text (MT), while all Greek quotations reflect the Septuagint translation (LXX).

13   It is a curious fact of New Testament scholarship that commentators who spend an otherwise enormous amount of time on Jesus' use of "Father" language almost never discuss this passage from Isaiah in which God is actually addressed as "our Father." Although Isaiah 63–64 is mentioned in many lists of textual parallels, it is not actually discussed by otherwise meticulous commentators such as Dunn, *Jesus Remembered*, 548–49; Darrell L. Bock, *Luke*, 2 vols., Baker Exegetical Commentary on the New Testament (Grand Rapids, MI: Baker, 1996), 2:1051–52; Davies and Allison, *Saint Matthew*, 1:600; Fitzmyer, *The Gospel according to Luke*, 2:902.

14   The Septuagint here reads: "And I said: You shall call me Father" (καὶ εἶπα Πατέρα καλέσετέ με).

although Tobit does not directly address God, he does refer to him as "our Father" (πατὴρ ἡμῶν) in a prayer regarding God's "kingdom" (Tob. 13:2, 4). This, as we will see, is surely noteworthy, given the centrality of God as "father" and God's "kingdom" in the Lord's Prayer.

Second, each of these three texts is describing *the future ingathering of Israel and the Gentiles in a new Exodus.* This is very clear in Isaiah, in which the new Exodus is a major theme.[15] In this context, the prophet calls upon God to look down "from heaven" and "return" the scattered "tribes" of Israel to the promised land, just as he had done in "the days of old, of Moses his servant" (Isa. 63:10, 17). It is important to note here that for Isaiah, this future Exodus will be tied to the establishment of a restored Temple, a gloriously new Jerusalem, and even a "new heaven and a new earth."[16] In other words, the future Exodus will not only be "new," it will be *eschatological.*

This hope for a new Exodus is equally clear in Jeremiah, who more than once speaks of future "days" when people will no longer speak about the first Exodus, when God "brought up the people out of the land of Egypt." Instead, they will speak about the new Exodus, when God will gather the scattered tribes of Israel "out of all the countries where he had driven them" (Jer. 16:14–16; 23:1–8). Jeremiah is describing this new Exodus when he says that people will no longer remember the Ark of the Covenant, the most visible sign of the Mosaic covenant and the Exodus from Egypt (Jer. 3:17). It is crucial to note here that in Jeremiah, the new Exodus will not only be eschatological, but specifically *messianic.* The future ingathering will be inaugurated by the coming of the Messiah, the "Branch" of David (Jer. 16:14–16; 23:1–8); it is a messianic Exodus.

Finally, although Tobit does not use any clear Exodus typology in the cited text, he is still describing the same basic series of eschatological events: the ingathering of the exiles, the conversion of the Gentiles and their pilgrimage to the new Jerusalem, and the building of a new temple (Tob. 13:5–10, 16–18; 14:5–7). To this extent, Tobit's vision for the future is rooted in the same concept of the new Exodus found in the prophets.

Third and finally—and this is significant—in all three texts, *the use of divine "Father" language only occurs in the context of their hope for the new Exodus.* Apart

---

15 See, for example Pao, *Acts and the Isaianic New Exodus,* 51–59, drawing on Rikki E. Watts, "Consolation or Confrontation? Isaiah 40–55 and the Delay of the New Exodus," *Tyndale Bulletin* 41 (1990): 31–59; Dale A. Patrick, "Epiphanic Imagery in Second Isaiah's Portrayal of a New Exodus," *Hebrew Annual Review* 8 (1984): 125–41; Carroll Stuhlmueller, *Creative Redemption in Deutero-Isaiah* (Rome: Pontifical Biblical Institute, 1970); Bernhard W. Anderson, "Exodus Typology in Second Isaiah," in *Israel's Prophetic Heritage: Essays in Honor of James Muilenberg,* ed. Bernhard W. Anderson and Walter Harrelson (New York: Harper, 1962), 177–95. See also Gerhard von Rad, who speaks of "the message of the new Exodus" as "one of Deutero-Isaiah's main topics." *Old Testament Theology,* 2 vols., trans. D. M. G. Stalker (New York: Harper & Row, 1965), 2:244–50, 261–2.

16 See, for example, Isaiah 52–54, 56, 65–66.

from these passages, neither Isaiah nor Tobit describes God as "father" anywhere else, despite the fact that both books contain numerous other prayers. Although such language does occur one other time in the book of Jeremiah,[17] it does so, remarkably, in another passage about the new Exodus:

> *The Lord has saved his people, the remnant of Israel.*
> "Behold, I will bring them from the north country,
>   and gather them from the farthest parts of the earth . . .
> a great company, they shall return here.
> With weeping they shall come,
>   and with consolations I will lead them back,
> I will make them walk by brooks of water,
>   in a straight path in which they shall not stumble;
> for I am a father to Israel, and Ephraim is my first-born son."
>   (Jer. 31:7–9)

This is an extremely significant text, for it makes explicit the implicit connection between the fatherhood of God and the new Exodus. The reason God will one day bring his people home to the promised land is because he is Israel's "father," and Israel is his "first-born son." The echoes of Exodus 4:22 here are unmistakable. Moreover, the context of this occurrence is important as well, for it takes place in the midst of Jeremiah's famous extended prophecy of the coming of the Messiah, the ingathering of the twelve tribes of Israel, and the inauguration of a "new covenant" that will be greater than the covenant with Moses (Jer. 30:1–8, 18–21, 31:31–33).

Taken together, these parallels suggest that Jesus' use of "father" language in the Lord's Prayer was not incidental or the result of Old Testament custom. The occurrences are too infrequent for that. Rather, it was a deliberate act that drew on the typological eschatology of the Old Testament and was meant to indicate to his disciples that the time for the inauguration of the new Exodus had come at last. Just as God's fatherly love for Israel had compelled him to deliver them from Egypt and bring them home in the first Exodus, so too, in the latter days, he will gather his children home to the promised land once more—although this time, he would bring the Gentiles with them. Seen in the light of this ancient hope, Jesus' address to God as "Father" may signal that he is not merely teaching the disciples about the nature of their relationship with God. More broadly, he is teaching them to pray for the new Exodus and everything it entailed: the ingathering of the tribes of Israel, the conversion of the Gentiles, the building of a new Jerusalem, and—by no means least important—the coming of the Messiah. In short, the inaugura-

---

17   The only other instance of "father" language (Jer. 3:4) is not actually a separate instance but a preface to the first citation in Jer 3:19.

tion of the new Exodus would mean nothing less than the advent of the messianic kingdom of God.

If there is any doubt about the possibility of the opening address having such deep messianic significance, one final example of "father" language from the Old Testament, used in the context of a prayer, should lay it to rest. It comes from the lips of King David in the book of Chronicles, during the great assembly that was held when Solomon was anointed king over Israel:

> Therefore David blessed the Lord in the presence of all the assembly; and David said: "Blessed are you, O Lord, the God of Israel, *our Father* forever and ever. *Yours, O Lord, is the greatness, and the power, and the glory,* and the victory, and the majesty; for all that is in the heavens and in the earth is yours; *yours is the kingdom, O Lord,* and you are exalted as head above all. Both riches and honor come from you, and you rule over all . . . And now we thank you, our God, and praise your glorious name. (1 Chron. 29:10–13)

The number of parallels with the Lord's Prayer are striking. First and foremost, of course is the *direct address* of God as "our Father" (אָבִינוּ; πατὴρ ἡμῶν) in the context of a prayer (1 Chron. 29:10), found elsewhere in the Old Testament only in Isaiah. Second, the focus of the prayer is on *the kingdom* of the Lord, a direct parallel to Jesus' prayer for the coming of God's kingdom. Lest this seem insignificant, scholars have pointed out that the expression, "the kingdom of God," never occurs anywhere in the Hebrew of the Old Testament, and that the "kingdom of the Lord"—the closest equivalent—only occurs *once*, in 1 Chronicles 28:5, immediately before our passage.[18]

Hence, when David prays to "Our Father" about his kingdom, the context directly ties this image to the kingdom of God as established in and through the anointed Son of David.[19] This suggests a connection between *praying to God as "Our Father"* and *the establishment of the Davidic kingdom under the messianic king*.[20] Should there be any doubt about this connection, recall that more than once, the Davidic king is singled out as the "son" who will call God "my Father" (2 Sam. 7:14; Ps. 89:26–27).

Finally, this link between the prayer of David and that of Jesus was evidently not lost on the early Church. David's words provide the basic content of the doxol-

---

18 Meier, *A Marginal Jew*, 2:243.

19 See 1 Chron. 28:1–8, 28:10–25.

20 Meier, *A Marginal Jew*, 2:276, n. 32, cites Odo Camponovo, *Königtum, Königsherrschaft und Reich Gottes in den frühjüdischen Schriften*, Orbis biblicus et Orientalis 58 (Freiburg: Universitätsverlag; Göttingen: Vandenhoeck & Ruprecht, 1984), 90–91, as seeing "a messianic conception connected with the idea of Yahweh's eschatological kingship" based on 1 Chron. 28:5.

ogy that was later attached to the Lord's Prayer: "For yours is the kingdom, and the power, and the glory forever."[21] Although modern scholars frequently overlook this Davidic background to the Lord's Prayer, the earliest Christians apparently saw quite clearly that the eschatological "kingdom of God" was the fulfillment of the Davidic "kingdom of the Lord," to be restored in the new Exodus.

"Hallowed Be Thy Name"

These connections between the fatherhood of God and the new Exodus can be confirmed by turning to the first actual petition in the Lord's Prayer: "Hallowed be thy name" (Matt. 6:10; Luke 11:2). Although the traditional translation of this line comes across in English as a declarative statement, the Greek is very clearly an imperative request: "May your name be hallowed!"[22] In this case, familiarity may breed a certain lack of awareness for just how peculiar this line of the prayer is. Why should Jesus instruct his disciples to pray that God's name be "hallowed" or "made holy"? Is not the divine name already holy?[23] What might it mean for God to "hallow" his own name?

Here again the answer can be found by recourse to the Old Testament background of Jesus' words. With regard to the first Exodus, few would doubt the prominence and importance of the revelation of God's "name" to Moses in the famous theophany at Mount Sinai (Exod. 3:13–22). With regard to the new Exodus, many commentators agree that the language of "hallowing" God's "name" is drawing on an eschatological prophecy from the book of Ezekiel, in which the Lord promises to one day vindicate the holiness of his name (Ezek. 36:23).[24] However, while Ezekiel 36 is widely recognized as a direct parallel to Jesus' words, commentators often ignore the larger context of the parallel, and the precise *event* that accompanies the hallowing of God's name—the ingathering of the scattered tribes of Israel:

> Therefore say to the house of Israel, Thus says the Lord GOD: It
> is not for your sake, O house of Israel, that I am about to act, but

---

21 This doxology is present in *Didache* 8:2 and some manuscripts of Matthew's Gospel. See Davies and Allison, *Saint Matthew*, 1:615, n. 54; Jeremias, *New Testament Theology*, 202–203.

22 Joseph Fitzmyer translates the line as "May your name be sanctified!" and comments that it "expresses a punctiliar mode of action suited for the eschatological nuance of this wish." Fitzmyer, *The Gospel according to Luke*, 2:903.

23 See 1 *Enoch* 9:4. See 1 *Enoch: A New Translation Based on the Hermeneia Commentary*, ed. G. W. E. Nickelsburg and J.C. VanderKam (Minneapolis: Fortress, 2004).

24 See, for example, Meier, *A Marginal Jew*, 2:296–97; Dunn, *Jesus Remembered*, 476–77; Fitzmyer, *The Gospel According to Luke*, 2:898. Wright does not discuss the echo of Ezekiel in his article, but he does admit that the first petition "evokes the prophecy of Ezekiel 36" in *Jesus and the Victory of God*, 293, although it does not significantly inform his exegesis of the text. While Brown notes the parallel, he does not highlight it as the principle background of Jesus' words. See Brown, "The Pater Noster as an Eschatological Prayer," 291.

for the sake of *my holy name*, which you have profaned among the Gentiles to which you came. *And I will hallow my great name, which has been profaned among the Gentiles, and which you have profaned among them; and the Gentiles will know that I am the Lord, says the Lord GOD, when I vindicate my holiness before their eyes. For I will take you from the Gentiles, and gather you from all the countries, and bring you into your own land. I will sprinkle clean water upon you, and you shall be clean from all your uncleannesses, and from all your idols I will cleanse you.* A new heart I will give you, and a new spirit I will put within you; and I will take out of your flesh the heart of stone and give you a heart of flesh. And I will put my spirit within you, and cause you to walk in my statutes and be careful to observe my ordinances. *You shall dwell in the land which I gave to your fathers; and you shall be my people, and I will be your God.* (Ezek. 36:22-28)[25]

This is a striking vision of the coming age of salvation: the people of Israel will be set free from exile among the Gentiles and be gathered "from all the countries" into a renewed and restored promised land, a paradise that will be "like the garden of Eden" (Ezek. 36:35). Although in this particular passage Ezekiel does not explicitly use Exodus typology, he has already described this "gathering" of Israel "out of the countries" by drawing on imagery from the first Exodus from Egypt (see Ezek. 20:1-38, esp. 33-38). Hence, the final ingathering will truly be a new Exodus. Moreover, just as the first Exodus included Israel's passing through the waters of the Red Sea (Exod. 14), so too this future restoration will be accompanied by the cleansing of Israel from its sins by "clean water" (Ezek. 36:25). This new Exodus, and all the events that will accompany it, will take place *when* God "hallows" his "name" by saving his people.

There are several important connections between this passage and the Lord's Prayer. First, the precise verbal parallels with Jesus' words are very strong. In Ezekiel, God declares that he will "make holy" or "hallow" his "name" (וְקִדַּשְׁתִּי אֶת שְׁמִי; ἁγιάσω τὸ ὄνομά μου) (Ezek. 36:23). In similar fashion, Jesus teaches his disciples to pray: "May your name be hallowed" (ἁγιασθήτω τὸ ὄνομά σου) (Matt. 6:9; Luke 11:2). Although the language of people "hallowing" the name of God is found on a couple of occasions in the Old Testament,[26] in the Lord's Prayer,

---

25 RSVCE, slightly altered.

26 See Lev. 22:32; Isa. 29:22-23. In both cases, the subject of the verb is not God but human beings. Among later Jewish literature, see *b. Yeb.* 79a which says that : "It is better that a single jot of the Torah be rooted out of its place so that the Name of heaven be sanctified in public." Translated by Jacob Neusner, *The Babylonian Talmud: A Translation and Commentary,* 22 vols (Peabody: Hendrickson, 2005). See also, Dunn, *Jesus Remembered,* 547, who also cites 1 *Enoch.* 61:12 which, intriguingly, occurs in the midst of a vision of the revelation and enthronement of the Messiah.

we appear to have a divine passive, with the sense being, "May *God* hallow his name." There is, to my knowledge, only one place in the Old Testament where such a concept occurs: Ezekiel 36. Hence, Jesus seems to be drawing on this particular prophecy and instructing his disciples to pray for its fulfillment.

In addition to these linguistic parallels, there are also strong thematic connections. It is surely no coincidence that Ezekiel's prophecy not only contains a description of the new Exodus, but other elements that parallel the Lord's Prayer: abundance of grain/bread for sustenance (Ezek. 26:29–30), forgiveness of sins (Ezek. 36:33), and "deliverance" from evil and idolatry (Ezek 26:29). In light of such connections, some scholars have even suggested that the entire Lord's Prayer is based upon Ezekiel 36.[27] While I would argue that there are other texts that provide more direct parallels with the other petitions, the basic insight is correct. Jesus is teaching the disciples to pray for the whole series of events that will accompany Ezekiel's new Exodus and encapsulating them in the initial plea for God to hallow his name.

Finally, and perhaps most intriguingly, the allusion to Ezekiel 36 may also support our earlier suggestion that the future Exodus envisioned by Jesus is not only eschatological but specifically messianic. For if the prophecy from Ezekiel is read in its wider context, one finds that the final ingathering of Israel is also tied to the coming of the Messiah and the establishment of his kingdom:

> Behold, I am about to take the stick of Joseph and the tribes of Israel associated with him [10 tribes of the northern kingdom]; and I will join with it the stick of Judah [2 tribes of the southern kingdom], and make them one stick, that they may be one in my hand. . . . Behold, *I will take the people of Israel from Gentiles among which they have gone, and will gather them from all sides, and bring them to their own land*; and I will make them one nation in the land, upon the mountains of Israel; and *one king shall be king over them all* . . . *My servant David shall be king over them; and they shall all have one shepherd* . . . I will make a covenant of peace with them; it shall be *an everlasting covenant* with them. (Ezek. 37:19-26)

We see here that the new Exodus is directly tied to three key eschatological events: the restoration of the twelve "tribes" of Israel, the coming of a future Davidic "king," and the forging of an "everlasting covenant." In other words, for Ezekiel, the new Exodus is directly tied to the advent of *the messianic kingdom*. This background gives us an indispensable clue as to the specific events Jesus may have had in mind when he instructed the disciples to pray for the hallowing of God's

---

27   See James Swetnam, "Hallowed be Thy Name," *Biblica* 52 (1972), 556–63.

name. In light of its Old Testament background, the first petition of the Lord's Prayer is not a plea for some vague "divine action" in history, but a specific request for the *messianic new Exodus*, in which God would restore the twelve tribes of Israel and send the Messiah to establish his everlasting kingdom. This is perhaps why Jesus, in the very next line, turns to the coming of this kingdom.

"Thy Kingdom Come"

Perhaps no line from the Lord's Prayer has been more vigorously debated than the petition: "May your kingdom come" (Matt. 6:10; Luke 11:2). As many scholars would agree, the hope for the "coming" of God's "kingdom" is arguably the heart not only of the Lord's Prayer, but of Jesus' entire mission and message. But what might Jesus have meant by instructing his disciples to pray for the coming of the kingdom?

A host of answers have been proposed, far too many to be discussed in this brief essay.[28] For our purposes here, I will simply attempt to interpret the petition by asking the same questions as above: namely, is there an Old Testament text behind Jesus' words? And, if so, does the context shed any possible light on their meaning?

The answer to these questions is a resounding, "Yes." An extremely important Old Testament prophecy appears to lie behind Jesus' words. Despite the erroneous claim of some scholars that Jesus' combination of noun "kingdom" and the verb "to come" cannot be found in the Old Testament, there is, in fact, one biblical text in which precisely such a conjunction takes place: Micah 4:8.[29] Admittedly, this is (to my knowledge) the *only* time the Old Testament ever speaks about the "coming" of a "kingdom," but this only heightens the importance of Micah's prophecy for interpreting Jesus' words. Because the passage is woefully under-discussed and because the surrounding context is so crucial, I cite it below as fully as possible:

> It shall come to pass in the latter days
> that the mountain of the house of the Lord
> shall be established as the highest of the mountains,
> and shall be raised up above the hills;
> and peoples shall flow to it, and many Gentiles shall come, and say:
> "Let us go up to the mountain of the Lord,

---

28 The bibliography on the kingdom of God is enormous. For a sampling of some of the more significant discussions with reference to Jesus, see Dunn, *Jesus Remembered*, 383–47; Meier, *A Marginal Jew*, 2:237–506; E. P. Sanders, "Jesus and the Kingdom: The Restoration of Israel and the New People of God," in *Jesus, the Gospels, and the Church*, ed. E. P. Sanders (Macon, GA: Mercer University, 1987), 225–39. See also Bruce Chilton, "The Kingdom of God in Recent Scholarship," in *Studying the Historical Jesus: Evaluations of the State of Current Research*, eds. Bruce Chilton and Craig A. Evans, New Testament Tools and Studies 19 (Leiden: E. J. Brill, 1994), 255–80.

29 See Meier, *A Marginal Jew*, 2:294.

to the house of the God of Jacob;
that he may teach us his ways and we may walk in his paths."
For out of Zion shall go forth the Law,
and the word of the Lord from Jerusalem . . .
In that day, says the Lord, I will assemble the lame
and gather those who have been driven away,
and those whom I have afflicted;
and the lame I will make the remnant;
and those who were cast off, a strong nation;
and the Lord will reign over them in Mount Zion
from this time forth forever more.
And you, O tower of the flock, hill of the daughter of Zion,
to you it shall come, the former dominion shall come,
and *the kingdom of the daughter of Jerusalem.* (Mic. 4:1–8)

Several aspects of this striking text provide important background for Jesus'
words. First, it contains the sole occurrence in the Old Testament of a parallel to
Jesus' prayer for the "coming" (ἔρχομαι) of the "kingdom" (βασιλεία) of God
(Matt. 6:10; Luke 11:2). Although this might be easy to overlook in the English
translation, the final line of the passage very clearly connects the verb "come" (בוא;
εἰσέρχομαι) to the nouns "dominion" and "kingdom" (ממלכת; βασιλέα) (Mic.
4:8). In the context of just having proclaimed that "the Lord will reign" in Mount
Zion (Mic. 4:7), this is very clearly an image of *the coming of the kingdom of the
Lord*—that is, the kingdom of God.

Micah also links the coming of the kingdom to several other eschatological
events that we have seen before: the advent of "the latter days" or end-times, the
building of a new Temple, and the conversion and pilgrimage of the Gentiles to
a new Jerusalem. These are important, because they show that the "coming" of
the "kingdom" of God cannot be reduced to a single event, but is, so to speak,
the *sum total* of several eschatological events that would signal the fulfillment of
the promises of God.[30] Finally, Micah describes the "coming" of the "kingdom"
primarily in terms of the ingathering of the scattered tribes of Israel, whom the
Lord had "driven away" into exile (Mic. 4:6–7). In this particular text, Micah does
not make the Exodus typology clear, but later in the book, he explicitly describes
this "coming" of the scattered children of Jerusalem as a new Exodus that will

---

30   See Dunn, *Jesus Remembered*, 393–96. I owe this formulation to the massive (but now forgotten)
work of the German Franciscan Hilarin Felder: "The dominion of God over the world, or the
kingdom of God in the world, was in general *the sum total of all hopes for the future.* The whole
Old Testament is filled with the idea, which Jesus summarized in the words: 'Thy kingdom
come.'" Hilarin Felder, *Christ and the Critic*, 2 vols., trans. John L. Stoddard (London: Burns
Oates and Washbourne, 1924), 153 (emphasis added).

surpass the wonders that took place "when [Israel] came out of the land of Egypt" (see Mic. 7:12-16).

It is difficult to overestimate the significance of this passage for understanding the Lord's Prayer. It not only shows that, once again, Jesus is drawing on Old Testament imagery to depict the coming of the kingdom of God. More importantly, it reveals that, in a certain sense, *the expectation of the coming of the kingdom of God and the hope for the new Exodus are one and the same.* They are two ways of speaking about the same eschatological event or series of events. The image of the "kingdom" emphasizes the Davidic dimensions of the dominion of God: the reign of the Messiah, the new Temple, and the establishment of a universal messianic kingdom.[31] The other image of the return of the exiled tribes to the promised land emphasizes the Mosaic dimensions of salvation. God will save his people in the latter days in much the same way he saved them in the Exodus: he will forgive their sins, release them from slavery, and then lead them home to the promised land. Both the Mosaic and the Davidic dimensions of salvation are important for understanding the shape of the messianic kingdom, for they both have typological as well as eschatological significance.

In short, Jesus' hope for the coming of the kingdom needs to be understood from within the context of *the typological eschatology of the Old Testament.* When this is done, we find that the coming of the kingdom of God is nothing less than the concrete and definitive fulfillment of all of God's promises to Israel, and, through Israel, to the whole world. It is the fulfillment of the promise to gather the scattered children of God together and bring them home to a new Zion, a new Temple, and a new Jerusalem, so that "all peoples" might walk in his ways, learn his "law," and worship in his "house," in an everlasting era of peace (Mic. 4:1-8). When seen in this light, the kingdom's "coming" will not only be an eschatological event, it will be a *liturgical* and *ecclesial* event as well—in the proper sense of the latter word[32]—as was the Exodus from Egypt and, for that matter, the establishment of the kingdom of David.

Once all this is clear, we can easily explain Jesus' otherwise awkward language of the "coming" of a "kingdom"—language which continues to puzzle scholars.[33] How can a "kingdom" be said to "come"? The answer is: quite easily, if "the kingdom" in question refers primarily to a *people*—namely, the scattered children of God. This is especially true if the people in question are in exile, as the tribes of Israel had been for centuries, spread among the Gentile nations. In this light, the coming of

---

31 This is not to exclude "kingdom" imagery from the Exodus; it is, of course, quite prominent (Exod. 19:5–6). But note the importance of the Davidic "Zion" imagery in Micah 4:8.

32 The Greek version of the Pentateuch more than once refers to the gathering of the twelve tribes of Israel to "worship" the Lord at Mount Sinai as the great "day of the *ekklesia*" or "day of the assembly" (Deut. 4:10; 9:10; 18:16). The Hebrew term behind the Greek is the word for "assembly" (קְהֹל).

33 For scholarly perplexity on this point, see, for example, Meier, *A Marginal Jew*, 2:298.

God's kingdom for which Jesus instructs his disciples to pray means nothing less than the ingathering of Israel and the Gentiles in a new Exodus.

"Give Us This Day Our Daily Bread"

Perhaps the most obvious sign of the presence of a new Exodus typology in the Lord's Prayer can be found in the third common petition: "Give us this day our daily bread" (Matt. 6:11), or "Give us each day our daily bread" (Luke 11:3). Again, while this line may be extremely familiar, it too is perhaps more curious than it appears at first glance. Why, in the midst of this great eschatological prayer for the coming of God's kingdom, does Jesus suddenly switch focus to a seemingly mundane request for daily food? Is not this the same Jesus who has commanded his disciples elsewhere: "Do not be anxious about your life, what you shall eat and what you shall drink" (Matt. 6:25; Luke 12:22)?[34] And why does he emphasize receiving this "daily" bread "each day"? Why the seeming redundancy?

The answer to these questions can be found once again by examining the Old Testament and ancient Jewish background of the petition. With regard to the Old Testament, there are few more memorable images of the Exodus from Egypt than that of the miraculous *manna from heaven*, which was given each day to the people of Israel during their journey through the wilderness toward the promised land. With the Lord's Prayer in mind, compare the following passages:

> Then the Lord said to Moses, "Behold, *I will rain bread from heaven* for you; and the people shall go out and gather *a day's portion every day*, that I may test them, whether they will walk in my law or not. On the sixth *day*, when they prepare what they bring in, it will be twice as much as they gather *daily* . . . " In the evenings quail came up and covered the camp; and in the morning dew lay round about the camp. And when the dew had gone up, there was on the face of the wilderness a fine, flake–like thing, fine as hoarfrost on the ground. When the people of Israel saw it, they said to one another, "What is it?" For they did not know what it was. And Moses said to them, "It is *the bread which the Lord has given you to eat* . . . " Now the house of Israel called its name manna; it was like coriander seed, white, and the taste of it was like wafers made with honey. (Exod. 16:4–5, 13–15, 31)

> [God] commanded the skies above,
> and opened the doors of heaven;
> and *he rained down upon them manna to eat,*

---

34 I owe this point to Albert Schweitzer, *The Mysticism of Paul the Apostle*, trans. W. M. Montgomery (London: A. & C. Black, 1931), 240.

> and gave them the grain of heaven.
> Man ate the bread of the angels; he sent them food in
>   abundance . . .
> And they ate and were well filled,
> for he gave them what they craved. (Ps. 78:23–25, 29)

In these two key descriptions of the Old Testament manna, we see several parallels with the Lord's Prayer. Just as during the Exodus, God would "give" (δίδομι) the "bread" (ἀρτός) to the people of Israel each "day" (ἡμέρα), so too Jesus commands his disciples to pray that God "give" (δίδου΄ / δὸς) them "bread" (τὸν ἄρτον) "today" (σήμερον) or "each day" (τὸ καθ᾽ ἡμέραν) (Matt. 6:11; Luke 11:3).

As other scholars have pointed out, this emphasis on the daily nature of the bread of the Lord's Prayer is surely evocative of the manna of the Exodus.[35] This is important, because the manna of the first Exodus was *no ordinary bread*; it was miraculous "bread from heaven," given as food for the people on the way to the promised land. Seen in this light, Jesus is not merely instructing the disciples to pray for the mundane bread of daily existence. Rather, he is teaching them to pray for *the new manna of the new Exodus.* As God had provided sustenance for his people during the first Exodus, when Israel "ate the bread of angels" (Ps. 78:23–25, 29), so too would God feed the people of his kingdom during the eschatological Exodus.

Should there be any doubt about this connection between the "bread" of the Lord's Prayer and the new manna, we need only turn to ancient Jewish eschatology to confirm the suggestion. Many ancient Jews expected that *when the Messiah finally came, he would cause the manna to come down from heaven again.* One of the most explicit descriptions of this comes to us from the first-century Jewish writing known as *2 Baruch.* In a vision of the messianic age, the text states:

> And it will happen that when all that which should come to
> pass in these parts is accomplished, *the Messiah* will begin to be
> revealed. . . . And those who are hungry will enjoy themselves
> and they will, moreover, see marvels every day. . . . *And it will
> happen at that time that the treasury of manna will come down
> again from on high, and they will eat of it* in those years because
> these are they who will have arrived at the consummation of
> time. (*2 Baruch* 29:3–8)[36]

---

35 "In the LXX account [of the manna] ἡμέρα appears repeatedly (vv. 1, 4, 5, 22, 26, 27, 29, 30), and δίδομι is used (vv. 8, 15, 29; LXX Ps. 77:24; John 6:32). Further, Luke's redactional 'daily' (τὸ καθ᾽ ἡμέραν) appears in LXX Exod 16, 5." Dale Allison, "Q's New Exodus and the Historical Jesus," 399.

36 The text can be found in Charlesworth, *The Old Testament Pseudepigrapha*, 2 vols. (Garden City:

Other later Jewish texts also bear witness to the same expectation:[37]

> As the first redeemer [Moses] caused manna to descend, as it is stated, "Because I shall cause to rain bread from heaven for you" [Exod. 16:4], *so will the latter redeemer* [the Messiah] *cause manna to descend.*[38]

> You will not find it [manna] in this age, but *you shall find it in the age to come.*[39]

> It [the manna] has been prepared for the righteous *in the age to come. Everyone who believes is worthy and eats of it.*[40]

In light of these striking texts, we see yet again that for many ancient Jews, the long-awaited new Exodus would not only be eschatological, but *messianic.* It, and the new manna that would accompany it, were directly tied to the coming of the Messiah. As C. H. Dodd puts it, these Jewish texts clearly depict the righteous eating the manna during "the period of the temporary messianic kingdom on earth."[41]

It is fascinating to note that there was a related Jewish tradition which held that the new manna would return not just at any time, but *at Passover.*[42] It does not take much to connect these ancient Jewish expectations with Jesus' own actions during Passover at the Last Supper, when he gave the disciples the "bread" of the

---

Doubleday, 1983), 1:630–31.

37   These examples are taken from Raymond E. Brown, *The Gospel according to John*, The Anchor Bible 29–29A (New York: Doubleday, 1966, 1970), 1:265–66, and C. H. Dodd, *The Interpretation of the Fourth Gospel* (Cambridge: Cambridge University, 1953), 83–84, n. 2, 335. See Craig S. Keener, *The Gospel of John*, 2 vols. (Peabody: Hendrickson, 2003), 1:682, for more Jewish parallels. For an exhaustive study, see Bruce J. Malina, *The Palestinian Manna Tradition: The Manna Tradition in the Palestinian Targums and its Relationship to the New Testament*, Arbeiten zur Geschichte des späteren Judentums und des Urchristentums 7 (Leiden: Brill, 1968).

38   *Midrash Rabbah* on Eccl. 1:9.

39   *Mekilta* on Exod. 16:25.

40   Midrash *Tanchuma, Beshallach* 21:66.

41   Dodd, *The Interpretation of the Fourth Gospel*, 335.

42   "Besides the general eschatological expectation of the manna, it seems that the manna was particularly associated with Passover time . . . Midrash Mekilta on Exodus 16:1 says that manna fell for the first time on the fifteenth day of the second month, a date associated with the celebration of Passover by those who missed the regular date (Num. 9:11). Joshua 5:10–12 says that manna fell for the last time on Passover eve. The expectation grew that the Messiah would come on Passover, and that the manna would begin to fall again on Passover." Brown, *The Gospel according to John*, 1:265, citing B. Gärtner, *John 6 and the Jewish Passover*, Coniectanea Neotestamentica 17 (Lund: Gleerup, 1959), 19.

coming "kingdom" of God and declared it to be his "body."[43] Although it would take us too far afield to delve any further into these connections, it is worth noting in passing that if Jesus and the twelve saw the bread of the Last Supper as the new manna of the new Exodus, it follows that *they would not have viewed it as mere ordinary bread*, but as miraculous bread from heaven.[44]

In any case, by instructing his disciples to say each day, "Give us this day our daily bread," Jesus is teaching them to ask God for the miraculous food that the Messiah himself would give them during their journey to the new promised land. To use an ancient Jewish expression, he is teaching them to pray for "the Bread of the Age to Come."[45] As Wright concludes:

> Manna was not needed in Egypt. Nor would it be needed in the promised land. It is the food of inaugurated eschatology, the food that is needed because the kingdom has already broken in and because it is not yet consummated. The daily provision of manna signals that the Exodus has begun, but also that we are not yet living in the land.[46]

It should go without saying that if this was the meaning Jesus intended for this petition, then he saw himself as the Jewish Messiah who would once again rain down the new manna from heaven, the "food of inaugurated eschatology."

"Forgive Us Our Debts As We Forgive Our Debtors"

We now turn to the fourth common petition, in which Jesus instructs the disciples to pray to God for the forgiveness of "debts" (so Matthew) or "sins" (so Luke) based on one's willingness to forgive "debtors" or "those indebted to us" (Matt. 6:12; Luke 11:4). Although a prayer for the forgiveness of sins is certainly nothing remarkable, it is curious that Jesus utilizes the language of "debt" (ὀφειλή) and "debtor" (ὀφειλέτης) (Matt. 6:12; Luke 11:4). Whence the economic terminology in an eschatological prayer?

On one level, a linguistic answer to the question is possible. As many scholars have pointed out, in the Old Testament and ancient Judaism, the language and imagery of "debt" was sometimes used as a metaphor for "sin."[47] Although not

---

43 See Matt. 26:26–29; Mark 14:22–25; Luke 22:14–22; 1 Cor. 11:23–25.

44 I am currently exploring these connections in a monograph tentatively entitled, "Jesus and the Jewish Roots of the Eucharist."

45 According to *Genesis Rabbah* 82:8, Rabbi Joshua interpreted Proverbs 28:19, "He that tills his land shall have plenty of bread," to mean that "He who serves God to the day of his death will be satisfied with the bread of the age to come" (לחמו של עולם הבא). Dodd, *The Interpretation of the Fourth Gospel*, 83–84, n. 2. Rabbi H. Freedman translates this as "bread of the future world." See his *Midrash Rabbah: Genesis*, vol. 2 (London: Soncino, 1983), 758.

46 Wright, "The Lord's Prayer," 143.

47 See Davies and Allison, *Saint Matthew*, 1:611, citing 11QTargumJob 34:4; Luke 7:41–43; Col.

exactly common, this usage is not unique to the Lord's Prayer. On a deeper level, however, the answer may yet again be rooted in Jesus' typological eschatology. The choice of "debt" imagery may be meant to evoke the most obvious image of the "forgiveness of debts" from the Old Testament: *the year of the Jubilee*, when every Israelite would be set free from debt-slavery and allowed to return to their own land. This year of economic redemption and deliverance, which took place every fifty years, signaled the joy of being forgiven one's debts and being set free from bondage (see Lev. 25:1-55).[48]

Two aspects of the Jubilee year need to be emphasized as background to Jesus' words. First, the Jubilee did not only mean freedom from debt, as important as that was. It also meant a *return to one's land*: the Jubilee was to be "a redemption of the land," when every man shall "return to his property" (Lev. 25:24, 28). This element of return is sometimes overshadowed by the release from slavery, but it is actually quite significant. For in Leviticus, the practices of the Jubilee year were not merely an act of kindness on the part of Israelites; they were directly rooted in the redemption of Israel from Egypt in *the Exodus*.

Three times in the course of his instructions regarding the Jubilee year, God emphasizes this connection by declaring: "I am the Lord your God who brought you forth out of the land of Egypt to give you the land of Canaan, and to be your God" (Lev. 25:38, 42, 55). As Wright points out, "The Jubilee provisions . . . look back to the fact that Israel had been enslaved in Egypt and that God had rescued and delivered her. They were part of the Exodus theology."[49] Just as the Lord had set Israel free from slavery in Egypt and returned them to their land, the promised land, so too, during the Jubilee year, the people of Israel were to remember their salvation by freeing those enslaved and forgiving those in debt.[50]

Second, the Jubilee was not only something that had happened in the past; it was also a future event that was directly tied to the inauguration of the new Exodus. The basis for this connection is found in the prophet Isaiah, who describes the Servant of the Lord as one who is "anointed" (מָשַׁח) to proclaim a great *eschatological* Jubilee that would precede the restoration of Israel to the promised land:

2:13–14; *m. 'Abot* 3:17. See 1 Macc 15:8 for the use of "forgive" with the terminology of "debt."

48   See also Lev. 27:16–25; Num. 36:4; Ezek. 46:16–18; Isa. 49:8–9; 61:1–2; Jer. 34:8–22; Neh. 5:1–13; *11QMelchizedek* 2:1–9. For a full treatment of the Jubilee in both the Old Testament and Second Temple Judaism, see John S. Bergsma, *The Jubilee from Leviticus to Qumran: A History of Interpretation*, Supplements to Vetus Testamentum (Leiden: E. J. Brill, 2006).

49   Wright, "The Lord's Prayer," 143.

50   The same principle is at work in the seven-year sabbatical debt-release. In this case the connection with the Exodus is even more explicit: "At the end of every seven years you shall grant a release. . . . You shall remember that you were a slave in the land of Egypt, and the Lord your God redeemed you; therefore I command you this day" (Deut. 15:1, 15).

> *The Spirit of the Lord GOD is upon me,*
> *because the Lord has anointed me*
> *to bring good news to the afflicted;*
> he has sent me to bind up the brokenhearted,
> *to proclaim liberty to the captives,*
> *and the opening of the prison to those who are bound;*
> *to proclaim the year of the Lord's favor...*
> They shall build up the ancient ruins,
> they shall raise up the former devastations;
> they shall repair the ruined cities...
> Therefore *in their land* they shall posses a double portion;
> theirs shall be everlasting joy. (Isa. 61:1–2, 4, 7)[51]

While modern Old Testament scholars continue to debate the precise identity of this "anointed" one, there is no doubt that he inaugurates the Jubilee year, "the year of the Lord's favor" (שנת רצון) (Isa. 61:2). This Jubilee is not merely tied to release of various individuals, but to the central hope of Isaiah: the return of the entire people of Israel to the promised land in a new Exodus. Perhaps most intriguing, the most ancient Jewish interpretation of this passage, found in the Dead Sea Scrolls, not only connects Isaiah 61 with a new Exodus, but with the coming of *the Messiah*, who is depicted as a new Melchizedek:

> And as for what he said: "*In [this] year of Jubilee, [you shall return, each one, to his respective property*" (Lev. 25:13), concerning it he said: "*Th]is is* [the manner of the release:] *every creditor shall release what he lent* [to his neighbour. He shall not coerce his neighbour or his brother, for it has been proclaimed] *a release for G[od]*" (Deut. 15:2). [*Its interpretation] for the last days refers to the captives. . .they are the inherita[nce of Melchize]dek, who will make them return. And liberty will be proclaimed for them, to free them from [the debt of] all their iniquities. And this [wil]l [happen] in the first week of the Jubilee. . .in which atonement shall be made for all the sons of [light and] for the men [of] the lot of Melchizedek. . .for it is the time for "the year of favor*" (Isa. 61:2). . .(11QMelchizedek 2:1–9)[52]

In this fascinating text, we find several key eschatological events that help to shed light on the future Jubilee. The "the last days" will see the coming of the Messiah,

---

51 RSVCE, slightly altered.

52 The translation here is taken from Florentino García Martínez and Eibert J. C. Tigchelaar, *The Dead Sea Scrolls Study Edition*, 2 vols. (Grand Rapids, MI: Eerdmans, 2000), 2:1207. Brackets represent portions of the text which are damaged or missing.

the "anointed one" (מָשִׁיחַ), who is depicted as an eschatological Melchizedek, the famous priest-king from the time of Abraham (Gen. 14:18; 11QMelch. 2:18). This messianic priest-king will inaugurate an *eschatological* Jubilee; it will take place in "the last days" in order to set "the captives" free. In addition—and this is important—the "liberty" of this eschatological Jubilee will not be merely economic, but *spiritual*: it will be proclaimed "to free them from [the debt of] all their iniquities (עוונותיהמה)."

Hence, the messianic Jubilee is oriented toward "atonement" for *sin*, and freedom from the power of "Belial," the chief of the evil spirits (11QMelch. 2:7,11–13). This "release" will not only mean the forgiveness of sins, but a return to the promised land. Indeed, it is the Messiah himself who "will make them return" to the land, thereby inaugurating a new Exodus (11QMelch. 2:5-6). All of this will take place during "the year of favor," the very Jubilee that Isaiah himself had tied to the coming of one who would be "anointed" by the Spirit of the Lord (Isa. 61:2).[53]

The upshot of this Old Testament and Jewish background is simple: by teaching his disciples to pray for the forgiveness of their "debts," Jesus is not merely instructing them to pray for absolution of one's individual sins—although he is certainly doing that. He is also situating that forgiveness within the broader covenantal context of the eschatological Jubilee and the new Exodus. As the Dead Sea Scrolls show, at least some Jews living at the time of Jesus would have understood this new Exodus in terms of a spiritual Jubilee—a deliverance from the debt of sin—that would be inaugurated by *the Messiah himself*. Along these lines, we cannot fail to note that this Isaianic vision of the Jubilee is the very same passage that Jesus himself reads at his inaugural sermon in the synagogue at Nazareth (Luke 4:16–30). In this famous sermon, Jesus declares that the messianic Jubilee—and hence, the new Exodus it would inaugurate—is now at hand, and that Isaiah's prophecy has been "fulfilled" (Luke 4:21). In effect, Jesus is identifying himself as the long-awaited Messiah who would inaugurate the eschatological Jubilee, the year of release from iniquity.[54] And in the Lord's Prayer, he is calling on his disciples to live out this redemption by daring to ask God to forgive them their "debts" as they forgive their "debtors."[55]

---

53   I have also altered the translation of "year of grace" (שנת הרצון) in 11QMelch. 2:9 to "year of favor" to reflect more clearly that the author is alluding to the "year of favor" (שנת רצון) in Isa. 61:2. Despite the explicit use of "messiah" terminology in this document, it receives little or no treatment in otherwise thorough studies of the Messiah in early Judaism, such as Gerbern S. Oegema, *The Anointed and His People: Messianic Expectations from the Maccabees to Bar Kochba*, Journal for the Study of the Pseudepigrapha Supplement Series 27 (Sheffield: Sheffield Academic, 1998). Compare, however, Timothy H. Lim, "11 QMelch, Luke 4 and the Dying Messiah," *Journal of Jewish Studies* 43 (1992): 90–92.

54   David E. Aune, "A Note on Jesus' Messianic Consciousness and 11Q Melchizedek," *Evangelical Quarterly* 45 (1973), 161–65.

55   It is worth noting here that N. T. Wright has argued quite vigorously that throughout the Old Testament, the very notion of "forgiveness of sins" is not only tied to the redemption of the

"Lead Us Not Into Temptation"

The fifth and final common petition in the Lord's Prayer which points us to the presence of an Exodus typology is also the last line of Luke's shorter version: "Lead us not into temptation," or *peirasmos* (πειρασμός)" (Matt. 6:13; Luke 11:4). Of all the petitions in this prayer, this one is by far the most difficult to understand.

This is particularly true of the traditional English translation, which at first blush seems to imply that God somehow "leads" human beings into "temptation" to *sin*, and that humans should ask him not to do so. Both common sense and the New Testament itself make clear that this cannot be the proper interpretation. The letter of James says that God "tempts (πειράζει) no one" (James 1:13–14). And most commentators agree that temptation to sin is not what Jesus means in the Lord's Prayer.[56] But, given that this is true, what does Jesus mean?[57]

The key to understanding the petition lies in grasping the dual meaning of the Greek word *peirasmos*, traditionally translated as "temptation." Although this word can mean "temptation" to sin, it is also quite frequently used to refer to "testing" or "trial." When this latter definition is taken into account, Jesus' instruction makes much more sense: he is teaching the disciples to pray that they be spared future "testing" or "trials" in which they would have to undergo tribulation, suffering, and maybe even death.

Given the eschatological orientation of the Lord's Prayer as a whole, it is likely that the time of "trial" envisioned by Jesus refers to the period of eschatological tribulation that was expected to precede the coming of the kingdom of God.[58] Indeed, over the course of the last century, this eschatological interpretation of the time of "testing" has become widely accepted and even worked its way into recent English translations of the Bible.[59] In this light, Jesus is teaching the disciples to pray to be delivered, not just from daily trials, but from the great tribulation that was to precede the coming of the Messiah and the dawn of the kingdom of God.[60]

The significance of this interpretation for our study is that the Greek word for "trial" not only has ties to ancient Jewish eschatology, but to the Exodus from

---

individual Israelite in the eyes of God (see Sir. 28:1–7) but to the *corporate* forgiveness of Israel's sins which led them into exile among the Gentile nations (Sir. 47:24; 48:15). He argues that, for the Old Testament, "Forgiveness of sins is another way of saying 'return from exile.'" Wright, *Jesus and the Victory of God*, 268 (emphasis eliminated).

56 See, for example, Davies and Allison, *Saint Matthew*, 1:613.

57 See Pitre, *Jesus, the Tribulation, and the End of the Exile*, 146–53, where I treat this issue in greater detail than herein and provide bibliography on the subject.

58 Among others, see Wright, "The Lord's Prayer," 144.

59 "Do not subject us to the final test" (NAB); "Do not bring us to the time of trial" (NRSV); "Do not bring us to the test" (NEB).

60 Compare Revelation 3:10: "Because you have kept my word of patient endurance, I will keep you from the hour of trial (πειρασμοῦ) that is coming on the whole world to test (πειράσαι) the inhabitants of the earth."

Egypt. Although this connection is regularly overlooked by commentators on the Lord's Prayer, the terminology of "trial" or "testing" (πειρασμός) is used at least three times in the Pentateuch to refer to *the period of plagues and tribulation that preceded the first Exodus.* The third of these is the most significant, since it not only ties the time of "trial" or "testing" both to the Passover and to a future time of tribulation in which Israel will be delivered from Exile:

> Just remember what the Lord your God did to Pharaoh and to all Egypt, *the great trials* that your eyes saw, the signs and wonders, the mighty hand and the outstretched arm by which the Lord your God brought you out. (Deut. 7:19)

> Moses summoned all Israel and said to them: You have seen all that the Lord did before your eyes in the land of Egypt, to Pharaoh and to all his servants and to all his land, *the great trials* that your eyes saw, the signs, and those great wonders. (Deut. 29:3)

> *And the Lord will scatter you among the peoples, and you will be left few in number among the Gentiles where the Lord will drive you.* . . . But from there you will seek the Lord your God, and you will find him, if you search after him with all your heart and with all your soul. *When you are in tribulation, and all these things come upon you in the latter days, you will return to the Lord your God and obey his voice,* for the Lord your God is a merciful God; he will not fail you or destroy you or forget the covenant with your fathers which he swore to them. For ask now about former ages, long before your own, ever since the day that God created human beings on the earth; ask from one end of heaven to the other:. . .[H]as any god ever attempted *to go and take a nation for himself from the midst of another nation, by trials,* by signs and wonders, by war, by a mighty hand and outstretched arm, and by terrifying displays of power, *as the Lord your God did for you in Egypt* before your very eyes? (Deut. 4:27–34)

Taken together, these texts suggest that the biblical notion of "trials" or "testings" (מסות; πειρασμούς) could be easily connected with the plagues of the Exodus—the greatest of which was, of course, the death of the first-born son in the Passover (see Exod. 12). Moreover, these "trials" could also serve as a prototype for a future time of "tribulation" that would take place "in the latter days" when God would restore Israel by gathering them in from "among the Gentiles" (see

Deut. 30:1–8). In other words, there would one day come a new Exodus, in which God would once again redeem his people through a time of *peirasmos* accompanied by signs and wonders: that is, through a period of suffering and death that would inaugurate the age of salvation.

This Old Testament background is crucial for grasping the typological and eschatological nature of the Lord's Prayer. If it is really a prayer for the new Exodus that would take place "in the latter days" (Deut. 4:30), then the "time of trial" or "testing" of which Jesus speaks can be none other than the time of tribulation that would precede the restoration of Israel and the coming of the messianic kingdom.[61] In fact, in typological terms, one could even suggest that *there could be no new Exodus without a new Passover*—a *paschal* time of trial that would precede the redemption of Israel and the Gentiles. If this is true, then in the Lord's Prayer, Jesus is urging his disciples to pray that the new Exodus may take place, but that, if at all possible, it might come without the tribulation of the new Passover: the eschatological trial in which the first-born son would be put to death for the sins of Israel and Egypt (see Exodus 12).

Should there be any doubt about this connection between the future "trial" and an eschatological Passover, we need only turn to the words of Jesus on the night of the Last Supper to confirm it. For it was on this night—during Passover—that Jesus himself uttered a prayer and a command in the Garden of Gethsemane which strikingly parallels the Lord's Prayer and gives us a contextual clue to the meaning of the *peirasmos*. Compare the words of the Lord's Prayer with Jesus' prayer in Gethsemane and his words to the disciples (Matt. 26:36-46; Mark 14:32-42):

The Lord's Prayer	*Jesus in Gethsemane*
"Father"	"Abba, Father"
(πάτερ)	(ἀββα ὁ πατήρ)
"Your will be done"	"Your will be done"
(γεηθήτω τὸ θέλημά σου)	(γεηθήτω τὸ θέλημά σου)
"Lead us not into temptation"	"Pray that you not enter into temptation"
(εἰς πειρασμόν)	(εἰς πειρασμόν)

In light of such parallels, when Jesus warns the disciples in Gethsemane about entering into *peirasmos* on this Passover night, immediately following the paschal Last Supper, after his prayer for God to take from him the paschal cup

---

61   This is Wright's position. See "The Lord's Prayer," 146.

and deliver him from the paschal hour of suffering and death, the implications should be clear.

The *peirasmos* that is spoken of by Jesus in Mark 14:38 is not merely the coming period of eschatological tribulation, it is also *an eschatological Passover*, which is intrinsically linked to the prophetic sign Jesus has just enacted in the Last Supper. Hence, the "cup" of which he speaks in Gethsemane and the Upper Room are one and the same: the cup of *peirasmos* and the cup of the paschal tribulation which will bring about the redemption of Israel and, therefore, a new Exodus.[62] In other words, *it is the passion and death of Jesus himself—as the new Passover lamb—that will inaugurate the new Exodus.* As is clear in Jesus' words to James and John in Mark 10:38, he holds out the possibility that Peter, James, and John might also have to drink of this cup of suffering. They too may well be caught up in the Passover tribulation that Jesus is about to undergo if they do not keep awake and earnestly pray to be delivered from it. Having uttered his own prayer of acceptance, however, Jesus recognizes that his fate is sealed. He will suffer the trial immediately, and says as much when, after praying a third time, he declares: "It is enough. The hour has come. Behold, the Son of Man is given over into the hands of sinners" (Mark 14:41).[63]

In short, when the Old Testament background of the line "Lead us not into temptation" is adequately taken into account and is compared with Jesus' words elsewhere, the Lord's Prayer also shows itself to be a prayer for divine mercy, a plea for God to spare his people the sufferings of the great *peirasmos* that would precede the coming of the messianic kingdom and the paschal trial that would accompany the new Exodus.

Typological Eschatology in The Lord's Prayer

Many years ago, Raymond Brown published a now-famous article in which he argued very convincingly that the Lord's Prayer should be interpreted as an "eschatological prayer": that is, as a prayer focused on the last days, the destruction of evil, and the definitive establishment of the kingdom of God.[64] This is certainly correct, but, as New Testament scholarship has amply demonstrated, "eschatology"

---

62 Paschal language may even be present in the Markan summary of Jesus' initial petition regarding the hour: he prayed "the hour might pass (παρέλθῃ) from him" (Mark 14:35). Surely it is no coincidence that this very language of παρέρχομαι is used in the Old Testament to describe the "passing" of the destroying angel in the final trial of Passover night, the death of the firstborn son: "For the Lord will pass over (παρελεύσεται) to strike the Egyptians; and when he sees the blood on the lintel and on both doorposts, the Lord will pass over (παρελεύσεται) the door, and will not allow the destroyer to enter your houses to strike you down (Exod. 12:23 LXX [Author's trans.])."

63 For a more detailed discussion of the connections between the eschatological Passover, the great tribulation, and Jesus' prayer in the Garden of Gethsemane, see Pitre, *Jesus, the Tribulation, and the End of the Exile*, 478–504.

64 Brown, "The Pater Noster as an Eschatological Prayer," 275–76.

is a broad concept that can be understood in vastly different ways, sometimes diametrically opposed to one another.[65]

In this essay, I have tried to show that while the Lord's Prayer is most certainly an eschatological prayer, it is also much more than that. It is also a typological prayer, a messianic prayer, and a Davidic prayer. That is, it is rooted in the eschatology of the Old Testament, which held that God would act in the future in ways that would parallel how he had acted in the past.[66]

This is an important conclusion, for it suggests a possible solution to the long-standing debate over the nature of Jesus' own eschatology. Scholars continue to battle over whether to describe Jesus' outlook as "apocalyptic eschatology," "restoration eschatology," "ethical eschatology," or no eschatology at all. Although we have not been able to take up the issue in detail, a close analysis of the language and imagery of the Lord's Prayer suggests that Jesus' view of the future might be best described as a *typological eschatology* that was deeply rooted in the salvation history and covenantal theology of the Old Testament. As such, his vision of the kingdom of God was primarily and fundamentally shaped by the prophetic hopes for the new Exodus, the coming of the Messiah, and the restoration of the Davidic "kingdom of the Lord."

When seen in this light, the Lord's Prayer is not just a prayer to the Creator to save his people in the last days. It is a prayer to the God of the Exodus to see the plight of his suffering children and release them from slavery to sin and death. It is a plea for the Father to hallow his name by giving his children a new heart and a new spirit and bring them home to a land that will be more glorious than Eden of old. It is a prayer for the coming of the messianic kingdom, when both Israel and the Gentiles will pilgrimage together to a new Temple and a glorious new Jerusalem. It is a prayer for the new manna—the new "bread from heaven"—that the Messiah himself will give to the new Israel during the messianic age. It is a prayer for the great eschatological Jubilee, when the Messiah would free his people, not just from their debt, but from the even heavier burden of their iniquity. Finally, it is a prayer for divine mercy, for God to spare his people the eschatological *peirasmos*, the "final Passover" of suffering and death that will precede the ultimate entry of the new Israel into "the glory of the kingdom."[67]

---

65   Compare, for example, the work of N. T. Wright in *Jesus and the Victory of God* and Dale C. Allison, Jr. in his work *Jesus of Nazareth: Millenarian Prophet* (Minneapolis: Fortress, 1998). Both of these scholars affirm that Jesus was "eschatological" in outlook, but they draw very different conclusions about what this meant for his vision of the future.

66   As the Lord says in Isaiah: "I am God, and there is none like me, declaring the end from the beginning" (Isa. 46:9–10).

67   For a fascinating description of the eschatological tribulation as an eschatological Passover, see the *Catechism of the Catholic Church*, no. 677: "The Church will enter the glory of the kingdom

In short, the Lord's Prayer is nothing less than a prayer for the fulfillment of *all* God's covenant promises to Israel and the world, as contained in the Old Testament and inaugurated by the new Exodus of Jesus' own passion, death, and resurrection. It is in this light, the light of the Old Testament, that the words of St. Augustine ring true:

> Run through all the words of the holy prayers [in Scripture], and I do not think that you will find anything in them that is not contained and included in the Lord's Prayer.[68]

---

only through this *final Passover*, when she will follow her Lord in his death and Resurrection" (emphasis added).

68 St. Augustine, *Letter* 130, 12, 22, cited in the *Catechism of the Catholic Church*, no. 2762.

Letter & Spirit 2 (2006): 97–140

THE AUTHORITY OF MYSTERY:
The Biblical Theology of Benedict XVI

~: Scott W. Hahn :~

St. Paul Center for Biblical Theology

Never before in the history of the Catholic Church has a world-class biblical theologian been elevated to the papacy. The election of Pope Benedict XVI, on April 19, 2005, brought to the Chair of St. Peter one of the world's finest theological minds, a public intellectual long engaged in dialogue over the crucial issues of the modern period, especially the relationship between freedom and truth.

The former Joseph Ratzinger was a young academic theologian with a very bright future when, in 1977, he was chosen to be archbishop of the historic Bavarian diocese of Munich and Freising. At the time, he expressly identified a continuity between his scholarly work and his new service in the hierarchy of the Church, taking for his episcopal motto a biblical expression: "cooperators in the truth."[1]

In practical terms, however, his election to the episcopacy brought to an end his promising career as an academic theologian. He would seldom again have the opportunity for sustained scholarly research and writing, a situation about which he occasionally expresses regret.[2] Nonetheless, in the last quarter-century, Benedict has produced a substantial body of biblical-theological work—articles, speeches, homilies, and more—that reflect the wide range of his study and interests, and the keen, systematic nature of his thought.

Close study of this body of writings suggests that, had Professor Ratzinger been left alone to pursue his scholarly interests and ambitions, his achievements would have rivaled or surpassed those of the greatest Catholic theologians of the last century—figures such as Hans Urs von Balthasar and Karl Rahner. That said, I believe this paper will help us to appreciate that there has been no other Catholic

---

1   In explaining his episcopal motto, which is found in 3 John 8, he has said that "it seemed to be the connection between my previous task as teacher and my new mission. Despite all the differences in modality, what is involved was and remains the same: to follow the truth, to be at its service. And, because in today's world the theme of truth has all but disappeared, because truth appears to be too great for man and yet everything falls apart if there is no truth; for these reasons, this motto also seemed timely in the good sense of the word." Joseph Cardinal Ratzinger, *Milestones: Memoirs, 1927–1977*, trans. Erasmo Leiva-Merkiakis (San Francisco: Ignatius, 1998), 153.

2   In forewords or afterwords to collections of his articles and talks, he sometimes expresses disappointment that his professional obligations make it impossible to develop his ideas as systematically or with the depth and precision that he would like. See, for example, Joseph Cardinal Ratzinger, *The Nature and Mission of Theology: Approaches to Understanding Its Role in the Light of Present Controversy*, trans. Adrian Walker (San Francisco: Ignatius, 1995 [Original German publication, 1993]), 8.

theologian in the last century, if ever, whose theology is as highly developed and integrated in explicitly biblical terms. We would be hard pressed to find another thinker who has so allowed sacred Scripture to shape and direct his theologizing.

Benedict's command of the biblical texts, the patristic interpretive tradition, and the findings of historical and literary scholarship, represents the full flowering of the Catholic biblical renewal promoted by the popes and culminating in *Dei Verbum*, the Second Vatican Council's constitution on divine revelation. If the first half of the twentieth century was marked by the *emergence* of three renewal movements—the biblical, the patristic, and the liturgical, we see the *convergence* of these movements in *Dei Verbum*; and in the theology of Benedict we see their integration and coordination. As the result, perhaps more than any other theologian in his time, Benedict has articulated a biblical theology that synthesizes modern scientific methods with the theological hermeneutic of spiritual exegesis that began in the New Testament writers and patristic commentators and has continued throughout the Church's tradition.[3]

His pontificate has thus far borne the distinctive stamp of his biblical theology. For Benedict, the Church lives, moves, and takes its being from the Word of God—through whom all things were created in the beginning, through whom the face of God was revealed in the flesh of Jesus Christ, and through whom God's new covenant is witnessed to in the inspired texts of Scripture and made present in the divine liturgy.

In the context of the liturgy, Benedict has spoken of "the authority of mystery."[4] But this is also an evocative expression for describing his integral vision of the Church as the handmaiden of the Word of God. The Church, as he sees it, lives under the authority of mystery—in dialogue with the Word that revealed the mystery of God's saving plan in history, and in obedient service to the Word as it seeks final accomplishment of God's plan in the life and age of the Church.

In what follows, I will explore the foundations and essential principles of Benedict's biblical vision. After a brief overview of his academic and ecclesial career, I will consider Benedict's critique of the methods and presumptions of historical and literary criticism of the Bible. I will then consider the key elements of what he calls a "hermeneutic of faith"—which restores theology and exegesis to their original ecclesial and liturgical locus. Finally, I will sketch in broad outlines the

---

3   For the purposes of this paper, I will be considering almost exclusively the theological opinions and insights that Benedict articulated prior to his pontificate. I will restrict myself to articles and addresses authored under his own name and will not consider decisions or other writings issued in his official capacity as prefect of the Vatican's Congregation for the Doctrine of the Faith. The theological and exegetical judgments and conclusions discussed herein, while reflective of and in accord with Catholic dogma and teaching, are not necessarily considered binding on Catholics.

4   Joseph Cardinal Ratzinger, *A New Song for the Lord: Faith in Christ and Liturgy Today*, trans. Martha M. Matesich (New York: Crossroad Herder, 1997 [1995]), 32.

biblical theology that grows out of Benedict's new hermeneutic, before concluding with a consideration of its implications and promise for exegesis and theology.

A Brief Theological and Ecclesial Résumé

While most popes in the modern era have hailed from the Vatican's diplomatic corps, Benedict, like his immediate predecessor Pope John Paul II, was an influential scholar and university professor before being named a bishop. As John Paul continued to make important scholarly contributions to the field of philosophy throughout his career as a Church official, Benedict, too, has been arguably among the seminal thinkers in theology and biblical interpretation in the last half-century.

It is beyond my scope here to provide a complete résumé of Benedict's career, but I should note a few highlights.[5] He received his doctorate in theology from the University of Munich in 1953, writing his dissertation on Augustine's exegesis and ecclesiology. He lectured in fundamental theology at several German universities before assuming the chair in dogmatic theology at the University of Tübingen in 1966. He was an expert theological adviser at the Second Vatican Council (1963–1965) and contributed to the Council's document on divine revelation, *Dei Verbum*. In addition to hundreds of articles published in academic and ecclesial journals, he is the author of books of enduring importance and influence on patristic theology and exegesis,[6] ecclesiology,[7] dogmatic theology,[8] and the Christian symbol of faith.[9] He was the co-founder of an important theological journal, *Communio*, in collaboration with some of the last century's most influential theologians, including Henri de Lubac and Hans Urs von Balthasar.

As the highest ranking doctrinal official in the Catholic Church for nearly twenty-four years, he helped oversee the teaching of the faith in Catholic universities and seminaries throughout the world and played an important role in the work of the International Theological Commission and the Pontifical Biblical Commission. He was a decisive intellectual force in the development of the

---

5   For a good overview, especially of his early academic writings, see Aidan Nichols, *The Thought of Benedict XVI: An Introduction to the Theology of Joseph Ratzinger* (London: Burns & Oates, 2005). For comprehensive bibliographies, see Nichols, 297–330, and Joseph Cardinal Ratzinger, *Pilgrim Fellowship of Faith: The Church as Communion*, ed. Stephan Otto Horn and Vinzenz Pfnür, trans. Henry Taylor (San Francisco: Ignatius, 2005 [2002]), 299–379.

6   Joseph Ratzinger, *The Theology of History in St. Bonaventure*, trans. Zachary Hayes (Chicago: Franciscan Herald, 1971).

7   Joseph Cardinal Ratzinger, *The Meaning of Christian Brotherhood* (San Francisco: Ignatius, 1993 [1960]).

8   Joseph Ratzinger, *Eschatology: Death and Eternal Life*, trans. Michael Waldstein (Washington: Catholic University of America, 1988 [1977]).

9   Joseph Cardinal Ratzinger, *Introduction to Christianity*, trans. J. R. Foster (San Francisco: Ignatius, 1990 [1968]).

Catechism of the Catholic Church, the first comprehensive statement of Catholic belief and practice to be published in more than 450 years.

Benedict's theological training and career were shaped by his encounter with the historical-critical method, which by the late 1940s had become the dominant theoretical model in the academy.[10] In autobiographical reflections, he has related how confident scholars then were that the method gave them "the last word" on the meaning of biblical texts. He relates a story, for instance, about a leading Tübingen exegete who announced he would no longer entertain dissertation proposals because "everything in the New Testament had already been researched."[11]

Well schooled in its techniques and findings, Benedict has nonetheless emerged as a forceful critic of what he describes as the theoretical hubris and practical limitations of historical criticism. For him, the issues involved are far from academic. Indeed, the stakes in the debate could hardly be more grave. How we read and interpret the Bible has a direct implication for what we believe about Christ, the Church, the sacraments, and the liturgy, about the ways and means of salvation.[12]

He knows and often quotes the solemn truth expressed memorably by St. Jerome: "Ignorance of the Scriptures is ignorance of Christ."[13] And he has gone so far as to suggest that a near exclusive reliance on the historical-critical method has resulted in widespread ignorance about the true nature, identity, and mission of Christ: "The crisis of faith in Christ in recent times began with a modified way of reading sacred Scripture—seemingly the sole scientific way."[14]

This perhaps explains why Benedict took the unprecedented step of devoting a key passage in his inaugural homily as Bishop of Rome to the insufficiency of "science alone" in biblical interpretation. Only the "voice of the living Church," he affirmed, can deliver "a definitive and binding interpretation . . . that certainty with which we can live and for which we can even die."[15]

---

10   *Eschatology*, 271–272.

11   *Pilgrim Fellowship of Faith*, 27.

12   "The historical Jesus can only be a non-Christ, a non-Son [of God]. . . . As a result, the Church falls apart all by herself; now she can only be an organization made by humans that tries, more or less skillfully and more or less benevolently, to put this Jesus to use. The sacraments, of course, fall by the wayside—how could there be a real presence of this 'historical Jesus' in the Eucharist?" *A New Song for the Lord*, 30.

13   Jerome, *Commentary on Isaiah 1:1*, quoted in Second Vatican Council, *Dei Verbum*, Dogmatic Constitution on Divine Revelation, (November 18, 1965), 25, in *The Scripture Documents: An Anthology of Official Catholic Teachings*, ed. Dean P. Béchard, S.J. (Collegeville, MN: Liturgical Press, 2002), 19–31, at 30. For an example of Benedict's use of Jerome, see his Address to the Participants in the International Congress Organized to Commemorate the Fortieth Anniversary of the Dogmatic Constitution on Divine Revelation, *Dei Verbum*, (September 16, 2005), in *L'Osservatore Romano*, Weekly Edition in English (September 21, 2005), 7.

14   Joseph Ratzinger, *On the Way to Jesus Christ*, trans. Michael Miller (San Francisco: Ignatius, 2005 [2004]), 9.

15   Homily. Mass of Possession of the Chair of the Bishop of Rome (May 7, 2005), in *L'Osservatore*

The Critique of Criticism

Benedict's own theological writings, as we will see, are deeply informed by historical and critical research. Indeed, one of the distinctive features of his thought is its
appreciation for the "historicity" of Christian revelation.[16] God has revealed himself in human history, and the vehicle for this revelation has been the Scriptures of
the Church. Hence, Benedict insists that the historical context and literary form
in which revelation comes to us must be attended to in order for us to grasp its
meaning and appropriate that meaning for ourselves. The insights of historical
criticism, Benedict argues, are invaluable and even indispensable for helping us
understand how biblical texts came to be written and what these texts might have
meant to their original audience.[17]

His work demonstrates a commanding grasp of New Testament exegesis,
especially scholarship on the Gospel of John and exegetical study of the relationship between the Old and New Testaments. He frequently employs or assumes
scholarly hypotheses concerning the dating, compositional form, and original
setting of biblical texts. Often he will find insightful clues to meaning in philology
or in the text's interpretive history, especially in rabbinic and liturgical traditions.
He avails himself of such contextualizations as ancient Near Eastern notions of
covenant and kinship, concepts in Greek philosophy, and definitions in Roman law;
he has even been known to bring anthropological studies to bear on his subjects.[18]

Benedict, then, does not at all seek to invalidate the historical-critical method,
only to "purify" it through self-examination, so that it can truly serve its proper
function in the search for the truth. He observes that, while they freely submit

---

Romano, Weekly Edition in English (May 11, 2005), 3. Frequently in his teaching Benedict
appears to be in "dialogue" with the ideas of influential exegetes, sometimes even referring to
them by name. See, for instance, his criticism of Adolf von Harnack and the "the individualism of
liberal theology," during the course of his General Audience of March 15, 2006, in *L'Osservatore
Romano,* Weekly Edition in English (March 22, 2006), 11.

16 Nichols, *The Thought of Benedict XVI,* 292.

17 Joseph Cardinal Ratzinger, *Behold the Pierced One: An Approach to a Spiritual Christology,* trans.
Graham Harrison (San Francisco: Ignatius, 1986 [1984]), 43–44.

18 See, for instance, his discussion of the "anthropological basis" of tradition in Joseph Cardinal
Ratzinger, *Principles of Catholic Theology: Building Stones for a Fundamental Theology,* trans. Mary
Frances McCarthy (San Francisco: Ignatius, 1987 [1982]), 86–88. See also, Joseph Cardinal
Ratzinger, *The Spirit of the Liturgy,* trans. John Saward (San Francisco: Ignatius, 2000), 117.
This natural deployment of the findings of historical and literary study has become a signature
of even his minor catechetical works as pope. For example, in a homily on the meaning of the
priesthood, he considers not only the use of royal and shepherd imagery in Oriental cultures, but
also the use of this imagery in the biblical portraits of Moses and David, and the "exilic" context
of Ezekiel's famous prophecy against Israel's shepherds (Ezek. 34). See Pope Benedict XVI,
Homily. Holy Mass for the Ordination to the Priesthood of Fifteen Deacons of the Diocese of
Rome (May 7, 2006), in *L'Osservatore Romano,* Weekly Edition in English (May 10, 2006), 3.

the biblical text to all manner of probing and analysis, biblical scholars have been remarkably unreflective about their own methods and preunderstandings.[19]

His critique shows him to be conversant not only with the long history of biblical interpretation, but also with the broader currents in the post-Reformation history of ideas. He roots what he calls the "crisis" in modern biblical interpretation in philosophical, epistemological, and historical assumptions inherited from the Enlightenment. His most basic criticism of criticism is that it is far from what it purports to be—a value-neutral science akin to the natural sciences, the findings of which are objective and rendered with a high degree of certitude.

Invoking the Heisenberg principle of uncertainty or indeterminacy, he notes that even experiments in the natural sciences have been found to be influenced by researchers' own involvement and presuppositions. It should be no surprise, then, that in "scientific" biblical criticism, no less than in any other area of human inquiry, researchers' own subjectivity shapes the object of their study, including the questions they pose, the methods they develop to seek answers, and the eventual outcome of their study.

In the case of biblical criticism, Benedict pinpoints several deep-seated, yet unquestioned presuppositions that scholars bring to their work. The first they inherit from the natural sciences which they seem so anxious to emulate—the evolutionary model of natural development.

Evolution posits that later, more complex life-forms evolve from earlier, simpler forms. Applied to Scripture study, this has led exegetes to suppose that, in Benedict's words, "the more theologically considered and sophisticated a text is, the more recent it is, and the simpler something is, the easier it is to reckon it original."[20]

---

19   "The historico-critical method is essentially a tool, and its usefulness depends on the way in which it is used, that is, on the hermeneutical and philosophical presuppositions one adopts in applying it. In fact there is no such thing as a pure historical method; it is always carried on in a hermeneutical or philosophical context, even when people are not aware of it or expressly deny it." *Behold the Pierced One*, 43. See further his gentle rebuke of the early-twentieth century Catholic scholar, Friedrich Wilhelm Maier: "He did not ask himself to what extent the outlook of the questioner determines access to the text, making it necessary to clarify, above all, the correct way to ask and how best to purify one's own questioning." Cardinal Joseph Ratzinger, "Relationship between Magisterium and Exegetes," Address to the Pontifical Biblical Commission, in *L'Osservatore Romano*, Weekly Edition in English (July 23, 2003), 8.

20   *Biblical Interpretation in Crisis*, 10. It is not difficult to see how this evolutionary hypothesis has influenced such articles of modern exegetical faith as the priority of Mark's shorter, narratively more skeletal Gospel, or the presumed existence of a more primitive "Q" source supposedly relied upon by Matthew and Luke's Gospels. For his part, Benedict sees the evolutionary theory underlying the penchant for distinguishing between "Jewish" elements in the Gospel—which are presumably original and historical because Jesus was a Jew—and supposedly later interpolations from "Hellenistic" or Greek thought. This latter example perhaps explains why modern scholars for many years could not see clearly what centuries of earlier Church interpreters had been able to see, namely the deep Old Testament substratum to the New Testament. Elements that scholars for much of the modern period have confidently asserted to be Hellenistic imports,

Benedict is not out to score points by identifying discarded scholarly opinions. He wants us to see something more fundamental—how the findings of modern exegesis are shaped by the prior hermeneutical and philosophical positions of the exegetes. He questions why modern scholarship would even presume that religious and spiritual texts and ideas develop along the same lines, or according to the same rules, as organisms are observed to develop in nature. Such a conjecture is hardly self-evident and, as Benedict points out, there are many contrary examples in the history of Christian spirituality, and more generally in the history of ideas.

> First and foremost, one must challenge that basic notion dependent upon a simplistic transferal of science's evolutionary model to spiritual history. Spiritual processes do not follow the rule of zoological genealogies.[21]

Indeed, studying the historical development of the *symbol*, or the Christian confession of faith, reveals a diametrically opposite process, one that might even be described as anti-evolutionary. As Benedict notes, the early Church's beliefs about the identity of Jesus started from an original multiplicity of complex names and concepts found in Scripture and in the early liturgical and creedal tradition—Jesus as Prophet, Priest, Paraclete, Angel, Lord, and Son of Man. Finally, through a process of what Benedict calls "increasing simplification and concentration," Church authorities settled on the three titles found in the earliest creeds—Christ, Lord, and Son of God.[22]

This historical footnote is intriguing on a number of levels. First, it decisively disproves the assumption of some original, primitive simplicity in Christian faith and belief. Also, it challenges the modern exegetical presumption that creeds and liturgical formulas are later "ecclesial" additions that are "discontinuous" with and distort Jesus' original witness. As Benedict shows in this brief example, the earliest Christian witness was decidedly more complex and theologically layered, while the later work of Church authorities was one of articulating the core or heart of the Gospel witness. This not only calls into question the evolutionary hypothesis that underlies modern exegesis, it also raises interesting questions about the central importance of ecclesial tradition in the formation and redaction of biblical texts.

Separation of Church and Scripture

This brings us to Benedict's second major criticism of criticism: the assumed neces-

---

such as the "Logos" theology in John's prologue, or cultic and mystery language, and notions of divine sonship, are now widely recognized to reflect deep Old Testament themes. *Behold the Pierced One*, 33; see also Joseph Ratzinger, *Gospel, Catechesis, Catechism: Sidelights on* The Catechism of the Catholic Church (San Francisco: Ignatius, 1997 [1995]), 75.

21 *Biblical Interpretation in Crisis*, 10.
22 *Behold the Pierced One*, 15–17.

sity of studying the biblical texts apart from their original ecclesial and liturgical context. Here Benedict sees the critical method laboring under mistaken assumptions rooted in the Enlightenment's anticlerical wing, and perhaps even earlier, in the French encyclopedists' critique of organized religion.[23]

There is more at work here than the methodological operation of isolating the texts for study.

There is a prior question: Why would students of the Bible establish, as a methodological principle, the necessity of deliberately excluding reference to the texts' original and living "habitats" in the faith communities that gave rise to these texts and still regard them to be sacred and authoritative? A natural scientist, by comparison, would never presume to study an animal or plant without considering its surrounding environment or ecosystem. Yet this is precisely the *modus operandi* of "scientific" exegesis.

Moreover, the "scientific" exegete adopts a hermeneutic of suspicion toward the larger ecclesial and liturgical tradition. It is presumed that we cannot trust the plain sense of the biblical texts. The Church's traditional use of texts in its dogmas, moral teachings, and liturgical rituals comes to be seen as an impediment to a true understanding of their original meanings. While seldom stated in such stark terms, it is implicit in the basic operation of biblical "science" that the received biblical texts are a species of ideology, part of ecclesiastical machinery used to legitimate and consolidate power and control by religious elites.[24]

The root of the problem is a refusal, on methodological grounds, to engage the divine nature of the religious text. Benedict traces this to the epistemological agnosticism of the German Enlightenment philosopher, Immanuel Kant, who believed it was impossible for human reason to know the truth and reality of "things in themselves," especially God. As Kant believed we can never know things that transcend our sensory perceptions, historical criticism starts with the supposition that it can only analyze the "human element" in Scripture, defined as those things that conform to the evidence of our senses and our understanding of natural laws.[25] This philosophical starting point, Benedict believes, is of "great consequence."

23 See the sources assembled in *Principles of Catholic Theology*, 92, n. 5.

24 In fact, as Benedict notes, the earliest attempts to study the historical Jesus had an explicitly anticlerical aim, "the aim of using history to correct dogma, setting up a purely human, historical Jesus against the Christ of faith." *Behold the Pierced One*, 43. See also, Joseph Cardinal Ratzinger with Vittorio Messori, *The Ratzinger Report: An Exclusive Interview on the State of the Church*, trans. Salvator Attanasio and Graham Harrison (San Francisco: Ignatius, 1985), 74–76; Joseph Cardinal Ratzinger, "Introduction" in Romano Guardini, *The Lord* (Washington, DC: Regnery, 1996 [1954]), xi–xii.

25 Again, for Benedict, the roots of this suspicion of Church dogma run deep and are tied to an anti-ecclesiastical agenda. "For [Hermann] Reimarus, the Church's faith was no longer the way to find Jesus but a mythical smokescreen that concealed the historical reality. Jesus was to be sought, not *through* dogma, but *against* it, if one wanted to arrive at historical knowledge of him. Historical reason became the corrective of dogma; critical reason became the antipode of traditional faith." *Principles of Catholic Theology*, 92.

[I]t is assumed that history is fundamentally and always uniform and that therefore nothing can take place in history but what is possible as a result of causes known to us in nature and in human activity. Aberrations from that, for instance, divine interventions that go beyond the constant interaction of natural and human causes, therefore cannot be historical. . . . According to this assumption, it is not possible for a man really to be God and to perform deeds that require divine power—actions that would disrupt the general complex of causes. Accordingly, words attributed to Jesus in which he makes divine claims and the corresponding deeds must be "explained". . . . [E]verything in the figure of Jesus that transcends mere humanity is . . . thus not really historical.[26]

Because of this prior assumption, the method is compelled to bracket off as pious exaggerations or legends every claim made in the texts about miracles, or about God's work in the world and in history. This puts historical critics in the position of having to explain away rather than to explicate the plain sense of many biblical texts, such as those of Christ walking on water, multiplying loaves and fishes, healing the sick, and raising persons from the dead.[27] Again, the question is why such a posture towards the texts would be considered necessary or even desirable. Why would we want to study religious texts in such a way as to exclude in advance any reference to divine or supernatural phenomena?

The Hermeneutic of Faith

The power of Benedict's critique lies in its insistence that we evaluate the merits of modern exegesis purely on "scientific" methodological grounds. As a scholar, he invites us to consider whether the method is capable of really explaining as much as it claims to explain. At the most basic level, he suggests, to study a religious text and not be able to explain its religious meaning is to have failed, or at least to have completed only half the task.

From a purely scientific point of view, the legitimacy of an interpretation depends on its power to explain things. In other words, the less it needs to interfere with the sources, the more it respects the corpus as given and is able to show it to be intel-

---

26 *On the Way to Jesus Christ*, 61–62. "Modern exegesis . . . completely relegated God to the incomprehensible in order to be able to treat the biblical text as an entirely worldly reality according to natural-scientific methods." *Biblical Interpretation in Crisis*, 17.

27 *A New Song for the Lord*, 30.

ligible from within, by its own logic, the more apposite such an interpretation is. Conversely, the more it interferes with the sources, the more it feels obliged to excise and throw doubt on things found there, the more alien to the subject it is. To that extent, its explanatory power is also its ability to maintain the inner unity of the corpus in question. It involves the ability to unify, to achieve a synthesis, which is the reverse of superficial harmonization. Indeed, only faith's hermeneutic is sufficient to measure up to these criteria.[28]

On the simple measure of its "power to explain things," the historical-critical method is found to be sorely deficient. The hermeneutic of suspicion vis-à-vis the Church, the presumed "evolution" of individual texts, the excising of reference to supernatural phenomena—all of these methodological assumptions represent a high degree of interference with the texts as they have been given to us. Nor do the operations of the method preserve or identify any inner unity or inner logic in the texts.

For Benedict, another fatal defect in the method is its severing of the bond that unites the Bible and the Church. This, he suggests, may represent one of the polemical legacies of the Reformation and its influence, especially on modern Protestant biblical interpreters. Whatever the origin, Benedict argues that studying biblical texts in isolation—with no reference to the way these texts have been and continue to be used in the Church's liturgy, preaching, and practice—makes the Bible a dead letter, an artifact from a long extinct, if nonetheless exotic, culture. The process of biblical exegesis becomes an exercise in "antiquarianism" or "archaeology" or even "necrophilia."[29]

In the end, Benedict notes the fact that "the history of exegesis is a history of contradictions"—a constantly shifting succession of competing hypotheses con-

---

28 *Behold the Pierced One*, 44–45.

29 *The Nature and Mission of Theology*, 65, 95. "We cannot reach Christ through historical reconstruction. It may be helpful, but it is not sufficient and, on its own, becomes necrophilia." Joseph Cardinal Ratzinger, *Feast of Faith: Approaches to a Theology of the Liturgy*, trans. Graham Harrison (San Francisco: Ignatius, 1986 [1981]), 28. Benedict believes, too, there are lessons to be learned from the fourth-century debate between the Church father, St. Gregory of Nyssa, and a rationalist interlocutor, Eunomius, who believed he could develop an accurate understanding of God by using exclusively rational and scientific means. Gregory demurred, charging that his opponent's scientific approach "transforms each mystery into a 'thing.'" Gregory called this approach, *physiologein*, that is, "to treat in a scientific way." Benedict sees the same transforming of mysteries into "things" going on in modern academic exegesis. "Is there not too much physiologein in our exegesis and our modern way of dealing with Scripture? Are we not in fact treating it as we treat matter in the laboratory . . . [as] a dead thing that we assemble and disassemble at our pleasure?" *A New Song for the Lord*, 50–51; see also *Biblical Interpretation in Crisis*, 17.

cerning the meaning of texts. And the method, as he sees it, cannot yield much more, unless yoked to a faith perspective.

> By its very nature, historical interpretation can never take us beyond hypotheses. After all, none of us was there when it happened; only physical science can repeat events in the laboratory. Faith makes us Jesus' contemporaries. It can and must integrate all true historical discoveries, and it becomes richer for doing so. But faith gives us knowledge of something more than a hypothesis; it gives us the right to trust the revealed Word as such.[30]

Hence, he calls for a "hermeneutic of faith,"[31] one in which historical and critical methods are subordinated to, and harnessed by, the living faith of the Church. In his own theological writing, we see him unfolding such a hermeneutic, always making use of contemporary exegesis, but refusing to abide by the artificial limits the method imposes on inquiry. In his writing we see the full explanatory power of the hermeneutic of faith, which respects the biblical texts as they are given in the Church, and is able to show their inner unity and logic. He insists forcefully that faith itself is a legitimate source of knowledge and inquiry. To reduce all human knowledge to the realm of the subjective and empirical, as the critical method presumes to do, marks a distortion of reason.

> Faith has a contribution to make with regard to the interpretation of Scripture. . . . To reduce all of reality as we meet it to pure material causes, to confine the Creator Spirit to the sphere of mere subjectivity, is irreconcilable with the fundamental message of the Bible. This involves, however, a debate on the very nature of true rationality; since, if a purely materialistic explanation of reality is presented as the only possible expression of reason, then reason itself is falsely understood. . . . *Faith itself is a way of knowing.* Wanting to set it aside does not produce pure objectivity, but comprises a point of view which excludes a particular perspective while not wanting to take into account the accompanying conditions of the chosen point of view. If one takes into account, however, that the sacred Scriptures come from God through a subject which lives continually—the pilgrim people of God—then it becomes clear rationally as well that this subject has something to say about the understanding of the book.[32]

---

30   *Gospel, Catechesis, Catechism,* 67–68; *On the Way to Jesus Christ,* 152.

31   *Eschatology,* 272.

32   "Relationship between Magisterium and Exegetes." Emphasis added.

We see here the fundamentals of Benedict's approach to the biblical text—the avowal that the Word of God cannot be separated from the people of God in which the Scriptures are given and revered; the assertion that God is active not only in the creation of these texts but also in the life of the Church that reveres these texts; and, finally, that faith is required for a full understanding of the texts, which in their most literal sense speak of things and realities that transcend human experience. There is, then, an "absolute necessity" for the exegete to have recourse to the historical method—it is "an indispensable part of the exegetical effort."[33] But because the sacred texts are more than human words, this historical study is not enough. The text must be read in light of the living faith of the Church.

> Of course, exegesis can and must also investigate the internal history of the texts in order to trace their development and thought patterns. We all know that there is much to learn from such work. But it must not lead us to neglect the principal task, which is to understand the text as it now stands, as a totality in itself with its own particular message. Whoever reads Scripture in faith as a Bible must make a further step.[34]

The Ecclesial Locus of Theology and Exegesis

Benedict does not base his hermeneutic of faith and biblical theology on philosophical or methodological preconceptions of his own. Indeed, his approach to the biblical text grows organically from the historical structure of revelation, that is, from the actual manner in which the Word of God was created and handed on. The recognition of the structure of revelation is, in fact, one of the important findings of modern form and redaction criticism. However, due to its philosophical prejudices, modern exegesis, unfortunately, in practice has chosen to turn a blind eye to its own findings.

As Benedict notes, the clear finding of critical exegesis is that Scripture is the product of the Church, that its contents originated in an ecclesial context and were shaped over long years by the Church's proclamation, confession, catechesis, and liturgical worship. Considered historically, then, there is an obvious and undeniable "interwoven relationship between Church and Bible, between the people of God and the Word of God."[35]

---

33 "Relationship between Magisterium and Exegetes."

34 *Gospel, Catechesis, Catechism,* 67.

35 "Two things have above all become clear about the nature of the biblical Word in the process of critical exegesis. First of all, that the Word of the Bible, at the moment it was set down in writing, already had behind it a more or less long process of shaping by oral tradition and that it was not frozen at the moment it was written down, but entered into new processes of interpretation— 'relectures'—that further develop its hidden potential. Thus, the extent of the Word's meaning cannot be reduced to the thoughts of a single author in a specific historical moment; it is not

Benedict bids us to pay close attention to the history of the early Church and the original inner unity of Word, sacrament, and Church order and authority. That history demonstrates that the institutions and practices of the Church are not artificial or arbitrary later constructs, but organic developments of the people of God's encounter with the Word of God. Put another way, the structure of revelation and of the faith—how the early Church heard the Word and responded to it—is itself the source of the Church's sacramental worship, its teaching office, and its principles of governance.

Benedict notes the interdependence of three critical "establishments" in the early Church—*apostolic succession*, the means by which responsibility and authority for bearing witness to the Word is handed on in the Church; the *canon* of Scriptures determined to be authoritative written expressions of that Word; and the "rule of faith" (*regula fidei*) established to guarantee the integrity and orthodoxy of that witness.[36] Establishment of the canon acknowledged the "sovereignty of the Word," and the Church as servant of the Word. At the same time it fixed the form of that Word, establishing the New Testament and the Hebrew Scriptures as "a single Scripture" and the "master text." Word and witness cannot be separated, and the continuity of that witness through history is guaranteed by the establishment of apostolic succession and the episcopal ministry. Finally, the truth of that witness is guaranteed by the rule of faith which becomes "a key for interpretation."[37]

From this "reciprocal compenetration"[38] of Word, witness, and rule of faith, come the distinctive characteristics of the Bible. Scripture, as "Scripture," is entrusted to and enacted by the Church.[39] The Bible—the canon of scriptural texts that make up the Old and New Testaments—is composed, edited, and organized

---

the property of a single author at all; rather, it lives in a history that is ever moving onward and, thus, has dimensions and depths of meaning in past and future that ultimately pass into the realm of the unforeseen. . . . Certainly, Scripture carries God's thoughts within it: that makes it unique and constitutes it an 'authority.' Yet it is transmitted by a human history. It carries within it the life and thought of a historical society that we call the 'People of God,' because they are brought together, and held together, by the coming of the divine Word. There is a reciprocal relationship: This society is the essential condition for the origin and the growth of the biblical Word; and conversely, this Word gives the society its identity and continuity. Thus, the analysis of the structure of the biblical Word has brought to light an interwoven relationship between Church and Bible, between the People of God and the Word of God." *Pilgrim Fellowship of Faith*, 32–33.

36 Pope Benedict XVI, Address to Ecumenical Meeting at the Archbishopric of Cologne (August 19, 2005), in *L'Osservatore Romano*, Weekly Edition in English (August 24, 2005), 8–9.

37 Address to Ecumenical Meeting at the Archbishopric of Cologne; *Principles of Catholic Theology*, 148–149.

38 Address to Ecumenical Meeting at the Archbishopric of Cologne.

39 In this regard, Benedict quotes Heinrich Schlier, the student of Rudolf Bultmann and courageous member of the Christian opposition to Hitler: "It is unlikely that any sensible Christian would contest that the care for the Word of God among men is entrusted to the Church alone." *The Nature and Mission of Theology*, 45.

in furtherance of the Church's mission to proclaim "the presence of the Word in the world."[40] As Benedict notes, the criteria for determining which books were truly the Word of God were primarily liturgical:

> A book was recognized as "canonical" if it was sanctioned by the Church for use in public worship. . . . In the ancient Church, the reading of Scripture and the confession of faith were primarily liturgical acts of the whole assembly gathered around the risen Lord.[41]

The Church, then, from the beginning, was understood as the *viva vox*, the living voice of Scripture, proclaiming the Word but also protecting the Word from manipulation and distortion.[42] As the confessional and sacramental life of the Church were the criterion by which the canon was formed, the Scriptures were intended from the beginning to be interpreted according to the rule of faith or the Creed, under the authority of the apostles' successors. And again, historically speaking, the Church's proclamation and interpretation of the Word was ordered to a liturgical or sacramental end—the profession of faith and baptism.

> The original sphere of existence of the Christian profession of faith . . . was the sacramental life of the Church. It is by this criterion that the canon was shaped, and that is why the Creed is the primary authority for the interpretation of the Bible. . . . Thus the authority of the Church that speaks out, the authority of apostolic succession, is written into Scripture through the Creed and is indivisible from it. The teaching office of the apostles' successors does not represent a secondary authority alongside Scripture but is inwardly a part of it. This *viva vox* is not there to restrict the authority of Scripture or to limit it or even replace it by the existence of another—on the contrary, it is its task to ensure that Scripture is not disposable, cannot be manipulated, to preserve its proper *perspicuitas*, its clear meaning, from the conflict of hypotheses. Thus, there is a secret relationship of reciprocity. Scripture sets limits and a standard for the *viva vox*; the living voice guarantees that it cannot be manipulated.[43]

---

40 "The establishment of the canon and the establishment of the early Church are one and the same process but viewed from different perspectives." *Principles of Catholic Theology*, 148.

41 *Principles of Catholic Theology*, 148, 150.

42 *Pilgrim Fellowship of Faith*, 35.

43 *Pilgrim Fellowship of Faith*, 35.

Memoria Ecclesiae

This original interwoven unity of the Word of God and the people of God forms the foundation for Benedict's reflections on the nature of Scripture and the function and mission of theology and exegesis in the Church. Basing himself on the historical record of early Christianity, Benedict describes the Church as called into being by Christ's Gospel and the salvation-historical event of his death and resurrection.

He speaks of "the *memoria Ecclesiae* . . . the Church as memory."[44] It is the memory of Christ's saving actions—preserved in the written testimony of Scripture and renewed in the Church's sacramental liturgy—that gives the Church its "common identity as God's family."[45] As the "living, historical subject" of God's Word,[46] the Church lives by and for the Word, bearing witness to the Word that others might experience its saving power.

The notion of the Church as living voice and memory distinguishes Benedict's ideas about Church tradition. Benedict holds to the Church's ancient understanding that divine revelation is not reserved only to the written Word of God, but includes the sacred tradition handed on in the Church's teachings, sacramental worship, and life of faith.[47] However, Benedict identifies a deeper, dialogic dynamic as characteristic of the relationship between Word and Church.

Tradition, he argues, cannot be reduced to a treasure chest, a static collection of ancient texts, legislations, and venerable practices. Rather, it is a living dialogue in which the Church constantly listens to the Word addressed to her and responds to the claims the Word makes on her life. The Church's response to the Word—its preaching and proclamation, its teachings and liturgical life—forms the "stuff" of tradition. But tradition is more than these things. Tradition is nothing other than

---

44 "Christian faith, by its very nature, includes the act of remembering; in this way, it brings about the unity of history and the unity of man before God, or rather: it can bring about the unity of history because God has given it memory. The seat of all faith is, then, the *memoria Ecclesiae*, the memory of the Church, the Church as memory. It exists through all ages, waxing and waning but never ceasing to be the common situs of faith." *Principles of Catholic Theology*, 23.

45 *Gospel, Catechesis, Catechism*, 63.

46 *The Spirit of the Liturgy*, 168. "The faith of the Church does not exist as an ensemble of texts, rather, the texts—the words—exist because there is a corresponding subject which gives them their basis and their inner coherence. Empirically speaking, the preaching of the apostles called into existence the social organization 'Church' as a kind of historical subject. One becomes a believer by joining this community of tradition, thought, and life, by living personally from its continuity of life throughout history, and by acquiring a share in its way of understanding, its speech and its thought." *The Nature and Mission of Theology*, 94.

47 For a classical treatment of the relationship between Scripture and tradition, see *Dei Verbum*, 7–10.

the fulfillment of Christ's promise to be with his Church until the end of the age (Matt. 28:20). It is Christ's permanent, living, and saving presence in the Church.

Benedict describes this presence using the biblical imagery of the river of life, which he associates with the blood and water that flowed from the side of the Crucified.[48]

> Tradition is the living Gospel. . . . Thanks to tradition . . . the water of life that flowed from Christ's side and his saving blood reach the women and men of all times. . . . Tradition is the living river that links us to the origins, the living river in which the origins are ever present, the great river that leads us to the gates of eternity.[49]

Tradition, therefore, is a sort of ongoing divine intervention in history that ensures that every succeeding generation may have the same contact with the risen Christ experienced by the first disciples. This experience, a true and personal encounter with the saving presence of Christ, forms the "content" of the Church's tradition, as bringing about this encounter constitutes the mission of the Church.

In the Church's proclamation and liturgical celebration, the Word of salvation spoken 2,000 years ago is always "a present reality."[50] In the sacramental liturgy of the Church we have "contemporaneity with Christ."[51] Indeed, the Church's identity is defined by its liturgical remembrance in the Eucharist of the salvific event that the Word speaks of. This liturgical remembrance, of course, was mandated by Christ himself at the Last Supper. As Benedict points out: "The universalism of salvation . . . requires that the Easter memorial be celebrated in history without interruption until Christ's glorious return (1 Cor. 11:26)."[52] In this "solemn remembrance, *the means of salvation history*—the death and resurrection of the Lord—is truly present."[53]

"A Word about the Word"

We see, then, that in Benedict's historical reconstruction of primitive Christianity,

---

48   See John 7:38; 19:34; Rev. 21:6; 22:1, 17.

49   Pope Benedict XVI, General Audience (April 26, 2006), in *L'Osservatore Romano*, Weekly Edition in English (May 3, 2006), 11.

50   Joseph Cardinal Ratzinger, *Called to Communion: Understanding the Church Today*, trans. Adrian Walker (San Francisco: Ignatius, 1996 [1991]), 19.

51   *The Nature and Mission of Theology*, 60; *Principles of Catholic Theology*, 88, 100.

52   General Audience (April 26, 2006).

53   *Principles of Catholic Theology*, 2. Emphasis added. See also, Joseph Ratzinger, *Church, Ecumenism and Politics: New Essays in Ecclesiology* (New York: Crossroad, 1988), 8.

the Church's missionary, liturgical, juridical, and organizational aspects are integrally related. We see, further, that his reconstruction recognizes the early Church's belief that it was guided, even "in-dwelt," by the presence or Spirit of Christ. And we see that the Church's original mission and tradition, again under the presence and tutelage of the Spirit, are ordered to liturgy—to the entrance of the believer into the family of God through Word and sacrament.

Benedict's historical study also draws out the original work of the Word in the Church's missionary, catechetical, and confessional efforts. He notices that the faith itself is not simply an intellectual assent to a set of principles or texts. The faith requires from each believer "a word about the Word"—a personal profession of faith in the Word that he or she has heard.[54] "The faith that comes to us as a Word must also become a word in us, a word that is simultaneously the expression of our life."[55]

As the Word cannot be heard unless it is heard *from* the Church, the confession of faith is likewise an ecclesial-liturgical action and saving event that takes place only *in* the Church. One does not confess faith in the Gospel by oneself, but in the presence of the community of those already living this faith; this confession takes place in the ritual context or form of the sacrament.[56] The communal celebration of baptism recognizes the historical and ecclesial character of conversion, that the faith of the Church precedes every individual believer's faith and is the instrument by which individuals come to the faith.

Benedict notes further that the confession of faith itself, the *symbol* or the Creed, is an interpretive synthesis of the biblical testimony by which the Church determined "what actually constituted Christianity."[57] Profession of the Creed, from the start, was preceded by a period of *catechumenate*, or instruction in the

---

54   *Gospel, Catechesis, Catechism*, 30–31.

55   "We do not think up faith on our own. It does not come *from* us as an idea of ours but *to* us as a word from outside. It is, as it were, a word about the Word; we are 'handed over' *into* this Word . . . that precedes us through an immersion in water symbolizing death . . . We cannot receive his Word as a theory in the same way that we learn, say, mathematical formulas or philosophical opinions. We can learn it only in accepting a share in Christ's destiny. But we can become sharers in Christ's destiny only where he has permanently committed himself to sharing in man's destiny: in the Church. In the language of the Church we call this event a 'sacrament.' The act of faith is unthinkable without the sacramental component. . . . That is, the faith that comes to us as a Word must also become a word in us, a word that is simultaneously the expression of our life." *Gospel, Catechesis, Catechism*, 30–31. See also, *Principles of Catholic Theology*, 26: "The life embraced the Word, and the Word formed the life. Indeed, it is only to one who has entered into the community of faith that the Word of faith reveals itself."

56   *The Nature and Mission of Theology*, 52.

57   *Principles of Catholic Theology*, 149.

truths of the faith.[58] The Church's catechesis—during the course of which many of its doctrines and dogmas originally arose[59]—was fundamentally scriptural, premised on a canonical belief in the unity of the Old and New Testaments.

In fact, Benedict helps us to see how the original confession of faith presumes not only a belief in the unity of Scripture, but also a belief that Scripture is to be interpreted in light of the cross and resurrection of Christ. In its simplest form, the Christian confession is summarized in the name, "Jesus Christ." In this confession, Jesus, the historical figure whose life and deeds are recorded in the New Testament, is acknowledged to be the "Christ," that is, the anointed messiah foretold in the Old Testament. The confession of faith in Jesus Christ, the very bedrock of "Christian identity . . . is founded on the unity of the testaments."[60]

Benedict again observes that the Church's most ancient practices cannot accurately be understood without reference to its faith in the saving presence of Christ. The sacrament of baptism, like the Eucharist, is believed to be a true and real initiation into the salvation-historical event that is the content of the Word. The Church's sacraments, Benedict reminds us, are held to be "the communications of him who . . . is God's visible Word."[61] By these acts, God establishes with men and women a covenant, a familial bond, making them children in "the great family" of the Church.[62] In the sacrament, the believer is united with God's larger salvific design—"a common history in which God brought the people together and became their way."[63]

Faith Seeking Understanding

With this historical foundation laid, we are ready to consider Benedict's understanding of the task and function of theology and exegesis. Again, Benedict wants to clear the path for a genuinely authentic exegesis and theology—one divested of philosophical blinders and true to what we know about the texts from historical and literary study. As a starting point, this requires that theology and exegesis

---

58   "Hand in hand with the sign there was always the instruction, the Word, that gave the sign its place in the history of Israel's covenant with God." *Principles of Catholic Theology*, 29.

59   *Principles of Catholic Theology*, 27. "To become a Christian is to enter into this one particular Creed, into the communal form of the faith. The inner bond between the community itself and this Creed is expressed by the fact that the acceptance into the community has the form of a sacrament: baptism and catechesis are inseparable. . . . By its very nature, the word of faith presupposes the community that lives it, that is bound to it, and adheres to it in its very power to bind mankind." *Principles of Catholic Theology*, 329–330.

60   Joseph Cardinal Ratzinger, *Many Religions, One Covenant: Israel, the Church and the World*, trans. Graham Harrison (San Francisco: Ignatius, 1999 [1998]), 18.

61   *Principles of Catholic Theology*, 47.

62   *Principles of Catholic Theology*, 32; *Behold the Pierced One*, 105–106; *Called to Communion*, 23.

63   *Principles of Catholic Theology*, 29–31.

reckon the integrity and inner coherence of the Word in its original ecclesial context, a context that is at once sacramental, confessional, and missionary; it requires
further that theology and exegesis account for the faith of the community that
has given us the sacred texts, specifically, the community's faith in the continuing
presence and guidance of the divine Word.

For Benedict, the Church is the living subject or "do-er" of theology, which
flows out of the Church's remembrance—its pondering, proclaiming, and "actual-
izing" of the Word of God. Theology stems from the very structure of the faith,
as a consequence, even an imperative, of the faith. It begins in the response to
God's gift, the divine Word that God has spoken to us in Jesus.[64] Theology is the
believer's response to the Word, who is a divine Person; and theology is, essentially,
a reflection on the "contents" of the Word—the revelation of God's love, expressed
in the new covenant made in the death and resurrection of Jesus Christ.

We "do" theology, in the first place, because we believe in and love the God
who has shown his face to us in Jesus Christ. Theology is faith seeking better
understanding of the One who reveals himself as love. It becomes an "imperative"
of the faith because there is an innate human desire to seek the truth and the most
intimate knowledge possible of the One we love.

> Faith can wish to understand because it is moved by love for the
> One upon whom it has bestowed its consent. Love seeks under-
> standing. It wishes to know ever better the one whom it loves.
> It "seeks his face," as Augustine never tires of repeating. Love
> is the desire for intimate knowledge, so that the quest for intel-
> ligence can even be an inner requirement of love. Put another
> way, there is a coherence of love and truth which has important
> consequences for theology and philosophy. Christian faith can
> say of itself, I have found love. Yet love for Christ and of one's
> neighbor for Christ's sake can enjoy stability and consistency
> only if its deepest motivation is love for the truth. This adds
> a new aspect to the missionary element: real love of neighbor
> also desires to give him the deepest thing man needs, namely,
> knowledge and truth.[65]

---

64 "Theology is a specifically Christian phenomenon which follows from the structure of faith.
. . . It is preceded by a Word which . . . has been granted . . . as a gift . . . Theology is pondering
what God has said and thought before us." *The Nature and Mission of Theology*, 103–104. "To
perceive the meaning of this Word, to understand this Word—that is the ultimate basis of
theology." *Pilgrim Fellowship of Faith*, 32; *Principles of Catholic Theology*, 325.

65 *The Nature and Mission of Theology*, 27.

We see, then, that theology for Benedict is far from a private affair. Theology's desire to better know and love God is always ordered to the Church's missionary proclamation of the saving Word—"to tell man who he is and . . . to disclose to him the truth about himself, that is, what he can base his life on and what he can die for."[66]

In Benedict's understanding, there is an original and inner dynamism that orients theology to proclamation and catechesis. This is not at all to reduce the work of theology to apologetics or catechetics. Instead, Benedict sees a missionary impulse issuing from the heart of the Christian faith experience. Faith, because it possesses the truth about human history and happiness, must necessarily express itself in proclamation and catechesis so that others may share in the truth.

The Authors of Scripture as the "Normative" Theologians

If the activity of theology flows from the inner structure of Christian faith, its content and methodology in a similar way issue from the inner structure of revelation. Benedict appropriates a distinction first drawn by Aristotle and later adopted by pseudo-Dionysius and Bonaventure: between *theology* proper (θεολογία), that is, the words of God, and *the study of theology* (θεολογιχή), our efforts to understand the divine discourse.[67]

He sees sacred Scripture as theology in its original and pure form, because it is "the discourse of God rendered in human words . . . it does not just speak of him but *is* his own speech. It lets God himself speak." He accepts the traditional Catholic notion of inspiration, of Scripture's dual, divine and human, authorship. But he draws out a deeper implication of that affirmation, namely that the human authors of Scripture are the original theologians—"they are 'theologoi,' those through whom God . . . as the Word that speaks itself, enters into history."

This fact of revelation has great significance for him: "the Bible becomes the model of all theology," and the authors of sacred Scripture become "the norm of the theologian, who accomplishes his task properly only to the extent that he makes God himself his subject." This in turn leads to perhaps his most daring and fruitful assertion of theological principle:

> [T]heology is a spiritual science. The normative theologians are the authors of Holy Scripture. This statement is valid not only with reference to the objective written document they left

---

66   *The Nature and Mission of Theology*, 63–64.

67   *Principles of Catholic Theology*, 320–322.

behind but also with reference to their manner of speaking, in which it is God himself who speaks.[68]

For Benedict that means that Scripture, and the human authors of Scripture, are meant to serve as the model—not only for how we should "do" theology, but also for what our theology should be about, and how the findings of theological inquiry should be expressed.

Taking the New Testament authors as "normative" means, in the first place, that the theologian must be a person who has heard and believed the Word, professed that faith in the Church, and made personal assent to the standards and teachings of the Church in its sacramental and moral life. Not only were the New Testament authors men of faith, but their written proclamation teaches us that the fullest knowledge of Christ is only possible in following him as disciples.[69] Of necessity, then, "theology presupposes faith. . . . There can be no theology without conversion."[70]

Following the New Testament writers, Benedict sees theology as essentially "about" Jesus Christ—who he is, the full meaning of the salvation-historical event of his resurrection, and how his presence remains in the world in his Church.[71] "All Christian theology, if it is to be true to its origin, must be first and foremost a theology of resurrection."[72] The primary data for theology becomes the words and deeds of Jesus as remembered and interpreted in the New Testament.[73]

In this sense, theology, following in the footsteps of the normative theologians, is a function of the Church as the living memory of Christ. Benedict illustrates his thought by reflecting on a passage in John's Gospel, a brief statement made after Christ's cleansing of the Temple: "When therefore he was raised from the dead, his disciples remembered that he had said this; and they believed the scripture and the word which Jesus had spoken" (John 2:22). The passage refers to Jesus' declaration that should his enemies destroy "this shrine," he would raise it in three days. Benedict reads this passage in light of the promise found later in John's

---

68 *Principles of Catholic Theology*, 320–322.

69 See the biblical citations in *On the Way to Jesus Christ*, 67. "[J]ust as we cannot learn to swim without water, so we cannot learn theology without the spiritual praxis in which it lives." *Principles of Catholic Theology*, 323.

70 *The Nature and Mission of Theology*, 55, 57.

71 *On the Way to Jesus Christ*, 76–77.

72 *Principles of Catholic Theology*, 184–185.

73 "[T]he remembrance and retention of the words of Jesus and of the course of his life, especially his passion, were from the beginning an essential factor in the formation of Christian tradition and in the norms applied to it." Joseph Ratzinger, *Dogma and Preaching*, trans. Matthew J. O'Connell (Chicago: Franciscan Herald, 1985), 4.

Gospel, that Jesus would send the Holy Spirit to lead the disciples to remembrance of all that he had said (John 14:26).

Benedict suggests that in this passage we have all the elements for a biblical-theological doctrine of the Church as *memoria ecclesiae*: belief in the salvation-historical event of the resurrection; belief in the unity of the Old Testament (the "scripture" Jesus referred them to) and the New Testament (the "word" spoken by Jesus); and remembrance in the Spirit, which takes place in the ecclesial context and authority established by Jesus.[74]

One could even develop Benedict's insights for theology further by delineating more precisely the *content* of the disciples' remembrance. The "word" that the Spirit brings them to remember is, in fact, a spiritual or typological interpretation of the Old Testament. In light of the resurrection, and under the guidance of the Spirit, the apostles understand Jesus' words about the Temple to have been referring to the "temple" of his body (see John 2:21).

The passage, then, gives us insight into Jesus' own preaching, which, as the Gospels illustrate in abundance, often involved typological or spiritual interpretation of his identity and mission in light of the Old Testament.[75] This method of interpretation, in turn, becomes the dominant pattern for the normative theologians, the New Testament authors. As we will see below, this pattern of spiritual exegesis is also one of the keys to Benedict's own exegesis and biblical theology.

Read through Benedict's eyes, we see the normative theologians of the New Testament in constant dialogue with the Old Testament texts. Indeed, the New Testament is seen by Benedict as a spiritual exegesis of the Old. "The New Testament is nothing other than an interpretation of 'the Law, the prophets, and the writings' found from or contained in the story of Jesus."[76] He notes that certain principles—"the internal unity of the Bible as a rule of interpretation, Christ as the meeting point of all the Old Testament pathways"—are the hallmarks of the New Testament authors' exegesis.[77]

The central salvation-historical event, Christ's resurrection, is both a mighty act of God and at the same time a vindication of Jesus' interpretation of the Old Testament. Or, as Benedict puts it more pointedly, the resurrection is "God's defense of Jesus against the official interpretation of the Old Testament as given by the competent Jewish authorities." By the resurrection, God "proves," so to speak,

---

74   See Benedict's discussion in *Principles of Catholic Theology*, 24–25.

75   See, in summary form, the post-resurrection catechesis to the Twelve in Luke 24:27, 44–45.

76   *Milestone: Memoirs, 1927–1977*, 53.

77   Cardinal Joseph Ratzinger, "Preface," Pontifical Biblical Commission, *The Jewish People and their Sacred Scriptures in the Christian Bible* (Boston: Pauline Books and Media, 2003), 11–19, at 14.

that Jesus is the suffering servant, the divine Son, and the Messiah from the line of David, as foretold by the prophets and the psalms. Of critical significance, in Benedict's mind, is the portrayal of Jesus as "the true lamb of sacrifice, the sacrifice in which the deepest meaning of all Old Testament liturgies is fulfilled." As we will see below, this has "essential significance for the Christian liturgy."[78]

As a final historical note, Benedict acknowledges that Jesus did not "invent" this way of reading the Scriptures. Already in the Old Testament, especially in the prophets and psalms, we find increasing anticipation of a messianic king who will be "the fulfilled image of the true Israel."[79] Nonetheless, Jesus does claim to be definitive interpreter of the Old Testament texts, and the New Testament authors employed certain interpretive methods, already present in rabbinic Judaism, to back up this claim. As we will see, the resulting original Christian pattern of reading the New Testament in light of the Old and the Old Testament in light of the New, becomes normative for Benedict's biblical theology.[80]

Benedict's New Synthesis

We are now in the position to sketch, if perhaps only in broad outlines, some of the fundamental elements of what I would describe as Benedict's biblical theology. The details of what I mean by "biblical theology" will hopefully become clear during the course of my discussion below. But I may state it preliminarily here: By biblical theology I mean a unified understanding of the saving truths of the inspired Scripture as they have been handed on in the tradition of the Church, an understanding based on the unity of the Old and New Testaments, on Christ as the interpretive key of the Scriptures, and on the Church's divine liturgy as the fulfillment and actualization of Scripture's saving truths.

For Benedict, following the normative theologians of the New Testament and the patristic authors, theology is essentially interpretation and commentary on

---

78 *Dogma and Preaching*, 3–5.

79 *The Meaning of Christian Brotherhood*, 48.

80 "Jesus of Nazareth claimed to be the true heir to the Old Testament—'the Scriptures'—and to offer a true interpretation, which, admittedly, was not that of the schools, but came from the authority of the Author himself: 'He taught them as one having authority, and not as the scribes' (Mark 1:22). The Emmaus narrative also expresses this claim: 'Beginning with Moses and all the prophets, he interpreted to them the things about himself in all the Scriptures' (Luke 24:27). The New Testament authors sought to ground this claim into details, in particular Matthew, but Paul as well, by using rabbinic methods of interpretation to show that the scribal interpretation led to Christ as the key to the 'Scriptures.' For the authors and founders of the New Testament, the Old Testament was simply 'the Scriptures': it was only later that the developing Church gradually formed a New Testament canon which was also Sacred Scripture, but in the sense that it still presupposed Israel's Bible to be such, the Bible read by the apostles and their disciples, and now called the Old Testament, which provided the interpretive key." "Preface," *The Jewish People and their Sacred Scriptures in the Christian Bible*, 17.

sacred Scripture. "Theology is interpretation,"[81] a reflection on the Word that has been given. In autobiographical remarks, he has acknowledged that exegesis has always been "the center of my theological work."[82] I would characterize Benedict in his exegetical theology as a "biblical realist." What he says about the "biblical realism" of the *Catechism of the Catholic Church*, which he was instrumental in conceiving and editing, is no less true of his own theological thought:

> The *Catechism* trusts the biblical word. It holds the Christ of the Gospels to be the real Jesus. It is also convinced that all the Gospels tell us about this same Jesus and that all of them together help us, each in its own way, to know the true Jesus of history, who is no other than the Christ of faith.[83]

For Benedict, "the biblical books . . . are, precisely, historical books."[84] He has often stated that the testimony of the New Testament is far more reliable that the constantly shifting hypotheses of historical-critical scholarship.[85] He accepts the Gospel testimony as "a written record of the most ancient catechesis,"[86] and assumes the historical reality of such events as the multiplication of loaves (Mark

---

81   *The Nature and Mission of Theology*, 93. Benedict's views on the object of theology were well reflected in these statements from the Congregation for the Doctrine of the Faith's *Instruction on the Ecclesial Vocation of the Theologian* (June 26, 1990), 6, 8: "[The theologian's] role is to pursue in a particular way an ever deeper understanding of the Word of God in the inspired Scriptures and handed on in the living tradition of the Church. . . . [T]he object of theology is the truth which is the living God and his plan for salvation revealed in Jesus Christ." In *L'Osservatore Romano*, Weekly Edition in English (July 2, 1990), 1.

82   *Milestones*, 52–53. Describing his thought to a journalist, he once said: "[E]xegesis was always very important. . . . The point of departure is first of all the Word. That we believe the Word of God, that we try really to get to know and understand it, and then . . . to think it together with the great masters of the faith. This gives my theology a somewhat biblical character and also bears the stamp of the fathers, especially Augustine." Joseph Cardinal Ratzinger with Peter Seewald, *Salt of the Earth: Christianity and the Catholic Church at the End of the Millennium*, trans. Adrian Walker (San Francisco: Ignatius, 1997), 66.

83   *Gospel, Catechesis, Catechism*, 64.

84   "Relationship between Magisterium and Exegetes."

85   "I credit biblical tradition with greater truthfulness than I do the attempts to reconstruct a chemically pure historical Jesus in the retort of historical reason. I trust the tradition in its entirety. And the more reconstructions I see come and go, the more I feel confirmed in my trust. . . . In the face of such partial authorities the vital power of the tradition carries incomparably greater weight with me. . . . I know that the Jesus of the Gospels is the real Jesus and that I can trust myself to him with far greater security than I can to the most learned reconstructions; he will outlast all of them. The Gospel tradition with its great breadth and its range of tone tells me who Jesus was and is. In it he is always present to be heard and seen anew." *Dogma and Preaching*, 9–10.

86   *Gospel, Catechesis, Catechism*, 61.

6:34–38).[87] The Old Testament witness, too, he likewise treats seriously as history.[88] He is quite conscious that in this stance he is at odds with the dominant model of "scientific" exegesis. But he rejects the notion that faith and history are somehow in dialectical opposition, that the biblical narrative cannot be a source of true historical knowledge.

> The opinion that faith as such knows absolutely nothing of historical facts and must leave all of this to historians is Gnosticism: this opinion disembodies faith and reduces it to pure idea. The reality of events is necessary precisely because the faith is founded on the Bible. *A God who cannot intervene in history and reveal himself in it is not the God of the Bible. . . .* That Jesus—in all that is essential—was effectively who the Gospels reveal him to be to us is not mere historical conjecture, but *a fact of faith.* Objections which seek to convince us to the contrary are not the expression of an effective scientific knowledge, but are an arbitrary over-evaluation of the method.[89]

Throughout the history recorded in Scripture, Benedict sees not only a series of events in the life of a people, but also the hand of God, "the great acts of God in history."[90] In this, we see Benedict's hermeneutic of faith, again in sharp contrast to the supposedly "scientific" worldview of biblical criticism. The exegete, he contends,

> may not exclude a priori that (almighty) God could speak in human words in the world. He may not exclude that God himself could enter into and work in human history, however improbable such a thing might at first appear. He must be ready to learn from the extraordinary. He must be ready to accept that the truly original may occur in history, something which cannot

---

87 See General Audience (May 24, 2006), in *L'Osservatore Romano*, Weekly Edition in English (May 31, 2006), 14.

88 For example, he writes of "the whole history recounted in the books of the Judges and Kings, which is taken up afresh and given a new interpretation in Chronicles," and uses the account of Israel's Exodus and settlement of the land as an insight into the meaning of worship. *The Spirit of the Liturgy,* 15–20. Likewise, he considers the history of liturgy from Genesis to the Christian era, *The Spirit of the Liturgy,* 35–45, and discusses the biblical nature of wisdom in light of Isaiah's prophecy and the Davidic monarchy. *Principles of Catholic Theology,* 356–358. See also, his discussion of Adam and Eve, Message for the Eightieth World Mission Sunday 2006, *L'Osservatore Romano,* Weekly Edition in English (June 14, 2006), 3.

89 "Relationship between Magisterium and Exegetes." Emphasis added.

90 *Principles of Catholic Theology,* 190.

be derived from precedents but which opens up out of itself. He may not deny to humanity the ability to be responsive beyond the categories of pure reason and to reach beyond ourselves toward the open and endless truth of being.[91]

Benedict shares the view of Bonaventure, that to understand the literal, historical text is not to understand Scripture as it is given, as revelation. What is needed is to understand the "spiritual meaning lying behind the letter."[92] He insists that "spiritual [interpretation] does not mean that the exegesis lacks realism or disregards history, but that it brings into view the spiritual depth of the historical events."[93]

As we have pointed out, Benedict reads biblical history using sophisticated tools of historical and literary criticism. However, in endeavoring to read the Bible with the normative theologians, the biblical authors, he does not stop with history, but reads also with the eyes of faith. Faith, informed by the tradition of the Church, especially the Creed, "gives us the right to trust the revealed Word as such."[94] Again and again, Benedict urges us not to oppose faith and reason. Faith does not exempt us from careful literary and historical analysis of the texts. Indeed, faith is a form of special knowledge that empowers us to undertake this analysis with deeper insight and lends to our work a greater unity and coherence.

The Transcendent Meaning of Biblical Words and Events

Following the biblical authors, Benedict's biblical theology is built on a series of *unities*—"the unity of the Old and New Testaments, of the New Testament and early Church dogma, of all these elements together and the ongoing life of faith." These "unities," as we saw above, are not an artificial philosophical construct imposed by Benedict; rather, they are observable in the structure of revelation and the origins

91   *Biblical Interpretation in Crisis*, 19.

92   *The Theology of History in St. Bonaventure*, 66–68, 78–79.

93   *Gospel, Catechesis, Catechism*, 65, n. 24.

94   "Of course, exegesis can and must also investigate the internal history of the texts in order to trace their development and thought patterns. We all know that there is much to learn from such work. But it must not lead us to neglect the principal task, which is to understand the text as it now stands, as a totality in itself with its own particular message. Whoever reads Scripture in faith as a Bible must make a further step. By its very nature, historical interpretation can never take us beyond hypotheses. After all, none of us was there when it happened; only physical science can repeat events in the laboratory. Faith makes us Jesus' contemporaries. It can and must integrate all true historical discoveries, and it becomes richer for doing so. But faith gives us knowledge of something more than a hypothesis; it gives us the right to trust the revealed Word as such." *Gospel, Catechesis, Catechism*, 67–68. He describes this spiritual reading as "a faith that does not set history aside but first opens its eyes so as to be able to understand it in its entirety." *On the Way to Jesus Christ*, 59.

of the Church. In his work, Benedict seeks to probe deeply into the mystery of these unities, which are the vehicles through which God's plan continues in the world. His goal is to "seek the inner unity and totality of the truth in the grand historical structure of the faith."[95]

We have seen how the New Testament witness presumes the "inner unity"[96] of the Old and New Testaments. The Bible, in its final canonical form, is essentially a historical narrative. It purports to tell a single story about events that have taken place in the history of a people—from the first day of creation to the last day, which is the beginning of a new heaven and a new earth. The canonical text claims to be more than an account of historical facts or the memoir of a particular people. It claims that God himself was at work in the events it records, and that the words of various characters and their deeds themselves represent actions of God.[97] This suggests, too, that within the very structure of biblical revelation, there is a twofold sense of meaning—the one literal and historical, and the other the sense of the text that can only be gained by faith, by belief in the claims made about God in these texts.

This consideration of the structure of biblical history also informs Benedict's particular contribution to the Church's understanding of inspiration. Because the sacred texts are the products of both divine and human authors, their testimony of necessity must transcend the limits of mere human language. Benedict explains this dynamic of the scriptural Word by referring to the "multidimensional nature of human language,"[98] in which words often convey more meanings than they literally express. This self-transcendent capacity of human language is heightened to an immeasurable degree in Scripture, which is the Word of God expressed in human language. "If even human speech boundlessly transcends itself the greater it is and refers to the unsaid and inexhaustible beyond the words themselves, how much more must this be true of the Word whose ultimate and real subject we believe to be God himself?"[99]

For Benedict, the meanings of the words of Scripture cannot be "fixed to a particular moment in history."[100] Instead, as we know from studying the history of biblical texts and the process of their composition, later Scriptures are always in dialogue with earlier ones, commenting on them and reinterpreting them. The meaning of individual texts "was not frozen at the moment it was written down,

---

95 *The Nature and Mission of Theology*, 96.

96 *Behold the Pierced One*, 44.

97 *On the Way to Jesus Christ*, 147–148.

98 "Preface," *The Jewish People and their Sacred Scriptures in the Christian Bible*, 17.

99 *A New Song for the Lord*, 50–51.

100 "Preface," *The Jewish People and their Sacred Scriptures in the Christian Bible*, 17.

but entered into new processes of interpretation—'relectures'—that further de-velop its hidden potential."[101]

As the words of Scripture, by their very nature, must admit of more than the literal level of meaning, the same is true of the historical events recorded in Scripture. This insight, too, naturally follows from the structure of biblical revela-tion, that is, from the fact that God is the ultimate "author," not only of the words of the inspired texts but of the historical agents and events detailed in its pages.

The events recorded are "real," but because God is their author their meaning far transcends "historical facticity." Indeed, because God is acting in the biblical narrative, "the events carry *within themselves* a surplus meaning. . .giving them significance for all time and for all men." It is important to understand that these surplus meanings are inseparable from the historical events. They are not arbitrary rereadings of the events or new interpretations of the events given after the fact. The surplus or divine meaning is *within* the original events—"present in the event, even though it transcends mere facticity."[102]

For Benedict, then, we must read the sacred page in such a way as to hear "the living Speaker himself." We must "once again develop methods that respect this inner self-transcending of the words into the Word of God."[103] Further, we must be vigilant in seeking "a greater understanding of how the Word of God can avail of the human word to confer on a history in progress a meaning that surpasses the present moment and yet brings out, precisely in this way, the unity of the whole."[104]

Reading the Scriptures as a single history of salvation, Benedict detects a kind of historical "pedagogy," a long, historical tutelage or "educational process" by which God prepared humanity for the revelation of Christ and his new covenant.[105] He sees in the "inner continuity and coherence"[106] of the Old and New Testaments a revelation of the divine intent in salvation history. "The totality of the Scriptures

---

101 *Pilgrim Fellowship of Faith*, 32–33.

102 See the important discussion in *On the Way to Jesus Christ*, 147–148.

103 *A New Song for the Lord*, 50–51; *Eschatology*, 42–44.

104 "Preface," *The Jewish People and their Sacred Scriptures in the Christian Bible*. While it is beyond my scope here, it should be noted that Benedict sees the danger of an incipient "Marcionism"—a heretical discarding of the Old Testament—in some of the assumptions and practices of historical criticism. See his discussion of Harnack, and the legacy of Luther's "antithesis between Law and Gospel" in this important "Preface," 17.

105 *Many Religions, One Covenant*, 55–56; *Pilgrim Fellowship of Faith*, 270; *Principles of Catholic Theology*, 344–345; Cardinal Joseph Ratzinger, *In the Beginning: A Catholic Understanding of the Story of Creation and the Fall*, trans. Boniface Ramsey (Grand Rapids, MI: Eerdmans, 1995 [1986]), 9, 16.

106 *Many Religions, One Covenant*, 36.

on which the Christian faith rests is God's 'testament' to mankind, issued in two stages, as a proclamation of his will to the world."[107]

In "the profound compenetration of the two testaments as the one Scripture of the Christian faith," Benedict sees the meaning of God's plan revealed in Jesus Christ.

> The real novelty of the New Testament lies not so much in new ideas as in the figure of Christ himself, who gives flesh and blood to these concepts—an unprecedented realism. In the Old Testament, the novelty of the Bible did not consist merely in abstract notions but in God's unpredictable and in some sense unprecedented activity. This divine activity now takes on dramatic form when, in Jesus Christ, it is God himself who goes in search of the "stray sheep," a suffering and lost humanity. . . . His death on the cross is the culmination of that turning of God against himself in which he gives himself in order to raise man up and save him. This is love in its most radical form.[108]

Covenant, the Bible's Central Theme and Key

God's will for the world is the *covenant*, a relationship of communion in love that embraces heaven and earth, spirit and matter, the divine and the human. Benedict reads God's covenant will and desire on the first pages of Scripture, in the account of creation. He expresses the meaning of the creation account in a series of statements: "Creation is oriented to the sabbath, which is the sign of the covenant between God and humankind. . . . Creation is designed in such a way that it is oriented to worship. It fulfills its purpose and assumes its significance when it is lived, ever new, with a view to worship. Creation exists for the sake of worship."[109]

Fashioned in the image of God, the human person was created for relation-

---

107 *Many Religions, One Covenant,* 47. "The synthesis of the testaments worked out in the early Church corresponds solely to the fundamental intention of the New Testament message, and it alone can give Christianity its own historical force." *A New Song for the Lord,* 72. "[T]he understanding of Holy Scripture as an inner unity in which one part sustains the other, has its existence in it, so that each part can be read and understood only in terms of the whole." *Principles of Catholic Theology,* 135–136. "[T]he New Testament itself wished to be no more than the complete and full understanding of the Old Testament, now made possible in Christ. The whole Old Testament is a movement of transition to Christ, a waiting for the One in whom all its words would come true, in whom the 'covenant' would attain fulfillment as the new covenant." *Feast of Faith,* 58.

108 Pope Benedict XVI, *Deus Caritas Est,* Encyclical Letter on Christian Love (December 25, 2005), 12, in *L'Osservatore Romano* Weekly Edition in English (February 1, 2006).

109 *In the Beginning,* 27–28.

ship with God. Men and women, too, were created for worship, which is an expression of "the pure relationship of love"[110] of the creature with the Creator. "The goal of creation is the covenant, the love story of God and man."[111] For Benedict, the God who reveals himself to us, the God who creates and redeems, reveals himself in Scripture as a "God-in-relationship." He reveals himself in word and deed in the acts of creation and redemption, acts solemnly expressed in the making of covenant. Covenant is the goal of creation and the way of God's self-revelation, of his entering into relationship with his creation.[112]

Benedict's biblical theology of covenant synthesizes a great deal of scholarship. He presents the covenant, not as a reciprocal partnership, but as the initiative and gift of the divine will. The covenant is a "creative act of God's love," Benedict says, noting that the prophets often described God's "passionate love" for Israel in terms of a husband's love for his bride.[113] In the covenant, we see the perfect "manifestation of his self, the 'radiance of his countenance.'"[114]

God's covenant is always expressed in words and sign, in law and liturgy, Benedict notes. Beginning with the sabbath ordinances, there is a profound inner connection in the covenant structure of revelation between the "legal and cultic" orders, between the moral order and the liturgical order, between the commands and ordinances of God and the sacrificial worship of God.[115] Law and worship are two sides of the covenant relationship. Each is

> an expression of God's love, of his "yes" to the human being that he created, so that he [the human being] could both love and receive love. . . . God created the universe in order to enter into a history of love with humankind. He created it so that love could exist.[116]

In Benedict's reading, God's testament or covenant is "the central theme of

---

110 "The true center, the power that moves and shapes from within the rhythm of the stars and of our lives, is worship. Our life's rhythm moves in proper measure when it is caught up in this." *In the Beginning*, 29–30.

111 *The Spirit of the Liturgy*, 26.

112 *Many Religions, One Covenant*, 75–77.

113 "The 'covenant' is not a two-sided contract but a gift, a creative act of God's love. . . . God, the king, receives nothing from man; but in giving him his law, he gives him the path of life." *Many Religions, One Covenant*, 50–51.

114 *Many Religions, One Covenant*, 77.

115 *In the Beginning*, 29; *Many Religions, One Covenant*, 68.

116 *In the Beginning*, 29–30.

Scripture itself, thus giving a key to the whole of it."[117] Covenant forms the narrative structure of Scripture, and the story of Scripture unfolds in the sequence of covenants that God makes—with Noah, with Abraham, with Jacob-Israel, with Moses at Sinai, and finally with David. The plurality and interrelatedness of these covenants makes up the one old covenant. Manifest in them is the truth of God's providential plan, the truth revealed in the covenant of creation.[118]

While each of these covenants is significant, the foundational covenant of salvation history is the covenant with Abraham who, by not withholding from God his beloved son, was blessed by God with the promise that he would become the father of many nations. This promise is fulfilled in Jesus Christ, who makes it possible for men and women of all nations to share in the spiritual destiny of Israel, as the children of Abraham.[119]

Benedict sees in Israel's prophets an insistent promise of universalism, that all the nations will come to worship the God of Israel. The work of Jesus thus becomes the fulfillment of the "prophetic thrust of the Old Testament itself."[120] Jesus' mission, indeed, can be understood only in light of the sacred Scriptures of Israel. Through his Gospel, which marks his interpretation of Israel's Scriptures, the promise that Abraham's descendants would be the source of blessing and salvation for all nations is realized.

The Deep Unity of Law and Gospel

The covenantal sequence of the canonical narrative indicates an "inner continuity" in salvation history—from Abraham and Israel to Jesus and the Church of Jews and Gentiles.[121] Benedict speaks of "the inner continuity and coherence of Law and Gospel" and the "deep unity between the good news of Jesus and the message of Sinai."[122] In fact, Christian identity is defined by reference to the old covenant. The Christian is joined to a history that began with Abraham and culminated in the kingdom of David.[123]

---

117 *Many Religions, One Covenant*, 48.

118 "[T]here is only *one* will of God for men, only *one* historical activity of God with and for men, though this activity employs interventions that are diverse and even contradictory—yet in truth they belong together." *Many Religions, One Covenant*, 57.

119 "'You will be a blessing,' God had said to Abraham at the beginning of salvation history (Gen. 12:2). In Christ, the son of Abraham, these words are completely fulfilled." *The Spirit of the Liturgy*, 183.

120 *Many Religions, One Covenant*, 28.

121 *Many Religions, One Covenant*, 68.

122 *Many Religions, One Covenant*, 33, 36.

123 *Truth and Tolerance*, 97.

[T]he mission of Jesus is to unite Jews and pagans into a single people of God in which the universalist promises of the Scriptures are fulfilled that speak again and again of the nations worshipping the God of Israel.... The mission of Jesus consists in bringing together the histories of the nations in the community of the history of Abraham, the history of Israel.... The history of Israel should become the history of all, Abraham's sonship is to be extended to the "many."... [A]ll nations...become brothers and receivers of the promises of the chosen people; they become people of God with Israel through adherence to the will of God and through acceptance of the Davidic kingdom.[124]

Thus the old covenant is fulfilled in the new covenant made in the blood of Christ. The cross by which the new covenant is enacted can only be understood in light of the old covenant. Benedict explains the meaning of the new covenant in light of the Exodus and Passover, and in light of the covenant made with Israel at Sinai. Christ is the new Passover and indeed, all of Israel's liturgical forms and feasts point to the new Passover of Jesus Christ.[125]

Here we see Benedict presuming the dynamic of the scriptural Word as discussed above. For Benedict, the historical event of the Passover, contained within it a surplus, divine meaning. The cross and resurrection of Jesus are "the inner meaning of the Passover...the ultimate Passover in which what has always been meant by that is seen for the first time in its true light." In this beautifully evocative passage, which I cannot possibly do justice to here, Benedict explains how the cross and resurrection are the ultimate meaning, not only of the Exodus and Passover, but of all the salvation history recorded in the Bible.

The resurrection is the reawakening of him who had first died on the cross; its "hour" is the Passover of the Jews.... Jesus' cross and resurrection are seen by faith in the context of the inner meaning of the Passover, as the ultimate Passover in which what has always been meant by that is seen for the first time in its true light. All salvation history is gathered here, as it were, in the one point of this ultimate Passover that thus includes and interprets salvation history, just as it is itself interpreted and illumined by salvation history. For it is evident now that this whole history is likewise an exodus history; a history that begins with the call of Abraham to go out from his country—and this

---

124 *Many Religions, One Covenant*, 26, 27–28; *Gospel Catechesis, Catechism*, 78–79.
125 *A New Song for the Lord*, 16.

going-out-from has been, ever since, its characteristic movement. It attains its deepest significance in the Passover of Jesus Christ . . .in the radical love that became a total exodus from himself, a going-out-from-himself toward the other even to the radical delivery of himself to death so that it can be explained in the words: "I am going away and shall return" (John 14:28)—by going, I come. The "living opening through the curtain," as the epistle to the Hebrews explains the Lord's going-away on the cross (Heb. 10:20), reveals itself in this way as the true Exodus that is meant by all the exoduses of history.

Thus we see how the theology of resurrection gathers all salvation history within itself and. . .in a very literal sense, it becomes a theology of existence, a theology of *ex–sistere*, of that exodus by which the human individual goes out from himself and through which alone he can find himself. In this movement of *ex–sistere*, faith and love are ultimately united—the deepest significance of each is that *Exi*, that call to transcend and sacrifice the *I* that is the basic law of the history of God's covenant with man and, *ipso facto*, the truly basic law of all human existence. . . .

God's action . . . implies, of necessity, that "is" that faith soon formulated explicitly: Jesus *is* Christ, God *is* man. Hence man's future means being one with God and so being one with mankind, which will be a single, final man in the manifold unity that is created by the Exodus of love. God 'is' man—it is in this formula that the whole greatness of the Easter reality has first been fully apprehended and has become, from a passing point in history, its axis, which bears us all.[126]

This long and extraordinarily rich passage indicates the powerful heights to which Benedict's biblical theology is capable of soaring. However, for my purposes here, I must limit myself to pointing out only a few salient points. First, Benedict presumes a unity of the scriptural Word, a unity that constitutes a "salvation history" at the same time that it enables texts from the Gospel of John and Hebrews to illuminate ancient Scriptures concerning the call of Abraham and the Exodus. All is interpreted in light of the revelation of divine love on the cross. His theo-

---

126 *Principles of Catholic Theology*, 189–190.

logical discussion includes consideration of the meaning of the Greek text and a concise yet creative meditation on the philosophical concept of "existence." We notice, too, Benedict's sweeping spiritual exegesis, which holds the Exodus to be the fundamental meaning of "the history of God's covenant with man," revealed in Christ's "exodus of love." In this particular exegesis, Benedict, as is typical, presumes knowledge of an important strain of historical and literary exegesis on the exodus motif in Scripture.[127] But Benedict does not stop there; rather, through a theological hermeneutic of faith, he yolks these exegetical findings to the Church's confession of faith that Jesus is true God and true man.

Benedict makes a similar spiritual exegesis in considering the relationship between the memorials instituted in the Last Supper and the Passover. Again, he synthesizes a wealth of scholarship in considering Jesus' quotation from the Sinai covenant (Matt. 26:28). He sees in the covenant at Sinai parallels with ideas of treaty and covenant-making in the ancient Near East. In sprinkling the sacrificial "blood of the covenant" on the altar and then on the people (Exod. 24:8), Moses was evoking the ancient notion of covenant as forming a "blood association" between the covenant partners—in a literal and symbolic sense making Israel and God "brothers of the same blood," Benedict contends.[128]

At the Last Supper, when Jesus refers to the cup as the blood of the covenant, Benedict continues, "*the words of Sinai are heightened to a staggering realism*, and at the same time we begin to see a totally unsuspected depth in them."[129] What the sacrifices of the old covenant all pointed to, is made a "reality" in Christ's death. "[A]ll cultic ordinances of the Old Testament are seen to be taken up into his death and brought to their deepest meaning."[130]

Again, we notice Benedict's theological hermeneutic at work. The language and actions of the original covenant at Sinai bear within themselves their fuller, spiritual significance—the new covenant made in the blood of Christ on the cross, represented in the eucharistic sacrifice. At the Last Supper, Jesus announces the final covenant in biblical salvation history. This covenant does not abrogate the covenant at Sinai. Rather it prolongs and renews it. The blood of the covenant is Christ's, given for the sake of the world. He is the new covenant by which "God binds himself irrevocably" to his creation.[131]

---

127 On the exodus motif, see Scott W. Hahn, "Worship in the Word: Toward a Liturgical Hermeneutic," *Letter & Spirit* 1 (2005): 101–136, especially at 122–124, and the current research summarized there at n. 59.

128 Quoting Gottfried Quell, in *Many Religions, One Covenant*, 59–60.

129 *Many Religions, One Covenant*, 60. Emphasis added.

130 *Many Religions, One Covenant*, 41.

131 *Many Religions, One Covenant*, 62–65.

In Benedict's reading of the canonical text of Scripture, we see a liturgical trajectory and teleology to creation.[132] As the covenant blood at Sinai symbolized the sharing of flesh and blood between God and Israel, this sharing is universalized and made real, literal, in the blood of Christ—in which all nations come to worship the God of Israel and are made kin, flesh and blood, one body with Christ through "sacramental blood fellowship."[133]

The Embrace of Salvation

For Benedict, the sacramental liturgy of the Church, the worship of the new covenant, is the goal and consummation of the biblical story. If everything in Scripture is ordered to the covenant that God wants to make with his creation, then everything in the Church is ordered to proclaiming that new covenant and initiating people into it through the sacramental liturgy. The mission of the Church is thus liturgical, its identity and actions defined by the Word revealed in history.[134] In a sense, Benedict says, the revelation of God is not "complete" without the response of the Church in the liturgy, the primary expression of the tradition.[135]

In all his writings, Benedict stresses the unity of the old and new covenant liturgies. The Eucharistic liturgy "places us in continuity with Israel and the whole of salvation history,"[136] revealing the Eucharist as the fulfillment of all the liturgies of the old covenant. Israel's liturgical worship was ordered to remembrance, memorial, and "renewal of the covenant."[137] Christian worship, too, becomes a remembrance of God's mighty works in history. And like Israel's worship, especially the Passover Haggadah, the Eucharist is both a remembrance of the past and a thanksgiving for God's continued presence among his people.[138]

---

132 Compare Hahn, "Worship in the Word," at 130.

133 *Many Religions, One Covenant*, 60. "In the Last Supper he recapitulates the covenant of Sinai, or rather what had there been an approximation in symbol now becomes reality: the community of blood and life between God and man." *Church, Ecumenism and Politics*, 8.

134 "The Church. . .is there so that the world may become a sphere for God's presence, the sphere of the covenant between God and men. . .in order that the covenant may come to be in which God freely gives his love and receives the response of love." *Pilgrim Fellowship of Faith*, 288–289.

135 "Christians know that God has spoken through man and that the human and historical factor is, therefore, part of the way God acts. That, too, is why *the Word of the Bible becomes complete only in that responsive word of the Church which we call tradition*. That is why the accounts of the Last Supper in the Bible become a concrete reality only when they are appropriated by the Church in her celebration." *The Spirit of the Liturgy*, 169. Emphasis added.

136 Pope Benedict XVI, Homily, Eucharistic Celebration at Cologne-Marienfeld, Germany (August 21, 2005), in *L'Osservatore Romano*, Weekly Edition in English (August 24, 2005), 11–12.

137 *Many Religions, One Covenant*, 62–65.

138 Joseph Cardinal Ratzinger, *God Is Near Us: The Eucharist, the Heart of Life*, ed. S.O. Horn and

Christian liturgy, he notes, follows the basic pattern of Old Testament covenant worship—the service including both the reading of the Word of God and the offering of sacrifice. Benedict sees this outline reflected also in Jesus' Easter appearance to his disciples on the road to Emmaus (Luke 24:25–31), in which Jesus reads and interprets the Scriptures in light of his resurrection, and then reveals himself in the breaking of the bread.[139]

Benedict acknowledges, as well, the important role Scripture plays in the eucharistic celebration. During the course of the liturgical year, the Scripture readings "enable man to go through the whole history of salvation in step with the rhythm of creation."[140] Through the Word read and prayed in the liturgy, the believer is slowly transformed into the person that God intends him or her to be.[141] In the liturgy, Benedict notes, the Old Testament is read typologically, as it is in the New Testament. And the liturgy is not merely evocative, representative, or commemorative. More than that, it brings about a kind of communion with the events narrated in the sacred pages. What Benedict has written in connection with early Christian liturgical art seems all the more applicable to the function of Scripture in the Christian liturgy:

> On liturgical feasts the deeds of God in the past are made present. The feasts are a participation in God's action in time. . . . The individual events are now ordered toward the Christian sacraments and to Christ himself. Noah's ark and the crossing of the Red Sea now point to baptism. The sacrifice of Isaac and the meal of the three angels with Abraham speak of Christ's sacrifice and the Eucharist. Shining through the rescue of the three young men from the fiery furnace and of Daniel from the lions' den we see Christ's resurrection and our own. Still more than in the synagogue, the point of the images is not to tell a story about something in the past, but to incorporate the events of history into the sacrament. . . . We are taken into the events.

V. Pfnur, trans. Henry Taylor (San Francisco: Ignatius, 2003 [2001]), 48–49.

139 "First we have the searching of the Scriptures, explained and made present by the risen Lord; their minds enlightened, the disciples are moved to invite the Lord to stay with them, and he responds by breaking the bread for his disciples, giving them his presence and then withdrawing again, sending them out as his messengers." *Feast of Faith*, 47.

140 Joseph Cardinal Ratzinger, *Co-Workers of the Truth: Meditations for Every Day of the Year*, ed. Irene Grass (San Francisco: Ignatius, 1992 [1990]), 2.

141 Through the liturgy, "the language of our Mother [the Church] becomes ours; we learn to speak it along with her, so that gradually, her words on our lips become our words. We are given an anticipatory share in the Church's perennial dialogue of love with him who desired to be one flesh with her." *Feast of Faith*, 30.

> . . . The centering of all history in Christ is both the liturgical
> transmission of that history and the expression of a new experi-
> ence of time, in which past, present, and future make contact,
> because they have been inserted into the presence of the risen
> Lord.[142]

As we can see, Benedict notices how the New Testament's typological interpretation of the Old is often ordered to the sacramental liturgy, especially as
regards the central sacraments of Christian initiation, baptism and the Eucharist.
We also see in this passage his sense of the mystery of the Word as living and
active, bringing about the very promises that it speaks of in the life of the believer.
"Scripture alive in the living Church is also God's present power in the world
today—a power which remains an inexhaustible source of hope throughout all
generations."[143]

It follows naturally that liturgy is the privileged context in which the community hears the Word and its authentic interpretation. This was the pattern of Christ
at Emmaus, in which "beginning with Moses and all the prophets, he interpreted
to them in all the Scriptures the things concerning himself" (Luke 24:27). In the
eucharistic liturgy, the New Testament readings are still heard as interpreting the
Old Testament in light of Christ. And it is in the liturgy that the texts are "realized"
or "actualized" as Scripture, as divine, salvific communications.

> [T]he liturgy is the true, living environment for the Bible.
> . . . [T]he Bible can be properly understood only in this living
> context within which it first emerged. The texts of the Bible, this
> great book of Christ, are not to be seen as the literary products
> of some scribes at their desks, but rather as the words of Christ
> himself delivered in the celebration of holy Mass. *The scriptural
> texts are thoroughly imbued with the awe of divine worship* resulting
> from the believer's interior attentiveness to the living voice of the
> present Lord.[144]

In his writings on the Eucharist as sacrifice, Benedict again shows himself to
be conversant with the breadth of scholarship on the continuities between Jewish
and Christian worship. He is impressed, for instance, by the evident influence of
the old covenant todah ("thanksgiving sacrifice"), by which Israelites gave thanks
to God after having been delivered from suffering or some life-threatening situa-

---

142 *The Spirit of the Liturgy,* 117.

143 *A New Song for the Lord,* 52.

144 "Introduction," *The Lord,* xii. Emphasis added.

tion.[145] In this, Benedict shows the Eucharist to be an eloquent fulfillment of the Old Testament understanding of sacrifice, as expressed in the psalms and prophets. In offering his life on the cross, and in establishing the Eucharist as a perpetual memorial of that self-offering, Jesus revealed that the worship God desires is "the transformation of existence into thanksgiving,"[146] our "giv[ing] ourselves back to him" in love and thanksgiving.

In the unity of the Last Supper and the crucifixion, Benedict sees the true depth of the Bible as the saving Word of God. For in the crucifixion, intended by Christ to be represented in the sacrificial offering of the Eucharist, we have, in effect, "the death of death." By this action, which will be perpetuated in the sacramental form of the Eucharist, Christ transforms death itself into a life-giving word. The Gospel of Christ is, thus, the good news that love is stronger than death. Thus, salvation history culminates in the transformation of death into the saving word of life.

> [T]]he indissoluble bond between the supper and the death of Jesus is. . .plain: his dying words fuse with his words at the supper, the reality of his death fuses with the reality of the supper. For the event of the supper consists in Jesus sharing his body and his blood, that is, his earthly existence; he gives and communicates himself. In other words, the event of the supper is an anticipation of death, the transformation of death into an act of love. Only in this context can we understand what John means by calling Jesus' death the glorification of God and the glorification of the Son (John 12:28; 17:21). Death, which by its very nature, is the end, the destruction of every communication, is changed by him into an act of self-communication; and this is man's redemption, for it signifies the triumph of love over death. We can put the same thing another way: death, which puts an end to words and to meaning, itself becomes a word, becomes the place where meaning communicates itself.[147]

The sacred Word heard in the Mass, and the sacrificial offering of that Word on the cross, come together in the canon or Eucharistic Prayer of the Church. Here, too, Benedict explains the Christian liturgy in terms of Old Testament

---

145 *Feast of Faith*, 51–60. Benedict's discussion includes a long and appreciative review of the scholarship of Hartmut Gese.

146 *God Is Near Us*, 48, 51.

147 *Behold the Pierced One*, 24–25.

belief in the creative power of the Word of God as both speech and deed.[148]As God's Word created the heavens and the earth, and as Jesus' word healed the sick and raised the dead, the divine Word spoken in the liturgy also possesses creative and transformative power.[149]

Notice in the following long passage, how Benedict easily integrates modern rhetorical insights into Scripture, especially speech-act theories, with the perspectives of liturgical theology and metaphysics in order to articulate a compelling, biblically grounded understanding of what happens in the divine liturgy:

> This *oratio*—the Eucharistic Prayer, the "Canon" is really more than speech; it is *actio* in the highest sense of the word. For what happens in it is that the human *actio*. . .steps back and makes way for the *actio divina*, the action of God. In this *oratio*, the priest speaks with the *I* of the Lord—"This is my body," "This is my blood." He knows that he is not now speaking from his own resources but in virtue of the sacrament that he has received, he has become the voice of someone else, who is now speaking and acting. This action of God, which takes place through human speech, is the real "action" for which all of creation is an expectation. The elements of the earth are transubstantiated, pulled, so to speak, from their creaturely anchorage, grasped at the deepest ground of their being, and changed into the body and blood of the Lord. The new heaven and new earth are anticipated.
>
> The real "action" in the liturgy in which we are all supposed to participate is the action of God himself. This is what is new and distinctive about the Christian liturgy: God himself acts and does what is essential. He inaugurates the new creation, makes himself accessible to us, so that, through the things of the earth, through our gifts, we can communicate with him in a personal way. . . . [P]recisely because God himself has become man, be-

---

148 "God reveals himself in history. He speaks to humankind, and the word he speaks has creative power. The Hebrew concept '*dabar*,' usually translated as 'word,' really conveys both the meaning of *word* and *act*. God says what he does and does what he says." Pope Benedict XVI, Message to the Youth of the World on the Occasion of the Twenty-first World Youth Day (April 9, 2006), in *L'Osservatore Romano*, Weekly Edition in English (March 1, 2006), 3.

149 In the liturgy, the scriptural word is truly "the Word of transformation, enabling us to participate in the 'hour' of Christ. . . . It is the Word of power which transforms the gifts of the earth in an entirely new way into God's gift of himself, and it draws us into this process of transformation." Homily, Eucharistic Celebration at Cologne-Marienfeld (August 21, 2005).

come body. . .he comes through his body to us who live in the body. The whole event of the incarnation, cross, resurrection, and second coming is present as the way by which God draws man into cooperation with himself. . . . True, the sacrifice of the *Logos* is accepted already and forever. But we must still pray for it to become *our* sacrifice, that we ourselves. . .may be transformed into the *Logos*, conformed to the *Logos*, and so made the true body of Christ. . . . There is only *one* action, which is at the same time his and ours—ours because we have become "one body and one spirit" with him. The uniqueness of the eucharistic liturgy lies precisely in the fact that God himself is acting and that we are drawn into that action of God.[150]

Here we have reached the summit of the liturgy and the summit of Benedict's biblical theology. In the liturgy, we are drawn into contact with the very means of salvation history, the saving act of Christ on the cross. In the liturgy, the desire of God's condescension meets the desire of the human person for transcendence. Benedict even suggests that this might be a kind of definition for liturgy. The liturgy is that divine-human action that brings about "an embrace of salvation between God and man."[151]

The Cosmic Liturgy

In Benedict's biblical theology, liturgy is the goal of creation and of the human person. In the liturgy, the purposes of salvation history are realized—heaven and earth are filled with God's glory, each participant is swept up into the embrace of salvation, into the communion of God's eternal love. The communion that God has desired since before the foundation of the world—between heaven and earth, between the visible and invisible, between the divine and human—is revealed and effected in the liturgy.

Every celebration of the Eucharist on the earth becomes "a cosmic liturgy . . .an entry into the liturgy of heaven."[152] In the liturgy, the eschatological orientation of Scriptures is actualized. "In the celebration of the liturgy, the Church moves toward the Lord; liturgy is virtually this act of approaching his coming.

---

150 *The Spirit of the Liturgy*, 172–174.

151 Pope Benedict XVI, General Audience (September 28, 2005), in *L'Osservatore Romano*, Weekly Edition in English (October 5, 2005), 8.

152 *The Spirit of the Liturgy*, 70.

In the liturgy the Lord is already anticipating his promised coming. Liturgy is anticipated *parousia*."[153]

Benedict observes that in the modern period there has arisen a fundamental misunderstanding about the nature of liturgy and the Church, due in large part to faulty exegetical conclusions. Indeed, the *parousia*, the coming again or presence of Christ, and the general character of New Testament eschatological expectation have been sharply debated questions in modern biblical scholarship. For much of the last century it has been an exegetical commonplace that the oldest New Testament writings are shot through with expectation of the imminent end of the world and return of Christ, leading many scholars to conclude that "in his ideas about time Jesus was mistaken...[and] that Jesus' message is intrinsically incapable of being appropriated by us."[154]

I do not have the space here to rehearse Benedict's thorough critique of this crucial exegetical mistake. But at work he sees many of the fallacious philosophical presumptions discussed earlier in considering his critique of criticism. The chief deficiency is the methodological decision to consider the texts apart from the liturgy and the tradition of the Church. This has caused exegetes to ignore or downplay the fact that eschatological expressions like *parousia* and *maranatha* properly "belong in the context of early Christian eucharistic celebration."[155]

Again, Benedict builds his argument on solid philological and historical grounds. He even brings in comparative religious and cultural data concerning the imperial liturgy of the Roman state and traditions of emperor-worship in the ancient Near East. He agrees that the normative theologians who authored the New Testament expected a second coming or *parousia* of Christ. But, he adds, it is clear from the language and the contexts of the various texts, that this coming and presence was anticipated, and in some way experienced, in every celebration of the Eucharist.

The cosmic imagery of the New Testament cannot be used as

---

153 *A New Song for the Lord*, 129. "Christian liturgy is never just an event organized by a particular group or set of people or even by a particular local Church. Mankind's movement toward Christ meets Christ's movement toward men. He wants to unite mankind and bring about the one Church, the one divine assembly, of all men...the communion of all who worship in spirit and in truth. . . . Christian liturgy is a liturgy of promise fulfilled, of a quest, the religious quest of human history, reaching its goal. But it remains a liturgy of hope. . . . Christian liturgy is liturgy on the way, a liturgy of pilgrimage toward the transfiguration of the world, which will only take place when God is 'all in all.'" *The Spirit of the Liturgy*, 49–50.

154 *Eschatology*, 271. On *parousia* (translated "coming" in Matt. 24:27 and "presence" in 2 Cor. 10:10 and Phil. 2:12), see Scott Hahn, *Letter and Spirit: From Written Text to Living Word in the Liturgy* (New York: Doubleday, 2006), 104–121.

155 *Eschatology*, 6; 202–203. For Benedict's critique, see *Eschatology*, 35–45; 271–272. For the Aramaic expression, *maranatha* ("Our Lord, come!"), see 1 Cor. 16:22; Rev. 22:20.

a source for the description of a future chain of cosmic events. All attempts of this kind are misplaced. Instead, these texts form part of a description of the mystery of the *parousia* in the language of liturgical tradition. The New Testament conceals and reveals the unspeakable coming of Christ, using language borrowed from that sphere which is graciously enabled to express in this world the point of contact with God. The *parousia* is the highest intensification and fulfillment of the liturgy. And the liturgy is *parousia*, a *parousia*-like event taking place in our midst. . . . Every Eucharist is *parousia*, the Lord's coming, and yet the Eucharist is even more truly the tensed yearning that he would reveal his hidden glory. . . . In touching the risen Jesus, the Church makes contact with the *parousia* of the Lord.[156]

"The Beauty and Necessity of the Theologian's Task"

Benedict's "critique of criticism" and his own biblical theology open up fresh new possibilities for the study of sacred Scripture and the practice of theology. What we see in his writings are "the essential elements for a synthesis between historical method and theological hermeneutics," which he has said can be found in the official teaching of the Church, as expressed in *Dei Verbum*.[157]

His synthesis promises a way of reading Scripture authentically as it was written—as a divine, living Word spoken in history to the Church, a Word whose meaning is understood within the broad unity of the Church's experience of the faith, an experience that includes liturgy and dogma, and is not limited to the expectations and contexts of a text's original audience. He promises the theologian that reading in continuity with this ecclesial tradition "increases the excitement and fecundity of inquiry."[158]

[H]ow exciting exegesis becomes when it dares to read the Bible as a unified whole. If the Bible originates from the one subject formed by the people of God and, through it, from the divine subject himself, then it speaks of the present. If this is so, moreover, even what we know about the diversity of its underlying historical constellations yields its harvest; there is a unity to be discovered in this diversity, and diversity appears as the wealth

---

156 *Eschatology*, 202–204.

157 Joseph Ratzinger, ed., *Schriftauslegung im Widerstreit*. Quaestiones Disputatae 117 (Freiburg: Herder, 1989), 20–21.

158 *The Nature and Mission of Theology*, 97.

of unity. This opens up a wide field of action both to historical research and to its hypotheses, with the sole limit that it may not destroy the unity of the whole, which is situated on another plane than what can be called the 'nuts and bolts' of the various texts. Unity is found on another plane, yet it belongs to the literary reality of the Bible itself.[159]

For the theologian and exegete of faith, the work of theology and exegesis assumes a place within the grand unity of God's plan as it is revealed in Scripture—that of bringing about the "divinization" of creation in the liturgical offering of the sacrifice of praise.[160]

> The unity of the person of Jesus, embracing man and God, prefigures that synthesis of man and world to which theology is meant to minister. It is my belief that the beauty and necessity of the theologian's task could be made visible at this point. . . . But [the theologian] can only do this provided he himself enters that "laboratory" of unity and freedom. . .where his own will is refashioned, where he allows himself to be expropriated and inserted into the divine will, where he advances toward that God-likeness through which the kingdom of God can come.[161]

Benedict bids the theologian and exegete to place himself in service to this divine plan. "We have to enter into a relationship of awe and obedience toward the Bible. . . . Historical-critical exegesis can be a wonderful means for a deeper understanding of the Bible if its instruments are used with that reverent love which seeks to know God's gift in the most exact and careful way possible."[162]

Hence, we understand Benedict's frequent exhortations concerning the need to retrieve the ancient practice of *lectio divina*, the loving contemplation of Scripture in which study is transformed into prayer.[163] Benedict presents us with a vision of a profound spiritual and scientific exegesis, a faith seeking understanding of the deepest mysteries of the cosmos, in conversation with the living God.

And if we take Benedict's thought seriously and consider the New Testament

---

159 *The Nature and Mission of Theology*, 64–65.

160 *The Spirit of the Liturgy*, 28.

161 *Behold the Pierced One*, 46.

162 *A New Song for the Lord*, 50.

163 Pope Benedict XVI, Reflection on the Opening of the Eleventh Ordinary General Assembly of the Synod of Bishops (October 3, 2005), in *L'Osservatore Romano*, Weekly Edition in English (October 12, 2005), 7.

authors to be the normative theologians, then the academic study of theology and Scripture brings us into the heart of what might be called the sacerdotal nature of the biblical texts. I will close with a particularly fertile passage, one that indicates the beauty and necessity of the theological and exegetical task, as well as the excitement and fecundity of Benedict's own research. Through a close reading of the text, he notes the curious preponderance of cultic and priestly language in Romans 15:16, where Paul describes his purpose in writing his letter as part of his mission "to be a minister of Christ Jesus in the priestly service of the Gospel of God, so that the offering of the Gentiles may be acceptable."

> The letter to the Romans, this word that has been written that it may then be proclaimed, is an apostolic action; more, it is a liturgical—even a cultic—event. This it is because it helps the world of the pagans to change so as to be a renewal of mankind and, as such, a cosmic liturgy in which mankind shall become adoration, become the radiance of the glory of God. If the apostle is handing on the Gospel by means of this letter. . .*this is a priestly sacrificial action, an eschatological service of ministry.* . . . [N]ow it is the specifically apostolic service of preaching the faith that appears as a priestly activity, as actually performing the new liturgy, open to all the world and likewise worldwide, which has been founded by Christ.[164]

Here Benedict opens a new window into the scriptural text, one in which we see the unity of the Old and New Testaments, of Church and Scripture, Word and sacrament, the Bible and the liturgy—a unity in service of the divine plan, which is a participation, a communion, in the mystery of God.

---

164 *Pilgrim Fellowship of Faith*, 118–119.

Letter & Spirit 2 (2006): 141–158

NOTES

∾:∾

"THE LORD WILL ACCOMPLISH HIS WORD":
Paul's Argumentation and Use of Scripture in Romans 9:24–29

∾: Pablo T. Gadenz :∾

Doctoral Candidate, Pontifical Gregorian University, Rome

Romans 9–11 is one of the more challenging areas of New Testament studies. From the perspective of Jewish-Christian dialogue, there is great interest because these chapters involve Paul's most extended discussion of Israel, including his enigmatic statement that "all Israel will be saved" (Rom. 11:26). Romans 9–11 is also of considerable significance to scholars studying the use of Old Testament texts by the New Testament writers, since Paul cites the Old Testament more in these chapters than in any other section in his letters, as he seeks to explain God's plan of salvation for Israel and the nations.

For the exegete, a primary challenge comes with regard to the internal coherence of these chapters. Paul's argument does, at first, seem contradictory. For example, he says that "the remnant will be saved" (Rom. 9:27), but later asserts that "all Israel will be saved" (Rom. 11:26).[1] Because of such challenges, many scholars in recent years have concluded that Paul's argument in these chapters is simply inconsistent or deliberately ambiguous.

Already in 1986, James W. Aageson suggested that the "impasse" in the study of Romans 9–11 was "the result of too little attention being devoted to Paul's method of developing a theological statement and, in particular, to his technique of scriptural argumentation."[2] Since that time, much work has been done to try to remedy this situation.

In this paper, I would like to draw upon this recent work to make a close

---

1   See Heikki Räisänen, "Paul, God, and Israel: Romans 9–11 in Recent Research," in *The Social World of Formative Christianity and Judaism: Essays in Tribute to Howard Clark Kee*, eds. Jacob Neusner, et al. (Philadelphia: Fortress, 1988), 178–206, at 192: "it would seem that there are considerable internal contradictions in Romans 9–11."

2   James W. Aageson, "Scripture and Structure in the Development of the Argument in Romans 9–11," *Catholic Biblical Quarterly* 48 (1986): 265–289, at 266.

study of Romans 9:24–29.[3] I have chosen this passage because it involves several of the key issues found in the whole section. For instance, with regard to his use of the Old Testament, Paul cites in vv. 25–26 two texts from Hosea that were originally addressed to Israel, yet he seemingly applies them to the Gentiles. Another difficulty, which touches upon the coherence of his argument, is whether Paul's citation of Isaiah in vv. 27–29 should be interpreted as favorable or unfavorable to Israel. The positions one takes with regard to these difficulties will significantly affect one's overall interpretation of Romans 9–11.

My aim, then, is to explain Romans 9:24–29 within the larger context of Romans 9–11. Through an exegesis of the passage, I wish to make a case for the internal coherence of Paul's argument. I will argue that there is a progression of thought, not a contradiction, between chapters 9 and 11.

Throughout the study, I will also examine some aspects of Paul's use of Scripture, such as his application of Jewish techniques of exegesis, which enable us to better understand how he interprets and deploys Old Testament texts in this section of the letter.

Models of Composition in Romans 9:6–29

Jean-Noël Aletti has shown how three models together help to understand Romans 9:6–29— the *midrashic*, the *chiastic*, and the *rhetorical*.[4]

Romans 9:6–29 is not a midrash in the strict sense, since it is not a Scripture commentary. But Aletti suggests that it, nonetheless, has features in common with the midrashim, so that one may conclude that Paul was familiar with, and intentionally used, Jewish techniques of exegesis.[5] For example, Paul follows the basic pattern of the homiletic midrash: a number of scriptural passages are cited to support a thesis, such as the string of Old Testament passages in vv. 7–13, which support the thesis in v. 6b regarding the identity of Israel. In addition, Paul uses "catchwords," such as the verb καλέω ("to call"), which serve to link different parts of his argument. Also, as we will see, he applies the rule of *gezerah shawah*, which joins two passages of Scripture that contain the same or similar words. Finally, Paul uses an "inclusion" to connect the beginning and end of the passage (note the use of the word σπέρμα, "seed," in vv. 7 and 29), and adds a concluding word of consolation or *ḥatima* (see v. 29).

---

3 A full discussion of what will be presented here in summary fashion can be found in Pablo T. Gadenz, "'The Lord Will Accomplish His Word': Paul's Argumentation and Use of Scripture in Romans 9:24–29" (S.S.L. thesis, Pontifical Biblical Institute, 2005).

4 See Jean-Noël Aletti, *Comment Dieu est-il juste? Clefs pour interpréter l'épître aux Romains* (Paris: Seuil, 1991), 157–178; and his article "L'argumentation paulinienne en Rm 9," *Biblica* 68 (1987): 41–56. For a summary presentation, see also Aletti's commentary, "Romans," in *The International Bible Commentary: A Catholic and Ecumenical Commentary for the Twenty–First Century*, ed. William R. Farmer (Collegeville, MN: Liturgical Press, 1998), 1553–1600, at 1589–1591.

5 Aletti, *Comment Dieu*, 158–160.

In addition to these characteristics of rabbinic exegesis, Aletti detects in Romans 9:6–29 a chiastic literary structure, which, through a deliberate, repetitious ordering of ideas and vocabulary, directs the reader to Paul's main points. This model, too, emerges from the Old Testament and rabbinic interpretive milieu with which Paul was familiar. From a study of the vocabulary of the small units within this section, the chiastic structure summarized in the table below can be observed.[6]

A: vv. 6–9	9:6,9	λόγος	word	λόγος	9:28	A': vv. 27–29
	9:6²ˣ	Ἰσραήλ	Israel	Ἰσραήλ	9:27²ˣ	
	9:7²ˣ,8	σπέρμα	seed-descendants	σπέρμα	9:29	
	9:9	υἱός	son	υἱός	9:(26),27	
B: vv. 10–13	9:(7),12	καλέω	to call	καλέω	9:24,25,26	B': vv. 24–26
	9:13	ἀγαπάω	to love	ἀγαπάω	9:25²ˣ	
C: vv. 4–18	9:15²ˣ,16,18	ἐλεέω	to have mercy/mercy	ἔλεος	9:23	C': vv. 19–23
	9:16,18²ˣ	θέλω	to will	θέλω	9:22	
	9:17	ἐνδείκνυμι	to show	ἐνδείκνυμι	9:22	
	9:17	δύναμις	power	δυνατόν	9:22	

Of particular interest for our purposes are the links in vocabulary between units AB (vv. 6–13) and B'A' (vv. 24–29). These links highlight important themes of the passage, such as the efficacy of God's word, which has not failed (v. 6a) and which God will accomplish (v. 28).

Aletti also finds a rhetorical model (*dispositio*) which shows how Paul develops his argument in this section of the letter. Aletti emphasizes the importance of identifying the thesis statements (*propositiones*) that govern individual argumentative units and the proofs (*probationes*) that support these thesis statements.[7] In the first part of Romans 9–11,[8] namely Romans 9:6–29, the *propositio* occurs in v. 6a (the word of God has not failed) and is followed by a *probatio* in vv. 7–29.[9] Whereas the chiastic model shows the parallelism between the beginning and the end of the section, the rhetorical model reveals the development of the argumentation.[10]

---

6   See Aletti, "Romans," 1590–1591.

7   See the articles by Jean-Noël Aletti, "La *dispositio* rhétorique dans les épîtres pauliniennes. Propositions de méthode," *New Testament Studies* 38 (1992): 385–401, at 390–391; "La présence d'un modèle rhétorique en Romains: Son rôle et son importance," *Biblica* 71 (1990): 1–24, at 8–12. On the importance of the *propositiones* in the argument of Romans 9–11, see Aletti, *Comment Dieu*, 148–150.

8   Aletti's rhetorical model for Romans 9–11 is as follows: introduction (*exordium*) 9:1–5; a three-part *probatio*: 9:6–29 (*propositio* in 9:6a), 9:30–10:21 (*propositio* in 10:4), 11:1–32 (*propositio* in 11:1a); and conclusion (*peroratio*) 11:33–36. See "Romans," 1589. Compare the outline in Aageson, "Scripture and Structure," 286–287.

9   See Aletti, *Comment Dieu*, 160–162. Aletti explains that the *probatio* itself consists of three stages: 9:6b–13 (assertions based on Scripture); 9:14–23 (questions/answers with imaginary interlocutor); 9:24–29 (proof from Scripture).

10   Aletti, "Romans," 1591.

The Rhetorical Structure of Romans 9:24–29

The compositional models proposed by Aletti provide a framework for understanding the main lines of Paul's argument and for interpreting the individual verses of the text. It is to these individual verses that we now turn.

In the Revised Standard Version (RSV), Romans 9:24–29 reads as follows:

> ₂₄[God has called us] not from the Jews only but also from the Gentiles. ₂₅As indeed he says in Hosea, "Those who were not my people I will call 'my people,' and her who was not beloved I will call 'my beloved.'" ₂₆"And in the very place where it was said to them, 'You are not my people,' they will be called 'sons of the living God.'" ₂₇And Isaiah cries out concerning Israel: "Though the number of the sons of Israel be as the sand of the sea, only a remnant of them will be saved; ₂₈for the Lord will execute his sentence upon the earth with rigor and dispatch." ₂₉And as Isaiah predicted, "If the Lord of hosts had not left us children, we would have fared like Sodom and been made like Gomorrah."

In these verses, v. 24 serves as a thesis statement which is supported in vv. 25–29 by a chain of scriptural citations from Hosea and Isaiah. The citations also confirm the governing thesis (*propositio*) of the broader passage (Rom. 9:6–29), namely, that God's word has not failed (v. 6). Paul's argument has two parts. First, he has to show that God's word has not failed with regard to the rejection of the Gospel by the majority of Jews. Secondly, he has to show that God's word has not failed in regards to the acceptance of the Gospel by Gentiles, who are mentioned for the first time in Romans 9 in v. 24.

Paul develops the second part of his argument first. Note the rhetorical *reversio*: while the Jews are mentioned first and then the Gentiles in v. 24, in the scriptural proofs, the Gentiles are treated first (vv. 25–26) and then the Jews (vv. 27–29). Many scholars agree with this breakdown of Paul's argument; they understand vv. 25–26 to refer to Gentile-Christians and vv. 27–29 (the "remnant" and the "seed") to refer to Judeo-Christians.[11] Others scholars, however, disagree.[12]

These other positions will be considered below in the exegesis of the individual verses. Obviously, proper identification of the groups to which vv. 25–29 refer is essential for a correct understanding of the passage. It is also important for

---

11   See, for example, C. E. B. Cranfield, *A Critical and Exegetical Commentary on the Epistle to the Romans*, 2 vols., International Critical Commentary (Edinburgh: T. & T. Clark, 1975, 1979), 2:501.

12   See, for example, J. Ross Wagner, *Heralds of the Good News: Isaiah and Paul "In Concert" in the Letter to the Romans*, Novum Testamentum Supplements 101 (Leiden: Brill, 2002), 79.

examining the alleged contradiction in Romans 9–11 and for determining whether Romans 9:6–29 concludes on a favorable or unfavorable note with regard to Israel.

The "Call" of God (Romans 9:24)

In v. 24, the "catchword" καλέω ("to call"), reappears after its absence in vv. 14–23. The verb is used to indicate the scope of God's call. Paul writes that God calls "us"— that is, Paul and those to whom he writes—hence, those who believe in Christ. The end of the verse specifies that these believers in Christ are taken ἐξ Ἰουδαίων . . . καὶ ἐξ ἐθνῶν. Since one of the challenges in this passage is the correct identification of the groups to whom Paul refers, it is helpful to say a word about these two groups mentioned in v. 24.

The word ἔθνος occurs in Romans a total of 29 times, 27 of which (including 9:24) are in the plural. The words typically used to translate the plural form ἔθνη are "Gentiles," "pagans," or "nations." Often, a particular translation is determined by considering whether or not the term in a given context carries a positive or negative connotation. For example, the translation "pagans" is used especially when the word has a negative connotation (see 1 Cor. 5:1).

Of more importance, however, may be the quantitative distinction between the collective ("nations") and individualizing ("Gentiles"). James M. Scott, after reviewing the usage of the term in the Septuagint (LXX), in Hellenistic-Jewish literature, and in Paul, distinguishes three uses of ἔθνη.[13] The term can refer to the "nations" of the world, including Israel (Exod. 19:5–6 LXX); the non-Jewish "nations" (Rom. 15:10); or individuals ("Gentiles") of any nation apart from the nation of the Jews (Rom. 2:14; 9:30; 11:13). Often, when Paul speaks of individual Gentiles, he prefers the term "Greeks" (Ἑλληνες; see Rom. 1:14; 3:9) or the singular Ἑλλην (Rom. 1:16; 2:9–10; 10:12). Concerning Romans 9:24, Scott favors the third sense because of "the antithesis between Ἰουδαῖοι and ἔθνη." Scott's overall conclusion, however, should be kept in mind: "Paul clearly thinks in terms of 'nations,' not just of individual 'Gentiles.'"[14]

The word Ἰουδαῖος occurs in Romans eleven times,[15] but only twice in Romans 9–11 where instead the terms Ἰσραηλίτης and Ἰσραήλ are used; these terms, on the other hand, do not occur in Romans outside of chapters 9–11. We will return to a consideration of the term "Israel" in the discussion of v. 27 below.

Regarding the meaning of Ἰουδαῖος, of interest is Shaye Cohen's study of the use of the term in the Hellenistic era. Cohen indicates that the word has three basic meanings: a Judean (an ethnic-geographical term); a Jew (a religious-cultural

---

13   See the discussion in James M. Scott, *Paul and the Nations: The Old Testament and Jewish Background of Paul's Mission to the Nations with Special Reference to the Destination of Galatians*, Wissenschaftliche Untersuchungen zum Neuen Testament 84 (Tübingen: Mohr Siebeck, 1995), 120–124.

14   Scott, *Paul and the Nations*, 134.

15   Rom. 1:16; 2:9, 10, 17, 28, 29; 3:1, 9, 29; 9:24; 10:12.

term); or a citizen of the Judean state (a political term).[16] In all occurrences before the end of the second century B.C., Cohen argues, the ethnic-geographic meaning is the correct one.[17] Only in the Hasmonean era does the religious meaning emerge.[18] Nonetheless, Cohen says that the term Ἰουδαῖος always "retained its ethnic component" even when the religious meaning became more prominent.[19] In Romans 9:24, it is helpful, therefore, not to exclude the ethnic-geographic component from the term Ἰουδαῖοι, and to keep in mind the possible dual sense (ethnic-geographic and religious) of the word. Because of the parallelism in the construction of v. 24, such a dual understanding of Ἰουδαῖοι also contributes to a possible understanding of ἔθνη which is ethnic-geographic and collective ("nations"), on the one hand, and religious and individual ("Gentiles"), on the other.

A final question in the text is how to interpret the preposition ἐκ in the parallel expressions ἐξ Ἰουδαίων and ἐξ ἐθνῶν. Whereas Paul uses ἐκ at times (even in Romans 9–11) to indicate origin as to race or family (for example, οἱ ἐξ Ἰσραήλ in Romans 9:6), here in Romans 9:24, it is rather to be understood as indicating separation ("out of," "from among").[20]

In summary, then, Romans 9:24 explains who the recipients of God's call are in Paul's own time, namely, believers in Christ, who come "from among the Judeans/Jews" and "from among the nations/Gentiles."[21] The verses that follow (vv. 25–29) provide Scriptural support for God's calling of believers from these two groups.

Calling Believers Out of the Nations (Romans 9:25–26)

Following the two-part thesis statement in v. 24, Paul now moves to the *probatio*, the "proof," in which he cites in succession a number of carefully interwoven Scriptural texts. In vv. 25–26, he begins by supporting the second part of the thesis statement, the part that involves the Gentiles. He combines two citations from

---

16 Shaye J. D. Cohen, *The Beginnings of Jewishness: Boundaries, Varieties, Uncertainties*, Hellenistic Culture and Society 31 (Berkeley: University of California, 1999), 70–71.

17 Cohen, *Jewishness*, 69–106.

18 Cohen, *Jewishness*, 109–139.

19 Cohen, *Jewishness*, 133.

20 See James D. G. Dunn, *Romans 9–16*, Word Biblical Commentary 38B (Dallas: Word Books, 1988), 570: "The ἐκ indicates a calling 'out of,' with implication of separation, from a larger body."

21 In passing, it is interesting to speculate (especially in view of the citations from Hosea in vv. 25–26 whose original context is the restoration of the northern tribes) whether the expression ἐξ ἐθνῶν might not also echo Old Testament prophecies in which God gathers the Israelites from among the nations. In Ezekiel LXX, for example, the phrase ἐκ τῶν ἐθνῶν occurs five times (Ezek. 11:17; 28:25; 34:13; 36:24; 39:27), and the phrase ἐξ ἐθνῶν once (Ezek. 38:8) with this meaning. Also, in Ezek 37:21, in the prophecy of the "two sticks," there is the expression ἐκ μέσου τῶν ἐθνῶν. Could Paul have thought of the fulfillment of this prophecy when writing that God has called "us" ἐξ Ἰουδαίων ...καὶ ἐξ ἐθνῶν?

the prophet Hosea to substantiate the claim that God has called "vessels of mercy" from among the Gentiles.

In v. 25, after an introductory formula, Paul loosely quotes from the Septuagint translation of Hosea 2:23. For our purposes here, of interest is Paul's change of the verb from ἐρῶ ("I will say") to καλέσω ("I will call"). This change links the citation both to v. 24 and to the citation of Hosea 1:10 LXX in v. 26 (in both vv. 24 and 26, the verb καλέω also occurs).[22]

The most serious point of debate in these verses is the identity of those addressed. In their original context, the texts from Hosea refer to the promised restoration of the ten northern tribes of Israel.[23] Does Paul disregard this original context? To what group does Paul apply these texts of Hosea?

This issue has particularly interested scholars because of its implications regarding Paul's hermeneutics. Reviewing the literature, three basic positions can be enumerated: first, that Paul applies the Hosea texts to currently unbelieving Israel, and hence, in continuity with their original context;[24] second, that he applies the texts to believers from among both Jews and Gentiles (see v. 24);[25] and third, that he applies the texts to Gentile believers (those ἐξ ἐθνῶν in v. 24).[26]

There are several difficulties with the first position.[27] First, it appears from the words ὡς καί, ("as indeed") at the beginning of v. 25 that Paul invokes the texts from Hosea to support what he has just said in v. 24 regarding God's calling of believers from among the Gentiles. It also appears from the mention of "Israel" in v. 27 that vv. 27–29 apply to a different group than vv. 25–26, and that the conjunction δέ, at the beginning of v. 27 should be interpreted adversatively ("but"). Also, as we will see below, Paul modifies the citation of Isaiah 10:22 in v. 27, the result of which is to avoid referring to Israel with the word λαός ("people"), which is already used in vv. 25–26; this change seems to reflect the intention to distinguish two different groups in vv. 25–26 and vv. 27–29. Finally, it seems difficult to reconcile what v. 27 says about the salvation of the remnant with the promise of Israel's restoration in vv. 25–26, if indeed vv. 25–26 are meant to apply to Israel.

The second position can also be critiqued. The chief difficulty here is that if

---

22 See Aageson, "Scripture and Structure," 272–273.

23 See, for example, Simon Légasse, *L'Épître de Paul aux Romains*, Lectio Divina Commentaires 10 (Paris: Cerf, 2002), 618; Joseph A. Fitzmyer, *Romans: A New Translation with Introduction and Commentary*, Anchor Bible 33 (New York: Doubleday, 1993), 573.

24 John A. Battle, Jr., "Paul's Use of the Old Testament in Romans 9:25–26," *Grace Theological Journal* 2 (1981): 115–129.

25 Wagner, *Heralds*, 86; Nils Alstrup Dahl, *Studies in Paul: Theology for the Early Christian Mission* (Minneapolis: Augsburg, 1977), 146.

26 Many scholars fall into this category, but they offer different explanations. While some think that Paul disregards the original context of the Hosea texts, others understand the application of the texts to the Gentiles by way of analogy, since the same principle is at work for the Gentiles that once applied to northern Israel; see, for example, Dunn, *Romans*, 571–572.

27 Aletti, "L'argumentation paulinienne," 48–50.

vv. 25–26 apply to believing Jews, and not just believing Gentiles, then it follows that the believing Jews, who are among those called by God (v. 24), were at one time among the "not my people" and have now become "my people." This would imply, however, that there was not always at least a group of Jews called by God, and hence that God's word had failed (v. 6a).[28]

Because of the difficulties with positions one and two, the only viable interpretation seems to be the third one, namely, that Paul applies the Hosea texts to Gentile believers. We have already seen above how the rhetorical structure of vv. 24–29 (*reversio*) leads to such a conclusion. This position is also supported by consideration of how the Hosea texts were interpreted in other Jewish and Christian texts. For example, 1 Peter 2:10 clearly alludes to Hosea 2:25 (2:23 LXX) to refer to Christians generally, even though there is not a direct citation of Hosea as there is in Romans 9:25.[29]

Also, it is interesting to note that the Pesachim tractate of the Babylonian Talmud is witness to a tradition that understands Hosea 2:25 with respect to God's plan for the Gentiles: God sowed (that is, exiled) Israel among the nations in order that there might be a harvest among the Gentiles.[30] From this last consideration, it is possible to think that Paul, in applying the Hosea texts to the Gentiles, did not disregard the original context but actually had it very much in mind. Since the ten northern tribes of Israel about whom Hosea prophesied were dispersed among the nations, God had to call believers from among the nations (ἐξ ἐθνῶν in v. 24) in order to bring about the restoration of Israel.[31] Now, a number of scholars suggest that Paul, while primarily applying the Hosea texts in vv. 25–26 to the Gentiles, may also have in mind the original context in Hosea of the ten northern tribes.[32] What is being suggested here is that such a consideration need not look elsewhere for another referent for the citations, since it is already contained in the same referent, namely, those called ἐξ ἐθνῶν. This suggestion respects the rhetorical structure of Romans 9:24–29, and at the same time, tries to take more fully into consideration the biblical context of Paul's Old Testament citations. With this suggestion, it is perhaps already possible, therefore, to see that in Romans 9, Paul is preparing for what will follow in Romans 11 regarding the salvation of Israel.

---

28   Aletti, "L'argumentation paulinienne," 49–50.

29   See John Hall Elliott, *1 Peter: A New Translation with Introduction and Commentary*, Anchor Bible 37B (New York: Doubleday, 2000), 20–23, 37–40, 442.

30   See b. Pes. 87b.; see, for example, *New Edition of the Babylonian Talmud*, ed. Michael L. Rodkinson, 18 vols. (New York: New Amsterdam Book Co., 1896–1903), 5:177.

31   Recall the discussion above regarding ἐκ in v. 24 as indicating separation, and ἐξ ἐθνῶν possibly being understood as "out of the nations."

32   See, for example, Cranfield, *Romans*, 2:500. J. Paul Tanner, "The New Covenant and Paul's Quotations from Hosea in Romans 9:25–26," *Bibliotheca Sacra* 162 (2005): 95–110, at 101, says that Paul's "*point in Romans 9 was not to deny a fulfillment with Israel but only to affirm a fulfillment also with Gentiles.*"

In summary, Paul does indeed apply the Hosea texts to the Gentiles in order to provide Scriptural support for the call of believers ἐξ ἐθνῶν (v. 24). Nonetheless, we have seen that Paul may still have the original context of the Hosea prophecies in mind, and understands the restoration of the northern tribes (and hence, "all Israel") to come about through the call of the Gentiles (see Rom. 11:25–26).

Salvation of the Remnant (Romans 9:27)

Having discussed in vv. 25–26 how God has called believers from among the Gentiles, Paul moves in vv. 27–29 to consider the other group mentioned in v. 24, namely, those called from among the Jews. After an introductory formula, Paul quotes in vv. 27–28 an abbreviated and adapted form of Isaiah 10:22–23.

Paul exchanges Isaiah's phrase ὁ λαὸς Ἰσραήλ ("the people of Israel," Isa. 10:22 LXX) with the phrase ὁ ἀριθμὸς τῶν υἱῶν Ἰσραήλ ("the number of the sons of Israel"). This phrase is taken from the first half of Hosea 1:10 LXX, the same verse that was quoted in v. 26.[33] The change results from Paul's application of the rabbinic exegetical rule of *gezerah shawah*,[34] which finds a literary analogy between two passages of Scripture that contain the same or similar words. In this case, the Hebrew text of Isaiah contains the phrase יִשְׂרָאֵל כְּחוֹל הַיָּם ("Israel as the sand of the sea"), which only occurs elsewhere in Hosea 2:1 (Hos. 1:10 LXX).[35] A link is thus established between the verses such that one verse can be used in the interpretation of the other. As noted above, an effect of the change is that it enables Paul to avoid designating Israel with the word λαός, a term applied to the Gentiles in vv. 25–26, thereby emphasizing the distinction between the group referred to in vv. 25–26 and that referred to in vv. 27–29.

Also of significance for the interpretation of the verse is the translation of Isaiah's phrase τὸ ὑπόλειμμα σωθήσεται ("the remnant will be saved") and the connotation to be associated with the concept of "remnant." Many modern versions translate: "*only* a remnant will be saved."[36] A few commentators correctly insist,

---

33 See Christopher D. Stanley, *Paul and the Language of Scripture: Citation Technique in the Pauline Epistles and Contemporary Literature*, Society for New Testament Studies Monograph Series 69 (Cambridge: Cambridge University Press, 1992), 114–115.

34 Moses Mielziner, *Introduction to the Talmud*, ed. Alexander Guttmann (New York: Bloch, 1968), 143, explains that the rule of *gezerah shawah* denotes "an analogy based on identical or similar words occurring in two different passages of Scripture"; one of the rule's uses is to construe laws "with reference to each other." See also Dan Cohn-Sherbok, "Paul and Rabbinic Exegesis," *Scottish Journal of Theology* 35 (1982): 117–132, especially 127–128 for the rule of *gezerah shawah*. For Paul's use of the rule in this verse, see Aletti, *Comment Dieu*, 170, 219–222.

35 In this case, the literary analogy works also with the Greek texts.

36 For example, see the translation of v. 27 in the following versions: New Revised Standard Version (NRSV), Revised Standard Version (RSV), New American Bible (NAB), and New International Version (NIV).

however, that while the insertion of "only" *may* be a fitting part of an interpretation, it is not properly part of the translation itself.[37]

Before considering the connotation of v. 27, however, it is helpful to clarify the identity of the actors (Israel and the remnant) in Paul's application of Isaiah. As discussed above, Paul in vv. 27–29 turns his attention to believers called from among the Jews (v. 24). These Judeo-Christians are identified with the "remnant" (v. 27) and the "seed" (v. 29).[38] By contrast, the term "Israel"[39] in v. 27 refers to a larger group, of which the remnant is a small part.

The distinction between a larger group and a smaller subset recalls that made by Paul in 9:6b: "for not all who are descended from Israel belong to Israel." Indeed, throughout Romans 9–11, Paul at times uses the term "Israel" for the larger group, despite the distinction made in 9:6b.[40] A key question then arises regarding which sense Paul means in 11:26 when he refers to the salvation of "all Israel."

From the perspective of the Old Testament background, scholars agree that "all Israel" is to be understood in a historical and ethnic sense—that is, "the *tribal structure* of the descendants of Jacob/Israel, whether to all twelve tribes, to the northern tribes, or to the southern tribes."[41] The term can also "be used to denote a representative selection from the full complement of the tribes."[42] From the perspective of Paul's argumentation in Romans 9–11, the phrase "all Israel" can be interpreted in a quantitative sense to mean the sum of the remnant plus "the others" (οἱ λοιποί in 11:7) who are presently hardened.[43]

We now turn to a consideration of whether v. 27 should be interpreted as a positive word of hope, emphasizing the salvation of the remnant, or a negative word of judgment, emphasizing the non-salvation of the non-remnant majority of

---

37   For grammatical issues related to whether the clause should be understood concessively ("though" or "even if") or conditionally ("if"), see James Hope Moulton and Nigel Turner, *A Grammar of New Testament Greek: III. Syntax* (Edinburgh: T. & T. Clark, 1963), 114. See also Richard B. Hays, *Echoes of Scripture in the Letters of Paul* (New Haven: Yale University Press, 1989), 68.

38   Many scholars identify the remnant with Judeo-Christians like Paul himself; see, for example, Fitzmyer, *Romans*, 574.

39   The term Ἰσραήλ occurs eleven times in the letter (Rom. 9:6²ˣ,27²ˣ,31; 10:19, 21; 11:2, 7, 25–26) and the term Ἰσραηλίτης occurs twice (Rom. 9:4; 11:1). It is noteworthy that Paul uses these terms only in chapters 9–11. Scholars generally explain the change in terminological emphasis from Ἰουδαῖος to Ἰσραήλ by saying that Paul uses the term "Israel" in Romans 9–11 because he is considering the question from the perspective of salvation history; see, for example, James D. G. Dunn, *The Theology of Paul the Apostle* (Edinburgh: T. & T. Clark, 1998), 505–506.

40   Jean-Noël Aletti, *Israël et la loi dans la lettre aux Romains*, Lectio Divina 173 (Paris: Cerf, 1998), 237.

41   James M. Scott, "'And then All Israel will be Saved' (Rom 11:26)," in *Restoration: Old Testament, Jewish, and Christian Perspectives*, ed., James M. Scott, Supplements to the Journal for the Study of Judaism 72 (Leiden: Brill, 2001), 489–527, at 507. See the whole section, 498–507, for Scott's analysis of the Old Testament texts.

42   Scott, "All Israel," 507.

43   Scott, "All Israel," 518; Aletti, *Comment Dieu*, 186–187.

Israel. The text of Isaiah 10:22–23, cited by Paul in v. 27, is generally interpreted to combine both dimensions.[44] Some scholars therefore suggest that Romans 9:27 likewise contains both a positive and a negative aspect, while others emphasize one aspect or the other.[45]

For various reasons, however, the positive understanding of the remnant concept appears indeed to be the one emphasized by Paul. First, considering Paul's rhetorical structure, it is important to recall that vv. 25–29 function to support the thesis in v. 24 regarding God's calling of believers from among the Gentiles (vv. 25–26) and from among the Jews (vv. 27–29). Paul's discussion of the remnant, considered in light of his thesis, is therefore not focused on those rejected but on those called; hence, the positive aspect is emphasized.[46]

Moreover, several scholars suggest that Paul's use of the remnant concept should be understood in light of the hope for the promised restoration of Israel, a dominant theme in the Second Temple Period.[47] Seen in this context, the remnant does not imply destruction for those in Israel who are not part of the remnant. Rather, the salvation of the remnant becomes a sign and pledge of the salvation of Israel as a whole.[48] For these reasons, one can argue that already in Romans 9:27, Paul is preparing the way for his statement regarding the salvation of "all Israel" in 11:26. There is thus a progression, not a contradiction between the two verses.

Decisive Fulfillment of the Word of God (Romans 9:28)

In v. 28, Paul continues with the abbreviated citation of Isaiah 10:22–23 begun in v. 27. Of interest is the change at the end of the citation. Here it can be argued that Paul modified the text under the influence of Isaiah 28:22, once again applying the principle of *gezerah shawah*.[49] The Hebrew phrase כִּי כָלָה וְנֶחֱרָצָה ("for decreed de-

---

44 See Gerhard F. Hasel, *The Remnant: The History and Theology of the Remnant Idea from Genesis to Isaiah*, Andrews University Monographs 5 (Berrien Springs, MI: Andrews University Press, 1972), especially 318–331 and 398–399 for Hasel's treatment of Isaiah 10:20–23. Hasel writes that "[t]he juxtaposition of salvation and judgment in 10:20–23 is typical of Isaiah's thought and theology" (399).

45 Among scholars who see both positive and negative aspects in Paul's use of the remnant concept in Romans 9:27–28 is James W. Aageson, "Typology, Correspondence, and the Application of Scripture in Romans 9–11," *Journal for the Study of the New Testament* 31 (1987): 51–72, at 57–58, 69, n. 28. Among those emphasizing the negative aspect of judgment are Ernst Käsemann, *Commentary on Romans*, trans. and ed. Geoffrey W. Bromiley (Grand Rapids, MI: Eerdmans, 1980), 275; and Cranfield, *Romans*, 2:501. Among those emphasizing the positive aspect of hope are Aletti, "L'argumentation paulinienne," 51–52; and Dunn, *Romans*, 573.

46 Aletti, *Israël*, 183; Wagner, *Heralds*, 107.

47 See Wagner, *Heralds*, 108; Scott, "All Israel," 520; and James W. Watts, "The Remnant Theme: A Survey of New Testament Research, 1921–1987," *Perspectives in Religious Studies* 15 (1988): 109–129, at 123–124.

48 Wagner, *Heralds*, 109: "For Paul, the salvation of the remnant upholds God's covenant faithfulness and pledges the eventual salvation of 'all Israel' (11:26)."

49 See John Paul Heil, "From Remnant to Seed of Hope for Israel: Romans 9:27–29," *Catholic*

struction") occurs only in these two verses. As a result of the *gezerah shawah*, Isaiah 10:23 and 28:22 are linked as being mutually interpretive. Thus, Paul substitutes certain words at the end of the citation in order, it seems, to strengthen the positive sense of the text.[50]

The chief difficulties in the verse are semantic: what is the precise meaning of λόγος and of the participial pair συντελῶν and συντέμνων? Many versions translate λόγος, not as "word," but as "sentence."[51] Such a translation clearly carries a connotation of God's judgment on Israel and hence contributes to an overall negative interpretation of the whole passage. Certainly, if v. 27 is understood as a word of judgment, then v. 28—which functions syntactically to confirm v. 27 (γάρ)—will also be understood that way. However, in the discussion above, it was argued that v. 27 should be interpreted positively; in this case, v. 28 should confirm this positive interpretation.

Another problem with translating λόγος as "sentence," is that it obscures the link to the occurrence of λόγος in Paul's thesis statement (the *propositio* "the word of God has not failed," v. 6a).[52] The word λόγος also occurs in v. 9, where it refers specifically to God's word of promise to Abraham regarding a descendant (Gen. 18:10, 14). It is better, therefore, to take λόγος in v. 28 also as referring to God's word, not a word of judgment (a "sentence") but rather a word of promise, namely, the one just mentioned in v. 27 regarding the salvation of the remnant.[53]

Turning to a consideration of the participles, the meaning of συντελῶν is more easily understood than that of συντέμνων. The verb συντελέω occurs six times in the New Testament,[54] and its meaning is "to complete/finish," "to fulfill/execute/accomplish," or "to end/be over." Hence, the phrase λόγον … συντελῶν … ποιήσει κύριος in Romans 9:28 means that the Lord will carry out his word, that he will bring it to fulfillment.[55]

The verb συντέμνω, on the other hand, is rare, not occurring elsewhere in the New Testament and occurring in the LXX only several times.[56] Its meaning

---

   Biblical Quarterly 64 (2002): 703–720, at 713–714. Heil, however, considers the *gezerah shawah* at the level of the Greek LXX text.

50 See Wagner, *Heralds*, 105: "the reverberations of Isaiah 28:22b in Romans 9:28 enrich and amplify the note of imminent deliverance." Also, the LXX translation of vv. 22–23 lacks the words of destruction (כִּלָּיוֹן and כָּלָה) found in the Hebrew, thus contributing to the positive sense of Romans 9:28; see Aletti, "L'argumentation paulinienne," 51, n. 22.

51 See, for example, the NRSV, RSV, NAB, and NIV.

52 Recall the chiastic structure of 9:6–29 in the table above.

53 Erich Seitz, "λόγον συντέμνων—eine Gerichtsankündigung? (Zu Römer 9, 27/28)," *Biblische Notizen* 109 (2001): 56–82, at 66.

54 The six occurrences are in Mark 13:4; Luke 4:2, 13; Acts 21:27; Rom. 9:28; and Heb. 8:8.

55 Seitz, "Gerichtsankündigung?" 64.

56 In the LXX, the verb συντέμνω occurs in the following passages: 2 Macc. 10:10; Isa. 10:22, 23; 28:22; and Dan. 5:27; and Dan. 9:24,26 (Theodotion).

is usually given as "to cut short/shorten," and "to limit/curtail." The problem, then, in Romans 9:28 seems to be to determine the object of the shortening or limiting action of the verb.

Many scholars understand "time" as the implied object of συντέμνω, so that the idea is that God will accomplish his word by curtailing the time, and hence the word is accomplished "quickly" (NRSV, NAB) or "with speed" (NIV).[57] Together with the translation of λόγος as "sentence," this temporal understanding of the participle leads to the idea of "swift judgment" — hence, a negative interpretation. Arguing against this common interpretation, however, is Paul's statement, only a few verses earlier, that God's way of fulfilling his word is just the opposite of swift; God instead exercises much patience (9:22; see 2:4).[58]

A second suggestion is to consider λόγος as the object of the participle, with the idea that God fulfills and curtails his word; in other words, that the scope of the promise is limited.[59] This would seem to imply, however, that God's word (9:6a) had, for the most part, failed.[60] To get around this difficulty, it is suggested that "Israel" (in v. 27) is really the object of συντέμνων, rather than λόγος: the idea is that the fulfillment of God's word or promise applies to a "curtailed" Israel; that is, to a remnant. A negative interpretation is also associated with this understanding: if God's word is fulfilled in only a diminished Israel, then the majority of Israel has no hope of salvation.[61] The difficulty with this interpretation, however, is that there is not a good grammatical basis for understanding the object of the participle to be "Israel."

Since it is grammatically easier to take λόγος as the object of the participle (indeed, as the object of both participles), it is worthwhile to take a closer look at this option, taking into account the objection just mentioned, namely, that the interpretation "curtailing the word" contradicts Paul's earlier claim that God's word has not failed (9:6a). It is necessary, therefore, to study more closely the meaning of συντέμνω as it is used in the Greek Old Testament.

On four occasions (Isa. 10:22, 23; 28:22; Dan. 9:26 Theodotion), the verb συντέμνω appears as part of a translation in which appears the Hebrew root חרץ. This root can mean "to cut/sharpen," but in these four passages has the meaning "to decide/determine."[62] Also, on one occasion (Dan. 9:24 Theodotion), συντέμνω is used to translate the root חתך, which means "to determine." The usage of the

57   See the discussion in Wagner, *Heralds*, 103–104.

58   Seitz, "Gerichtsankündigung?" 68.

59   Heinrich Schlier, *Der Römerbrief*, Herders theologischer Kommentar zum Neuen Testament 6 (Freiburg: Herder, 1977), 304–305.

60   Ulrich Wilckens, *Der Brief an die Römer*, 3 vols., Evangelisch-katholischer Kommentar zum Neuen Testament 6 (Zürich: Benziger Verlag, 1978, 1980, 1982), 2:207.

61   Wilckens, *Römer*, 2:207.

62   See Seitz, "Gerichtsankündigung?" 68–70; Heil, "From Remnant to Seed," 715.

verb συντέμνω in the Greek Bible, therefore, suggests that the correct meaning of συντέμνω in Romans 9:28 may be "to decide" or "to determine."[63]

Another important observation regarding the use of συντέμνω in the Greek Old Testament is that several times it appears together with συντελέω, so that the two verbs can be understood as forming a hendiadys related to the Hebrew hendiadys כָלָה וְנֶחֱרָצָה.[64] In addition to Isaiah 10:22 LXX (συντελῶν καὶ συντέμνων), the two Greek verbs also occur together in Isaiah 28:22 and Daniel 5:27 LXX. In a hendiadys, two ideas are coordinated, and one of them is dependent on the other as a further determination of it.[65] In our case, the "fulfilling" (συντελῶν) is dependent on the "deciding/determining" (συντέμνων) since the logical order would be that one first makes a decision and then carries it out. This logical order is the order of the participles in the last-mentioned verse (Dan. 5:27 LXX). In Romans 9:28 (and in Isaiah 28:22), however, the participles are reversed, apparently to put emphasis on the fulfilling (συντελῶν) of the word, an idea which parallels the action of the main verb ποιήσει.[66] A possible translation of the Greek participial pair in Romans 9:28, therefore, could be "fulfilling and deciding," or, considering the pair as a hendiadys, "fulfilling decisively"; all of v. 28 might therefore be rendered: "For decisively fulfilling [his] word, the Lord will accomplish [it] on the earth."[67]

In summary, the function of v. 28 is to confirm (γάρ) the "word" expressed in v. 27 regarding the salvation of the remnant by indicating that God will accomplish this word on the earth, bringing it to decisive fulfillment. The citation from Isaiah in Romans 9:28, therefore, highlights the efficacy of God's word (9:6a),[68] a word which is here a positive word of salvation. The results of our study of the meaning of λόγος and of the participial pair συντελῶν καὶ συντέμνων rule out the negative interpretation of the verse that understands it in terms of a sentence of swift judgment on Israel. The results regarding v. 28 also confirm the positive interpretation of v. 27 given earlier.

The Sign of Hope (Romans 9:29)

In contrast to the earlier citations in 9:25–28, Paul in v. 29 cites the LXX text of Isaiah 1:9 exactly. This citation corroborates the citation of Isaiah 10:22–23 in vv. 27–28, since the two citations are linked by the comparative conjunctive phrase

---

63   See Seitz, "Gerichtsankündigung?" 73; Heil, "From Remnant to Seed," 715.

64   Heil, "From Remnant to Seed," 714.

65   See Friedrich Blass and Albert Debrunner, *A Greek Grammar of the New Testament and Other Early Christian Literature*, ed. and trans. Robert W. Funk (Chicago: University of Chicago Press, 1961), §442,16.

66   Seitz, "Gerichtsankündigung?" 71-72; Heil, "From Remnant to Seed," 715.

67   Compare Seitz, "Gerichtsankündigung?" 73; Heil, "From Remnant to Seed," 720.

68   Aletti, "L'argumentation paulinienne," 51.

καὶ καθώς ("and just as"). The syntax suggests, therefore, that v. 29 and vv. 27–28 express parallel rather than antithetical ideas.[69]

From the parallelism, it follows that the key words ὑπόλειμμα ("remnant") in v. 27 and σπέρμα ("seed") in v. 29 refer to the same group of people. The link between the two words is also indicated by the verb in v. 29, ἐγκατέλιπεν, from the lexical form ἐγκαταλείπω ("to leave behind"), a cognate of λεῖμμα (the word for "remnant" used in 11:5) and ὑπόλειμμα.[70] The recurrence of the word σπέρμα in v. 29 functions as an inclusion, linking this final unit (A': vv. 27–29) with the first unit (A: vv. 6–9), in which σπέρμα occurs twice in v. 7 and once in v. 8. Because of the syntactical and semantic links between v. 29 and vv. 27–28, it follows that if v. 29 is understood positively as a word of reassurance, then vv. 27–28 should also be so understood, and not as a word of judgment on Israel.[71] Verse 29 can thus provide a further reason for understanding the more difficult vv. 27–28 in a positive way.

However, in interpreting v. 29, some scholars believe that Paul here affirms that there is no longer any hope of salvation for Israel, apart from the believing remnant.[72] Does v. 29, however, really yield such a negative assessment? To answer this question, it is helpful to note that, grammatically, the citation of Isaiah 1:9 LXX in Romans 9:29 is an unreal conditional sentence.[73] The part of the citation which is interpreted as a judgment on Israel (the reference to Sodom and Gomorrah) is in the apodosis of the conditional clause, and hence, never occurs because the unreal condition is never fulfilled. Those who argue in favor of the negative interpretation nevertheless interpret the conditional clause to mean that, except for the "seed" which is spared, the same fate as that of Sodom and Gomorrah will fall on Israel.[74]

The conditional clause, however, can be interpreted to mean that since God has left a "seed" of Israel, the judgment, like that of Sodom and Gomorrah, will not fall on Israel at all.[75] To substantiate this positive interpretation of the conditional clause, one can consider that, in reference to Israel, the "seed" language in the Old

---

69 Some commentators, apparently failing to see the parallelism, contrast vv. 27–28 and v. 29, seeing the former negatively, and the latter positively; for example, James W. Aageson, *Written Also for Our Sake: Paul and the Art of Biblical Interpretation* (Louisville, KY: Westminster/John Knox, 1993), 93–94.

70 See also the excursus on the seed-remnant relationship in Paul Edward Dinter, "The Remnant of Israel and the Stone of Stumbling in Zion According to Paul (Romans 9–11)" (Ph.D. diss., Union Theological Seminary in the City of New York, 1980), 347–356.

71 Seitz, "Gerichtsankündigung?" 58.

72 For example, Wilckens, *Römer*, 2:207.

73 See Blass and Debrunner, *Greek Grammar*, §360.

74 See Fitzmyer, *Romans*, 575.

75 Wagner, *Heralds*, 110: "the citation of Isaiah 1:9 provides decisive evidence that Paul's appeal to Isaiah in Romans 9:27–29 is intended as a word of *hope* for the remnant—and ultimately for Israel as a whole."

Testament and in other Jewish literature has a positive connotation: it indicates not only the continued survival of Israel, but also its future growth.[76]

One can also arrive at the positive interpretation by referring once again to Paul's use of compositional models. With regard to the rhetorical and chiastic models, v. 29 functions in a positive way to show that God's word has not failed (v. 6a): the promise of "seed" (v. 7) has become a reality experienced by the "seed"-remnant itself.[77] With regard to the midrashic model, recall that the conclusion of a midrashic homily contains a word of consolation (ḥatima)[78]; Paul's citation of Isaiah 1:9 is meant also to function as a concluding word of hope at the end of the section, Romans 9:6–29.[79]

Both on account of the Old Testament background and on account of Paul's argumentation, therefore, the positive interpretation of v. 29 is to be favored over the negative interpretation. Finally, because of the syntactical and semantic links between v. 29 and vv. 27–28, the positive interpretation of vv. 27–28 is also confirmed. In summary, Paul's citation of the "seed" text from Isaiah 1:9 serves as a sign of hope for Israel, and thus prepares for what Paul will say in Romans 11:26 regarding the salvation of all Israel.[80]

Romans 9:24–29: Directions for Future Research

At the end of this paper, I wish to note some conclusions and suggestions for future work in Romans 9–11, not only at the levels of exegesis and theology, but also at the level of methodology.

At the level of exegesis, one of the difficulties examined here in detail is the apparent disregard of the original context of the Hosea citations in Romans 9:25–26. The exegesis of vv. 25–26 showed that while Paul indeed does apply the texts to the Gentiles, he does not ignore Hosea's original context, which refers to the restoration of the northern tribes of Israel. Since the ten northern tribes of Israel were dispersed among the nations or Gentiles, God had to call believers from among the nations in order to bring about the restoration of all Israel. In Paul's mind, the restoration of Israel is, therefore, closely connected to the calling of the Gentiles (see Rom. 11:25–26).

More work is needed in this area, especially with regard to the possibility that Paul is thinking of the restoration of the northern tribes throughout Romans

---

76 Wagner, *Heralds*, 112–115.

77 Aletti, "L'argumentation paulinienne," 52.

78 On the *ḥatima*, see Hermann L. Strack and Günter Stemberger, *Introduction to the Talmud and Midrash*, trans. Markus Bockmuehl (Edinburgh: T. & T. Clark, 1991), 266–268.

79 Aletti, *Israël*, 183.

80 Aletti, "L'argumentation paulinienne," 52. Also, Wagner, *Heralds*, 116: "it is clear that Paul's reference to the 'seed' in Romans 9:29 carries with it the germ of his conclusion in 11:26 that God will certainly redeem 'all Israel.'"

9–11.[81] More study is also needed of the distinctions between terms such as Ἰουδαῖος (Jew/Judean) and Ἰσραήλ (Israel).[82] Paul's shift in terminology from Jew to Israel in Romans 9–11 was noted above, but an understanding of the full significance of the shift requires further investigation in the Jewish literature of the time-period.

With regard to issues of theology arising from a study of Romans 9–11, of particular interest are ecclesiological questions, especially in light of ongoing Jewish-Christian dialogue. Since Paul affirms that Israel continues to have a role in God's plan of salvation (see Rom. 11:11–15), scholars often consider the relationship between Israel and the Church, and the models that can be used to describe this relationship. However, more attention should also be given to the relationship between Israel and *the nations* or *Gentiles*, since this is the relationship about which Paul speaks more directly—especially in Romans 11.[83] Indeed, the Church consists of believers called both from among the Jews and from among the Gentiles or the nations (9:24). Further work is needed, then, to understand the respective roles of Israel and the nations in God's plan of salvation, and to understand how Paul viewed his own mission as "apostle to the nations" (Rom. 11:13).[84]

With regard to methodology, one of the concerns of this study has been to show the importance of paying close attention to *how* Paul develops an argument, in order to understand better *what* he is truly affirming. Studies which do not attend closely to the logic of Paul's argument run the risk of either seriously misunderstanding it or concluding prematurely that it is inconsistent.

The exegesis in this study made use of three compositional models (midrashic, chiastic, and rhetorical) that have been proposed by Jean-Noël Aletti to aid in understanding Romans 9:6–29, the first part of Romans 9–11. It is important to emphasize that these models are not imposed on the text from outside, but are developed from observations within the text itself. The explanatory power of these models was confirmed in the exegetical analysis of Romans 9:24–29.

---

81 Scott, "All Israel," 518, n. 78, notes the lack of work done in this area: "The fact that 'all Israel' includes the northern tribes is made plausible by Rom 11:2, which introduces citations from 1 Kings 19. . . .Elijah the Tishbite is, of course, the prophet who was active in the *Northern Kingdom* of Israel. . . .Hence, 'Israel' refers here particularly to the northern tribes. Surprisingly, this fundamentally important observation seems to have escaped notice in the secondary literature."

82 For example, see Cohen, *Jewishness*, 71: "the relationship between the term *Ioudaios/oi* and the terms *Hebraios* and *Israel* must be determined; and the occurrences of the terms must be catalogued by chronology, geography, and language."

83 See Aletti, *Israël*, 236–242; and Dunn, *Theology*, 504–509.

84 Regarding Paul's understanding of his own mission, see, for example, the two articles by Craig A. Evans, "Paul and the Hermeneutics of 'True Prophecy': A Study of Romans 9–11," *Biblica* 65 (1984): 560–570; and "Paul and the Prophets: Prophetic Criticism in the Epistle to the Romans (with special reference to Romans 9–11)," in *Romans and the People of God: Essays in Honor of Gordon D. Fee on the Occasion of His 65th Birthday*, eds. Sven K. Soderlund and N. T. Wright (Grand Rapids, MI.: Eerdmans, 1999), 115–128.

Together with the focus on Paul's argumentation and use of compositional models, attention was also given in this study to Paul's use of Scripture, since about one-third of all of Paul's citations of the Old Testament occur in Romans 9–11. We saw how Paul understands texts of Scripture in relation to one another (for example, through the rule of *gezerah shawah*) and how he rereads Scripture in light of his conversion and missionary experiences.

Certainly, more work needs to be done, in order to extend to all of Romans 9–11 the combination attempted here of formal analysis of Paul's argumentation and study of the material content of his scriptural citations. It is hoped, nonetheless, that a contribution has been made to help move beyond the "impasse" in the study of Romans 9–11. Through the consideration of Paul's argumentation and his use of Scripture in Romans 9:24–29, this study has defended the coherence of Paul's argument, especially with regard to the apparent contradiction between 9:27 and 11:26. There is continuity and progression between the words in Romans 9 and the words in Romans 11. God's word has not failed. Indeed, as Paul affirms, the Lord will accomplish his word.

Letter & Spirit 2 (2006): 159–173

A Liturgical Approach to Hebrews 13

~: James Swetnam, S.J. :~
Pontifical Biblical Institute, Rome

The thirteenth chapter of the Epistle to the Hebrews has long been a source of contention.[1] Its apparently heterogeneous content is a source of perplexity.[2] Its relation with the rest of the epistle has been subject to a variety of interpretations.[3] It would seem advisable to try to come to grips with what the chapter says in itself before trying to assess its place at the end of the entire work. The present study will therefore confine itself to trying to arrive at a plausible interpretation of what the chapter is trying to convey. Subsequent study will be needed to evaluate its place in the structure of the entire epistle.[4]

The relevant portion of chapter 13 for purposes of the present study comprises vv. 1–21. This means that for the present writer, the benediction at vv. 20–21 is part of the text to be elucidated. Verses 22–25, on the other hand, are a brief set of remarks and a valediction, not uncommon in letters of the period, and to be evaluated accordingly.[5]

This article is composed of three parts: First, vv. 1–21 are viewed in terms of the chapter's structure. Secondly, vv. 1–21 are viewed in the perspective of the biblical sacrifice known as *tôdâ*. Finally, these verses are viewed in the context of the Latin Rite Mass of the Roman Catholic Church.

The Structure of Heb. 13:1–21

The following, preliminary assessment of structure is offered:

---

1   "One of the key literary problems of Hebrews is the relationship between chap. 13 and what precedes....Many scholars have maintained that all or part of the chapter is a secondary addition to the text. Some have argued that this addition was made by a pseudepigraphist, in order to bring the whole document into conformity with the Pauline corpus; others, that an authentic Pauline text has been appended." H. W. Attridge, *The Epistle to the Hebrews*, (Philadelphia: Fortress, 1989), 384. See also: W. L. Lane, *Hebrews 9–13* (Dallas: Word Books, 1991), 495–497; P. Ellingworth, *The Epistle to the Hebrews: A Commentary on the Greek Text* (Grand Rapids: Eerdmans / Carlisle, UK: Paternoster, 1993), 692–693.

2   "A formless collection of the ethical precepts and theological reflections scarcely seems congruous with the careful development of argument in chaps. 1–12." Lane, *Hebrews 9–13*, 496.

3   Some have even argued that chapter 13 is alien to Hebrews: "...it is asserted that considerations of coherence, form, and content call into question the integrity of Hebrews and the authenticity or appropriateness of chap. 13." Lane, *Hebrews 9–13*, 496.

4   It seems desirable at this point to make explicit the presuppositions with which the present writer approaches this text. They are those of a believer in the traditions and teaching authority of the Roman Catholic Church.

5   Attridge, *The Epistle to the Hebrews*, 408–409.

Verses 1–5a form a section composed of a series of admonitions concerning conduct;

Verses 5b–6 form a section composed of two citations from Scripture; vv. 7–17 form a section composed of a series of statements framed by mention of the community's "leaders" (ἡγούμενοι); this section stands, obviously, at the heart of the chapter by reason of its length and position.

Verses 18–19 form a section composed of a personal appeal for prayer by the author of the epistle.

Verses 20–21 form a section composed of a blessing.

The challenge, then, is to find a coherent structure for these five sections which will indicate a plausible explanation for the role of each of them in the chapter as a whole. Further, the central section, framed by mention of the community's leaders, needs a coherent structure itself, given its length.

A Call to Brotherly Love (Heb. 13:1–5a)

With Hebrews 13:1, a series of moral admonitions suddenly becomes the center of attention. These admonitions follow from what immediately precedes, 12:29, with its reminder that the addressees, like all Christians, stand under God's judgmental fire. But this sobering thought, in turn, would seem to follow in the mind of the author of Hebrews from the liturgical context expressed in 12:28, with its mention of worship with "reverence" (εὐλάβεια) and "awe" (δέος). Thus 12:28, with its overtones of worship, is the underlying introduction to vv. 1–5a.[6]

The passage in question would seem to consist of four couplets, combining direct admonitions with explanatory comments:

First Couplet: "Let love of the brethren remain. Hospitality do not forget, for through this some have played host to angels unawares" (vv. 1–2).[7]

Second Couplet: "Remember those who are in chains as chained with them, those who are ill–treated as being yourselves in a body"[8] (v. 3).

---

6   "The connection of 13:1–21 to the preceding section, 12:14–29, is established through 12:28. There the community is summoned to be thankful, and through thanksgiving to serve God in an acceptable manner." Lane, *Hebrews 9–13*, 496.

7   Translation of Scripture is by the present writer.

8   There seems to be no reference to Christ's mystical body. See Ellingworth, *The Epistle to the Hebrews*, 696. But there may be theological implications in the context of Hebrews. See J.

Third Couplet: "Let marriage be honored by all and let the marital bed be undefiled, for God will judge fornicators and adulterers" (v. 4).

Fourth Couplet: "Do not be a money-lover, be content with what you have" (v. 5a).

In the light of Hebrews 12:28–29, which would seem to be the introduction to the admonitions, these moral strictures are designed to respond to the call to show gratitude for the gift of an unshakeable kingdom. The addressees are to offer to God worship like the faith which motivated Jesus in his suffering.

An Exhortation to Courage (Heb. 13:5b–6)

For he himself has said, "I shall not desert you and I shall not abandon you," hence we should take courage and say, "The Lord is my helper and I shall not fear. What will a human do to me?" (vv. 5b–6)

After the admonitions of 1–5a the author introduces two citations from Scripture. The use of the word γάρ ("for") coupled to αὐτός ("he himself") seems to refer implicitly to what is understood in the final admonition: one should be content with what one has because, as expressed in v. 5b, each one is under God's providential care.

The source of the citation in v. 5b is not clear. One view traces it back to Genesis 28:15 as modified from Deuteronomy 31:6, 8; another is that it is dependent on Joshua 1:5 as modified by Deuteronomy 31:8. In the context of a writing by and for persons who were, clearly, deeply versed in the language of the Greek Old Testament, such fine distinctions are probably misleading. All the sources can be adduced as playing a part.

The language of v. 5b is intriguing. God is presented as speaking to an individual. The individual, in the context of Hebrews, would seem to be Christ understood as the new Joshua who is leading the new people of God into God's definitive rest.[9]

Verse 6 contains a citation from Psalm 118:6. It is in the singular number,

---

Thurén, *Das Lobopfer der Hebräer. Studien zum Aufbau und Anliegen von Hebräer 13* (Åbo: Åbo Akademi, 1973), 210–211, n. 721.

9   See the comment by Lane, *Hebrews 9–13*, 520: "The writer could have understood the oracle as the word of God to a new Joshua who will lead the people into rest (4:8). It is important in any case that the singular of address ('I will never fail you; I will never forsake you') has in view an individual who represents the whole people. If the writer read the oracle in this manner he may have understood it as the word of God addressed to the Son (so Thurén, *Lobopfer*, 218). Christians share in this word and its response, in so far as they are partners with Christ (see 3:14)."

and should thus be best taken as the response of the individual addressed in v. 5b, Christ. Christ responds to the word of God, but in the name of the entire community. This is to be inferred from the introduction to the citation in the first part of the verse, "hence we should take courage and say." The words of the psalm, cited as they are in response to the more particularized context of the citation in v. 5b, have the effect of generalizing and radicalizing the attitude of both Christ and the Christians so that they are without fear in any context.[10]

With Christ "Outside the Camp" (Heb. 13:7–17)

After the admonitions and the citations comes the portion of the chapter which is central, as is indicated by its placement and size. The section is bounded by the mention of the "leaders" (ἡγούμενοι) in vv. 7 and 17.[11] Further, the phrase "outside the camp" (ἔξω τῆς παρεμβολῆς) would seem to act as frames for v. 12 with its mention of the sacrificial death of Christ, the only mention of such an important teaching of the epistle in this section of the chapter framed by "leaders." Further, the phrase "outside the gate" (ἔξω τῆς πύλης) would seem to occupy a central position with regard to the two occurrences of "outside the camp". That is to say, it is not simply the death of Jesus which is of basic concern to the author, but the fact that this death occurred outside the camp/city.

The result looks like this:

> Verse 7: Principal framing verse ("leaders");
>
> Verse 11: Secondary framing verse ("outside the camp");
>
> Verse 12: Central verse portraying the death of Christ ("outside the gate");
>
> Verse 13: Secondary framing verse ("outside the camp");
>
> Verse 17: Principal framing verse ("leaders").

A translation of the passage which reflects the arrangement presented above is as follows:

> 7 Remember your *leaders*, who spoke to you the word of God;
> in reflecting on the outcome of their conduct imitate their faith.
> 8 Jesus Christ yesterday and today the same, and forever.

---

10   See Lane, *Hebrews 9–13*, 529: "The Christian is to be free both from the love of money and from the fear of death (see 2:14–15)."

11   Attridge, *The Epistle to the Hebrews*, 390–391: "The central section of chap. 13 concludes the thematic development of Hebrews and provides a climactic exhortation. The boundaries of the section, which have been analyzed in a variety of ways, are indicated by an inclusion formed by the references to leaders past (v. 7) and present (v. 17)."

9Do not be led astray by a variety of strange teachings; for is good that the heart be sustained by grace, not by foods in which those who live by them are not helped. 10We have an altar from which those serving the tent have no right to eat. 11For while the blood of the animals is brought as a sin-offering into the Holy of Holies by the high priest, their bodies are burned *outside the camp*. 12For this reason Jesus also, so that he might sanctify the people through his own blood, suffered *outside the gate*.

13For that very reason, then, let us go to him *outside the camp*, taking on his shame. 14For we have not here a city which remains but one which is to come.

15Through him, then, let us offer up a sacrifice of praise regularly to God, that is, fruit of lips which confess his name. 16The doing of good and fellowship do not forget. Now with such sacrifices as these is God pleased. 17Obey your *leaders* and be subject to them, for they are vigilant over your souls as ones having to give an account, that they may do this with joy and not sighing, for this would not be of any help to you.

The cruces in this passage are numerous. Among them are:

Verse 8: Its mention of Jesus Christ seems gratuitous; the precise force of the time references is not clear.[12]

Verse 9: Its mention of "strange teachings" and "foods" has provided bases for endless discussions, some of which touch on the Eucharist.[13]

Verse 10: The nature of the "altar" has been the cause of much controversy as well; again, some of it touches on the Eucharist.[14]

Verse 13: The point the author wishes to make with the emphasis on the need to go "outside the camp" is much debated.[15]

Verse 15: The precise nature of the "sacrifice of praise" has

---

12   Attridge, *The Epistle to the Hebrews*, 393.

13   Attridge, *The Epistle to the Hebrews*, 393–396.

14   Attridge, *The Epistle to the Hebrews*, 396–397.

15   Attridge, *The Epistle to the Hebrews*, 398–399.

been discussed, again with reference to the Eucharist in some cases.[16]

It would seem desirable to discuss these cruces later in this paper, from the standpoint of the *tôdâ* (Part II) and from the standpoint of the Latin Rite Mass of the Roman Catholic Church (Part III).

A Request for Prayer (Heb. 13:18–19)

These two verses contain a request for prayer. A translation follows:

> Pray for us: for we are persuaded that we have a clear conscience, desiring to behave well in all matters. I in particular urge you to do this so that I may be restored to you all the sooner.

The plural has been interpreted as "authorial," that is, the author is speaking for himself alone, as he does elsewhere in the epistle.[17] But in view of the apparent reference in v. 23 to Timothy's release from prison, it seems more appropriate to view it as a genuine plural. This gives to the verses a more justifiable tone, avoiding connotations of self-pitying pleading. The author thinks that not only he, but his fellow Christians in prison as well, are there unjustly. In v. 19 he personally hopes that, as an individual, the prayer which he requests may result in his visiting the addressees sooner than he could otherwise foresee.

Blessing and Glory (Heb. 13:20–21)

This passage contains a benediction (vv. 20–21a) and a doxology (v. 21b). A natural question is whether this passage serves to end the theological content of the epistle and is to be linked structurally with this general content somehow, or structurally is part of chapter 13.[18]

From the structure given above, the present writer would opt for the latter position. The death of Jesus is clearly the center of the chapter. This death stands within the frame indicated by the word "leaders." Before the verse in which the word "leaders" occurs (v. 7), there occur two sections, vv. 1–5a and vv. 5b–6, each with its distinct physiognomy. Hence, it would seem reasonable, in a work so obviously crafted with care, that two sections should follow the verse in which the word "leader" occurs (v. 17). These are vv. 18–19 and vv. 20–21.

This does not prevent the benediction and doxology of vv. 20–21 from also serving as a fitting conclusion to an intensely theological writing. The verses in question are extraordinarily rich:

---

16   Attridge, *The Epistle to the Hebrews*, 399–401.

17   Heb. 5:11; 6:9. See Attridge, *The Epistle to the Hebrews*, 402–403. In Heb. 4:13 the author seems to be speaking for himself and all Christians.

18   For a view linking it with other epistles, see Attridge, *The Epistle to the Hebrews*, 404–405.

Now may the God of peace, the one who led up from the dead
the great shepherd of the sheep in the blood of the eternal covenant, our Lord Jesus, provide you with every good thing to do
his will, as he brings about in you that which is pleasing before
him through Jesus Christ, to whom be glory for ever. Amen.

The word, "Amen," is a fitting conclusion to the contents of the chapter as a
sign of a break with the four verses of a personal nature which follow and which
terminate the epistle.

A proper commentary on these verses is beyond the scope of this paper,
but one question seems worth discussing: the antecedent of the relative pronoun
"whom" in v. 21. Does it refer to God or to Jesus? In the context of the epistle, the
answer would seem to be Jesus. That the phenomenon of glory is proper to God
is taken for granted in the epistle (see Heb. 1:3). But a major point of the epistle is
that the man Jesus becomes the Christ by being invested with God's glory (2:7, 9,
10; 3:3). The explicit mention of "Jesus Christ" immediately before the relative, as
opposed to the use of the simple "Jesus" in the previous verse to refer to Jesus who
was raised from the dead, would seem to indicate this meaning.[19]

The Tôdâ and the "Sacrifice of Praise" in Hebrews

The זבח תודה (*zebach tôdâ* or *tôdâ* for short) is one of the more moving cultic
practices of the Old Testament.[20] This is a type of bloody sacrifice proper to the
worship of the temple which is intrinsically connected with ceremonies which in
themselves are not bloody. These ceremonies consist of a ritual offering and consumption of bread that is accompanied normally by a hymn or hymns of praise and
thanksgiving. These non-bloody ceremonies constitute, with the bloody temple
sacrifice, an integral religious ceremony of public praise and thanksgiving. It is
offered by a Jewish male, priest or layman, as a public act in order to acknowledge
with his friends a signal act of salvation (for example, from war or disease) performed by God in his favor. This signal act of salvation can be of the past or of the
future. In the latter instance, of course, it is a sign of trust in God's saving designs
on his behalf.

The full expression, *zebach tôdâ*, and the abbreviated expression, *tôdâ*, occur
a number of times in the Hebrew text of the Old Testament. The basic texts are
found in Leviticus.[21] There are also several important occurrences in the Psalms.

---

19 For the present writer the title "Jesus" indicates Jesus' earthly priesthood, while "Jesus Christ"
   indicates his heavenly priesthood in which the earthly priesthood is, of course, subsumed. See
   James Swetnam, "Christology and the Eucharist in the Epistle to the Hebrews," *Biblica* 70
   (1989), 75–79.

20 H. Gese, "Der Herkunft des Herrenmahls," in *Zur biblischen Theologie. Alttestamentliche
   Vorträge* (Tübingen: J.C.B. Mohr [Paul Siebeck], 1989), 107–127.

21 For a full discussion of what is here presented in summary fashion, see James Swetnam, "*Zebach*

Arguments have been mounted to show that the use of *tôdâ* in these psalm texts is "spiritualized," that is, the texts do not refer to physical ceremonies but only to the spirit of the physical ceremonies. But a study of the arguments shows that they are by no means conclusive. There is no reason to suppose that the ceremony outlined in Leviticus was not a regular feature of Jewish life into the Second Temple period and as such plays a part in the prayers of the Psalms.[22]

The Hebrew expression *zebach tôdâ* was translated θυσία αἰνέσεως by the Septuagint translators. There is no indication that the translators distinguished between a "material sacrifice" and a "spiritual sacrifice".[23]

The warrant for the introduction of the *zebach tôdâ* in the present study is that it appears in its standard Greek translation, θυσία αἰνέσεως, in Hebrews 13:15.

This article will argue that, given the occurrence of θυσία αἰνέσεως in the section of chapter 13 framed by the word "leaders," the section is centered on the Christian version of the *zebach tôdâ*. The principal reason for this line of argument is the fact that the three aspects of the *zebach tôdâ* are found in the section, delineated with reasonable clarity. Verses 9–10 refer to the ritual consumption of bread; vv. 11–13 refer to the bloody sacrifice; vv. 15–16 refer to the accompanying hymns and prayers. The central element is the bloody sacrifice of Jesus; the bloody or expiatory aspect is explicitly mentioned.

The *zebach tôdâ* has been modified, of course. It is no longer a Jewish ceremony, but a Christian ceremony. To emphasize this change, the fact that Jesus suffered "outside the camp/gate" is repeated. This not only indicates the connection of Jesus' sacrifice with the expiatory offering of the Old Testament, but serves as a metaphor for the change from Judaism to Christianity.[24] That is to say, those who, with regard to the fourth crux mentioned above, hold that the emphasis on going "outside the camp/gate" refers in part to a going out of the world of Judaism, would seem to be correct. The Old Testament matrix still serves as the recognizable basis for the sacrifice, but the content has been radically changed, and the image of going out of the camp is used, in part, to indicate this.

The fact that the author of Hebrews seems to make use of the three aspects of the *tôdâ* would seem to indicate several things:

First, that the *tôdâ* was in use among the Jews of the time as part of their own ritual. To assume that the author of Hebrews invokes it as part of an exercise in archaizing seems improbable, given the way he seems to presume the contemporary

---

Tôdâ [זבח תודה] in Tradition. A Study of 'Sacrifice of Praise' in Hebrew, Greek and Latin", *Filologia Neotestamentaria* 15 (2002): 65–86.

22   Swetnam, "*Zebach tôdâ* in Tradition," 76.

23   Swetnam, "*Zebach tôdâ* in Tradition," 77–78.

24   Lane, *Hebrews 9–13*, 545–546.

existence of the Levitical priesthood in chapter 7 and the contemporary existence of those "serving the tent," that is, the temple (v. 10).

Secondly, it indicates that the *tôdâ* was the background, or at least *a* background, for Jesus as he instituted the Eucharist.[25] Otherwise the coincidence between the three aspects of the *tôdâ* and these three aspects in regards to the Eucharist would seem highly improbable—the Eucharist involving, as it does, among other things, the consumption of food, the bloody sacrifice of Christ, and the use of verbal prayer/hymnody.

Finally, the *tôdâ* is used in Hebrews 13 in the same integrity that it has in Leviticus 7, that is, there is no indication that the bloody death of Jesus is being "spiritualized," and thus there is no reason to think that the other two aspects are being "spiritualized" either.

These general considerations are not sufficient to settle the controversies in regards to vv. 9, 10, and 15, mentioned above, but would seem to warrant a renewed investigation of these alleged allusions.

Specifically, in v. 9, the contrast is not between foods and non-foods as a means of strengthening the heart, but between Christian food and non-Christian food. That is to say, the relative clause beginning ἐν οἷς is restrictive, not non-restrictive.[26] In v. 10, the "eating" indicated by φαγεῖν is physical, and the altar is the eucharistic table.[27]

In v. 15, the use of the term θυσία αἰνέσεως in connection with the phrase, "that is, fruit of lips which confess his name," has been taken as a certain indication of the "spiritualized" interpretation being given to the "sacrifice of praise" in the verse. However, a "sacrifice of praise," taken in the restricted sense indicated here, given the context, of necessity takes in the other two aspects by implication. There are other difficulties with this "spiritualized" interpretation. The phrase διὰ παντός in the Old Testament is used, for, among other things, an indication of the

---

25 For a preliminary and incidental attempt to situate the *tôdâ* as background for the institution of the Eucharist in Matthew and Mark, see James Swetnam, "The Crux at Hebrews 5:7–8, *Biblica* 81 (2000): 347–361.

26 Against Attridge, *The Epistle to the Hebrews*, 393–394; Lane, *Hebrews 9–13*, 530–537. Ellingworth (*The Epistle to the Hebrews*, 708) makes this interesting observation: "The parallel with [the use of βρῶμα] in 9:9f suggests that the reference is to the place of food in the Levitical cultus," but does not elaborate. As is clear from the mass of material marshaled by Lane, the background for this discussion is complicated. The interpretation involving the *tôdâ* which is being proposed in the present paper is intended to provide a new and perhaps decisive element in the discussion.

27 Against Attridge, *The Epistle to the Hebrews*, 396: "As the exposition develops it becomes clear that 'altar' is used in a symbolic fashion typical of the early church to refer to the sacrifice of Christ in all of the complexity with which that is understood in Hebrews"; Lane, *Hebrews 9–13*, 538: ". . .[the word θυσιαστήριον] is employed metaphorically for the event of the sacrificial death of Christ outside the city gate." Ellingworth (*The Epistle to the Hebrews*, 708–712) is less categorical and holds for a "flexible" interpretation of θυσιαστήριον. He and Lane give a wealth of references to background material.

occurrence of the daily sacrifices of the temple, where it is appropriately translated "regularly" (Num. 28:15, 23, 24, 31).[28] To translate the phrase as "continually" or "constantly" on the assumption that it refers to a "spiritualized" reality is unwarranted.[29] On the supposition that a distinct ceremony is involved—the Christian "sacrifice of praise"—the translation "regularly" in imitation of the regularity of the temple sacrifices, makes good sense.

This apparently minor detail in the understanding of the text can lead to a major change in the interpretation of v. 16, for it implicitly indicates that θυσία is plural: the sacrifice of praise is to be offered regularly, that is, a multiplicity of sacrifices are to be offered. This suggests that the plural of θυσία in v. 16 could refer appropriately back to the θυσία of v. 15. What seems to stand in the way of this is the clause τῆς δὲ εὐποιίας καὶ κοινωνίας μὴ ἐπιλανθάνεσθε ("The doing of good and fellowship do not forget") in 16a. But this clause need not negate the basic reference which the θυσίας of v. 16 has to the θυσία of v. 15: a sacrifice of praise made with fixed regularity and made with a spirit of doing good and fellowship pleases God.[30] The interposing clause, "the doing of good and fellowship do not forget," would be a legitimate addition making explicit what should be understood in any community sacrifice, but in this instance preparing the way specifically for the author's request for prayer in vv. 18–19. The comment, "now with such sacrifices as these is God pleased," is a fitting summary for the whole section comprising vv. 9–15 and outlining the Christian sacrifice of praise.

From Hebrews to the Canon of the Roman Mass

The translation history of זֶבַח תּוֹדָה and θυσία αἰνέσεως can be traced on to the Latin versions of the New Testament for Hebrews 13:15. For the Old Latin, the translations found are *laudes hostias, hostias laudis* and *sacrificium laudis*.[31] In the Vulgate the principal reading is *hostiam laudis*, and the principal variants are *sacrificium laudis* and *laudes hostias*.[32]

A study of the phrase in the Latin tradition would not be complete, however, without noting that the version *sacrificium laudis* is also found in the Roman Canon of the Latin Rite Mass. It occurs in the remembrance of the living:

---

28   Lane, *Hebrews 9–13*, 559–560.

29   Against Attridge, *The Epistle to the Hebrews*, 390; Lane, *Hebrews 9–13*, 522. The translation "continually" could be justified in the sense of "fixed regularity," referring to discrete sacrifices repeated on a constant basis.

30   A case could be made that τῆς δὲ εὐποιίας καὶ κοινωνίας μὴ ἐπιλανθάνεσθε is parenthetical, as, for example, clauses introduced by δέ at 3:4 and 4:13.

31   Swetnam, "*Zebach Tôdâ* in Tradition," 83. A study of the Latin versions of the Old Testament would obviously be useful as well, but in the context of the present article it seems sufficient to consider how the Old Latin and the Vulgate translate the phrase θυσία αἰνέσεως in the context of the interpretation being given Heb. 13:7–17.

32   Swetnam, "*Zebach Tôdâ* in Tradition," 83.

Memento, Domine, famulorum famularumque tuarum
Et omnium circum adstantium,
Quorum tibi fides cognita est et nota devotio,
Qui tibi offerunt hoc sacrificium laudis
Pro se suisque omnibus,
Pro redemptione animarum suarum,
Pro spe salutis et incolumitatis suae,
Tibi reddunt vota sua aeterna Deo vivo et vero.[33]

[Remember, Lord, your people.
Remember all of us gathered here before you
You know how firmly we believe in you
and dedicate ourselves to you.
We offer you this sacrifice of praise
for ourselves and those who are dear to us.
We pray to you, our living and true God,
For our well-being and redemption.][34]

The use of the phrase "sacrifice of praise" in the heart of the Latin Rite Mass would seem to indicate that the Mass was considered as such a sacrifice. This fact does not weaken the case of those who would see allusions to the Eucharist in chapter 13 of Hebrews.

But the use of "sacrifice of praise" in the heart of the Latin Rite Mass might yield a valuable clue to the structure of chapter 13 of Hebrews as well. For the structure of chapter 13 as outlined above seems to mirror the basic structure of the Latin Rite Mass:

> Verses 1–5a mirror the examination of conscience which is part
> of the beginning of every Latin Mass;[35]

---

33   Text and arrangement after C. Giraudo, *La struttura letteraria della preghiera eucaristica. Saggio sulla genesi letteraria di una forma. Toda veterotestamentaria, beraka giudaica, anaphora cristiana* (Rome: Biblical Institute Press, 1981), 345–346.

34   This translation of the Latin found in *Daily Roman Missal*, ed. James Socias (Chicago: Midwest Theological Forum, 1993), 683–685.

35   See J. A. Jungmann, *Missarum Sollemnia. Eine genetische Erklärung der römischen Messe. Erster Band. Messe im Wandel der Jahrhunderte. Messe und Kirchliche Gemeinschaft. Vormesse* (Wien: Herder, 1949), 370–386 ("Confiteor"). Jungmann's treatment is largely centered on the Mass as it existed in medieval times. Much would need to be done to verify a relationship between chapter 13 of Hebrews and the early eucharistic celebrations that were later codified as the Mass of the Latin Rite. But the coincidences between the structure of Hebrews and the structure of the Latin Rite Mass are too striking to ignore.

Verses 5b–6 mirror the second main part of the Mass, the readings from Scripture;[36]

Verses 7–17 mirror the central, sacrificial part of the Mass;[37]

Verses 18–19 mirror the "Remembrance of the Living" in which the phrase *sacrificium laudis* occurs, as cited above;[38]

Verses 20–21 mirror the final blessing given by the priest at each Mass.[39]

Thus, chapter 13 appears to be structured according to a liturgical pattern similar to, if not dependent on, what came to be established as the Roman Latin Rite Mass. Further, the central section of chapter 13 would seem to be dependent on the Jewish זֶבַח תּוֹדָה (θυσία αἰνέσεως, *sacrificium laudis*) for its historical antecedents.

Instead of being an apparent welter of unrelated material, chapter 13 thus emerges as a tightly organized and well-conceived literary unity centering on the physical death of Christ and its sacramental participation by the Christians in the Eucharist. As the concluding climax of the epistle, the chapter would thus seem logically to presume previous discussion of the Eucharist. This has been the contention of the present writer for decades, but progress in his thinking his way into the mind of the author of Hebrews has been slow.[40]

If—granted, a large "if" but one not made recklessly—there is some connection besides coincidence between the early eucharistic celebrations which became codified as the Mass of the Latin Rite and chapter 13 of Hebrews, the discussion of possible eucharistic references would seem to be placed in a new perspective. This new perspective, when added to the new perspective of the *tôdâ*, calls for fresh

---

36 Jungmann, *Missarum Sollemnia*, Erster Band, 484–562 ("Der Lesegottesdienst"). Other elements are treated by Jungmann under this heading at. 563–610.

37 J. A. Jungmann, *Missarum Sollemnia. Eine genetische Erklärung der römischen Messe.* Zweiter Band. *Opfermesse* (Wien: Herder, 1949), 123–332 ("Der Canon actionis").

38 Cf. Jungmann, *Missarum Sollemnia*, Zweiter Band, 194–207 ("Der Memento für die Lebenden"). This part of the Latin Rite Mass occurs within the Canon, but is placed here outside the section devoted to the Canon because the author of Hebrews has chosen to stress the sacrificial, strictly sacramental aspect of the Roman Canon in vv. 7–17. Mention of the remembrance of the living there would have interfered with the three-fold pattern based on the *tôdâ*. The use of the word "pray" (προσεύχομαι) as a request for prayers from the addressees is not unusual in Paul, where it is used in connection with a plea for freedom from danger (Rom. 15:30–31; 2 Thess. 3:1–2). It is also found in connection with "word" (λόγος) (2 Thess. 3:1–2; Col. 3:2–4). Here, in Hebrews, it is incorporated into a presentation of the Latin liturgy.

39 Jungmann, *Missarum Sollemnia*, Zweiter Band, 532–541 ("Der priesterliche Schlußsegen").

40 James Swetnam, "A Suggested Interpretation of Hebrews 9:15–18," *Catholic Biblical Quarterly* 27 (1965): 375, n. 8; James Swetnam, "Hebrews 9:2: Some Suggestions about Text and Context," *Melita Theologica* 51 (2000): 163–185.

discussion. With regard to the five cruces involving chapter 13 the following points suggest themselves:

In regards to verse 8, where the mention of Jesus Christ seems gratuitous, and the precise force of the time references is not clear, perhaps the following suggestions may be useful. Verse 7 states that the leaders of the community "spoke to us the word of God" (ἐλάλησεν ὑμῖν τὸ λόγον τοῦ θεοῦ). The use of the verb ties in with the use of the same verb at 2:3. There, the author says a "great salvation" was first spoken (λαλεῖσθαι) through the Lord, confirmed by those who heard it, that is, the first generation of Christians, and is now heard by the present generation, those addressed in the letter. The leaders of the community spoken of in 13:7 are the leaders of the first generation, and their speaking the "word" to "us" is simply another way of saying what 2:3 says. The Lord himself is indicated by this "word" (λόγος), that is the "salvation" spoken of in 2:3.

This would explain why the mention of Jesus Christ at the beginning of 13:8 is not gratuitous. Perhaps the famous crux posed by the temporal sequences of the verse could be explained by thinking of the Jesus Christ of "yesterday" (ἐχθές) as being the Jesus Christ—the heavenly Jesus as distinguished from the earthly Jesus—spoken of by the first generation of leaders, referred to in v. 7. The Jesus Christ of "today" (σήμερον) is the Jesus Christ spoken of by the second generation, referred to in v. 17. But each eucharistic Jesus Christ is "the same" (ὁ αὐτός) and will be the same forever, no matter where the eucharistic *tôdâ* is celebrated.

In v. 9, where the mention of "strange teachings" and "foods" has provided bases for endless discussions, the relevance of "foods" becomes clearer in the perspective of the possible relevance of the *tôdâ* and the Roman Mass. Real food and real physical eating are in question, but the difference is between the Jewish foods and the Christian Eucharist. Likewise, in v. 10, where the nature of the "altar" has been the subject of dispute. In the possible perspective of a Christian *tôdâ* and the Roman Rite Mass, Paul's use of "altar" (θυσιαστήριον) at 1 Corinthians 10:18 in the context of his discussion of the Eucharist takes on a greater relevance.

The supposition of a *tôdâ* background to the Eucharist may also contribute to discussions of v. 13, where the author's point in stressing the need to go "outside the camp" is much debated. The emphasis of vv. 11–13 on the death of Jesus "outside the camp/gate" and the call to Christians to go out to him "outside the camp" is more intelligible in the light of this supposition. Other aspects of the theological connotations of Jesus' death "outside the camp/gate" are, of course, not to be overlooked: the basic symbolism of the rites of expiation for sin and the shame involved in following Jesus outside the traditions of Judaism are of fundamental importance for the understanding of these verses.

Finally, the inadequacy of a "spiritualizing" interpretation of the *tôdâ* in its Christian version as presented in v. 15 should be clearer in the context of possible allusion to the Roman Canon, particularly in view of the play on the singular and plural of "sacrifice" (θυσία) in vv. 15–16.

The Meaning of Hebrews 13

The primary goal of this article was to see if Hebrews 13:1–21 could be made more intelligible, preparatory to seeing if its place in the epistle as a whole could eventually be more securely assessed. This attempt to make chapter 13 more intelligible was made in three successive stages, each of which was based on a perspective.

The first stage approached the text in the perspective of its structure. Any text is presumed to have a structure or at least a non-structure. Determining the structure of a text generates perspectives, for a structure indicates the author's points of view. The structure which emerged from a study of formal criteria as well as content showed that the author was basing his exposition on the centrality of the death of Jesus and its role in Christian liturgy (vv. 11–14). Flanking this central concern were verses concerned with eating (vv. 9–10) and verbal prayer (vv. 15–16). Serving as a frame for all of this were verses which emphasized the role of the leaders of the community (vv. 7 and 17). Verses 1–5a indicated the author's concerns about moral conduct; vv. 5b–6 indicated his concern for Scripture; vv. 18–19 indicated the author's personal reliance on the community in prayer; and vv. 20–21 indicated his concern to invoke God's blessing in Christ on the addressees.

The second stage of the attempt to make chapter 13 more intelligible, approached the central portion of the text, vv. 7–17, from the perspective of the Jewish *tôdâ* ceremony. This resort to the *tôdâ* was justified by the occurrence of the phrase θυσία αἰνέσεως in v. 15. Thus the perspective of the "sacrifice of praise" was used to evaluate the structure resulting from a study of formal indications in the text combined with content. This use of the *tôdâ* perspective seemed confirmed by the apparent coincidence of its three elements—bloody sacrifice, food, and verbal prayer/hymns—with the three elements of eating, bloody death, and verbal prayer resulting from the analysis of structure.

The third and final stage approached the entire text, vv. 1–21, from the standpoint of the Latin Mass of the Roman Rite of the Catholic Church. The justification for this approach was the coincidence of the five sections of these verses with the basic outline of the Latin liturgy: act of repentance; reading from Scripture; central sacramental action; prayer based on remembrance of the living; final blessing. No statement was made about whether the epistle was influenced by the liturgical act or vice versa. The only thing asserted was that a coincidence in so many variables of such a varied nature seems improbable.

The interplay of these three perspectives makes possible a coherent exegesis of the entire chapter. Verses 1–21 are seen as a sophisticated presentation of the eucharistic liturgy of the Church, carefully structured and carefully argued. As such, the verses clearly were intended by the author to provide a concluding climax for the entire epistle. How such a climax is related to the rest of the epistle will require the elaboration of more perspectives which seem to reflect the mind of the author of the epistle in all of its several parts.

Chapter 13 of Hebrews will not become adequately understood until it is studied in detail so that the interplay of its sentences becomes plausibly coherent and until this adequate understanding of chapter 13 is shown to be plausibly coherent in the context of the entire epistle. The present study was written as a help for the first of these goals, that is, to provide a defensible hypothesis for an initial assessment of the chapter's meaning.

Letter & Spirit 2 (2006): 175–188

TRADITION & TRADITIONS

~:~

THE LADDER FROM EARTH TO HEAVEN

~: Guigo II :~

Translated by Jeremy Holmes[1]

Brother Guigo to his beloved brother Gervase: rejoice in the Lord. I am bound by debt to love you, brother, because you first began to love me; and I am compelled to write back to you, because you first invited me to write by your letter. So I decided to send you some things I had thought out concerning the spiritual exercise of cloistered monks, so that you, who have learned such things better by experiencing them than I have by discoursing learnedly about them, may be the judge and corrector of my thoughts. And it is right that I should offer you first of all these beginnings of our labor, that you may gather the first-fruits of the new plant[2]—which you stole by a laudable theft from servitude under Pharaoh[3] and pampered solitude, and called into the well-ordered rows of a military camp;[4] skillfully cutting off the wild-olive branch, you prudently grafted it onto a cultivated olive tree.[5]

---

1   *Translator's Note:* Guigo II (d. 1188) was the ninth prior of the Carthusian motherhouse, the Grande Chartreuse, in the second half of the twelfth century. Neither he nor his order were much concerned to leave a record about his life, and in the history of the order he is largely overshadowed by his predecessor, Guigo I. As a result, the work here translated, his *Scala Claustralium* ("The Ladder of Monks"), has been attributed to various authors over time, including St. Augustine and St. Bernard of Clairvaux. Its popularity has endured, however, and today it is seen as a classic work in *lectio divina*, or the technique of reading sacred Scripture accompanied by prayer. My translation is based on the critical edition of Guigo's work, Guigo II, *Lettre sur la vie contemplative (l'échelle des moines), Douze méditations,* Sources Chrétiennes 163, eds. Edmund Colledge and James Walsh (Paris: Éditions du Cerf, 1970). After the translation was complete, I compared it with the translation given by Colledge and Walsh in Guigo II, *The Ladder of Monks and Twelve Meditations,* Cistercian Studies Series 148 (Kalamazoo, MI: Cistercian Publications, 1981). Where appropriate, I have added further biblical references to the footnotes or omitted references that seem unlikely, and have supplied occasional interpretive comments. The better to serve academic study, this translation leans more towards a word-equivalence approach than Colledge and Walsh. I also attempt to bring out more clearly how the biblical allusions have impacted Guigo's choice of words.

2   Ps. 143:12.

3   Exod. 13:14.

4   Song of Sol. 6:3, 9; Num. 2.

5   Rom. 11:17, 24.

One day, while I was busy with the bodily labor of the hands, I began to think about man's spiritual exercise, and four spiritual steps suddenly presented themselves to my pondering soul: reading, meditation, prayer, and contemplation. This is the ladder of cloistered monks[6] whereby they are lifted up from earth into heaven; although it is divided into only a few steps, its length is nonetheless immense and incredible. Its lower part rests on the earth, but its upper part penetrates the clouds and probes the secrets of heaven.[7]

As these steps differ in name and number, so also are they distinguished by order and value. If anyone diligently considers their properties and functions, the various effects they have on us, and how one differs from and is better than another, he will consider any labor and study spent on them as short and easy in comparison to their tremendous usefulness and sweetness.[8]

Now *reading* is the diligent examination of Scripture with attentiveness of soul. *Meditation* is the studious action of the mind as it searches out the knowledge of hidden truth under the guidance of its own reasoning power. *Prayer* is the heart's devout reaching out to God for the removal of evils or the acquisition of goods. *Contemplation* is a certain elevation above itself of the mind suspended in God, as it tastes the joys of eternal sweetness.

Now that we have described the four steps, we must go on to look at their functions with respect to us.

The Four Steps

Reading seeks the sweetness of the blessed life, meditation finds it, prayer asks for it, and contemplation tastes it.[9] Reading places solid food in the mouth;[10] meditation chews and breaks it; prayer extracts the flavor; contemplation is the very sweetness that gives joy and refreshes. [The function of] reading is in the bark, meditation in the pith,[11] prayer in the request for what is desired, and contemplation in the enjoyment of the sweetness obtained. That one may grasp this more clearly, I will give one of many possible examples.

In reading I hear: *Blessed are the pure of heart, for they shall see God.*[12] Behold, this saying, brief but packed full with a sweet and multiple meaning for the soul

---

6   Guigo's letter is often named from this phrase, "the ladder of monks," or in Latin: *scala claustralium.*

7   Gen. 28:12; Sir. 35:21.

8   Gen. 29:20.

9   A 15th-century manuscript found at the abbey of Melk contains the following wonderful insertion: "Hence the Lord himself said: Seek, and you shall find; knock and it shall be opened to you (Matt. 7:7). Seek by reading, and you shall find by meditating; knock by praying, and it shall be opened to you by contemplation."

10   1 Cor. 3:2; Heb. 5:12.

11   Compare the use of the word *adipe* ("pith" or "fat") in Pss. 80:17; 147:14.

12   Matt. 5:8.

to graze upon, provides, as it were, a cluster of grapes, and when the soul has diligently examined it she says to herself: "There could be something good here. I will withdraw into my heart and see whether perhaps I can find and understand this purity. For [most] precious and desirable is that thing whose possessors are called blessed, to which the vision of God—which is eternal life—is promised, which is highly praised by so many passages in sacred Scripture." Desiring, therefore, to elaborate this more clearly for herself, she begins to chew and break this cluster of grapes, and places it, so to speak, in a wine press by arousing the power of reason to search out what this very precious purity is, and how it can be possessed.

As diligent meditation goes to work, it does not remain outside, does not linger on the surface, but climbs higher, penetrates the interior [truths], and probes each one. Paying close attention, it considers that he did not say, *Blessed are the pure of body*, but *the pure of heart*; for to have hands innocent of evil deeds is not enough unless we be cleansed in mind from wicked thoughts. It confirms this by the authority of the prophet, when he says, *Who shall ascend the mountain of God, or who shall stand in his holy place? He who is innocent in hands and pure of heart.*[13] It also considers how much that same prophet longs for this purity of heart, praying, *A pure heart create in me, O God,*[14] and again, *If I have contemplated iniquity in my heart, the Lord will not hear me.*[15] It thinks how anxious blessed Job was to guard [this purity] when he said, *I made a covenant with my eyes that I would not so much as think about a virgin.*[16] See how much the holy man restrained himself: he shut his eyes lest he should see vanity,[17] lest he should carelessly gaze upon what he would then unwillingly desire.

After [meditation] has studied these and similar [truths] regarding purity of heart, it begins to think about the reward, how glorious and delightful it would be to see the longed-for face of the Lord, beautiful above the sons of men,[18] no longer downcast and despicable, no longer clothed in the appearance[19] given him by his mother, but wearing the robe of immortality[20] and crowned with the diadem given him by his Father on the day of resurrection and glory,[21] the day which the Lord

---

13   Ps. 23:3–4.

14   Ps. 50:12.

15   Ps. 65:18.

16   Job 31:1.

17   Ps. 118:37.

18   Ps. 44:3.

19   Colledge and Walsh render *species* as "earthly beauty," thus taking the rhetorical contrast here as between earthly and heavenly beauty. I have chosen the more basic lexical meaning of *species*, namely "appearance," because I understand the contrast as between unglorified and glorified appearance.

20   Sir. 6:32.

21   Song of Sol. 3:11.

has made.[22] It ponders that this vision will offer that satisfaction of which the prophet says, *I will be satisfied when your glory appears.*[23]

Do you see how much juice has come from the smallest grape, how much fire has arisen from a spark, how much this small mass, *Blessed are the pure of heart, for they shall see God,* has been stretched out on the anvil of meditation? But how much further it could still be stretched if someone experienced approached it! I perceive that the well is deep,[24] but I am still a clumsy beginner and have scarcely found a small amount to draw from it. Inflamed by these fires, incited by these desires, the alabaster broken,[25] the soul begins to have a presentiment of the ointment's sweetness—not by the sense of taste as yet, but as it were by the sense of smell.

Thence she infers how sweet it would be to experience this purity, if simply meditating upon it is so delightful. But what shall she do? The desire to have it consumes her, but she does not find within herself the means of having it; and the more she seeks, the more she thirsts. When she takes up meditation, she takes up sorrow,[26] because she does not experience the sweetness that meditation shows to be in purity of heart without itself providing it. For to experience this sweetness belongs neither to the one who reads nor to the one who meditates unless it be given from above.[27]

For to read and to meditate is common to the good and to the wicked. Even the Gentile philosophers discovered what the main part[28] of the true good consisted in, guided by the power of reason; but since when they had known God, they did not glorify him as God,[29] and placing confidence in their own powers, they said, *We will make our tongue great, our lips are from ourselves,*[30] they did not deserve to obtain what they were able to see. They became vain in their thoughts, and their wisdom was swallowed up[31]—the wisdom that the pursuit of human learning gained for them, not the Spirit of wisdom, who alone gives true wisdom—that is, savory knowledge,[32] which delights and refreshes the soul that possesses it with an invaluable flavor.

---

22 Ps. 117:24.

23 Ps. 16:15.

24 John 4:11.

25 Mark 14:3; John 12:3.

26 Eccles. 1:18.

27 John 19:11.

28 "Main part": *summa* could also mean "height," but I have rendered it in such a way as to credit the Gentile philosophers with only a partial insight.

29 Rom. 1:21.

30 Ps. 11:5.

31 Rom. 1:21.

32 Guigo alludes here to a popular etymology according to which the word *sapientia* ("wisdom") is formed from the combination of *sapidus* ("savory" or "sweet") and *scientia* ("knowledge").

Of this [wisdom] it is said, *Wisdom will not enter a wicked soul.*[33] It comes only from God. And as the Lord has bestowed the faculty of baptizing on many, but has reserved the power and authority to remit sins in baptism for himself alone—hence John said, speaking antonomastically[34] and by way of distinction, *This is he who baptizes*[35]—so also can we say of him, "This is he who gives the flavor of wisdom, and makes knowledge savory to the soul." Words are given to all, but wisdom of soul only to a few; the Lord dispenses it to whom he wills, and when he wills.[36]

The Heart Burning with Love

Seeing that she cannot obtain the desired sweetness of knowledge and experience on her own, and [that] the more she approaches a lowly heart,[37] the more God is exalted,[38] the soul humbles herself, and has recourse to prayer, saying, "O Lord, seen only by the pure of heart, I search by reading, meditating on what true purity of heart is and how it may be had, that by purity of heart I may know you at least to some small extent. I was searching for your face, O Lord, your face, O Lord, did I seek;[39] for a long time I have meditated in my heart,[40] and in my meditation the fire and the desire of knowing you more has blazed up.[41] When you break for me the bread of sacred Scripture,[42] you are known to me in the breaking of the bread;[43] and the more I know you, the more I desire to know you, no longer in the bark of the letter but in the knowledge[44] of experience. Nor do I ask this on the basis of my own merits, O Lord, but in virtue of your mercy. For I confess that I am an unworthy sinner; but even the little dogs eat of the crumbs that fall from their

---

33 Wisd. of Sol. 1:4.

34 Antonomasia is a figure of speech whereby a title or epithet is substituted for a proper name; in this case "he who baptizes" replaces "Jesus."

35 John 1:33.

36 1 Cor. 12:11.

37 Ps. 63:7.

38 Ps. 63:8.

39 Ps. 26:8.

40 Ps. 76:7.

41 Ps. 38:4; Luke 24:32.

42 Luke 24:30–31.

43 Luke 24:35.

44 "Knowledge": Guigo may be playing here on the double signification of *sensus*, which could be rendered either "meaning" (as opposed to the "letter") or "knowledge" (aligned in connotation with "experience").

masters' table.[45] Give me therefore, O Lord, a pledge of the future inheritance,[46] at least a drop of the heavenly rain to cool my thirst[47]—for I burn with love."[48]

By these and similar blazing words, [the soul] inflames her desire; thus she demonstrates her fervor, and, by these incantations, summons her spouse. But the Lord, whose eyes are upon the just, whose ears are directed not only toward their prayers[49] but into the prayers themselves,[50] does not wait until she has finished speaking, but interrupting in the middle of the prayer he thrusts himself in and rushes to the desiring soul, soaked in the dew of heavenly sweetness,[51] steeped in the best of ointments;[52] he revives the weary soul, refreshes her that was hungry, fattens her that was withered, causes her to forget earthly things, marvelously vivifies the self-forgetful soul by slaying her and sobers by inebriating her.

And, as in certain bodily functions the soul is so overcome by carnal desire that she loses all use of reason, and a man becomes, as it were, entirely carnal, so conversely, the motions arising from the urges of the flesh are so overcome and swallowed up by the soul in this exalted contemplation that the body in no way opposes the spirit, and man becomes, as it were, entirely spiritual.

But, O Lord, how shall we discover when you do this, and what will be the sign of your coming?[53] Are sighs and tears the messenger and witnesses of this consolation and joy? If so, this is a novel antiphrasis,[54] and unusual signification. For what agreement is there between consolation and sighs, between joy and tears?—if indeed these should be called tears and not rather the overflowing abundance of interior dew infused from above as a proof of interior cleansing and a purification of the exterior man; so that as in the baptism of infants an exterior washing signifies and represents the washing of the interior man, so here, conversely, an interior washing gives rise to an exterior cleansing.

O happy tears, that purify interior stains and extinguish the flames of sins! Blessed are you who so weep, for you shall laugh.[55] Recognize in these tears, O

---

45 Matt.15:27.

46 2 Cor. 1:22, 5:5; Eph. 1:14.

47 Luke 16:24.

48 Song of Sol. 2:5.

49 Ps. 87:3, *ad precem* ("toward their prayers").

50 Ps. 33:16; 1 Pet. 3:12, *in precem* ("into the prayers").

51 Song of Sol. 5:2; Gen. 27:28.

52 Song of Sol. 4:14; Amos 6:6.

53 Matt. 24:3. It is worth noting here that the tradition distinguishes three "comings" of Christ: the first coming is the Incarnation, the last is the coming in glory at the end of time (the original context of Guigo's Matthean allusion), and in between these is his invisible coming in grace to the individual believer.

54 Antiphrasis is the use of an expression where its exact opposite would be appropriate, usually intended to produce an ironic or humorous effect.

55 Matt. 5:5.

soul, your spouse, and embrace the one whom you desired, inebriate yourself now with a torrent of pleasure,[56] suck the honey and milk[57] of consolation from the breast.[58] These are the marvelous little gifts and comforts that your spouse brings and bestows upon you, namely groans and tears. He brings you for your drink tears in measure.[59] Let these tears be for you bread day and night,[60] bread that strengthens a man's heart,[61] and sweeter than honey and honeycomb.[62]

O Lord Jesus, if these tears provoked by remembering and desiring you are so sweet, how sweet shall the joy be that comes from open vision of you! If it is so sweet to weep for you, how sweet shall it be to rejoice over you! But why do we divulge such secret conversations to the public? Why do we try to express indescribable affections in common words? The inexperienced will not understand such things, for they would read them more clearly in the book of experience, where the unction itself teaches them.[63] For otherwise exterior letters will not profit the reader at all: reading exterior letters has little flavor unless the tongue takes an interior gloss[64] from the heart.

The Hidden Grace

O my soul, we have prolonged this discourse a long while. For it would have been good for us to be here and to contemplate the glory of the spouse with Peter and with John[65] and to remain with him a long time, if he wished to have built here not two, not three tents,[66] but one, in which we would be together, and together would delight. But now, the spouse says, "Release me, for now the dawn is rising;[67] now you have received the light of grace and the visitation you desired."

Having given the blessing, wounded the sinew of the thigh, and changed the

---

56 Ps. 35:8.

57 Song of Sol. 4:11. Note that the word order is "honey and milk" rather than the common biblical phrase "milk and honey."

58 Isa. 66:11.

59 Ps. 79:6.

60 Ps. 41:4.

61 Ps. 103:15.

62 Ps. 18:11.

63 1 John 2:27.

64 A reader of Scripture in the 12th-century might have consulted a gloss, a brief line-by-line commentary. Guigo's point is that even a commentary will not help unless the reader already has an "interior gloss" in his heart in the form of spiritual and experiential understanding.

65 The mention of Peter and John at the transfiguration sets the reader up to expect the name "James," which in Latin is *Jacobus*; Guigo takes advantage of this to transition into a mystical comment on the story of the patriarch Jacob. He repeats this pattern the next time he mentions the scene of the transfiguration.

66 Matt. 17:4.

67 Gen. 32:26.

name from Jacob to Israel,[68] the long-desired spouse withdraws for a little while, having suddenly escaped. He withdraws himself as regards the aforementioned vision, as regards the sweetness of contemplation, but remains present as regards governance [of the soul], as regards grace, as regards union.

But do not fear, O bride, do not despair, do not suppose that you are despised because [your] spouse has withdrawn his face from you for a little while. All things work together for your good,[69] and you profit both by his coming and by his departure. He comes to you, and he withdraws from you. He comes for consolation, and withdraws as a precaution, lest the greatness of the consolation should puff you up;[70] lest, having the spouse with you all the time, you should begin to despise your companions, and attribute this consolation no longer to grace, but to nature. The spouse dispenses this grace when he wills and to whom he wills; it is not possessed as though by right of inheritance.

There is a common saying that too much familiarity breeds contempt. He withdraws, therefore, lest he be despised while too constantly present, that when absent he may be all the more desired, that being desired he may be more eagerly sought, that being sought for a long time he may be found at last with more gratitude. Furthermore, if this consolation were never lacking, which in comparison with the future glory to be revealed in us[71] is enigmatic and partial,[72] we might think that we have here an abiding city and would think about the future [city] less.[73]

Therefore, lest we should confuse exile with the homeland, a pledge with the chief part of the reward, the spouse comes and withdraws successively; one moment he brings consolation, another moment he turns all our bed in sickness.[74] For a little while he permits us to taste how sweet he is,[75] and before we fully experience him, he withdraws himself; and thus hovering over us with outstretched wings, so to speak, he encourages us to fly,[76] as though he were to say, "Behold,

---

68   Gen. 32:25–32.

69   Rom. 8:28.

70   2 Cor. 12:7.

71   Rom. 8:18.

72   1 Cor. 13:12.

73   Heb. 13:14.

74   This cryptic phrase is an allusion to Ps. 40:4. As Augustine interprets it, the image is of a feverish man who tosses and turns on his bed unable to find a comfortable position. The meaning is that we try to find our rest in earthly things, but God sometimes deprives us of comfort so that our restlessness will lead us to seek the things of heaven. *Enarrationes in Psalmos* ["On the Psalms"], in *Patrologiae Cursus Completus. Series Latina*, ed. J.P. Migne (Paris: Garnier and J.P. Migne, 1844–1864), 36:457–8.

75   Ps. 33:9.

76   Deut. 32:11.

you have barely tasted how pleasant and sweet I am,[77] but if you wish to be wholly satisfied with this sweetness, run after me in the aroma of my ointments,[78] lift up your hearts to where I am at the right hand of God the Father.[79] There you will see me,[80] not through a mirror in an enigma, but face to face:[81] your heart will rejoice fully, and no one will take your joy away."[82]

But take care, O bride: when the spouse withdraws himself, he does not go far. And though you do not see him, nonetheless he sees you at all times. He is full of eyes before and behind,[83] you cannot hide from him anywhere; he also keeps his spirit messengers around you at all times, like the most perceptive informants,[84] that they may see how you conduct yourself when the spouse is absent and accuse you before him if they detect in you any sign of wantoness and buffoonery.

He is a jealous spouse:[85] if by any chance you take on another lover, if you are more eager to please another, immediately he will leave you, and cleave to other young maidens. This spouse is fastidious, he is noble, he is rich, beautiful above the sons of men,[86] and so none but the beautiful is worthy to be his bride. If he sees any stain in you, any wrinkle,[87] he immediately averts his eyes.[88] He cannot abide any uncleanness. Therefore be chaste, be modest and humble, that you may deserve to be visited frequently by the spouse.

I fear that this discourse may have detained you too long, but a subject matter as fertile as it is sweet compelled me; I did not prolong it of my own accord, but its sweetness drew me unwillingly.

Climbing Step by Step

Let us summarize what has been said, that what was said in a scattered way may be better understood when brought together. As was pointed out in the foregoing examples, you can see how these steps are joined together, and how one comes before another not only in time, but in causation.

For reading comes first, being as it were the foundation, and once it has given

---

77 1 Pet. 2:3.

78 Song of Sol. 1:3.

79 Acts 7:55; Eph. 1:20.

80 John 16:19.

81 1 Cor. 13:12.

82 John 16:22.

83 Ezek. 1:18; Rev. 4:8; 5:6.

84 The critical text edited by Coledge and Walsh has *perlatores*, which would mean agents who bear messages or bring word of something, but many manuscripts have *exploratores*, "spies."

85 Exod. 34:14.

86 Ps. 44:3.

87 Eph. 5:27.

88 Isa. 1:15; Ps. 118:37.

us the subject matter it sends us on to meditation. Meditation then inquires more diligently about what should be desired, and like a man digging in the ground[89] it finds a treasure and displays it;[90] but when it cannot obtain [the treasure] on its own, it sends us on to prayer. Raising itself to God with all its powers, prayer begs for the desirable treasure, the sweetness of contemplation. When this comes, it rewards the labors of the three previous [steps], as it inebriates the thirsty soul with the dew of heavenly sweetness.

Reading has to do with exterior exercise; meditation has to do with interior understanding; prayer has to do with desire; contemplation is beyond all comprehension. The first step pertains to beginners, the second to the proficient, the third to the devout, and the fourth to the blessed.

Furthermore, these steps are interconnected and mutually supportive in such a way that the preceding steps benefit one little or not at all without the subsequent steps, while the subsequent steps can never or rarely be reached without the preceding ones. For what good does it do to spend all our time in continual reading, running through the lives and writings of the saints, if we do not draw out the sap by chewing and re-chewing, and transfer it into the deepest recesses of our heart by swallowing it down, that by means of them we may consider our own condition and strive to imitate the works of those whose deeds we desire to read so often?

But how shall we think about these things, or how shall we be on our guard lest by meditating on false or useless things we overstep the boundaries laid down by the holy fathers[91] unless we have previously been instructed about these things either by what we read or what we hear? For hearing pertains in a certain way to reading. Hence we often say that we have read not only the books that we read to ourselves or to others but also those we hear read by a teacher.

Similarly, what good does it do a man to see by meditation what he should do if he does not gain strength to do it by the help of prayer and the grace of God? For indeed, every best and perfect gift is from above, coming down from the Father of lights;[92] without him we can do nothing, but he himself works in us,[93] although not altogether without us. *For we are co-workers with God,*[94] as the apostle says. For God desires that we should pray to him; he desires that when grace comes and knocks at the door[95] we should open the inner recess of our will and consent to it.

He demanded this consent of the Samaritan woman, when he said, *Call your*

---

89   Prov. 2:4.

90   Matt. 13:44.

91   Prov. 22:28.

92   James 1:17.

93   Phil. 2:13.

94   1 Cor. 3:9.

95   Rev. 3:20.

husband,[96] as though to say, "I desire to pour out grace upon you; make use of your free will." He demanded prayer of her: *If you knew the gift of God, and who it is who says to you, "Give me a drink," you would have asked him for living water.*[97] When she heard this read to her by the Lord, so to speak, the woman thus instructed meditated in her heart that to have this water would be good for her, and useful. Inflamed, therefore, by the desire to have it, she betook herself to prayer, saying, *Lord, give me this water that I may not thirst anymore.*[98]

You can see that hearing the Lord's word and then meditating upon it aroused her to prayer. For how could she be eager about her request if meditation had not first inflamed her, or what good would the preceding meditation have done her if the prayer that followed had not obtained what was shown to be desirable? So for meditation to be fruitful, it must be followed by the devotion of prayer, whose effect, so to speak, is the sweetness of contemplation.

From all this we can gather that reading without meditation is arid, meditation without reading is prone to error, prayer without meditation is tepid, meditation without prayer is unfruitful; prayer with devotion obtains contemplation, while to obtain contemplation without prayer is rare or miraculous.

For God, whose power has no end and whose mercy is over all his works, sometimes raises up children to Abraham from the rocks,[99] when he forces those who were hard and did not want to consent to want it, and so like an extravagant man, he takes the bull by the horn, as the saying goes, when he thrusts himself in uninvited, when he pours himself out unsought. Even though we read that this has happened to some [people], as [it did] to Paul[100] and some others, still we should not take such [graces] for granted by tempting God, as it were; rather we should do what pertains to us, namely read and meditate on God's law, pray to him that he may strengthen our weakness[101] and look [kindly] upon our imperfect [efforts], as he himself teaches us to do when he says, *Ask and you shall receive, seek and you shall find, knock and it shall be opened to you.*[102] For now *the kingdom of God suffers violence, and violent men take it away by force.*[103]

The Perfection of the Blessed Life

By means of the distinctions made here one can perceive the properties of the aforementioned steps, how they are interrelated, and what each of them does in

---

96 John 4:16.

97 John 4:10.

98 John 4:15.

99 Matt. 3:9.

100 Acts 9, 22, 26, and Gal. 1.

101 Rom. 8:26.

102 Matt. 7:7.

103 Matt. 11:12.

us. Blessed the man whose soul is free from other affairs, who desires always to go over and over these four steps, who sells all that he has and buys the field wherein is hidden the desirable treasure,[104] namely to be free and to see how sweet is the Lord.[105]

The one who has labored on the first step, has pondered on the second, has been devoted on the third, and has been lifted above himself on the fourth—by these ascents which he has arranged in his heart he ascends from strength to strength until he sees the God of gods in Zion.[106] Blessed the one to whom it is granted to remain on this highest step even for a little while, who can truly say: "Behold, I experience the grace of God; behold, with Peter and John[107] I contemplate his glory on the mount; behold, with Jacob I delight in the embraces of beautiful Rachel."

But let this man take heed after this contemplation, which has raised him up even to heaven, lest he fall by disorderly conduct[108] even to the abyss; lest, after so great a visitation, he turn back to the wanton actions of the world and the allurements of the flesh. But since the weak gaze of the human mind cannot endure the brilliance of the true light for very long, let him descend in a gentle and orderly fashion to one of the three steps by which he ascended. Let him linger alternately, now on one and now on another, as he freely chooses in light of the time and place—since, as it seems to me, he is closer to God the further he is from the first step. But alas! How fragile and pitiable the human condition!

Thus we see clearly by the guidance of reason and the witness of the Scriptures that the perfection of the blessed life is contained in these four steps, and that man's spiritual exercise should revolve around them. But who is there who perseveres in this way of life? "Who is he, and we shall praise him."[109] Many find it within themselves to will, but few to accomplish.[110] Would that we were among those few!

Now there are four reasons that commonly draw us back from these steps, namely *inevitable necessity, useful and upright activities, human weakness,* and *worldly frivolity.* The first is excusable, the second tolerable, the third pitiable, and the fourth blameworthy. And blameworthy indeed: if a man draws back from his

---

104 Matt. 13:44.

105 Pss. 33:9; 45:11.

106 Ps. 83:6–8.

107 As before, Guigo names Peter and John at the scene of the transfiguration, and then uses the name of James (*Jacobus*) to transition into a mystical comment on the story of the patriarch Jacob.

108 "Disorderly conduct": *inordinato casu* would most literally mean "by a disordered fall." Coledge and Walsh render it as "violently."

109 Sir. 31:9.

110 Rom. 7:18.

intended course of action for such reasons, it would have been better never to have known the grace of God than to draw back after he knew it.

For what excuse will he have for his sin?[111] Can the Lord not justly say to him: "What more should I have done for you that I did not do?[112] You were not, and I created you; you sinned and made yourself the devil's servant and I redeemed you; you ran about in the world with wicked men[113] and I chose you;[114] I had given you favor in my sight and had desired to make my dwelling with you,[115] and you indeed have despised me, and you have cast behind you not only my words but me,[116] and have gone after your desires."[117]

But O my God, good, pleasant and meek, sweet friend, wise counselor, strong helper, how unfeeling, how rash is the one who casts you out, who drives so humble and meek a guest from his heart! O how unhappy and ruinous an exchange, to cast out his creator and receive instead perverse and harmful thoughts, so suddenly to hand over the hidden chamber of the Holy Spirit, the heart's hidden [place], to be trampled by unclean thoughts and swine—[this heart] which just a little before was contemplating heavenly joys![118] The spouse's footprints are still warm in the heart, and already adulterous desires are admitted. It is unfitting and indecent that the ears that just now heard the words which man is not permitted to speak[119] should so quickly bend to hear fables and slander,[120] that the eyes that just now were baptized with sacred tears should suddenly turn to gaze on vanities, that the tongue that just now sang the sweet nuptial song, that reconciled the bride with [her] spouse by its fiery and persuasive words and brought her into the wine cellar,[121] should turn again to immodest speech, to buffoonery, to devising treacheries, to slander. Far be it from us, Lord! But if we do fall back into such things out of human weakness, let us not despair because of it but let us run back again to the merciful doctor who raises the needy from the earth and lifts the poor out of the

---

111 John 15:22.

112 Isa. 5:4.

113 Ps. 11:9.

114 Isa. 43:7–11.

115 John 14:23.

116 Ps. 49:17.

117 Sir. 18:30.

118 Matt. 7:6.

119 2 Cor. 12:4.

120 2 Tim. 4:4.

121 Song of Sol. 2:4.

dunghill,[122] and he who does not desire the death of the sinner[123] will again cure and heal us.[124]

Now it is time for me to end this letter. Let us all pray to God that he may mitigate for the present the impediments that draw us back from contemplating him, and do away with them entirely in the future, leading us on by these steps from strength to strength until we see the God of gods in Zion,[125] where the elect will not perceive the sweetness of divine contemplation drop by drop and intermittently, but, in a torrent of pleasure, will unceasingly have that joy which no one will take away,[126] and unchangeable peace, peace in the selfsame.[127]

You therefore, my brother Gervase, if ever it is given you from above to ascend to the uppermost level of these steps, remember me and pray for me when things are going well for you. Thus curtain draws curtain,[128] and he who hears let him say: Come.[129]

---

122 Ps. 112:7.

123 Ezek. 33:11.

124 Hos. 6:2.

125 Ps. 83:8.

126 John 16:22.

127 Ps. 4:9.

128 Exod. 26.

129 Rev. 22:17. Guigo is cryptic in this last sentence because he is abbreviating a standard set of allusions. A traditional mystical interpretation understood the curtains of the Temple as representing a holy person, and just as one curtain draws another curtain after it, so one holy person can draw another after him by his good example or prayers. This allusion is often paired with the reference to Revelation, which is interpreted to mean that the one who has heard the divine invitation to the heavenly banquet should then extend that invitation to others. Guigo's readers are familiar enough with these traditions that he feels no need to spell them out.

Letter & Spirit 2 (2006): 189–202

The Word, Scripture, and Tradition

∾: Hans Urs von Balthasar :∾

Scripture is the Word of God that bears witness to God's Word. The one Word therefore makes its appearance as though dividing into a Word that testifies and into a Word to whom testimony is given. The Word testified to is Jesus Christ, the eternal Word of the Father, the Word who took flesh in order to witness, represent, and be, in the flesh, the truth and life of God.

The entire revelation concerning salvation is ordered to this manifestation of the Word, as to a central point—in a forward direction in the apostles and in the whole history of the Church to the end of time, in a backward direction in the Old Testament revelation in word and history, backward to the Law and the prophets and even to the creation; for God upholds all things by the Word of his power (Heb. 1:3), creates all things through, for, and by his Word. The Word is at the head of all things and by him all things consist (Col. 1:16–17); and not only is the Word the divine *Logos* [Word], for the Son of Man is the first and the last (Rev. 1:18).

The testifying Word is the sequence of Scripture from Genesis to the Apocalypse which accompanies the progressive revelation of the Word in the flesh and which reflects it as if a mirror—a function which distinguishes[1] it from the former Word. The word of revelation is the Word in the mode of action: God is apprehended in the act of self-communication. The word of Scripture is the Word in the mode of contemplating his own action, recording and elucidating it, something which can only be performed properly and perfectly by the Word himself, since God alone compasses the entire range of his revelation; and only he can assign a valid human expression for it.

The word of revelation is primarily the Son, who speaks of the Father through the Holy Spirit. The word of Scripture is primarily the work of the Holy Spirit who, as Spirit of the Father, effects, accompanies, illumines, and clarifies the Son's incarnation (before and after the event), and who, as Spirit of the Son, embodies his self-manifestation in permanent, timeless forms.

At first sight, therefore, the two lines of the testified and the testifying Word seem to run parallel, but this appearance is deceptive. For both forms of the Word are ultimately the one Word of God testifying to itself in the one revelation.

---

1   In this distinction, we part company with many Protestants. Scripture is not identical with revelation. And although it is truly God's Word, it is so only in the mode of testifying to his revelation. Scripture is, in fact, only the mode of God's self-witness in words, while there are besides other modes of his self-witness.

The Testifying Word and the Word Testified

Two sets of considerations can help clarify this concept. First, there are, it is true, certain passages in which the contrast between the two forms of the Word is plainly evident. In the Gospel, for example, the Lord speaks, acts, and suffers without reference to the written account, that is, to the Gospel. This account was written down only later by eyewitnesses under the guidance of the Holy Spirit, who is already active here as the Spirit of the Church. The Spirit has become, as it were, the most attentive hearer of the Word, but who, because he himself is a divine Person, sets down the divine truth in writing such as he heard it as Spirit and as he deems it important for the Church.

The same is true for all that the apostles did and for the book of the Acts, as well as for all the historical books of the Old Testament, although the two forms of the Word are far less distinct in the prophets and in the Apocalypse. It is true, of course, that even then the Word may first have come to the prophets personally, in a "private" revelation, and the publication made subsequently, in which case it makes no difference whether this revelation was first oral and afterward put into writing, or whether, on occasion, it was taken in writing form from the outset.

Revelation to the prophets and promulgation by the prophets tend to merge together, and form virtually a single act of revelation effected by the Spirit in the service of the coming or past incarnation of the Son. Both acts constitute so complete a unity that there is no reason to postulate a revelation prior to its committal to writing, as, for instance, in the sapiential books where the revelation is transmitted directly to the pen of the inspired writer.

The same is true for the epistles of the New Testament. Admittedly, in the seven letters of the Apocalypse, a certain distinction is required inasmuch as the Spirit first dictates the letters to the churches to the apostle John who then, either at once or at some later time, writes them down; the same is not true of the other epistles. Yet we must not overlook the expository, quasi-contemplative character of both the sapiential books and the apostolic epistles. Just as the former interprets the history of the Jews and their law for the people of God, so does the later interpret the Gospel for the Church. The upshot is that the relationship between the testified and the testifying Word is a fluid one, varying from clear contrast to actual identity. Revelation, then, is effected partly before the writing, partly in the actual writing; in other words, Scripture participates in God's self-revelation in Jesus Christ through the Spirit.

The second line of thought takes us deeper, and definitely rules out the idea of a parallelism between the testified and the testifying Word. The central Word, which God speaks and which comprises, as their unity and end, all the manifold words of God, is Jesus Christ, the incarnate God. He, however, made his appearance in the sign of obedience, to fulfill the will of the Father, and thereby to redeem and justify the creation.

He fulfills it inasmuch as he lets his earthly life as Word made flesh be fashioned, step by step, by all the forms of the Word in the Law and the prophets. His life is a fulfilling of Scripture.

Therefore, he assimilates the scriptural Word into his own life, making it live and there take flesh, become wholly actual and concrete. As his life proceeds, two things stand out: the Word more and more becomes flesh, inasmuch as he imparts to the abstract nature of the Law and the expectancy of prophecy the character of a divine, factual presence, and the flesh becomes more and more Word, inasmuch as he increasingly unifies the scriptural words in himself, making his earthly life the perfect expression of all the earlier revelations of God. He is their living commentary, their authentic exposition, intended as such from the beginning. He fulfills not only the Word of the Father coming down from heaven, but equally the Word stored up for him in history and the tradition of Scripture—the Word, that is to say, both in its vertical and horizontal provenance.

If he, as the One finally come, is the complete, definitive fulfillment, he is also, as a living person, the progressive, continual fulfillment. And since he is both of these in one, and always remains such, the possibility ensues of there being Scripture even after him, though of quite a different character. The Law and the prophets were like the formal presignifying of the Word that would, at some time, become man: they were God's Word in human form and, indeed, the adequate expression of revelation, a Word not to be superseded or regarded as of merely relative significance.

Jesus, the "Compendium of all the Scriptures"

In this respect, the word of the Old Testament served to define exactly the point of mediatorship, the place and the form in which God was to become accessible to man and of service to him. It was not without reason, then, that the Law drawn up for the men of that time had as one of its functions the foreshadowing of the Eucharist of the New Testament; see, for example, Psalm 118.

And, although Jesus made his life as man the compendium of all the Scriptures, and realized in himself all its promises of eternal life (John 5:39–40), still there can be a Scripture subsequent to him. This fact is proof that the fulfillment of the Father's decree does not imply its annihilation and that Jesus' fulfillment is not a conclusion (as in human affairs) but rather a new opening (as always with God). He makes fulfillment issue in a new promise so as to remain at all times what he is, namely, the One who ever and again fulfills beyond all expectation.[2]

---

2   "'My words shall not pass away': we may ask whether it is not the case that the words of
    Moses and the prophets have passed away, and those of Christ not passed away, for what they
    prophesied has passed away by being fulfilled, but the words of Christ are ever full, ever in
    process of fulfillment; they fulfill themselves every day, nor are they ever overfilled. It is they, in
    fact, that are fulfilled in the saints, that are being fulfilled, that will be fulfilled in the future. Or
    else perhaps we should say that the words of Moses and the prophets are perfectly fulfilled, since,

The Lord remains in the flesh what he is, the Word. He does not dissociate himself from what had been said before his coming, nor from what he himself has said or from what is said about him. The Gospel is the living doctrine proceeding from him, become Scripture, and abiding in the Church, but also a new "incarnate" Scripture, a living participation in his own corporeal nature (as the Church fathers repeatedly testify), and therefore in his own quality of being inspired. Just as the Word he spoke as man is inspired by the Holy Spirit, so also is the written Word; its inspiration is not something past and concluded but a permanent, vital quality adhering in it at all times. It is this quality which allows the Lord to adduce the Word as proof that, in his fulfillment in the Spirit, he transcends all boundaries, all verbal limitations, in his superabundance of life and power.

If then, the incarnate Son merges all Scripture in himself so as to make it fully what it is—namely the Word of God the Father in the Son—he also sends it forth from himself so as to make it fully what it is, namely, the Word of the Spirit whom he sends out at the end of his earthly course, upon his return to the Father. In both forms, therefore, Scripture is not a testifying word separated from the testified but rather the one Word of God in the unity of his incarnation.

In this connection, the patristic idea that Scripture is the body of the *Logos* receives added significance. If, however, we are not to view it as a merely arbitrary piece of allegorizing, we must place it more precisely in the whole setting of the incarnation. The expression, "body of Christ," can be used in many senses. The basic and primary meaning is the historical body which he took from Mary, in which he lived on earth, with which he ascended to heaven. The final form and purpose of his taking flesh is the mystical, but nonetheless real, body, the Church, the incorporation of humanity into the historical body, and thereby into the Spirit of Christ and of God.

And to make it plain that the historical and the mystical body are not two disparate things but are a unity in the strict sense, there exist two means to effect incorporation, two means which bring about the transition from the first to the second bodily form: the Eucharist and Scripture. They mediate the one, incarnate *Logos* to the faithful, and make him who of himself is both origin and end, the way (*via*); the Eucharist does so inasmuch as he is the divine life (*vita*), and Scripture inasmuch as he is the divine Word and the divine truth (*veritas*).

The Eucharist is the marvelous means of freeing Christ's historical humanity from the confines of space and time, of multiplying mysteriously its presence without forfeiting its unity and, since it is given to each Christian as his indispensable nourishment (John 6:53–58), of incorporating all into the body of Christ, making them in Christ one body through which courses the divine life. Through the

in their true sense, they are also the words of the Son of God, and are always being fulfilled."
Origen, *Commentary on Matthew*, 54, in *Ante-Nicene Fathers*, vol. 10, eds. Alexander Roberts and James Donaldson (Peabody, MA: Hendrickson, 2004), 504.

Eucharist, the Church comes into being as the body of Christ; and while the one flesh of the Lord is multiplied, mankind divided is unified in it. "And the bread that we break, is it not the partaking of the body of the Lord? Because the bread is one, we though many, are one body, all of us who partake of the one bread" (1 Cor. 10:16–17).

Bread from Two Tables

Scripture contains the Lord as Word and as Spirit, in the same marvelous transcendence of space and time, without the Word ceasing to be unique and individual. Just as the Eucharist does not mean that Christ's body ceases to be one, historical body, so his Word in Scripture does not detract from its being present as a unique concrete reality. The two modes of communication have this in common: they universalize the body of Christ without making it any the less concrete.

The universal validity of the words of Scripture is not to be attributed to the abstract and universal nature of general truths of the human order. Scripture makes the incarnate Lord present in a way analogous to that in which the eucharistic body makes present his historical body. Hence, Origen admonishes Christians to approach the Word in Scripture with the same reverence as they approach the Lord's body in the Eucharist. The patristic tradition is continued in these words of the *Imitation of Christ*:

> Two things are needful for me in this life, and without these two I cannot continue to live: God's word is light, and his sacrament living bread for my soul. We can also say that they are two tables set out in the room of God's Church. One is the table of the holy altar; on it lies the sacred bread, the precious body of Jesus Christ. The other is the table of the holy Law; on it lies the sacred doctrine which instructs us into the true faith, and reaches, behind the veil, into the inmost holy of holies.[3]

"The Catholic Church, next to the body and blood of the Lord, deems nothing so sublime and holy as God's Word in sacred Scripture" (Origen). Both of them are made possible only through the historical Christ and his body the Church; they are both exclusively the gift of the Bridegroom to the bride, and for those outside they are always inaccessible and alien. It is recorded of the martyrs that they died rather than surrender the sacred Scriptures to the heathens, just as Tarsicius died to prevent the Eucharist from falling into their hands.

Both forms are express results of the Spirit acting on what pertains to the Son; to the Spirit, is to be attributed equally the miracle of transubstantiation and the formation of the Word in Scripture. Indeed, it is the work of the Spirit to form

---

3   Thomas á Kempis, *The Imitation of Christ*, Bk. 4, chap. 11 (New York: Viking Penguin, 1987), 205–206.

the mystical body of Christ by spiritually universalizing the historical Christ. The profound truth of their relationship is not affected by the fact that Scripture does not contain the Word in the manner of a sacrament. For the Lord is, at all times, ready to give himself to and work in those who receive him in a lively spirit of faith; and he is no less ready to reveal himself in person, as Word and truth, to those who approach the Scripture praying, seeking, and thirsting. *Per evangelica dicta deleantur nostra delicta* ("May the words of the Gospel cleanse us of our faults").[4]

The Gift of the Bridegroom

All this brings out clearly the relationship between Scripture and tradition. The Word of Scripture is a gift of the bridegroom to his bride, the Church. It is destined for the Church and, in this respect, belongs to her; but it is also the Word of God, the Word of the head, and as such it is above the Church. This variable relationship in which the Church exercises control over Scripture, but only insofar as God's Word allows her to do so, is best clarified by the mysterious relationship between bride and bridegroom, a mystery of the divine love. For the more God, in human form and therefore divested of power, delivers himself over to the Church in order to exalt and enrich her, the more must the Church humble herself as his handmaid, and adore, in the Son's humiliation, his sublimest majesty.

If she then recognizes tradition as a source of the faith alongside Scripture, it is far from her intention to evade the authority of the Scriptures by appealing to traditions unknown, perhaps even formed by herself. What she really means is that the letter of Scripture can, after the incarnation, only be a function of his living humanity which, in any case, transcends mere literalness. Scripture itself witnesses to this: "Many other signs also Jesus worked in the sight of his disciples, which are not written in this book ... many other things that Jesus did; but if every one of these should be written, not even the world itself, I think, could hold the books that would have to be written" (John 20:30; 21:25).

Here, the Word that testifies asserts that the Word testified to, the Word of revelation, is infinitely richer than what can be drawn from Scripture. And here the Word after the incarnation is essentially different from the Word before it. The Old Testament Word was only coming, not a Word finally come and fulfilled. For that reason, it could not have been the subject of a "tradition" (meaning, thereby, the expression of the fullness of the Word manifested, a fullness that bursts all the bounds of Scripture.)[5]

---

4   Editor's note: These are the words said silently by the priest as he kisses the book of the Gospels after proclaiming the Gospel during the Divine Liturgy. See *The Daily Roman Missal*, ed. James Socias (Princeton, NJ: Scepter, 1993), 572–573.

5   There was, of course, tradition in the human sense, insofar as the fixing of the word in writing came later and harked back to the traditions of centuries—a normal procedure with ancient peoples. This kind of tradition is a sort of pregnancy whose purpose is the bringing forth of a child fully formed, namely, the word of Scripture. In the New Testament, however, Scripture

Regarding the Old Testament word's expression of the Law and the promises, it was on par with what could have been compromised in ordinary speech and writing—it being always understood that this also could only have been assimilated in faith and through the grace of God who spoke it. The Jews, however, had as an object of faith no other divine revelations to Abraham or Moses, no other divine Word to the prophets, than that contained (whether from the outset or subsequently) in their Scriptures. Consequently, there was, in the old covenant, no tradition as a source of faith: the scriptural principle was similar to that of Protestantism in relation to the New Testament.

For it is not so much the organic character of history, as the Tübingen theologians held, that makes tradition a source of faith from the time of the incarnation, but primarily the uniqueness of the person of Christ and of his relationship to his mystical body, the Church. Except for tradition, the Scriptures of the new covenant would resemble those of the old covenant, having its law and promises; it would not be the Word-body of him who also dwells and works in this Church as the living eucharistic body (not present in the old covenant).

In this, the eschatological character of strict Protestantism, which denies the Mass and transubstantiation, is perfectly logical. The God of the old covenant speaks from heaven in explicit language, but he does not deliver himself up to the people. But Christ delivers himself up to the Church because he has delivered himself up for her on the cross (Eph. 5:2, 25), because the Father delivered him up to the cross for her (Rom. 8:32), because he finally delivered up his Spirit on the cross (John 19:30), the Spirit he breathed on the Church at Easter (John 20:22).

So it is that he delivers himself over to the Church as Eucharist and as Scripture, places himself in her hands in these two corporeal forms in such wise that, in both forms, he creates a means of being present in the Church as the one, ever active, unchanging life, life that is yet increasingly manifold, ever manifesting itself in new, astonishing ways. The Word of revelation infinitely surpasses all that the Word that testifies can possibly contain; and in this superfluity becomes available to the Church in the living eucharistic presence of Christ; the necessary reflection of this vitality in verbal form is the principle of tradition.

Scripture is itself tradition inasmuch as it is a form whereby Christ gives himself to the Church, and since there was tradition before Scripture, and since there could have been no scriptural authority apart from tradition. At the same time, Scripture, as the divinely constituted mirror of God's revelation, becomes the warrant of all subsequent tradition; without it, the Church's transmission and proclamation of the truth would be imperiled, in fact made impossible—and the same is true for her holiness—without the presence of the Eucharist.

The Word of Scripture, as God's Word bearing witness to itself, is essentially

---

is present at the beginning of the Church's history, and is immersed in tradition, which is its vehicle.

threefold, being the Word of God, God's Word concerning the world, and God's utterance to man.

Word of God. It is word, not vision, not feeling, not mere halting speech, such as human speech about God would be at best. A word, that is, of unequaled clarity, simplicity, precision. This character of the Word derives from the two mysteries of the Trinity and the incarnation. Since God has in himself the eternal Word that expresses him eternally, he is most certainly expressible; and since this very Word has taken human form and expresses in human acts and words what it is in God, it is capable of being understood by men. The first would be of no avail for us without the second, the second unthinkable without the first.

The identity of Christ's person in his two natures as God and man is guarantee of the possibility and rightness of the reproduction of heavenly truth in earthly forms, and of its accuracy in Christ. "Amen, amen, I say to you, we speak of what we know, and we bear witness to what we have seen.... He who comes from heaven is over all. And he bears witness to that which he has seen and heard" (John 3:11, 32). But this truth of God, with all its precision, is yet personal (the Word being the person of the Son), and therefore sovereign and free.

The Son is not some kind of mechanical reproduction of the Father; he is that regiving which is effected only by perfect love in perfect sovereignty. For this reason, the translation of the divine Word into a human word is itself, through the Son, sovereign and free, and not verifiable other than in the Son himself. "I am the truth." "No man comes to the Father but by me." Faith, therefore, bringing acceptance of the Word, is demanded in that the truth proclaimed is primarily divine (and so surpassing human understanding) and, secondly, personal, that is to say, brought about only by trusting in the freedom of the divine Person who forms it; for, in fact, the exact correspondence between the divine content and the human expression is inseparable from the person of the incarnate Word of God, being itself the effect of the incarnation.

Christology and the Senses of Scripture

In other words, the relation between the human and the divine in Scripture finds its measure and norm in the relation between the divine and human natures in Christ. And just as the whole of Christ's humanity is a means of expressing (*principium quo*) his divine Person (*principium quod*), this, in turn, is a purely human word, but yet, as such, wholly the expression of a divine content.

This concept illustrates how the much-discussed relationship between the literal and spiritual senses of Scripture is a christological problem, one soluble only on the basis that the two senses are to each other what the two natures of Christ are to each other. The human nature we come into contact with first; it is the medium covering, yet revealing, the divine element, becoming transparent in the resurrection, but never, in all eternity, to be discarded or disparaged. The spiritual sense is never to be sought "behind" the letter but within it, just as the Father is not to be found behind the Son but in and through him. And to stick to the literal sense while spurning the spiritual would be to view the Son as man and nothing more. All that is human in Christ is a revelation of God and speaks to us of him. There is nothing whatever in his life, acts, passion, and resurrection that is not an expression and manifestation of God in the language of a created being.

The perfect correspondence the Son effects between expression and content does not imply that the content, which is divine and indeed God himself, does not surpass the expression, which is in created terms. Christ's divinity cannot be wholly comprehended through his humanity, and no more can the divine sense of Scripture ever be fully plumbed through the letter. It can only be grasped in the setting of faith, that is to say, in a mode of hearing that never issues in final vision, but in a progression without end, a progression ultimately dependent, in its scope, on the Holy Spirit (Rom. 12:3, Eph. 4:7).

Faith, the foundation of all our understanding of revelation, expands our created minds by making them participate in the mind of God, disclosing the inward divine meaning of the words through a kind of co-working with God (1 Cor. 2:9, 16); for this reason, it is the saint, the man most open to the working of the Spirit, who arrives at the closest understanding. He will not do what the ordinary man, so dominated by original sin, does almost unawares, yet with such desperate persistence. The ordinary man will confine the meaning of God's Word within human bounds, admitting its truth only to the extent that it corresponds to human forms of thought and ways of life, and content himself with the meaning he has managed to elicit at some time or other, as if it was the final one, attempting to do what the Magdalen was forbidden: "Touch me not (that is, do not keep clinging to me), for I am not yet ascended to my Father" (John 20:17).

The idea that one has understood a passage of Scripture finally and completely, and has drawn out all that God meant in it, is equivalent to denying that it is the Word of God and inspired by him. For the effect of inspiration is not to be seen principally in the absence of error from Scripture, which is only a by-product of inspiration—many a book is free from error without thereby being inspired. Inspiration involves a permanent quality, in virtue of which the Holy Spirit as *auctor primarius* ("primary author") is always behind the word, always ready to lead to deeper levels of divine truth those who seek to understand his Word in the Spirit of the Church, the Spirit she possesses as bride of Christ.

The primary content of Scripture is always God himself. Whether it is narrating historical events, enunciating laws or relating parables, God is speaking and speaking about himself, telling us what he is and about the manner in which he surveys and judges the world. To penetrate into the spirit of Scripture means to come to know the inner things of God and to make one's own God's way of seeing the world.

Scripture, then, as the Word of God, is also his *word concerning the world*, and this, once again, only in relation to its union with the Word of revelation, which is the incarnate Son, precisely because God has made the Son the source of the meaning of the world and sees it in no other connection than in the Son.

In him it was created: the "in the beginning" of creation (Gen 1:1). is to be seen in relation to the "in the beginning was the Word" (John 1:1). Consequently it was created for him as its end, just as, firstly, "we" the believers (Eph. 1:4), and then "all men" (1 Tim. 2:2–6), indeed "all things in heaven and on earth," were to be planned, chosen, created, and reestablished (Eph. 1:10) in him, so that he, as "first and last," holds the keys of all (Rev. 1:18). This he is not only as *Logos* but as incarnate and crucified.

> God did not plan the foundation of the world and bring it to pass without, in foreseeing sin, forming his decree for the redemption of the world, and this through the future incarnation of his only-begotten Son. Redemption, therefore, is not something in the mind of God posterior to the creation of the world. On the contrary, the world was created in the foreknowledge of its need for redemption, for it to be the stage on which redemption should be enacted. Consequently, it is not only through the eternal Word that this world was conceived from eternity and created by God, but, rather, for the sake of the Word, who was to take flesh, who became flesh and dwelt among us.[6]

Since, then, the whole creation is formed in, through, and for the Son, it participates, in its very root, in his formal character as Word. The Son as the Word incarnate is the supreme and dominant law of the world. This idea is like an eminence from which we may look back and see the Word of God—that is, the Law and the promise, the form of the Word selected by God to enshrine his dealings with mankind—as an anticipation and as a kind of basic setting of the incarnation. And we may also go back beyond the Old Testament and say the same of that form of the Word set in the heart of creation itself, in the "nature" of the creature, replacing for the Gentiles, in whose hearts it was engraved, the Law and promise given exclusively to the Jews (Rom. 2:14–15).

In both cases, that of the Jews and of the Gentiles, the presence of the Word of God within them was the center of gravity and ruling principle of their lives. A human being means one to whom God has spoken in the Word, one who is so made as to be able to hear and respond to the Word. The Alexandrian theology, which derives the rational character of the creation (in a wider sense also the rationality of the subhuman creation) from the presence of the *Logos* within it, agrees here

---

6   Valentin Loch and Wilhelm Reischl, *Die Heilige Schrift des Alten und Neuen Testaments* (Regensburg, 1889), regarding Eph. 1:4–5.

with modern philosophers such as Dilthey, Heidegger, and Kamlah, who see the significance of the derivation of *Vernunft* (reason) from *Vernehmen* (perception), or Buber and Ebner, who place the essence of created being in its capacity for and capability of the word.

Maximus the Confessor even declared that there are three stages in the realization of the Word in the world: the Word as nature, the Word as Scripture, and the Word made flesh in Christ. Accordingly, the law of history and that of nature is, ultimately, to be measured by the law of Christ, the final and definitive *Logos* of the entire creation, for man finds the word that expresses and "redeems" him only in hearing and vitally responding to the Word of God in Christ. However secular this human word may seem as culture, art, philosophy, pedagogy, and technology, it can yet be a response to God's call, and so a bringing back of man and the world to God.

Thus, in responding to God's Word, man will also be enabled to "redeem" the world lying deeply hidden in the nature of things, to say what each thing says (Claudel) and, himself infused through Christ by the Word, to express the creation subjected to him. But this ordering exacts from man that the more he approaches the summit, Christ, the more acute should become his perception of the Word's concretization in history. In nature, the Word is present in a permanent state; in history, it is present in individual events, in revelation, it has that actuality and singularity of God which transcends all the laws of historical time, just as God reveals himself in the "one man Jesus Christ" (1 Tim. 2:5) in an ever-present "today" (2 Cor. 6:2; Heb. 4:7) without any diminution or staleness.

Nourished by the Word of God

Scripture, therefore, is *God speaking to man*. It means a word that is not past, but present, because eternal—a word spoken to me personally and not simply to others. Just as the Eucharist is not merely a memorial of a past event but, rather, makes eternal and ever-present the single, living body and sacrifice of the Lord, so Scripture is not mere history, but the form and vehicle of God's Word addressing us here and now.

Man's life, at its deepest level, is a dialogue with God but one in which God's Word to man is infinitely more important than man's to God, and man can respond as he should only through a constant hearing of the Word (contemplation must here be understood as listening). Furthermore, all that God has to say to any man he has spoken once and for all in Christ (Heb. 1:1), so that each of us must individually acknowledge and make his own all the treasures of wisdom and knowledge hidden in Christ (Col. 2:3).

When, finally, we consider that Scripture is the divine testimony made by Christ, it is clear that reading and contemplating Scripture in the spirit and guidance of the Church is the most certain means of discerning what, in the concrete, is God's will for my individual life and destiny, of discovering the means appointed by him. It is here that God has spoken, here that he never ceases to speak in the fullness of his Word. From this source, the preacher steeps himself in the knowledge of the things he has to impart to his hearers, while here each individual believer encounters God's Word addressed to him personally in the most direct fashion. Every word that proceeds from the mouth of God is, as the Lord has said, nourishment for the soul (Matt. 4:4). Thomas Aquinas comments:

> One who does not nourish himself on the Word of God is no longer living. For, as the human body cannot live without earthly food, so the soul cannot live without the Word of God. But the Word proceeds from the mouth of God when he reveals his will through the witness of Scripture.[7]

The Word of Scripture is above any other word concerning God; in virtue of its christological form, it is a word opening into God and leading into him. To phrase this in human terms, it is selected by the Holy Spirit with such art that its precision never involves limitation (as is the case with human utterance), that the single truth it conveys does not rule out any other truth, whether allied, contrasting, or complementary; it never bolts any door but opens all locks.

Even the Church's definitions, though infallible and assisted by the Holy Spirit, do not share this special quality of Scripture, for their significance is mostly to put an end to a period of uncertainty, to solve a point of doubt or controversy, rather than to engender a fresh perspective.[8] However necessary these definitive pronouncements may be for the Church in history, they are by no means the basic sustenance of the Christian.

Since God's truth through Christ is imparted to the soul in Scripture, no dialogue between God and the soul, however interior or mystical, ever takes precedence over Scripture or replaces it. This must be asserted to counter the Protestant tendency to emphasize, on the one hand, the prophetic against the mystical element (Heiler), and on the other, the Word against mysticism (Brunner). To oppose the two is either to revert to an Old Testament idea of the Word, ignoring its aspect as food of the soul and, therefore, its likeness to the Eucharist, or else to misconceive the nature of Christian mysticism, whose only possible norm is revelation as contained in Scripture.

Scripture itself is mystical not only in its being inspired, inspiration being of the mystical order, but also because the whole of it, the Old Testament as well as

---

7   In *Catena Aurea: Commentary on the Four Gospels Collected Out of the Works of the Fathers*, trans. John Henry Newman, 4 vols. (Southampton: St. Austin, 1997), 1:123.

8   As Scheeben justly observes: "A diligent comparison and reflection on the expressions and indications of holy Scripture affords ... a fuller, deeper and more comprehensive understanding of revealed truth than is given in the authoritative dogmatic teaching of the Church. *Handbuch der Katholischen Dogmatik*, 3 vols. (Freiburg: Herder, 1873-1882), 1:122.

the New, describes the continuous sequence of mystical experiences undergone by the patriarchs, prophets, kings, apostles, and disciples. It would be far better for Christian mysticism to recognize in Scripture its true canon, instead of diverting into the obscurities of individual psychology. Christian mysticism is scriptural mysticism, that is to say, a special charismatic form of encounter with the Word. Its function, direct or indirect, is to convey the revelation of the Word to the Church; thus, it is essentially social.

The Spirit lives through the centuries in the Church as the inspired author of the Scriptures, and is ever at work in interpreting the revealed Word, leading the Church deeper "into all truth" (John 16:13); and it continues to act in the "prophets" of the New Testament—those who, along with the apostles, Paul considered foundations of the Church (Eph. 2:10; 3:5; 4:11), in the same manner that he included the prophets of the Old Testament. Admittedly, their writings are not sacred Scripture in the biblical sense, but only because, with the Lord and with his eyewitnesses, God's revelation had already reached his completion; and therefore Scripture, as the form of the Word testifying to this revelation, had likewise been completed.

However, where revelation is concerned, it is best to avoid speaking of a "conclusion." The word is inappropriate since the completion of fullness is not so much an end as a beginning. It is the beginning of the infinite pouring out of Christ's fullness into that of the Church, of the Church's growth into the fullness of Christ and of God, as described in the epistle to the Ephesians. It is, moreover, the beginning of the outpouring of the infinite riches of Scripture into the Church, whose range the whole of world history will never suffice to exhaust.

Every human book is finite in content. Each can be studied, read, committed to memory, until one day it is mastered and no longer needed. But Scripture is the Word of God; and the more we probe it, the more do its divine dimensions broaden and impose themselves. "Strengthened with power through his Spirit . . . you may be able to comprehend with all the saints what is the breadth and length and height and depth"—the four-dimensional space of divine truth!—"and to know Christ's love which surpasses all knowledge, in order that you may be filled unto all the fullness of God" (Eph. 3:18–19).

Letter & Spirit 2 (2006): 203–215

The Sacraments and the History of Salvation

❧ Jean Cardinal Daniélou, S. J. ❧

There are, of course, many aspects under which we may consider the relations between the Bible and the liturgy. First of all, there is the fact of the importance given to biblical texts in the ceremonies of the liturgy; in particular, the first part of the Mass is a liturgy of the Word, the essential content of which is the reading of texts from the Old and New Testaments. But the liturgy is at once word and action—*logos kai ergon*—and the Bible is at once a book and a history. It is this second aspect that we are going to consider—the relationship of the actions that make up sacred history in the Old and New Testaments to the actions that are the sacraments of the Church.

We should, first of all, recall the fact that liturgical tradition continually establishes analogies between sacramental actions and the works of God in the Old and New Testaments. Let us take some examples from baptism and the Eucharist, sacraments which the fathers of the Church continually relate to the essential events of the Bible. In the space available here, it is, of course, impossible to go into the details of this teaching which fills the sacramental catecheses and the liturgical texts; I can only indicate the great themes.[1]

In connection with baptism, let us take the blessing of the water given in our present ritual:

> O God, as thy Spirit hovered over the waters at the very beginning of the world, so that even then by their very nature they might have the power of sanctification. . . .

> O God, as thou didst wash away by water the crimes of the guilty world, and so by the flood didst give us an image of the new birth; for it was the same element that signified the destruction of sin and the beginning of virtue. . . .

> I bless you, O water, creature of God, by the living God, who caused you to flow from the fountain of paradise and commanded you to flow out in four rivers and water the whole earth; who changed you in the desert to a water fit to drink and caused you to flow from the rock to quench the people's thirst. . . .

---

1   I have given a survey of this teaching in my book, *Bible and Liturgy* (Notre Dame, IN: University of Notre Dame, 1956).

> I bless you through Jesus Christ, who in the wonderful miracle at
> Cana changed you by his power into wine ... who was baptized
> in you by John at the Jordan; who caused you to flow from his
> side together with his blood. ... .[2]

Let us go over these analogies. The first is that of the primordial waters
sanctified by the Spirit. As the Spirit of God, hovering over these waters, raised up
the first creation, so the same Spirit, hovering over the baptismal waters, raises up
the new creation, effects our rebirth. The Spirit of God is the creative Spirit.

Christ's word refers to this aspect: "Unless a man be born again of water
and the Spirit, he cannot enter the kingdom" (John 3:5). "Why are you immersed
in water?" St. Ambrose asks the neophyte. "We read: *Let the waters bring forth
living things* (Gen. 1:20). And things were born. This took place at the beginning
of creation. But it was reserved to our own times that water should give you a new
birth by grace."[3]

"Water is the Image of Death"

Here we can begin to see the dimension that is given to baptism by this analogy.
Baptism is of the same order as the creation of the world, because to create is an action properly divine. It is the same Spirit who raised up the first creation and who
will raise up the new creation. The Spirit descended on the waters of the Jordan,
thence to bring forth the new creation which is that of the Man-God. And baptism
is the continuation of this creative work in the era of the Church. The very context
of springtime, in which baptism is administered, expresses this analogy. Spring is
the yearly anniversary of the first creation and of the new creation as well.

Immediately after speaking of creation, the prayer of consecration alludes to
the flood—a new act of God's power and a new symbol of water. The relationship
between the flood and baptism goes back to 1 Peter, in which baptism is called the
antitype of the flood (1 Pet. 3:20–22). Optatus of Milan writes in the fifth century:
"The flood was a figure of baptism because the whole universe, soiled by the tide of
sin, by the intervention of water was restored to its pristine purity."[4] Water is the
instrument of God's judgment; it is water that destroys the sinful world. Baptism
is a mystery of death. It means the destruction of the ancient man, as the flood

---

2   See F. X. Lasance and Francis Augustine Walsh, *The New Roman Missal in Latin and English*
    (New York: Benziger Brothers, 1937), 526–529.

3   *On the Sacraments*, Bk. III, chap. 3, in *Saint Ambrose: Theological and Dogmatic Works*, trans.
    Roy J. Deferrari (Washington, DC: Catholic University of America, 1963).

4   *Against Paremenianum the Donatist*, Bk. 5, chap. 1, in *Optatus: Against the Donatists*, trans.
    Mark Edwards (Liverpool: Liverpool University, 1998). Also in *Patrologiae Cursus Completus.
    Series Latina*, ed. J.P. Migne (Paris: Garnier and J.P. Migne, 1844–1864), 11, 1041. Hereafter
    abbreviated *PL*.

meant the destruction of the ancient world, so that a new creature may appear, washed clean and renewed by the baptismal water.

The essential point here is the symbolism of water. Lactantius writes: "Water is the figure of death,"[5] and Ambrose: "In the water is the image of death."[6] Lundberg has brought out the importance of this theme of the waters of death, which seems strange to us until we remember the text of Paul showing us that baptism is at once death with Christ and resurrection with him (Rom. 6:3–5).

The prayer of consecration brings out the contrast between water as creative and destructive, between the creation and the flood: "It was the same element that signified the destruction of sin and the beginning of virtue." Thus the text of Paul refers to the baptismal rite; this is seen to be a putting to death by immersion in water and a new birth by arising from water. We rediscover the true symbolism of the rite by referring to the realities of the Old Testament.

But we have by no means exhausted the biblical analogies of baptism. The prayer of consecration goes on to speak of the rivers of paradise. Here we enter a whole new field. In the commentaries of the fathers no theme recurs more frequently than that of the analogy between Adam and the catechumen. Adam, after he had sinned, was driven out of paradise. Christ promised the good thief that he would be with him in paradise. Baptism is the return to paradise, which is the Church.

From the beginning, preparation for baptism was seen as the antitype of the temptation in the garden of Eden. St. Cyril of Jerusalem calls the baptismal renunciation of Satan the breaking of the pact which, since the fall, binds man to the devil. Baptism, as we all know, is the destruction of original sin. But the image is not that of the stain that the water washes away; it is the dramatic contrast between our exclusion from paradise and our return to paradise.

This theme of baptism as a return to paradise[7] is as essential to the liturgy as is the paschal theme. Christ is the new Adam, the first to re-enter paradise; and by baptism the catechumen enters also, for the Church is paradise. De Bruyne and other scholars have shown how the symbolism of the ancient baptistries is concerned with paradise, its tree of life, its four rivers. Cyprian writes: "The Church, like paradise, contains within its walls trees loaded with fruit. These trees are watered by four rivers, by which she dispenses the grace of baptism."[8] And

---

5   *The Divine Institutes*, Bk. 2, chap. 10, in *Ante-Nicene Fathers*, vol. 7, eds. Alexander Roberts and James Donaldson (Peabody, MA: Hendrickson, 2004), 57. *PL* 6, 311a.

6   *On the Holy Spirit*, Bk. 1, chap. 6, para. 76, in *The Nicene and Post-Nicene Fathers*, Second Series, vol. 10, eds. Philip Schaff and Henry Wace (Grand Rapids, MI: Eerdmans, 1997), 103. *PL*, 16, 722d.

7   See "Catechese Pascale et Retour au Paradis," *La Maison-Dieu* 45 (1956), 99- 120.

8   *Letter 73*, para. 10, in *The Letters of Cyprian of Carthage: Letters 67–82*, trans. G.W. Clarke, vol. 47 in *Ancient Christian Writers*, eds. Walter J. Burghardt and Thomas Comerford Lawler (New York, NY: Newman, 1989), 59.

Ephraim adds: "It is here that each day the fruit is gathered that gives life to all."[9] No theme is more ancient in the Church than this; it is to be found in the Odes of Solomon, in the Epistle to Diognetus; Papias got it from apostolic centers.

The prayer of consecration then alludes to the rock in the desert. We have come now to the cycle of Exodus; and first we have to consider a theme not mentioned in the prayer of consecration, but in the *Exsultet*. This is one of the most important of all: that of the crossing of the Red Sea; Paul, in 1 Corinthians, sees here a figure of baptism.

Redemption in the Waters of the Red Sea

This figure has recently been the subject of a lengthy study by Martelet.[10] I shall do no more than quote one of the most ancient patristic witnesses, Tertullian: "When the people, leaving Egypt without hindrance, escaped from the power of Pharaoh by passing across the water, the water destroyed the king and all his army. What clearer figure of baptism could we give? The nations are freed from the world; they are freed by water; they leave the devil, who once tyrannized over them, annihilated in the water."[11]

Here again we must be careful not to stop at the images but to discover the theological analogy. Tertullian points it out to us. What is the essence of the great work that God accomplished at the crossing of the Red Sea? The people were in a desperate situation, in imminent danger of destruction. By the power of God alone, a path was opened up through the sea, the people passed through and came to the further shore, there to sing the hymn of the redeemed. This was not a work of creation, nor a work of judgment, nor a work of sanctification; it was a work of redemption, in the etymological sense of the word. It was God who delivered the people, and he alone.

Now, the catechumen is in an analogous situation just before he is baptized. He is still under the domination of the prince of this world and so given up to death. Then, by an act of the power of God alone, the water of the baptismal pool opens and he passes through. And when he has arrived at the other side, he also sings the canticle of the redeemed. In both cases, we are in the presence of a divine act of salvation. And between the deliverance of the Red Sea and the deliverance of baptism, here again intervenes the deliverance of Christ, who made himself the prisoner of death and who, on this same paschal night, by the power of God, broke the iron bolts and the bronze locks of death's prison and arose to become the firstborn from the dead.

---

9   *Hymns on Paradise* 6, para. 9, in *Hymns on Paradise*, trans. Sebastian Brock (Crestwood, NY: St. Vladimir's Press, 1997).

10   Gustave Martelet, "Sacrements, Figures et Exhortation en 1 Cor. 10:1–11," *Recherches de Science Religieuse* 44 (1956), 323–359; 515–560.

11   *On Baptism*, chap. 9, in *Ante-Nicene Fathers*, 3:673.

The figure of the rock from which living water gushed forth introduces us to a new and equally essential perspective. Paul makes this also a figure of baptism: "Our fathers . . . all drank the same spiritual drink (for they drank from the spiritual rock which followed them, but the rock was Christ)" (1 Cor. 10:1–4). In the Old Testament, the outpouring of living water, united with the effusion of the Spirit, is a promise for the end of time, and the texts of Ezekiel and Isaiah referring to this are part of our present liturgy of baptism. Now it is very probable, as Lampe has shown,[12] that the baptism of John referred to this prophecy, for he also connected water and the Spirit. His baptism signified the fact that the eschatological times of the outpouring of the Spirit had now come. (And we know how dear this theme was to the community at Qumran.) But John baptized only in water. It is Christ who gives water and the Spirit.

Christ said this same thing of himself: "If anyone thirst, let him come to me and drink. He who believes in me, as the Scripture says, 'From within him shall flow rivers of living water.' He said this, however, of the Spirit whom they who believed in him were to receive; for the Spirit had not yet been given" (John 7:37–39). We may, with Cullmann, discover an announcement of baptism in the texts of John concerning living water, that of the Samaritan woman in particular.[13] And certainly we must, with him and with the whole of tradition, recognize in the water and blood flowing from the side of Christ the image of water united with the Spirit, for the blood is the figure of the Spirit (John 19:34). And so Christ crucified is the eschatological rock from whose pure side flows the water that refreshes us for everlasting life, the baptism that gives the Spirit.

We should notice in this connection that the gift of the Spirit is essentially connected with the outpouring of water. In the third century we find a tendency to distinguish the rite of water, which purifies, from another rite, the anointing or imposition of hands, which gives the Spirit. Gregory Dix makes use of these texts to distinguish within Christian initiation a sacrament of the Spirit, distinct from baptism, which would be confirmation. But this is contrary to primitive tradition and to tradition as a whole. It is the water, and it alone, that gives the Holy Spirit. The accompanying rites are illustrative only. Confirmation is a different sacrament, connected with spiritual growth and with participation in the ministry.

The biblical themes that we have been considering up to this point have been concerned with water. But, once again, this is not the essence of their relationship with baptism. In a theme such as that of the return to paradise, the mention of water is secondary; the emphasis is much more on the restoration of Adam to the realm of grace for which God had destined him from the beginning and to which

12   G. W. H. Lampe, *The Seal of the Spirit: A Study in the Doctrine of Baptism and Confirmation in the New Testament and the Fathers* (New York: Longmans, Green, 1951), 27–28.

13   Oscar Cullman, "Les Sacrements dans l'Evangile Johannique: La Vie de Jésus et le Culte de l'église Primitive," *Études d'Histoire et de Philosophie Religieuses* 42 (Paris, 1951), 51–55.

baptism restores him. Moreover, in this theme of paradise, the Eucharist appears as well as baptism, and both are closely associated. In the same way, the rock of living water is related to the Eucharist and to baptism as well.

Baptismal Grace and the New Covenant

It is the theological analogy that is essential in every case. This appears also in the other biblical themes which tradition relates to baptism and the Eucharist. For example, let us take that of the covenant. Gregory Nazianzen writes plainly: "We must call the grace of baptism a covenant, *diatheke.*"[14]

The covenant is the act by which God promises, in an irrevocable way, to establish communion of life between man and Himself. Christ realizes the new and eternal covenant by uniting in himself for ever the divine nature and a human nature in such a way that they will never be separated. We should not forget the fact that "the Covenant" was one of our Lord's names in primitive Christianity, following the text of Isaiah: "I have made you: Covenant of the peoples" (Isa. 42:6).

Baptism is our introduction into this covenant. Baptism establishes it by the pledge of God and that of man. When baptism was given in an interrogative form, this pledging formed part of the very form of baptism, which was given in faith and in water, as Justin says.

Later on, this aspect was connected with the pre-baptismal profession of faith: "You catechumens," writes John Chrysostom, "should learn to know the meaning of this word: I renounce Satan. For this word in fact is the covenant (*syntheke*) with the Lord."[15] This pledge is called *symbalon,* "pact," and it is from here that the term came to be applied to the profession of faith preceding baptism. John Chrysostom emphasizes the unconditional and irrevocable character of this engagement of God's: "God does not say: If this, or, if otherwise. Such were the words of Moses when he poured out the blood of the covenant. And God promises eternal life."[16]

We should take note of the allusion to the blood of the covenant poured out by Moses. The Old Covenant was sanctioned by a sacrament, by the sprinkling of the same blood on the people and on the altar, signifying and bringing about a communion of life. It is certainly in reference to this gesture of Moses that Christ, when he took the wine and blessed it, declared: "This is my blood, the blood of the New Covenant," before giving it to his disciples, a sign of the communion of life brought about between them and himself (Matt. 26:28; 1 Cor. 11:25). The Eucharist is truly the new rite which succeeds the Old Covenant and which at once

---

14   *Oration on Holy Baptism*, 8, in *The Nicene and Post-Nicene Fathers*, Second Series, 7:362.

15   *Second Instruction to the Catechumens*, 5, in *The Nicene and Post-Nicene Fathers*, First Series, 9:170. Also in *Patrologiae Cursus Completus, Series Graeca*, ed. J.P. Migne (Paris: Garnier and J.P. Migne, 1957–1866), 49, 239. Hereafter abbreviated *PG.*

16   *Homilies on Colossians* 6 (On Col. 2:6–7), in *The Nicene and Post-Nicene Fathers*, First Series, 13:287. PG 62, 342.

witnesses to and brings about the covenant made by Christ with mankind in his incarnation and his passion.

Here again we can see the irreplaceable value of the biblical analogy. It enables us to see the full significance of eucharistic communion as participation in the life of God, the participation that mankind has irrevocably gained in Christ himself and that is now offered to each man. It connects the Eucharist with Scripture by showing us that the Eucharist continues, in the era of the Church, the divine actions which took place in both testaments. It illuminates the symbolism of the sacramental rites by showing us the partaking of the eucharistic blood as being the supreme expression of communion of life, for blood is the expression of life itself.

And again, as the covenant is our bond with God, it is also our incorporation into the people of God. In the Old Covenant, this incorporation was expressed by circumcision. Cullmann, Sahlin, and many others have shown the connection of circumcision with baptism and the valuable elements which this connection brings to the theology of baptism.[17]

"The baptism of the Christian was expressed in the circumcision of the Hebrews," writes Optatus of Milevis.[18] But Ephesians had already brought out the parallelism:

> Wherefore bear in mind that once you, the Gentiles in flesh, who are called "uncircumcision" by the so-called "circumcision" in flesh made by human hand—bear in mind that you were at that time without Christ, excluded as aliens from the community of Israel and strangers to the covenants of the promise. . . .But now in Christ Jesus you, who were once afar off, have been brought near through the blood of Christ (Eph. 2:11–13).

It is baptism itself that is the new rite of incorporation into the people of God in the Church. But, as other aspects of the sacrament are expressed by particular ceremonies, such as the clothing with a white garment and the anointing, so with this one. The expression of our incorporation into the people of God by baptism is the ceremony of the *sphragis*, the Sign of the Cross marked on the forehead of the candidate.

Ezekiel had prophesied that the members of the eschatological community would wear on their foreheads the mark of the [Hebrew letter] *taw*, the sign signifying Yahweh, the *name* of Yahweh. It seems probable that the Sadocites of Damas actually bore this mark. And the Apocalypse of John shows us the elect as marked with the name of Yahweh, that is, with the *taw*. It is very likely that this was the

---

17 See "Circoncision et Bapteme," in *Theologie in Geschichte und Gegenwart: Michael Schmaus zum Sechzigsten Geburtstag Dargebracht von Seinen Freunden und Schülerne*, ed. Johann Auer and Hermann Volk (Munich, 1957), 755–777.

18 *Contra Parmenianum Donatistam*, Bk. 5, chap. 1, PG 11, 1045a.

sign with which Christians were marked originally as the sign of their incorporation into the eschatological community. Now this sign is in the form of a cross. This is why, in the Greek communities which no longer understood the meaning of the Hebrew letter, it was interpreted as being the sign of the Cross of Christ. But Hermas still says: "Those who are marked with the name."[19]

This leads us to another theme akin to that of the covenant, that of the dwelling, the *shekinah*. Yahweh had caused his name to dwell among his own. This is the mystery of the tabernacle. This presence abandoned the people of the Old Covenant when the veil of the Temple was rent. Henceforth its dwelling-place is the humanity of Christ, in whom the name has set up its tabernacle. And this dwelling-place is in our midst in the Eucharist.

We have already seen the Eucharist as communion, covenant. Now we see it as presence, *shekinah*. As the eucharistic prayer of the *Didache* expresses it: "We give thee thanks, O Father, for thy holy name which thou hast caused to dwell in our hearts."[20] Here the name is the Word, as Peterson has pointed out. But the expression "the name" is the older and the more fitting. For in the Old Testament it is the name, and not the Word, which is connected with the dwelling.

As for the last great aspect of the Eucharist—sacrifice—which is at once adoration, thanksgiving, and expiation, the liturgy of the Mass itself invites us to seek its prefiguring in the sacrifice of Abel, in that of Abraham, and in that of Melchizedek. Here again, the prophets had proclaimed that at the end of time the perfect sacrifice would be offered by the obedient servant, the new Isaac, and the true Lamb. It is this priestly act, by which all glory is forever rendered to the blessed Trinity, which the eucharistic sacrifice makes perpetually present in all times and all places.

The Bible and the Liturgy Are Sacred History

Thus we have brought out the traditional teaching. The sacraments are conceived in relation to the acts of God in the Old Testament and the New. God acts in the world; His actions are the *mirabilia*, the deeds that are his alone. God creates, judges, makes a covenant, is present, makes holy, delivers. These same acts are carried out in the different phases of the history of salvation. There is, then, a fundamental analogy between these actions. The sacraments are simply the continuation in the era of the Church of God's acts in the Old Testament and the New. This is the proper significance of the relationship between the Bible and the liturgy. The Bible is a sacred history; the liturgy is a sacred history.

---

19   *Similitude* 9, chap. 13, in *Ante-Nicene Fathers*, 2:48. See also Jean Daniélou, *The Theology of Jewish Christianity* (Philadelphia: Westminster Press, 1964), 330–331.

20   *The Teaching of the Twelve Apostles*, 10, in *The Didache, The Epistle of Barnabas, The Epistles and the Martyrdom of St. Polycarp, The Fragments of Papias, The Epistle to Diognetus*, trans. James A. Kleist, vol. 6 in *Ancient Christian Writers*, eds. Johannes Quasten and Joseph Plumpe (New York: Newman, 1948), 20.

The Bible is a witness given to real events; it is a sacred *history*. There is a profane history, which is that of civilizations, witnessing to the great deeds done by men. But the Bible is the history of divine actions; it witnesses to the great deeds carried out by God. It is all for the glory of God. And so it is the proper object of faith. For "to believe" does not mean only to believe that God exists, but also that he intervenes in human life. Faith is wholly concerned with these interventions of God: the covenant, the incarnation, the resurrection, the diffusion of the Spirit. And the Old Testament, in particular, is already essentially a sacred history.

This point needs to be emphasized today. For in Bultmann and his disciples, we find a tendency to see in the Old Testament, and in Scripture in general, only a word that God addresses to us here and now. Under the pretext that the divine events are presented in a stylized form, their very historicity is questioned. Demythization has become dehistorization. But Cullmann and Eichrodt[21]—the latter precisely in connection with the problem that concerns us here, that of typology—have brought out the primacy of the event over the word, of the *ergon* over the *logos*. The object of faith is the existence of a divine plan. It is the objective reality of the divine interventions which modifies ontologically the human situation, and to the reality of which faith causes us to adhere.

This history is properly the history of the works of God which are grasped only by faith. It does not consist in reconstituting the historical and archeological context of the people of Israel or of the primitive Church. This is a part of the history of civilizations and is of a different order. Sacred history reaches, beyond the order of bodies and minds, what Pascal calls the "order of charity"—which meant to him, good Augustinian that he was, the supernatural order. It is concerned, therefore, with the supernatural history of mankind, the most important history ultimately, since it is concerned with the final questions of the destiny of man and of mankind, the very depths of human nature.

Thus the Old Testament has as its purpose to recall to us the great deeds that God did for His people. But this represents only one aspect. It includes the Law, but it includes also the prophets. Prophecy is part of its very substance. We must give this word its true meaning; it is not merely prediction, not merely proclamation. Prophecy is the announcement of the fact that, at the end of time, God will accomplish works still greater than in the past. Here the movement of the Old Testament is quite different from that of natural religions. These are essentially, as Eliade and van den Leeuw have shown, the effort to defend primordial energies against the destructive action of time.

It is with the Bible that time acquires a positive content as being the setting in which the design of God is being carried out. But this orientation toward the future is an act of faith, founded on the promises of God. The great Biblical figure

---

21   W. Eichrodt, "Ist die Typologische Exegese Sachgemasse Exegese?" *Theologische Literaturzeittung* 81 (1956), 641–653.

Abraham is quite different from the Greek hero Ulysses. The title of Homer's poem is *Nostoi,* "the returns." The outstanding characteristic of Ulysses is nostalgia, and finally after his long journeying, he returns to the place from which he set out. Time destroys itself. But Abraham leaves Ur of the Chaldees forever and sets out on a journey to the land that God is to give him. For the man of the Bible, paradise and the state of innocence are not the points of departure; they are the end of the journey. Such a man cannot help having an eschatological attitude.

But, wonderful to say, these hoped-for future events are not unrelated to the events of the past. The promises of God remain unchanged. God said to Isaiah: "Remember no more what is past; behold, I will make a new wonder. I will make a path through the sea" (Isa. 43:16–29).

The New Exodus and God's Design

One of the deeds of the past was the crossing of the Red Sea, the act of deliverance by which Yahweh delivered his people from their hopeless condition. The eschatological event will be a new Exodus, a new deliverance, a new redemption. And so we begin to see what is the real basis of typology—as Goppelt and Eichrodt have pointed out—the analogy between the divine deeds carried out in the different epochs of the history of salvation.

Prophecy announces to us eschatological events. The New Testament is the paradoxical affirmation that these events have taken place in Jesus Christ. We have lost sight of the importance of the expression that continually recurs in the New Testament: "so that the prophecies might be fulfilled,"[22] and this is because we have lost the understanding of what prophecy really is. It is because prophecy announces the end of time—and not some one event to come—and because Christ *is* the end of time that Christ fulfills prophecy. What is essential, then, is the fact that Christ is proclaimed to us as being the end of time. This is the meaning of John's gesture: *Ecce Agnus Dei* ("behold the lamb of God," John 1:29, 36). Not: "There is a Lamb of God." But: "The Lamb of God is here."

We should remember here that the phrase, "the *end* of time," is to be taken in its full meaning: not only the end in the sense of the conclusion of time, but also in the sense of the goal of time, the definite and decisive event, that beyond which there is nothing more because there can be nothing beyond it. The paradoxical Christian affirmation is, as Cullmann has well shown, that the decisive event is already accomplished. No discovery, no revolution can ever bring about anything as important to mankind as the resurrection of Jesus Christ. In fact, in the resurrection of Christ two things were accomplished beyond which nothing further is possible: God is perfectly glorified and man is perfectly united to God. We can never go beyond Jesus Christ. He is the final goal of God's design.

But did sacred history stop with Jesus Christ? This is, indeed, what we

---

22   For example, John 12:38; 13:18; 19:36; Acts 1:16.

usually seem to ask. And this is because we do not place the sacraments in the perspective of sacred history. We forget that, although Jesus Christ is the goal of sacred history, his coming into the world is only the inauguration of his mysteries. In the Apostles' Creed, after the mysteries of the past, we speak of a mystery still to come: *inde ventúrus est* ("he will come again"). But between the two there is a mystery of the present: *sedet ad déxteram Patris* ("he is seated at the right hand of the Father").

For Christ's enthronement at the right hand of the Father is only the definitive installation of the incarnate Word, who at his ascension entered into the heavenly tabernacle, in his functions as king and priest. The glorious humanity of Christ, during the whole era of the Church, causes every grace, every illumination, every sanctification, every blessing. And these divine works carried out by Christ in glory are, above all, the works of the sacraments. These constitute the deeds properly divine being carried out in the heart of our world, the deeds by which God accomplishes our sanctification and builds up the Body of Christ. It is in their radiance that all holiness, all virtue, all ministry is developed.

Thus the nature of the sacraments is made clear to us in the perspective of the history of salvation. They are the divine acts corresponding to this particular era in the history of salvation, the era of the Church. These divine acts are the continuation of the acts of God in the Old and New Testaments, as Cullmann has already shown.[23] For the ways in which God acts are always the same: He creates, judges, saves, makes a covenant, is present. But these acts have a different modality in each era of the history of salvation.

What characterizes the era of the Church is, on the one hand, the fact that it comes *after* the essential event of sacred history, the event by which creation has attained its purpose in such a way that nothing can be added to it. The sacramental acts are, therefore, only saving actualizations of the passion and resurrection of Christ. Baptism plunges us into his death and resurrection. The Mass is not *another* sacrifice, but the *unique* sacrifice made present in the sacrament; in this sense it is true that the sacraments add nothing to Christ and that they are only the sacramental imitation of what has already been effectively accomplished in him.

On the other hand, the era of the Church is that in which what has already been accomplished in Christ, the head, is communicated to all men, who form the body. The era of the Church is the time of the mission, the growth of the Church, and the sacraments are the instruments of this growth, incorporating into Christ his new members. As Gregory of Nyssa says: "Christ builds Himself up by means of those who continually join themselves to the faith" by baptism.[24] And Methodius of Olympia shows us how the sacramental life is the continual espousal

---

23   Cullmann, *Les Sacrements dans l'Evangile Johannique*, 85.

24   *PG* 1397c.

of Christ and the Church.[25] We can understand why Cyril of Jerusalem made the Canticle of Canticles the sacramental text par excellence.[26]

But the last characteristic of the era of the Church is that the transformation carried out by Christ actually reaches mankind, but it is not yet made manifest: "You are now the sons of God, but it has not yet appeared what you shall be" (1 John 3:2). Thus the sacraments have a hidden aspect. They are a veil as well as a reality. *Jesu, quem velatum nunc aspicio . . . ut te revelata cernens facie . . .* ("Jesus, whom I now behold under a veil . . . may I [one day] behold you with your face unveiled . . . ").[27]

And this shows us one more aspect of the sacraments in the history of salvation. They are not the final stage. After the mysteries of the past, there are the mysteries of the future. Prefigured by the realities of the Old Testament and the New, the sacraments are themselves prefigurations of eternal life. Baptism anticipates the Judgment; the Eucharist is the eschatological banquet already made present in mystery. And so the sacraments recapitulate the whole history of salvation: *Recolitur memoria passionis, mens impletur gratia, et futurae gloriae nobis pignus datur* ("the memory of his passion is kept, the soul filled with grace, and a pledge of future glory given to us.").[28]

Thus, we see the sacraments as being the acts of God in the era of the Church. As we have said, God's ways of acting are always the same. This is what finally defines the right of the Church to bring out the analogies between the sacraments and the divine events recorded in Scripture. It is here that we find the ultimate basis of what we explained at the start of this article. The universe of the liturgy is a marvelous symphony in which appear the harmonies between the different eras of the history of salvation, in which we pass from the Old Testament to the sacraments, from eschatology to spirituality, from the New Testament to eschatology, in virtue of these fundamental analogies. Knowledge of these correspondences is *the* Christian wisdom as the fathers understood it, the spiritual understanding of Scripture. And this is where the liturgy is the mistress of exegesis.

To conclude: One of the greatest difficulties for many minds is to understand the connection between Scripture and the Church. They hold to Scripture, but they do not see the need for the Church. It is of the utmost importance that such people be shown the strict continuity between Scripture and the Church. And it is precisely this continuity that appears at the climax of the history of salvation. It is here that the realities spoken of by Scripture and the realities that constitute the

---

25   *The Banquet of the Ten Virgins*, Discourse 3, chap. 8, in *Ante-Nicene Fathers*, 6:320.

26   See Daniélou, *The Bible and the Liturgy*, 191–207.

27   Thomas Aquinas, "Adoro te Devote" ("I Adore You Devoutly"), in *Latin Hymns*, arr. and trans. Adrian Fortescue (Harrison, NY: Roman Catholic Books, n.d.), 76–77.

28   Thomas Aquinas, "Antiphon of the Magnificat at the Second Vespers of Corpus Christi," in *Latin Hymns*, 60–61.

Church appear as being various stages of one work. And, furthermore, by employing a unique language, which is that used by the Word of God, and by causing us to discover the scriptural categories in the sacraments, the continual reference to Scripture found in the explanation of the sacraments manifests the fact that they belong to the same universe.

Thus Bible and liturgy illuminate one another. The Bible both authorizes and clarifies the liturgy. It authorizes it by the authority of the prophets and the figures of which it is the fulfillment, and by thus placing it in the whole pattern of God's plan. It illuminates it by giving us the forms of expression by which we can understand the authentic meaning of the rites. In its turn, the liturgy illuminates the Bible. It gives us its authentic interpretation by showing us how it is a witness to the *mirabilia Dei*. And, much more, as these acts are continued in the sacraments, they actualize the Word of God by authorizing us to apply it to the present acts of God in the Church in virtue of the analogy between these acts in the different phases of history.

Letter & Spirit 2 (2006): 217–234

The Kingdom of God and the Heavenly-Earthly Church

~: Christoph Cardinal Schönborn, O. P. :~

"God, who is rich in mercy, out of the great love with which he loved us, has made even us, who were dead through our sins, alive together with Christ. . .and he has raised us up with him in Christ Jesus and given us a place with him in the heavens" (Eph. 2:4–6). Christian existence means being with Christ, and thus means being where he is, sitting at the right hand of the Father. The Church has her homeland where Christ is. In terms of her head and of her goal, she is a *heavenly* Church. Since she is an earthly Church, she knows that she is a *pilgrim* Church, stretching out to reach her goal.

The Second Vatican Council's Constitution on the Church, *Lumen Gentium*, contemplated the Church as the people of God. If one reads this great conciliar text as a whole, it is clear that the Council sees the Church as the people of God entirely on the basis of her *goal*, to be the heavenly, perfected Church (*Lumen Gentium*, 2). It is only the goal that gives meaning to the path. The Church is the pilgrim people of God, and her goal is the heavenly Jerusalem.

It is only when we contemplate the Church in her earthly-heavenly transitional existence that we have the *whole* Church in view. This is why we begin by presenting some witnesses for this way of seeing the Church; then we ask why the sensitivity to this perspective has been largely lost today, and above all why the heavenly dimension of the Church is often forgotten; finally, we should like to indicate some perspectives on how it is possible to regain this vision of the Church as heavenly-earthly reality. The seventh chapter of *Lumen Gentium* will give us special help in understanding here.

The Unity of the Pilgrim Church and the Heavenly Church

Andrea Pozzo has given a most beautiful expression, in a painting on the ceiling of Sant'Ignazio in Rome, to the unity of the pilgrim Church and the Church of heaven. On the ceiling of the central nave, a great Baroque architecture opens out onto an infinite heaven. Saint Ignatius ascends on clouds to the Holy Trinity. Other saints of the Society of Jesus join him; on all sides, angels ascend and descend, creating the link here to the allegorical representations of the four continents, which strive toward this heavenly fellowship and make their way toward it. While the Church of heaven descends, the pilgrim Church ascends to her native land; or rather, both make their way to meet one another, "grow together to form the one Church" to which all her members belong "to various extents and in various ways," whether they are pilgrims on earth or "have departed from this life and are being purified" or are already glorified in the vision of God (*Lumen Gentium*, 49).

In the church of Sant'Ignazio there is also the tomb of St. Robert Bellarmine, who dedicated an entire volume of his work, *De Controversiis Christianae Fidei*, to the three levels of the Church: the Church militant, the Church of the state of purification, and the triumphant Church.[1] The ecclesiology of the Counter-Reformation has often been accused of overemphasizing the societal, institutional character of the Church militant and giving too little prominence to her fundamentally eschatological character. By replacing the expression "Church militant" with the concept of "pilgrim Church",[2] the Council wanted to correct this vision and to show that the Church in her pilgrim state strives with all her might toward her fullness and perfection "in the heavenly glory" (*Lumen Gentium*, 48).

Chapter 7 of *Lumen Gentium* was edited in this perspective, even if "belatedly and hurriedly."[3] Popes John XXIII and Paul VI had personally insisted, with vigor, on the introduction of some remarks on the veneration of the saints at some place in the Constitution on the Church. The Council took the view that the question of the veneration of the saints must be situated against a wider theological horizon, namely, that of the eschatological character of the Church. Monsignor Gerard Philips makes the following comments on the outcome of this work:

> This idea leads us unexpectedly to a happy enrichment of the Constitution on the Church. Not only does this broadening permit us to see the Church in her totality, including her perfection: it also proffers us the meaning of her marching forward, in concrete terms, the meaning of hope. Only now are we able to understand completely chapter 2, on the pilgrim people of God. The second and the penultimate [seventh] chapters of *Lumen*

---

1   When the much-discussed definition of the Church by St. Robert Bellarmine ("The Church is an association of men which is just as visible and tangible as the association of the Roman people or of the kingdom of France or of the republic of Venice," in vol. II, *Contr.* 1a, Liber III, cap. II) is criticized today, it is all too easily forgotten that it concerns only the aspect of the Church militant and that it must be given its place within the totality of the three levels of the Church. Compare the observations by Charles Journet, *L'Église du Verbe Incarné: Essai de Théologie Speculative*, 2 vols. (Bruges, 1962), 2:61, 80.

2   The expression "militant" Church crops up again, a little surprisingly, in Leonardo Boff, *Iglesia: carisma y poder. Ensayos de ecclesiología militante* (1982). Eng. trans.: *Church, Charism and Power: Liberation Theology and the Institutional Church* (New York: Crossroad, 1987).

3   Henri de Lubac, *Geheimnis aus dem wir leben* (Einsiedeln, 1967), 105. Eng. trans.: *The Church: Paradox and Mystery* (Shannon: Ecclesia Press, 1969). See also the commentaries by Msgr. G. Philips, *L'Eglise et Son Mystère*, 2 vols. (Paris, 1968), 2:161–205, and O. Semmelroth in *Lexikon für Theologie und Kirche*, Supplement 1, Das Zweite Vatikanische Konzil, ed. Michael Buchberger (Freiburg, Herder, 1957-65), 314–25. It is striking that chap. 7 has found little echo in what has been written about *Lumen Gentium*. See however, C. Pozzo, *Teología del Más Allá*, 2d. ed. (Madrid, 1980), 538–78.

Gentium correspond to one another and achieve the equilibrium. Now we no longer merely consider whence we come and what has already been realized: we consider also the direction in which we are heading and what awaits us in the future.[4]

Although this vision does a little to correct the insufficiently eschatological view of the "Church militant" in the posttridentine theology, "it remains true that the decision to take 'people of God' as the fundamental and initial concept, linked with today's juxtaposition of the two Churches—the earthly, in which we live, and the heavenly Church of those who have already reached their 'native land'—has brought about a certain restriction of the patristic horizon."[5]

One must indeed take care not to exaggerate this antithesis and push it to extremes.[6] Nevertheless it is useful to point out.

In the New Jerusalem Above

Cardinal Henri de Lubac emphasizes a certain difference between the patristic view and the view presented by *Lumen Gentium*. What is this difference?

"You have come," says the letter to the Hebrews, "to Mount Zion, to the city of the living God, to the Jerusalem above." Our fathers believed these words and reflected on them. Thus, the Church that had given birth to them in the water of baptism—precisely this earthly, visible Church—was at the same time "the heavenly Church" for them, "the new Jerusalem above, our mother." "Let us already now, in the Church, live in the Jerusalem above," Augustine will say, "so that we may not perish for ever" (*On the Psalms*, 124, 4). And again: "The present Church is the kingdom of Christ and the kingdom of God" (*Sermon* 125). In this synthesizing vision of the mystery, the Church is identified with Christ her Bridegroom, who is himself the kingdom: *autobasileia*, in Origen's wonderful term. And precisely this vision corresponds to the deepest logic of Christian eschatology: if one were to abandon it, countless abuses in thought and deed would be the result.[7]

In my view, some of the directions taken by ecclesiology that have emerged since the Council justify the anxiety that Cardinal de Lubac had formulated already before the Council. I shall attempt to show that one cannot understand such

---

4   Philips, *L'Eglise*, 163.

5   De Lubac, *Geheimnis*, 110.

6   De Lubac, *Geheimnis*, 107.

7   De Lubac, *Geheimnis*, 111.

tendencies to be the view of the Council itself. Before we tackle these disputed questions, let us first remain with this vision of the Church as a reality that is essentially heavenly. The following testimonies—basically chance fruits of my reading—do not claim to offer a fully rounded picture, but feature here as harmonious voices (so to speak) in the immeasurable choir of the Church.

The Church is where Christ is. How then would it be possible for her not to be primarily in heaven, where Christ is? A nun who lived in secret in Hungary and died at the age of twenty-five writes in her diary:

> This Easter feast was the first that permitted me to experience what I have accepted with my understanding for a very long time: this life is only a brief passage of transition that flies quickly away. The only truth is the risen Lord. It is still painful to be far away from him, and how much do I feel this on this day! But I can never again forget this unique experience, which lasted only a few minutes. It is not this life that is reality for me: the other life, beyond the grave, is a thousand times more real.[8]

It is impossible not to be reminded of Paul here. "You have been raised up with Christ: therefore strive for the things that are of heaven, where Christ sits at the right hand of God" (Col. 3:1; *Lumen Gentium*, 6; 48); "Thus we are always confident, even though we know that we live in exile far from the Lord, as long as we are at home in this body; for we walk as those who believe, not as those who see. But because we are confident, we prefer to depart from the body and to be at home with the Lord" (2 Cor. 5:6–8; cf. *Lumen Gentium*, 6; 48; 49); "I yearn to depart and to be with Christ" (Phil. 1:23; *Lumen Gentium*, 48).

This experience, this faith, this burning desire, does not come from a pagan egotism that aims at one's own immortality (that was the objection of an Adolph von Harnack).[9] Their center is Christ himself and his promise: "There are many dwellings in my Father's house. . .I go to prepare a place for you. When I have gone and have prepared a place for you, I will come again and take you to myself, so that you too may be where I am" (John 14:2–3). The Jerusalem Bible comments on this text: "This entire expectation of the Church is based on this promise." For here is the place of her hope.

Thanks to Christ, the faithful here below have already their "native land in heaven" (Phil. 3:20; *Lumen Gentium*, 48); they are "no longer foreigners without the rights of citizens, but fellow-citizens of the saints and members of God's household" (Eph. 2:19; *Lumen Gentium*, 6); their names have been entered in the

---

8   *Monika. Ein Zeugnis in Ungarn*, with introduction by Hans Urs von Balthasar (Einsiedeln, 1982), 160.

9   *Das Wesen des Christentums*, (Leipzig, 1905), 146. Eng. trans: *What is Christianity?* (New York: Harper, 1957).

list of the citizens of the heavenly Jerusalem (Luke 10:20). "All the faithful who are pilgrims on this earth make for the 'city of the living God' and do not cease to go toward it (Heb. 12:22)."[10] "The heavenly Jerusalem. . .is our mother" (Gal. 4:26; *Lumen Gentium*, 6). Thus, to be a Christian means that one has set up his tent in heaven (Rev. 12:12; 13:6).[11] Because Christ is her head, and she his body, the Church is essentially heavenly. Augustine says this again and again: "'Jerusalem, which is constructed as a city': Christ is its foundation. The apostle Paul says: 'No one can lay any other foundation than that which is already laid: Jesus Christ' (1 Cor. 3:11). When the foundation is laid in the earth, the walls are built above it, and the weight of the walls pulls downward, because the foundation is laid below. But if our foundation is in heaven, we will be built up toward heaven. . .for. . .we are constructed in a spiritual manner; our foundation lies above. Let us then hasten to the place where we are being built!"[12]

This mighty vision of the Church is not in the least an evasion that would permit one to avoid the toils and vicissitudes of an active involvement in this world. It is only when one sees in faith the "heavenly" nature of the Church that the meaning of her earthly condition as a pilgrim Church becomes clear as well. Since she has her origin in the life of God himself, in the holy Trinity, the Church is "first of all a reality founded by heaven in time."[13] She is this because she is nothing other than what God intends to do with this world, according to the famous saying of Clement of Alexandria: "For as his will is a deed, and this deed is called 'world,' so is also his desire the salvation of men, and this is called 'Church.'"[14] In this ultimate vision there lies the final meaning of the "communion of saints" that we profess in the creed. Nicetas of Remesiana has expressed this vividly:

10   Ceslas Spicq, "Les chrétiens vivent en citoyens du ciel," in *Théologie morale du Nouveau Testament*, 2 vols. (Paris, 1970), 1:417–32, at 418; see also, Spicq, *Vie chrétienne et pérégrination selon le Nouveau Testament*, (Paris, 1972); Erik Peterson, "Von den Englen," in *Theologische Traktate* (Munich, 1951), 327–29.

11   According to E.-B. Allo, *L'Apocalypse* (Paris, 1933), 208, these passages (also Rev. 7:15) concern also "the dwelling of God in the hearts of the saints, already here below through grace, and then in heaven."

12   *On the Psalms*, 121, 4, in *Patrologiae Cursus Completus. Series Latina*, ed. J. P. Migne (Paris: Garnier and J. P. Migne, 1844–1864), 37, 1621. Hereafter abbreviated *PL*. See also the numerous texts in Henri de Lubac, *Die Kirche. Eine Betrachtung* (Einsiedeln, 1968), 66–71. Eng. trans.: *The Splendor of the Church* (San Francisco: Ignatius, 1986).

13   Hans Urs von Balthasar, *Theodramatik. Das Endspiel* (Einsiedeln, 1983), 114. Eng. trans.: *Theo-Drama: Theological Dramatic Theory*, vol. 5, *The Last Act* (San Francisco: Ignatius, 1999). See also the texts of Adrienne von Speyr quoted in Von Balthasar, *Theodramatik*, 114–22: The Church is "in a very proper sense the place where eternity begins within time"; "The Church with all her sacraments and institutions lives from the air of eternity of heaven; she cannot avoid mediating something of this." See also H. U. von Balthasar, "Die himmlische Kirche und ihre Erscheinung", in *Homo creatus est*, vol. 5 of *Skizzen zur Theologie* (Einsiedeln, 1986), 148–64.

14   *The Instructor*, Bk. I, chap. 6, in *Ante-Nicene Fathers*, vol. 2, eds. Alexander Roberts and James Donaldson (Peabody, MA: Hendrickson, 2004), 216.

After you have professed your faith in the most blessed Trinity, you declare that you believe in the holy Catholic Church. What is the Church other than the gathering together of all the saints? For since the beginning of the world, the patriarchs. . .the prophets, the martyrs, and all the righteous. . .form one single Church, since they are sanctified through one and the same faith and one and the same life, and are marked with the sign of one and the same Spirit, and thus form one single body. As is stated above, Christ is termed the head of this body. But there is still more to be said. Even the angels, the heavenly dominations, and authorities are members of this one single Church. . . .Believe therefore that you are to attain to the fellowship of the saints in this one Church. Know that this Catholic Church is *one*, established over the whole face of the earth; you must cling decisively to her fellowship.[15]

We asked whether in Andrea Pozzo's ceiling painting it is the Church of heaven that is descending or the Church of earth that is ascending. Now we can say: it is the one single Church of heaven and of earth. But since this one single Church has her true dwelling place in heaven, she is in her essence "the holy city, the new Jerusalem that comes down from God out of heaven" (Rev. 21:2). In the course of the centuries, Christian art and architecture have endeavored to express this, by making churches into images of the heavenly Jerusalem.

The Church and the Kingdom of God

"Who is the city of God, if not the holy Church?"[16] Is the Church identical with the kingdom of God? Augustine affirms this: "Thus, the Church is already now the kingdom of Christ and the kingdom of heaven."[17] Although it is true that the kingdom of Christ here below (*nunc*) is "in a state of war (*militae*)," it will be perfected only at the end of the ages (*in fine saeculorum, tunc*).[18]

Thomas Aquinas does not say anything different: "The kingdom of God is spoken of by preference (as it were) in a double sense: first, as the group of those who walk in faith, and in this sense the Church militant is called the 'kingdom of

---

15   *Explanation of the Symbol*, 10, in *PL* 52, 871 B; see also P.-Y. Emery, "L'unité des croyants au ciel et sur la terre," *Verbum Caro* 16 (1962), 1–240.

16   Augustine, *On the Psalms*, 92, 4; see also Augustine, *The City of God*, Bk. 16, chap. 2, in *A Select Library of the Nicene and Post-Nicene Fathers of the Christian Church*, vol. 2, ed. Philip Schaff (Grand Rapids, MI: Eerdmans, 1997), 310. See also "L'Eglise et la Cité de Dieu," vol. 37 of *Oeuvres de Saint Augustin* (Paris, 1960), 774–777, n. 28.

17   *The City of God*, Bk. 20, chap. 9, in *A Select Library of the Nicene and Post-Nicene Fathers*, 429.

18   Compare the note on "les deux états de l'Eglise 'qualis nunc' et 'qualis tunc,'" in *Oeuvres de Saint Augustin*, vol. 32 (Paris 1965), 723–25.

God'; but then also as the assembly of those who have already safely attained their goal, and in this sense the triumphant Church is called the 'kingdom of God.'"[19]

For both Augustine and Thomas, there are two successive states of the Church, *nunc et tunc*, now and then: the definitive and the provisional state of the kingdom of God. Jacques Bonsirven says the same in his book, *Le Règne de Dieu*: "Is the kingdom of God identical with the Church. . .? The answer can only be 'yes.'"[20] Cardinal Charles Journet is no less affirmative: "We do not believe that one can refuse to identify the Church and the kingdom. We have two concepts here, but only one single reality. The Church is the kingdom; the kingdom is the Church. The concept of 'kingdom' refers to eschatology. But it is precisely with Jesus that eschatology, which belongs above all to the qualitative order, has broken into time. From the time of Christ onward, the whole Church has entered the end time; she is eschatological."[21]

But now, precisely in the name of eschatology, this identification has been called into question for about the last one hundred years in a debate that is not at all concluded. Much is at stake here, for it is a question not only of the nature of the Church but also of very significant practical consequences.

If the Church is essentially heavenly, since she is "there where Christ is," if she is his body, and it is "not only the believers who are alive today that belong" to this body "but also those who have lived before us, and those who will come after us until the end of time,"[22] then it is not possible to grasp a reason *not* to identify the Church and the kingdom of God.

The objection has been made for a hundred years that one may not identify the Church with the kingdom, since this is a strictly eschatological reality, whereas the Church is only a sign of the kingdom and a pointer to it. We must attempt to clarify this very confused question, so we shall begin by listening carefully to the teaching of the Council, and then we shall ask about the reception of this teaching.

The Eschatological Character of the Pilgrim Church

One can often read the statement that the Council taught that the Church is *the sacrament of the kingdom*: "The Council has given new vigor to the old patristic view of the Church as the sacrament of the kingdom. . . .In her [the pilgrim Church], the kingdom of God is already present. She is, as Augustine says, already 'the reconciled world,' she is already the new creation; but she is not yet the kingdom

---

19 *Commentary on the Fourth Book of the Sentences of Peter Lombard*, Dist. 49, q. 1, a. 2, quaest. 5, sol. 5.

20 (Paris, 1957), 194f.

21 *L'Eglise du Verbe Incarné*, 2: 997, n. 1; compare 60–91 and *Nova et Vetera* 38 (1963), 307–10.

22 Augustine, *On the Psalms*, 62, 2.

in its fullness and its definitive realization."[23] But if the author of these lines had looked more closely, he could have seen that the council nowhere calls the Church the "sacrament of the kingdom."

The Constitution *Lumen Gentium* is clear on this point. It states: "In order to accomplish the Father's will, Christ founded the kingdom of heaven on earth, revealed his mystery to us and brought about our redemption through his obedience. The Church, that is, the kingdom of Christ which is already present in mystery, grows visibly in the world through the power of God" (*Lumen Gentium*, 3). Before we ask what "already present in mystery" may mean here, let us listen to two other texts of the Constitution.

Article 5, which was inserted in the schema after the discussions of the second conciliar session, is entirely concerned with the Church and the kingdom of God. The *Relatio commissionis doctrinalis* states that this article, which originally bore the title, "On the kingdom of God," was inserted because it expressed the simultaneously visible and spiritual character of the Church's fellowship, as well as her historical and eschatological aspect.[24]

Although one really should quote the whole text, which is very important for our subject, we limit ourselves to recalling the following striking passages: "For the Lord Jesus initiated his Church by proclaiming the good news, namely the coming of the kingdom of God, which had been promised from of old in the Scriptures: 'The time is fulfilled, and the kingdom of God has drawn near' (Mark 1:15; Matt. 4:17)." The presence of the kingdom is seen in the words and works, but above all in the person, of Christ himself. Christ's mission is continued in the Church: "The Church receives thence. . .the mission to proclaim the kingdom of God and of Christ and to establish it among all peoples. Thus she represents the seed and the beginning of the kingdom. As she gradually grows, she reaches out in longing for the perfected kingdom; with all her might she hopes and yearns to be united with her King in glory" (*Lumen Gentium*, 5).

The Church is here called the "seed and beginning of the kingdom" on earth. May one comment on this as follows: "This is why the Church can posit a distance between the Church and Christ: she is only the sacrament of salvation. It can proclaim the distance between the Church and the kingdom: here too we have an 'already and not yet' (*Lumen Gentium*, 5, above all the conclusion; see also *Unitatis Redintegratio*, 3, 5). Because the Church is not coterminous with the kingdom, she

---

23 I myself "perpetrated" these sentences in *Realizzare il Concilio. Il contributo di Communione e Liberazione* (Milan, 1982), in a lecture on "Il significato ecclesiologico del Concilio Ecumenico Vaticano II," at 23. This text, which I hereby withdraw, was also published as "Realizzare il Concilio," *L'Osservatore Romano* (October 2, 1982), 2.

24 Quoted from G. Alberigo and F. Magistretti, eds., *Constitutionis Dogmaticae Lumen Gentium Synopsis Historica*, (Bologna, 1975), 436.

renews and reforms herself unceasingly: *Lumen Gentium*, 8, conclusion; *Gaudium et Spes*, 21, 5; 43, 6."[25]

Is the purpose of the formulations, "present in mystery" (*Lumen Gentium*, 3) and "seed and beginning" (*Lumen Gentium*, 5), "to proclaim the distance between the Church and the kingdom"? A third text can complete the framework of this question. *Lumen Gentium* 9 says of the people of God: "This messianic people has Christ as its head. . . .It is destined to possess the kingdom of God, which was founded on earth by God himself and must continue to unfold until it is also perfected by him at the end of the ages." Is this text to be read in the sense of a distance between the Church and the kingdom? In my view, the answer can be given only on the basis of *Lumen Gentium* as a whole: for if we read these three passages in the light of chapter 7, it becomes clear that one can speak of a "distance" only when one is looking at the Church in her *pilgrim existence*. Seen in this way, she is not yet the *perfected* kingdom: "In her sacraments and institutions, which still belong to this period of the world, the pilgrim Church bears the figure of this world which is passing away" (*Lumen Gentium*, 48). Does this mean that she stands at a distance from the kingdom?

The pilgrim Church is nothing other than the "kingdom of heaven" that Christ has established on earth (*Lumen Gentium*, 3). When it is said of the pilgrim Church that she is "the kingdom of Christ which is already present in mystery" (*Lumen Gentium*, 3) and that she is the "seed and beginning of this kingdom on earth" (*Lumen Gentium*, 5), then the perfected kingdom will be nothing other than the perfected Church: "It is only in heavenly glory. . . that the Church will be perfected" (*Lumen Gentium*, 48). Will this Church, when she is "perfected in glory at the end of the ages of the world," be anything other than the totally realized kingdom? For "then will. . .all the righteous. . .be gathered together in the Father's presence in the all-embracing Church" (*Lumen Gentium*, 2). It is certainly true that the Church strives with all her power "to attain the perfected kingdom," but in this "she yearns to be united with her king in glory (*Lumen Gentium*, 5), and as long as she goes along the paths of her earthly pilgrimage, her life is nevertheless

---

25 Thus Yves Congar, "Les implications christologiques et pneumatologiques de l'Ecclésiologie de Vatican II," in *Le Concile de Vatican II: Son Eglise, Peuple de Dieu et Corps du Christ*, (Paris, 1984), 174. With the exception of the first (*Lumen Gentium*, 5), none of the passages adduced here speaks of the kingdom of God: *Unitatis Redintegratio*, 3, 5 states that the Church is on the pilgrimage of hope toward "the fullness of eternal glory in the heavenly Jerusalem"; *Lumen Gentium*, 8, 3 says that the Church is "at once holy and always in need of purification"; *Lumen Gentium*, 9 (Conclusion) adds that she is "ceaselessly renewing herself"; *Gaudium et Spes*, 21, 5 takes over *Lumen Gentium*, 8, 3; *Gaudium et Spes*, 43, 6 takes over *Lumen Gentium*, 15, where the members of the Church are summoned to purification. See Second Vatican Council, *Unitatis Redintegratio*, Decree on Ecumenism (November 21, 1964) and *Gaudium et Spes*, Pastoral Constitution on the Church in the Modern World (December 7, 1965) in *Vatican Council II: The Conciliar and Post Conciliar Documents*, ed. Austin Flannery (Northport, NY: Costello, 1987).

"hidden with Christ in God, until she appears in glory, united to her bridegroom (Col. 3:1–4)" (*Lumen Gentium*, 6).

Thus there lies no distance between the Church and the kingdom of God. Rather, we have different *status* both of the Church and of the kingdom: The *pilgrim* Church is the kingdom that "buds and grows until the time for the harvest (Mark 4:26–29)" (*Lumen Gentium*, 5), but the Church in the glory of heaven is the perfected kingdom, the final goal of the pilgrimage of the messianic people of God (*Lumen Gentium*, 9).

But what then shall we say about the fact that the Church, which "includes sinners within her own self, is at one and the same time holy and continuously in need of purification, and always takes the path of penitence and renewal" (*Lumen Gentium*, 8)? Is this "because the Church is not coterminous with the kingdom"?

As we have seen (note 25), the Council never makes such a connection. On the contrary, the Council clearly demonstrates, by appealing to the Gospel, that the kingdom that Christ initiated on earth has no other destiny than the Church: "The word of the Lord is like a seed that is sown in a field (Mark 4:14): those who hear it in faith and are counted among the little flock of Christ (Luke 12:32) have received the kingdom itself" (*Lumen Gentium*, 5).

The saints make known how the Church is already the kingdom received in faith. "In their life. . .God shows men, in a living manner, his presence and his countenance. In them, he himself speaks to us and gives us a sign of his kingdom, to which we are powerfully drawn, surrounded as we are by such a great cloud of witnesses (Heb. 12:1) and confronted with such a testimony to the truth of the Gospel" (*Lumen Gentium*, 50).

The Church *is* the kingdom, and the Council does not permit us to say that she is merely its sacrament. For the expression *sacrament* is in fact employed by the Council in another sense, which strengthens even further the identity between the Church and the kingdom: "Christ has. . .made his body, the Church, the all-embracing sacrament of salvation" (*Lumen Gentium*, 48). "For the Church is in Christ as it were the sacrament, that is, the sign and the instrument, for the most intimate uniting to God, the unity of the whole of humanity" (*Lumen Gentium*, 1). The sacramentality of the Church lies in her relationship to the world—not to the kingdom. Through her and in her, Christ calls all men to himself: "Sitting at the right hand of the Father, he works continuously in the world to lead men to the Church and to unite them more closely to himself through her" (*Lumen Gentium*, 48).

Paul VI summarized the teaching of the Council in his "Credo of the People of God": "We profess that the kingdom of God begins here on earth in the Church of Christ" (no. 35). [26] Cardinal Journet says the same in a summarizing formula-

---

26   See *Encyclical of Pope Paul VI, Humanae Vitae, on the Regulation of Birth, and Pope Paul VI's "Credo of the People of God*, Study Club Edition (Glen Rock, NJ: Paulist Press 1968).

tion: "The kingdom is already on earth, and the Church is already in heaven. To abandon the equal value of Church and kingdom would mean overlooking this important revelation."[27]

"The Fata Morgana of Eschatology"[28]

On January 28, 1979, Pope John Paul II addressed the following words to the Latin American bishops at Puebla:

> In the extensive material drawn up in preparation for this conference. . .one sometimes notices a certain confusion in the exposition of the nature and mission of the Church. For example, we find the reference to the separation that some make between the Church and the kingdom of God. This deprives the kingdom of its full contents, so that it is understood in a very secularized sense: thus we are told that one does not enter the kingdom of God through faith and through belonging to the Church.[29]

To what confusion does the Holy Father refer here? Which secularization of the concept "kingdom of God" is involved here? The problem to which he alludes is basically an old problem, but one that has taken on a new form in roughly the last hundred years. The secularization of the idea of the kingdom of God is one of the possible consequences of the radical eschatologism that has dominated the discussions about the relationship between the Church and the kingdom of God since Johannes Weiss, Alfred Loisy, and Albert Schweitzer. We cannot sketch here the history of this debate, which is not yet in the least closed. We limit ourselves to the presentation by Jean Carmignac (see note 27) and to the theses that Leonardo Boff has developed in his *Ecclesiogenesis*.[30]

Carmignac begins by recalling that the source of many obscurities about the kingdom of God is the fact that Greek has only one expression, *basileia*, to reproduce three Hebrew expressions that are close to but not identical with it: *melukah* (kingdom), *malkuth* (lordship), and *mamlakah* (the land ruled by a king).[31] Naturally, the interpretation of the scriptural texts acquires greater precision when one takes into account the particular aspect involved in each individual use of the

---

27 Jornet, *L'Eglise du Verbe Incarné*, 2:57.

28 *Le mirage de l'Eschatologie* is the title of what I consider a very important book by the French exegete Jean Carmignac (Paris, 1979). This well documented book has the subtitle "Royauté, Règne et Rouaume de Dieu. . .sans Eschatologie."

29 *Acta Apostolicae Sedis* 71:3 (February 1979), 194.

30 *Eclesiogênese. As comunidades de base reinventam a Igreja* (Petrópolis, 1977), quoted here from the German edition, *Die Neuentdeckung der Kirche. Basisgemeinden in Lateinamerika* (Mainz, 1980). Eng. trans.: *Ecclesiogenesis: The Base Communities Reinvent the Church* (Maryknoll, NY: Orbis, 1986).

31 Carmignac, *Le mirage*, 13–16.

expression *basileia*.[32] Then it becomes clear that, whereas one can distinguish the Church in some way from the lordship of God, one cannot distinguish her from the "sphere where the King rules." In fact, the various traits of this kingdom of God or of Christ correspond to those of the Church.[33] Carmignac summarizes the results of his exegetical investigation as follows:

> It is not permissible. . .as some writers do, to see the Church as a preparation for the kingdom, for then the kingdom would be temporally later than the Church, and that would contradict the words of Jesus and the apostles, who confirm that the kingdom already belongs to their time and is a present reality. Nor may one hold the view that the kingdom of God will be the continuation of the Church in the other world. The Church begins to exist at precisely the moment in which the kingdom of God was founded, and she will continue to exist for the whole of eternity. It is not at all possible to separate the Church and the kingdom from one another—at least, not if one holds to the New Testament as a whole, without giving some texts preference before others.
>
> But the identification of the Church and the kingdom of God does not in the least oblige us to see these two expressions as synonymous. They refer to the same reality, but from different perspectives. If ones speaks of the kingdom of God, one looks above all at the event of God's working, which is realized among men when they gather around Christ; if one speaks of the Church, one looks above all at these men who are gathered around Christ by God.[34]

Carmignac draws up an impressive list of authors from the Church fathers on into our own days who make statements in keeping with this identification.[35] Why, therefore, has this identity lost its evidential character from a certain point in time that does not lie very far in the past? Here begins what Carmignac calls "the fata morgana of eschatology."

The "formation of an error" begins with Reimarus; it consists in the idea, which has been vigorously propagated since then, that the entire Jewish people at the time of Jesus awaited this kingdom of the Messiah. Eduard Reuss extends this idea by means of the assertion that Jesus' contemporaries lived in an eschatological

---

32   Carmignac, *Le mirage*, 19–83.

33   Carmignac, *Le mirage*, 99.

34   Carmignac, *Le mirage*, 101.

35   Carmignac, *Le mirage*, 102–19.

"high tension." Ernest Renan popularizes the idea that Jesus too lived in this "high tension" and that he awaited the imminent, abrupt irruption of the kingdom of God as the total overthrowing of this world. "Basically, the considerations of these authors went astray because of two fundamental errors: (a) because of rationalistic prejudices, they bracketed off (consciously or not) those texts of the New Testament that opposed their theory and did not agree with their prefabricated syntheses; (b) they imagined that the Jews at the beginning of the Christian era were obsessed by the expectation of the kingdom of God and that Jesus shared their illusions."[36]

The "success of an error" was ensured by Johannes Weiss and Alfred Loisy. Both men "take one further step, because they begin to combine the concepts 'kingdom of God' (as something lying exclusively in the future) and 'eschatology' (reified to become the end of the world). For them, eschatology and the kingdom of God become two correlative concepts that cannot be separated from one another."[37] Two theses take on an uncritically accepted evidential character for many: "that Jesus' contemporaries lived *in the feverish expectation of the kingdom of God* and that Jesus could do no other than make *their illusions* his own."[38]

The "triumph of an error" arrives with Albert Schweitzer. "Schweitzer presupposes without further ado that the *kingdom of God* is a *purely eschatological* vision of faith, and he constructs inexorably a life of Jesus that goes in circles around this illusion, which was to be proved to be a lie by the historical reality."[39] The "logic of an error" reaches its zenith in Rudolph Bultmann. For him, it is clear "that *Jesus' proclamation of God's lordship* was an eschatological message" and that this was "the message of the coming end of the world." "All this means that in earliest Christianity *history was swallowed up by eschatology.*"[40]

W. G. Kümmel observes on this point: "The fundamentally futurist-eschatological understanding of Jesus' proclamation, with its basis laid by Johannes Weiss and Albert Schweitzer, seems to be for Bultmann so much a matter of course that he neither adduces any evidence in support of it nor mentions any dissenting opinions."[41]

The most striking thing about the dossier drawn up by Carmignac is the demonstration that there exists no evidence for this view of eschatology and of the kingdom of God. The few texts that are usually plucked out of the intertestamental literature and adduced as evidence do not in the least permit one to construct

---

36 Carmignac, *Le mirage,* 144.

37 Carmignac, *Le mirage,* 147.

38 Carmignac, *Le mirage,* 154.

39 Carmignac, *Le mirage,* 157.

40 *Geschichte und Eschatologie* (Tübingen, 1958), 36–42. Eng. trans.: *History and Eschatology* (Edinburgh: Edinburgh University, 1957).

41 "Die Naherwartung in der Verkündigung Jesu," in *Zeit und Geschichte* (Festschrift for Bultmann) (Tübingen, 1964), 31–46, at 31.

the entire theory of eschatologism upon them.[42] Thus the presumed apocalyptic horizon that Jesus allegedly shared with his contemporaries shrinks greatly, and one must ask whether eschatologism is not to a great extent an *a priori* construction. Before we return to this question, we shall look briefly at the consequences to which the "fata morgana of eschatology" can lead.

In his *Ecclesiogenesis*, Leonardo Boff takes over the theses of eschatologism and makes them his own without posing any questions—simply as a matter of course. The explosive quality of his views comes from the practical consequences that he draws from this position. Boff takes it for granted that Jesus lived in the imminent eschatological expectation of the kingdom of God:[43] "No one can deny that Jesus had the same temporal expectation as his entire generation."[44]

The necessary inference from the supposition that people at that period were expecting the kingdom of God, understood as the end of the world, and that it was precisely *this* kingdom of God that Jesus proclaimed, is that Jesus did not wish to found the Church, but rather to proclaim this kingdom. Jesus' "imminent expectation" seems of itself to exclude the idea that he thought of an institutionally established Church.[45]

For Boff, it is a fact that Jesus' expectation was not fulfilled. The kingdom did not come—at least, it did not come in the form in which it was expected. Thanks to the death and then the resurrection of Jesus, the kingdom of God became reality in the person of Jesus. But the kingdom has not become universally realized; it has found its personal realization in Jesus, and this realization is the anticipation of the fullness of the kingdom. And it is here that the Church finds her place and her possibility of existence: "Thus the Church has clearly the character of a substitute for the kingdom of God. On the one hand, she is the kingdom of God, since the Risen One lives in her; on the other hand, she is also not the kingdom, since it is only in the end time that the kingdom of God will come. The Church is at the service of the kingdom of God and is its sacrament, sign, and instrument, so that it can start and realize itself in the world."[46]

The Church—as the link that spans the gap between Easter and the delayed parousia—is thus the "substitute" for the kingdom, which is understood as a purely eschatological reality. One is, accordingly, not surprised when it is stated that the Church owes her existence not to any intention of the "pre-Easter Jesus" but to a decision taken by Peter and the apostles, namely, the decision to begin the mission to the Gentiles:[47] "As an institution, therefore, the Church is based not (as is

---

42 Carmignac, *Le mirage*, 160–65; compare 212.

43 Boff, *Die Neuentdeckung der Kirche*, 80.

44 Boff, *Eclesiogênse*, 90. One is surprised at the assuredness of this assertion.

45 Boff, *Eclesiogênse*, 82–84.

46 Boff, *Eclesiogênse*, 91.

47 Boff, *Eclesiogênse*, 87.

generally asserted) on the incarnation of the Word but on the faith and the power of the apostles, who transposed eschatology into the time of the Church, thanks to the might of the Spirit, and translated the message about the kingdom of God into the teaching about the Church—the Church, which is an imperfect and temporal realization of the kingdom."[48]

Here we see to the full the serious consequences of "The fata morgana of eschatology": a narrowed-down understanding of the kingdom (bereft of its present element as something that is "already there") is linked to a reductionist understanding of the Church (which is bereft of her "eschatological character"). This has grave consequences, for such a Church—detached from the plan of Jesus Christ and bound one-sidedly to the working of the Spirit[49]—is based on human, and thus mutable, decisions. Thus the ecclesiogenesis, the "new birth of the Church," which the author foresees can be brought about through new decisions: "The Church can organize herself in a manner different to that hitherto prevailing, because this is theologically possible and because this lies in the intention of Jesus Christ."[50] What institutional form is the Church to have? "Jesus wanted, and still wants, the form for which the apostolic fellowship decides, out of the power of the Spirit and in confrontation with the needs of each individual situation, and which this fellowship makes its own."[51]

Yves Congar observes, "This certainly does not correspond to the intention of the Council."[52] In my view, the fundamental defect in this view of the Church lies in its Christology. This ecclesiology is the product of a reductionist Christology.[53] If the Council's vision of the Church is to be received more fully and deeply, the christological bases of *Lumen Gentium* must be considered anew.

The Need for a Christocentric Eschatology

I limit myself to some suggestions that have been insufficiently elaborated and rather point to paths for future work.

The fundamental error of eschatologism is its subordination of Jesus' eschatology to the alleged apocalyptic horizon of his time. In a recent study, "On the Concept of Christian Eschatology,"[54] however, Hans Urs von Balthasar has shown how very christocentric the entire eschatology of the New Testament basically is, even where it makes use of the language of Jewish apocalyptic. Christ's eschatology

---

48 Boff, *Eclesiogênese*, 95.

49 Compare the criticism of this position in Congar, "Les implications," 165.

50 Boff, *Eclesiogênese*, 79.

51 Boff, *Eclesiogênese*, 97.

52 Congar, "Les implications," 166.

53 Hans Urs von Balthasar points out this christological deficit in *Test Everything: Hold Fast to What Is Good* (San Francisco: Ignatius, 1989), 43–47.

54 *Theodramatik* (Einsiedeln, 1983), 14–16.

determines the views of his disciples, more in its substance than in the literary modes of expression. Let us take the "little apocalypses" of the synoptic evangelists: "If one takes an overview of the texts without any preconceptions, he will be astonished to see how many of them. . .refer to the direct effect of the presence of Jesus in the world."[55]

This is not a scenario that would simply have been drawn from the world of apocalyptic images; it deals essentially with the consequences of the coming of Jesus Christ and of the *krisis* provoked by this coming. In the case of the "false prophets" (Matt. 24:4), for example, it seems to be a case of some who are calling into question the uniqueness of Christ, and even the words and the natural catastrophes (Matt. 24:6–8) have a "christological motivation," since they transpose to the societal and cosmic level the separations that Jesus already provokes on the level of the family.[56] There is no "neutral" apocalyptic—apocalyptic always has Christ as its center—and there is no serious reason to exclude the possibility that this "christocentrism" of the New Testament eschatology ultimately arose from the consciousness that Christ himself had of his mission, of his "hour."[57] Is it possible to avoid the conclusion that Jesus Christ was conscious of being himself the *eschaton*, in his mission and in his person?

Karl Barth, who was a "consistent eschatologist" in his *Römerbrief* (1922), altered his position totally,[58] in order to orient eschatology once again on the mystery of Christ: Jesus himself "is the kingdom, he was the kingdom, and will be the kingdom, and in him exist the entire establishment, all the salvation, all the perfection, all the joy of the kingdom. To speak precisely, there are no 'last things': no abstract, no autonomous 'last things' apart from and alongside him who is *the* Last."[59]

Once he has given back eschatology its own, definitive place in Jesus Christ as its center, Karl Barth can again discover what the older writers, both Catholic and Protestant, never lost from view: the Church is the kingdom. "'The kingdom of God' means the lordship set up in Jesus Christ in the world, God's ruling that takes place in him. He himself is the kingdom of God. One should therefore not

---

55   *Theodramatik*, 28.

56   *Theodramatik*, 31.

57   On this, see the document of the International Theological Commission, "Jesu Selbst-und Sendungsbewusstsein", in *IKZ Communio* 16 (1987), 38–49. Eng. trans.: "The Consciousness of Christ Concerning himself and his Mission." *Communio* 14:3 (1987): 316–25.

58   Karl Barth writes in his *Kirchliche Dogmatik*, vol. 8: 2, 562: "It is precisely a 'consistent' eschatology, which must look on the intervening time between 'now' and 'once in the future' as a time of emptiness, of nothingness, of a mere deprivation, of increasing disappointment which is laboriously concealed, that is *not* the eschatology of the New Testament Christianity." Eng. trans.: *Church Dogmatics* (London: T&T Clark, 2004).

59   *Kirchliche Dogmatik*, 589.

suppress the proposition that has often been attached too quickly and too heed-lessly in Protestant theology: the *kingdom of God* is the community."[60]

The Church of the Angels and Mary[61]

It is impossible to understand the Church in her mystery, which can be grasped only in faith,[62] if one fails to take into account that part of the Church, of the kingdom of God, which forms above all the Church of heaven: the holy angels. In order to quicken the sense to perceive the true nature of the Church, we must continually recall this fellowship between the pilgrim Church and the saints and angels of heaven—this is the theme of chapter 7 of *Lumen Gentium*.

When the mentions of the holy angels in the liturgy, where they had had a central place since the Apocalypse, were reduced and made almost void of sig-nificance, was not this an all too easy capitulation to a certain rationalism? "The *ekklesia* of the Eucharist would then be no mere assembly of men among themselves, but—as the Jews already believed and affirmed in their *berakoth*—the gathering of redeemed men with the angels who are the first servants of their salvation, as they also were the first to recognize the love of God and to respond to this with praise. This corresponds also to the vision of the Church offered us in the Christian Apocalypse: the earthly Eucharist that is perfected and is transposed into heaven and as it were drawn into the liturgy of the angels."[63]

How are we to keep alive the knowledge of the invisible dimension of the Church, when her invisible members are forgotten in our liturgical assemblies, at which they are present? The consciousness that the angels belong to the Church has "directly the wholly practical consequences that no one can be a prophet or an apostle unless he has *first been a contemplative and an intercessor* like the angels. For one cannot effectively transmit, on the level of man or on the level of an angel, anything that one has not first made most deeply one's own. It is only when *agape* has taken control of our entire being that God, thanks to the maternal grace that he wanted to communicate to his entire creation, to his entire heavenly and earthly Church, can bestow on us, if he wishes, the gift of the simple prophetic testimony or of the apostolic mission in the name of his Son. In this sense, the bishops ought to be the 'angels of the Church', according to the ancient interpretation of the Apocalypse (Rev. 2:1, 8, 12, 18, etc.)."[64]

Although the identity between Church and kingdom has its basis in Christ,

---

60   *Kirchliche Dogmatik*, IV, 2, 742; compare Carmignac, *Le mirage*, 184–88.

61   Cf. L. Bouyer, *Die Kirche*, vol. 2: *Theologie der Kirche* (Einsiedeln, 1977), in the chapter on *Lumen Gentium*, 7 and 8.

62   *Fide solum intelligimus*, says the Catechism of the Council of Trent with a view to the mystery of the Church. Karl Barth mentions this with acknowledgment and agreement in *Zwischen den Zeiten*, 5 (1927), 365–78.

63   Bouyer, *Die Kirche*, 402.

64   *Die Kirche*, 403.

there is no higher concretization of this identity for the Church than the Mother of God. It would not be possible to assert this identity if its only basis were Christ, the Head of the Church, and there was no real perfect correspondence on the side of the members of the Church. One may justly say that, if Mary did not exist in the Church, then there would be a distance between the Church and the kingdom, because of the presence of sinners in the Church. But "in the most Blessed Virgin the Church has already reached that perfection whereby she exists without spot or wrinkle (Eph. 5:27)" (*Lumen Gentium*, 65).

In Mary, the most perfect member of the Church, we are able to contemplate the Church's true nature. Thus, "by contemplating Mary's mysterious holiness, by imitating her love and faithfully carrying out the Father's will, the Church too herself becomes a mother through receiving the Word of God in faith" (*Lumen Gentium*, 64). If Mary did not exist in the Church, one could not speak with full correctness of the Church's motherhood. *"The Church's motherhood is something that already exists in reality only because the Church has found here her anticipated perfection*: the highest created holiness in a unique communication with Christ's own holiness, who communicates it to her who is not only the mother of us all, but is first of all his own mother."[65]

In Mary, the Council wanted to display to us the sign of the Church but also the Church's reality: both the eschatological character of the earthly, pilgrim Church and her inseparable unity with the Church of heaven. "As the Mother of Jesus, already glorified with body and soul in heaven, is the image and beginning of the Church, which will be perfected in the world to come, so she also shines here on earth in the intermediary time until the day of the Lord comes (2 Pet. 3:10) as a sign of sure hope and of consolation to the people of God on its pilgrim way" (*Lumen Gentium*, 68).

---

65   *Die Kirche*, 406.

Letter & Spirit 2 (2006): 235–248

Reviews & Notices

~: **Carol M. Kaminski** :~

From Noah to Israel:
Realization of the Primaeval Blessing after the Flood
(London: T & T Clark, 2004)

From the first pages to the last, the "story" told in Scripture is the history of God's plan to impart his saving blessing upon his people. The divine plan begins with the primaeval blessing of the first man and woman: "Be fruitful and multiply, and fill the earth and subdue it" (Gen. 1:28). It culminates in the blessings extended through the sacramental liturgy of the new people of God—in the washing of robes in baptism (see Rev. 22:14), and in the eucharistic marriage feast of the lamb (see Rev. 19:9). In between, God's covenant promises are expressed in terms of blessings—to Noah (Gen. 9:1), Abraham (Gen. 12:3), Israel (Num. 6:27), and David (2 Sam. 7:29).

In this intriguing study, which assumes the literary unity of the final form of the canonical texts, Kaminski traces the progress of the divine blessing at a crucial juncture in salvation history—from the great flood through the raising up of the children of Israel.

A key interpretive question is how the divine blessing was carried forward following its restatement to Noah and his sons (Gen. 9:1). The Tower of Babel incident (Gen. 11:1–9) shows Noah's descendants seemingly afraid or resisting the mandate to multiply and fill the earth (Gen. 11:4); thus, it appears that God is required to forcefully "scatter" them. However, Kaminski notices that this "scattering" motif is actually introduced earlier—in a summary statement about the career of Noah's sons (Gen. 9:19).

In an insightful and detailed discussion, Kaminski notes that, in older translations, the decisive Hebrew verb, נָפַץ, is rendered correctly as "scattered" or "dispersed." More recent translations, however, beginning with the Revised Standard Version, translate נָפַץ as "peopled" or "populated," thereby implying the primaeval blessing is fulfilled in Noah's three sons (". . . from these the whole earth was peopled" Gen. 9:19 RSV).

Kaminski argues for a return to the older translations, pointing out that elsewhere in the Old Testament, נָפַץ is often used to describe God's judgment against Israel and the nations (see Gen. 49:7; Deut. 4:27; 28:62, 64; Jer. 13:24; Ezek. 34:5, 6, 12).

If the scattering of Noah's sons is taken to be a judgment against them, a judgment confirmed by the scattering of Noah's descendants at Babel, how, if at all, does the primaeval blessing advance? Kaminski locates the clue in the table of nations (Gen. 10). She observes that the literary form of Shem's genealogy (Gen. 11:10–26) is "almost identical" with that of the antediluvian genealogy presented for Adam's son, Seth (Gen. 5:1–32). And she demonstrates that the two genealogies also share the same "theological function" in the Genesis narrative. As Seth's line was depicted bearing the divine blessing before the flood, Shem's line takes up the divine blessing after the flood.

This conclusion is bolstered by the restatement of the Shemite genealogy after Babel (Gen. 11:10–26), which reveals Abram to be the "goal" of Shem's line. Indeed, in Abraham's descendants, God renews his primaeval blessing (Gen. 17:20; 28:3; 35:11; 47:27; 48:4).

In her closely argued discussion, Kaminski does not explore the possible narrative implications of Noah's "fall" and the respective roles played by Ham and Shem (see Gen. 9:20–27). This "fall" could serve as a further clue as to why the blessing continued only in Shem's line (see Gen. 9:26). Perhaps it is no coincidence that the story of Shem and Ham is recounted immediately after the "scattering" of Noah's sons is described.

Kaminski is strong in showing how the biblical narrative identifies Israel as the bearer of God's primaeval blessing to the world. Israel's fecundity in Egypt (Exod. 1:7) is recalled in language that echoes both the original blessing (Gen. 1:28; 9:1), and the promise to Abram (Gen. 12:1–2). Thus, she helps establish an "intrinsic connection" between Genesis' history of creation (Gen. 1–11) and the salvation history that forms the rest of the book (Gen. 12–50). She further helps us see how God's original intentions for creation are borne forward by the redemption and election of Israel.

Kaminski's study is worthy of the deeper conclusion she leaves us with: "If the primaeval blessing is interpreted in narrative context, then it shows that God's particular blessing to Israel is the means through which his intention for creation—thwarted by sin and divine judgment in the primaeval history, but preserved by grace—will be restored to the world. . . . The particular blessing progresses by means of a divine promise, from Noah to Israel, but it is not for Israel's sake alone, but for the sake of the world."

～: Alice M. Sinnott :～

The Personification of Wisdom,
Society for Old Testament Study Monographs
(Burlington, VT: Ashgate, 2005).

The personification of Wisdom as a female figure is a powerful motif in the biblical books of Proverbs, Job, Sirach, the Wisdom of Solomon, and Baruch. This personification is "profound and dynamic," and has few true parallels in the literatures of the ancient Near East, Sinnott writes in this short study, which is based on her 1997 doctoral dissertation for Oxford University.

In the Scriptures, Wisdom is depicted as being enthroned in heaven (Sir. 24:4–5)—with God from all eternity (Sir. 1:4; 24:9), and "before the beginning of the earth" (Prov. 8:22–31). She is the artisan of creation (see Wis. of Sol. 7:21–22; 8:6; 14:2), and was sent to dwell with all flesh as a gift from God (Sir. 1:10; Bar. 3:37). She is a particular gift to Israel (Sir. 24:8), and is manifest in the Law given through Moses (Sir. 24:23; Bar. 4:1). By forsaking Wisdom, Israel was conquered and exiled (Bar. 3:9–13).

Wisdom will be the salvation of Israel (Wis. of Sol. 9:18; 10:1–21). But she is also the "tree of life" for all peoples (Prov. 3:18). Her ways cannot be found but for the revelation of God (Job 28:12–28; Bar. 3:31). Hence, she is sent as God's divine word or speech, to cry out in the marketplace, to announce her ways and to issue judgment on those who would prefer their own devices to her counsel (Prov. 1:20–33). Wisdom prepares a table and calls all people to eat her bread and drink her wine (Prov. 9:1–6; Sir. 24:19–21) She loves those who love her (Prov. 8:17), and promises to those who love her "a beautiful crown" (Prov. 4:6–9).

Sinnott traces lady Wisdom's appearance in Israel's Scriptures to the trauma of 586 B.C. and beyond, with the destruction of the Temple and the exile. In establishing a post-exilic context for these texts, Sinnott points out that there is little mention in this literature of the Temple, the sacrificial system, or the Davidic dynasty. It is telltale that Wisdom teaches, not in the Temple, but in the marketplace.

Sinnott finds in Proverbs, especially, echoes of the exilic and post-exilic prophets. She demonstrates the close parallels between Wisdom's condemnations and those of the prophets (compare, for example, Prov. 1:24–25; Isa. 65:12; Jer. 29:19). Likewise, Wisdom's threats are couched in language very similar to the prophets (compare Prov. 1:26–27; Hos. 5:6).

Although she acknowledges that most of the biblical descriptions of Wisdom as a female are written in poetic form, Sinnott draws no conclusions from this. In the same way, she suggests, but does not pursue, a liturgical locus for the rise of this unique understanding of Wisdom. "It is very likely that the new articulation took shape primarily in the people's liturgical celebrations, as it is in celebrations and rituals that the people of Israel would seek to give meaning to their lives by 're-membering' Yahweh's deeds on their behalf in the past and celebrating them in the present." This is a potentially fertile insight that, unfortunately, is left at that.

In general, Sinnott argues that the figure of Wisdom functioned during the exile to assure Israel of God's sovereignty over creation and his continued care and presence at a time of chaos and alienation. As for the later text, the Wisdom of Solomon, which dates to the first century B.C., Sinnott sees a similar function for the female figure of Wisdom—"to encourage and persuade [Jews] to remain devoted to their ancestral heritage while living in a Hellenist milieu."

Unfortunately, Sinnott does little to synthesize her findings on Wisdom or to suggest deeper conclusions than that these texts functioned to give assurance and comfort to Israel in a time of trial. As a result, she stops short of answering a crucial question—why was Wisdom portrayed in feminine rather than masculine terms? In passing, she suggests that it could have been a reaction to the goddess worship in surrounding cultures. But she never ventures to explain why Wisdom is portrayed as a woman rather than a man.

Sinnott does a good job in helping us to see how Wisdom is depicted as the active and saving presence of God in the world. One would have hoped to see her suggest how this Old Testament portrait was taken up in the New Testament and in the patristic writings. However, she gives no consideration to how these texts have been treated in the interpretive traditions of either Judaism or early Christianity.

Nor does she pursue other possible intertextual avenues. She notices that the depiction of Solomon's passionate courtship of Wisdom is replete with nuptial imagery (Wis. of Sol. 8:1–8). But she does not consider the possible connections between personified Wisdom and the imagery found in Israel's other ancient wisdom book, the Song of Solomon. In addition, one wishes she had considered the relation of personified Wisdom to the broader scriptural theme of God's nuptial relationship with Israel (Isa. 61:10; Hosea 2:15–22).

~: Ellen Bradshaw Aitken :~

Jesus' Death in Early Christian Memory: The Poetics of the Passion,
Novum Testamentum et Orbis Antiquus 53
(Fribourg: Academic Press, 2004).

Form criticism has helped us see that, before the New Testament was written down, primitive narratives of Christ's passion and death were performed or enacted in the liturgy of the early Church—especially in the baptismal rite and in the celebration of the Eucharist. Indeed, numerous fragments of hymns, ritual prayers, and confessions of faith have long been identified, especially in the epistles, but also in the Gospels and the Apocalypse.

In this understated and evocatively written study, Aitken explores the complex interrelations of narrative and ritual, Scripture and liturgy, communal reminiscence and self-identity. It is an area that has been studied previously by scholars. However, Aitken has made a real contribution by focusing on how the Scriptures of Israel shaped the early Church's liturgical remembrance and, in turn, the formation of several pivotal New Testament texts. To excellent effect, Aitken yokes recent scholarship on the use of the Old Testament in the New to the insights of "speech act" and "reader response" theories. She is especially effective in showing how primitive accounts of the passion functioned as "performative language," that is, as language that not only describes historical events but also accomplishes or reenacts those events in the life of the early Christian community.

In incisive readings of select passages from 1 Corinthians (11:23–26; 15:3–5), 1 Peter (2:22–25), Hebrews, and the noncanonical Epistle of Barnabas, she pays particular attention to the formative influence of the Exodus and Israel's trials in the wilderness, as well as to psalms and prophecies about the righteous who suffer and are vindicated by God. In the early Christian liturgy, she sees "the reactualization of Scripture in the context of its performance in ritual. This process of reactualization entails an identification between the 'there and then' of Scripture and the 'here and now' of the present situation of the community." She sees also that, in the eucharistic liturgy, especially, the Church is defined as "the people with whom, by Jesus' death, God makes the authentic covenant."

The book's centerpiece is Aitken's beautiful reading of Hebrews. With Ernst Käsemann (*The Wandering People of God* [1984]), she sees the letter as "a continuous allusion to the community's liturgy." Indeed, she goes further in identifying the letter as "a mystagogic text [that] seeks to lead its already initiated audience into further understanding of the narrative and practice of the community." The letter presupposes a liturgical basis for the Church's identity, she observes, namely that "the people of God are defined by cultic acts"—particularly the ritual act of covenant renewal around the memory of Jesus.

Aitken powerfully demonstrates how "psalms, stories, hymns, liturgical patterns, and ritual observances" form a kind of network of quotation and allusion that connects the experience of the Christian initiate with Christ's suffering and Israel's experience in the wilderness. She is especially perceptive on the letter's use of typology to show how the Exodus narrative is "transferred from a geographical dimension into a cosmological dimension. The promised land is now the heavenly realm, and the journey is now one into the heavenly temple where Jesus is seated at God's right hand and where true worship is offered."

Aitken's study of the "poetics of the passion" opens a promising avenue for future study of the liturgical influence on New Testament texts. Indeed, her work helps us to recover some of the most ancient traditions regarding the Bible and the liturgy.

One of the oldest traditions is preserved in the letter of Pliny the Younger to the emperor Trajan, circa 112. Pliny tells how Christians gather to "sing . . . a hymn to Christ as if to a god . . . and to bind themselves by oath." This is the process that Aitken helps to put us in touch with—how these primitive hymns and oaths, or confessions of faith, enacted in the liturgy, helped shape the early Church's identity and the composition of Scripture.

Aitken has advanced our appreciation of how the life of Christ, the history of salvation, and the destiny of the individual meet and embrace in the liturgy of the Church. In an insightful, if brief, discussion of the Emmaus story (Luke 24), she even suggests that Christ himself is the source of this profound Christian sacramental understanding.

As she writes: "The Emmaus story speaks of 'recognition'—the moment of saying 'this is that'—through scriptural interpretation and cultic action. It thus narrates the instant of mimesis—the reenactment of the words of the Scriptures and the ritual meal in terms of Jesus. Moreover, Luke's story presents the risen Jesus as the one who first, for these disciples, engages in this action. Jesus is the one who interprets his suffering and death out of the Scriptures and performs the ritual of the meal in such a way that it reveals Jesus. Thus, Jesus is portrayed here as the authoritative initiator and interpreter of the cultic reenactment, just as the tradition quoted in 1 Corinthians 11:23–26 shows the earthly Jesus, before his death, as the interpreter of the cult legend of Israel and the initiator of the eucharistic cult."

~: Jacob Neusner :~

How Important Was the Destruction of the Second Temple in the Formation of Rabbinic Judaism?
(Lanham, MD: University Press of America, 2006)

In 70 A.D., the Temple at Jerusalem was burned to the ground by occupying Roman forces, ending the complex religious system of sacrifice and prayer that had defined Jewish self-identity for centuries.

The received scholarly consensus is that 70 A.D. changed everything for the Jewish people, bringing about a virtually new religious and cultural form—rabbinic Judaism. In the rabbinic system, Torah-study replaced a cult organized around Temple prayer and sacrifice, rabbis replaced the priestly caste, and the synagogue replaced the Temple as the center of Israel's social and cultic life.

In his latest book, the prolific Rabbi Neusner challenges this established version of the story. He admits that he himself is among those responsible for helping to establish the scholarly consensus. Here, however, he painstakingly reviews every "canonical" rabbinic document from the first to the seventh centuries for all possible allusions and references to the events of 70. His findings, he argues, cannot be used to support the prevailing thesis; indeed, he says, close study of the rabbinic literature flatly contradicts the present scholarly consensus.

"The destruction of the second Temple in 70 cannot be assigned a critical place in the formative history of rabbinic Judaism," he writes provocatively. "It was more than a footnote, but less then a principal text: to be coped with, not to be confirmed, let alone affirmed, as enduring."

Neusner does not deny that the Temple's destruction changed how Jews lived and worshipped, and that it inflamed eschatological expectations, as expressed in apocryphal writings such as IV Ezra and II Baruch, and political uprisings like that led by Bar Kokhba in 132–135. His analysis of the Mishnah, the great body of rabbinic law which dates to around 200, proves the practical impact the Temple's destruction had on Israel's liturgical life and conduct.

But if the loss of the Temple created a crisis in Israel's liturgy, Neusner argues that it was viewed as "temporary and superficial and raise[d] only some few minor questions of accommodation." He points out that hundreds of legislative provisions in the Mishnah are written as if the Temple were still standing and its cult still functioning. Such passages admit the loss of the Temple, but nonetheless speak of Israel's priesthood, sacrificial system, and holy places "in an ideal present tense of realized reality."

Throughout the Halakhah the corpus of rabbinic religious law, Neusner finds the institutions and cult of the Temple portrayed as perpetual, subject to the laws of divine promise, beyond the vicissitudes of history. The overriding sense is that 70 was not "decisive in the supernatural life of holy Israel, which is lived beyond time and above history." The holy city is still prescribed as the goal of pilgrimage; there are rules relating to Temple architecture and liturgy. (By comparison, there are surprisingly few stipulations for synagogue rites and worship.) The Tosefta Berakhot, which dates to 250, still calls for prayer and meal-offerings in the Temple, and instructs Jews, no matter where they live, to direct their prayers toward the Temple—even though the Temple, at that point, lay in ruins beneath a pagan temple erected by the Romans.

What accounts for this seemingly sublime serenity at the heart of early rabbinic Judaism? Neusner locates his explanation in the Aggadah, the collection of rabbinic commentary on Israel's Scriptures. The rabbis, Neusner argues, were thoroughly imbued with a biblical, "covenantal theology." They looked at the events of 70 through the eyes of Moses and the prophets, especially Jeremiah. In fact, Neusner also studies how the rabbinic documents represent and interpret the destruction, in 586 B.C., of the first Temple, built by Solomon, and the subsequent Babylonian captivity.

He concludes that the rabbis interpreted the events of 70 by "recapitulating" the categories of Scripture's prophetic-theological response to the events of 586 B.C. The Temple once again had been destroyed as a punishment for Israel's sins. But Israel's unique covenant relationship with God remained unperturbed. Following the lead of the post-exilic prophets, the rabbis taught that Israel, post-70, could still make atonement and receive forgiveness through acts of repentance and love, and a return to the Law.

Neusner sees nothing at all original in the rabbinic response. "The event of 70 taught no lessons not already imparted in 586." The rabbis' applications of Scripture are "derivative, a mere adaptation of received theological principles." Their proposals for renewal and restoration were nothing more than restatements of the Mosaic Law. The project of rabbinic Judaism was to find a way to live and think between the second Temple and the anticipated third and final one. "And the [rabbinic] answer proves blatant: Israel is to think precisely how and what Moses and the other prophets had taught them to think."

Hence, Neusner concludes that the events of 70 "made no difference" in the formation of rabbinic Judaism. The decisive event in the formation of the rabbinic mind was not 70 A.D. but 586 B.C. "The prophetic-rabbinic Judaism began, not in 70, but in the aftermath of 586 with the formation of Scripture—the Torah of Moses and the teachings of the prophets."

Readers will no doubt form different interpretive judgments about the conclusions Neusner draws from his research. He has gathered an impressive sourcebook that, along with his pointed and even poignant commentary, at times reads like a new addition to the rabbinic canon. But the evidence he presents could easily be marshaled to support a contrary conclusion—namely that the rabbinic literature was indeed, as the conventional wisdom holds, "a massive reaction to the catastrophe of 70."

Even conceding his point—that the rabbis advanced no fresh theological insights apart from recapitulating biblical ideas about sin and suffering, atonement and repentance, exile and restoration—his study gives us greater insight into the profound depths of their biblical worldview. Further, he helps us to see how, in their interpretations and applications of Scripture, the Word of God continued to live, instruct, and make claims upon the people of God.

∾ Emmanuel Kaniyamparampil ∾

The Spirit of Life:
A Study of the Holy Spirit in the Early Syriac Tradition
(Kerala, India: Oriental Institute of Religious Studies, 2003)

Jean Daniélou, in his magisterial, *The Theology of Jewish Christianity* (1958), long ago suggested that the ancient Syriac Church is the theological heir to the original form of Christianity that developed among the apostles and first disciples in Jerusalem. As Kaniyamparampil amply demonstrates in this excellent book, the Syriac tradition preserves a precious patrimony of theological reflection and exegesis, rich in ancient biblical and Judaic symbolism and allusion.

Based on the author's doctoral dissertation at the Catholic University of Paris, this book surveys the earliest writings in Syriac Christianity—the second-century *Odes of Solomon* (some of the earliest Christian hymns); the *Acts of Thomas*, which dates to the early third century; and the apologetic works of the sage Aphrahat, who lived in the first half of the fourth century. Although not studied directly, there is a generous consideration, too, of the writings of St. Ephrem, the fourth-century sage and exegete.

In all these sources, Kaniyamparampil identifies deep biblical roots for early Syriac pneumatology. Especially important is the depiction of the Spirit hovering over the primordial waters in the creation account (Gen. 1:2). In fact, he sees this depiction as the source for an ancient liturgical practice—the priest gently waving his hands over the gifts of bread and wine during the epiclesis, that part of the eucharistic celebration in which the Holy Spirit is called down to sanctify the gifts.

In addition to a profound engagement with the scriptural texts, Kaniyamparampil identifies the liturgy as the chief inspiration for Syriac devotion to the Spirit. "The Syriac authors are steeped in the biblical understanding of the Holy Spirit. . . . For early Syriac tradition, the liturgy was the privileged place of expressing its theological experiences and convictions. And it is in the celebration of the holy mysteries that we primarily observe the active faith in the Holy Spirit that this tradition encapsulates."

In an intriguing consideration of the Spirit's role in the Christian life, Kaniyamparampil explores the early feminine or motherly symbolism used to describe the Spirit's work. For instance, God the Father is depicted as a nursing mother in both the *Odes* and in the writings of St. Ephrem.

Kaniyamparampil notes that there is abundant literary evidence that "Judaeo-Christians cherished a mother figure of the Holy Spirit." And, as he points out, the Spirit's work is also described in maternal terms in the early Western tradition—by such respected theological writers as Hippolytus of Rome and Marius Victorinus. As he explains it, such symbolism was far from a heterodox effort to cast the godhead in sexual or gender-oriented terms. Rather it was an effort to reflect, in the light of biblical revelation, on "the action of the Spirit in the divine economy."

Again he finds a deep biblical substratum for feminine imagery of the Spirit. He notes that the Hebrew word for Spirit, רוּחַ, is feminine in gender. Likewise, he notes that רָחַף the related verb used to describe the Spirit's hovering over creation (Gen. 1:2), is also used to describe God's maternal care for his people in the desert—as a mother eagle "flutters over its young" (Deut. 32:11). He also detects the influence of the biblical figure of Wisdom, personified as both feminine and Spirit (see Wisd. of Sol. 7:7; 9:17; Sir. 14:22; 24:7; Prov. 8).

At the heart of this imagery, Kaniyamparampil also sees a decisive liturgical influence. Aphrahat described the Spirit performing a maternal role in bringing Christians to new life as children of God in the "spiritual womb" of baptism. This maternal-feminine imagery, Kaniyamparampil argues convincingly, expresses an original Jewish-Christian belief in the life-giving, salvific action of the Spirit, whereby the believer is regenerated and constantly renewed as a child of God.

In this forceful work of retrieval, Kaniyamparampil helps us to listen anew to some of the first Christian theologians and exegetes, and recovers for us their faith in the divine vitality and fecundity of him whom Aphrahat called "the Spirit of life."

~: **John J. O'Keefe and R. R. Reno** :~

Sanctified Vision:
An Introduction to Early Christian Interpretation of the Bible
(Baltimore: John Hopkins University, 2005)

There is a wide gulf between the way we read Scripture today and the way it was read by the first Christian fathers and teachers. In this slender and useful volume, O'Keefe and Reno endeavor to bridge that gap. Through close readings of Church fathers such as Origen, Athanasius, Irenaeus, and Augustine, the authors seek to disclose the inner logic of patristic exegesis. Though they cover a scholarly terrain that is already well trod, O'Keefe and Reno consistently offer fresh insights and new perspectives.

Central to the fathers' biblical theology and hermeneutic is their belief in the divine economy—in God's orderly plan for human history, a plan that culminates in the incarnation and cross of Christ. This belief unifies the disparate texts of Scripture into a single narrative, and requires that each text of Scripture be read in the context of "a divine order of events that stretches from the fall of Adam and Eve, through the election of Abraham, the Exodus of the Israelites, the reign of King David, the Babylonian exile, to the coming of Jesus Christ and his fulfillment of all things." This conviction also explains the importance of allegory and typology to the patristic mind, as the fathers sought to read the events of the Old Testament in light of the New and the New Testament in light of the Old.

One could have hoped for a fuller treatment of how patristic habits of interpretation originated in the New Testament authors themselves. But this book is, nonetheless, an excellent introductory text. It is distinguished by its unique emphasis on patristic exegesis as a spiritual science and ascetic discipline. In this, the authors demonstrate an undeniable concord between the goal of the divine economy and the pedagogy of Scripture—each aiming at the sanctification of the believer in Christ.

Their conclusion is a challenge and inspiration to students of the sacred page: "Unlike most modern intellectuals, the Church fathers recognized that good interpretation is most likely to flow from a good person. Patristic exegesis was, finally, a religious exercise. Right reading was the fruit of righteousness. . . . Insofar as the meaning of Scripture directs our attention toward the holiness of God, a reader can only follow and expound that meaning if the soul is purified and prepared to turn its vision toward the divine. 'The mind should also be cleansed,' writes Augustine, 'so that it is able to see [divine] light and cling to it once it is seen.' [*On*

Christian Doctrine, 1.10] The eye of the reader can only follow the Scriptures if vision is sanctified."

~: **Kevin J. Vanhoozer** :~

The Drama of Doctrine:
A Canonical Linguistic Approach to Christian Theology
(Louisville, KY: Westminster John Knox, 2005)

This is a big and admirable book with a big and admirable ambition—to restore doctrine to the center of Christian life, not only in the thinking of pastors and Church leaders, but in the minds and hearts of believers.

Vanhoozer builds his argument around a metaphor that evokes Hans Urs von Balthasar's multi-volume "theo-drama." He recasts theology as a form of *drama*, or, as he puts it, "a performance practice . . . of corresponding one's speech and action to the Word of God." In Vanhoozer's theological drama, the canon of Scripture is the script, the Church (understood in strictly spiritual, not institutional terms) is the company of actors, and the pastor is the director.

His discussion of the canon as a "covenant document" and of the Church as a covenant community is strong. God's covenant promises form Scripture's narrative unity and the new covenant, like the old, establishes with each believer "a personal relationship structured by solemn promises accompanied by ritual ceremonies."

One is frustrated, however, by Vanhoozer's crimped treatment of the sacraments and liturgy. He rightly argues that the Church, through Word and sacrament, is called "to present the body of Christ," and to "insert Church members into the drama of redemptive history by recalling the words and acts of God." He further maintains that there is a *"real presentation"* of Christ in the sacraments and that believers are *"really* drawn into the ongoing theo-dramatic action by the Spirit."

But *how* the covenant relationship is effected by the liturgy, and the nature of Christ's presence and agency in the sacraments, remain fuzzy. We are left with an unsatisfying brand of neo-Calvinism, in which the sacraments are mere symbolic performances or "rehearsals" for some true participation that awaits the age to come.

This criticism is not denominational grousing. It goes, rather, to the central question of Vanhoozer's book—how, in their performance of the faith, are believers to remain faithful to the normative "script" of Scripture? No attempt is made to engage the perspectives of older, more widespread Christian traditions, such as Catholicism and Orthodoxy. Vanhoozer presumes the superiority of the

Reformation's answers on everything from ecclesiology to sacramentology. Yet how these answers square with the practice and beliefs expressed in Scripture is again presumed but not demonstrated, let alone proven.

This is disappointing since Vanhoozer claims at the outset to be advancing a new "Catholic-Evangelical Orthodoxy." One hopes that, in the future, he will see how his theological project would only be enhanced by engagement with the sacramental realism that lies at the heart of Catholic and Orthodox beliefs about the divine liturgy and its relation to biblical salvation history.

Still, there is much to be learned from this book, and much ecumenical common ground to be found in Vanhoozer's equation of doctrine with wisdom: "The drama of doctrine is about refining the dross of textual knowledge into the gold of Christian wisdom by putting one's understanding of the Scriptures into practice. . . . The proper end of the drama is wisdom: lived knowledge, a performance of the truth."

~: Kevin J. Vanhoozer, gen. ed. :~

Dictionary for Theological Interpretation of the Bible
(Grand Rapids, MI: Baker, 2005)

Overall, this nearly 900-page volume is a remarkable achievement, the first of its kind to treat theology and exegesis as integrated disciplines and to presume a way of reading that synthesizes literary and historical perspectives with traditional notions of divine authorship and inspiration.

The basic methodological ground is covered well, with thorough, competent articles on topics ranging from patristic and medieval exegesis to speech-act and reader-response theories. Key figures in the history of interpretation, especially in the modern era, are well treated. The volume includes a good topical and scriptural index, although one would have hoped for an index of persons, as well.

Scot McKnight's article on "covenant" is very strong, especially in showing how God's covenants reveal his "intent from the beginning of history," and how that intention is ultimately liturgical—"to lead all humans to bow before him in eternal worship and praise." Christopher Seitz, in an excellent treatment of the "canonical approach," emphasizes the decisive role of the "rule of faith" as compelling the Church to an "interlocking and associative interpretation" that embraces both the Old and the New Testaments. Craig Bartholomew's articles on "biblical theology," and "deconstruction," especially, are also well conceived and helpful.

In her illuminating entry on "Jesus and Scripture," Edith Humphrey stresses the essential relationship between "the incarnate and inscribed Word." Darrell

Bock's entry on "messianism," and Daniel Trier's on "theological hermeneutics," are likewise well done. Peter Williamson adds a solid entry on Catholic biblical interpretation. Francis Martin contributes a short but highly packed article on "the spiritual sense." Robert Gagnon's article on "sexuality" is also a standout.

Among the articles on key biblical theologians, the short entry on Augustine is a little disappointing—essentially a biographical backgrounder but offering no perspective on the hermeneutical ideas and influence of this giant of the patristic era. By comparison, the dictionary allots more space to the entries on the Yale school of criticism and the "hero story." Michael Rota's treatment of Aquinas, however, is well developed. One would have thought that the seminal figure of Origen merited his own entry; however, he is treated in good articles on patristic biblical interpretation, allegory, and the spiritual sense of Scripture. One wishes, too, that the editors had chosen to consider scriptural inspiration and inerrancy in a separate article, rather than treating them in the entry on biblical authority.

Conspicuously absent is any serious appreciation of the importance and role of the liturgy and the sacraments. Or perhaps it is better to say that, in this regard, the dictionary too obviously shows its editors' Protestant and Evangelical biases. The history of interpretation, beginning within the canon itself, demonstrates that the liturgical life of the community was the privileged locus not only for hearing the biblical word, but also for its interpretation and actualization. This commonplace of historical and literary criticism, unfortunately, is nowhere reflected in the editing of this volume. It is telling that the general editor's essay on Paul Ricouer almost runs as long as the total space devoted to all topics such as liturgy and the sacraments.

It is genuinely puzzling that there are no entries on the crucial biblical-theological topics of "sacrifice" or "priesthood." Bryan Spinks' article on "liturgy," and Jeremy Begbie's on "worship," are slight, and almost seem like afterthoughts. Overlooking the pervasiveness of the liturgy and worship in both the Old and New Testaments, Spinks treats liturgy as a kind of devotional accessory that "encapsulates the good news and challenge of the holy Scriptures." Michael Horton's contribution on the sacraments treats the fifteen centuries before the Reformation in five sentences. Similarly, Graham Cole's article on the "Lord's Supper," begins, not with the ancient Jewish roots of the Eucharist, but with the debates between Luther and Zwingli.

There is much to laud in this impressive volume, which gathers between its covers some of the finest theologians and exegetes in the world today. It is a good beginning, and inspires hope that future editions will be more reflective of the full breadth of the Christian biblical and liturgical tradition.

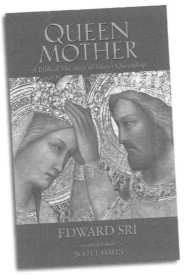

THE ST. PAUL CENTER
FOR BIBLICAL THEOLOGY
Reading the Bible from the Heart of the Church

Promoting Biblical Literacy for Ordinary Catholics . . .

- Free Online Bible Studies—*for beginners, intermediate, and advanced students*
- Online Library of Scripture, Prayer, and Apologetics—*more than 1,000 resources*
- Online Bookstore—*hundreds of titles*
- Popular Books & Textbooks—*on the Bible, the sacraments, and more*
- Workshops—*including parish-based training for Bible-study leaders*
- Pilgrimages—*to Rome and other biblical sites*

. . . and Biblical 'Fluency' for Clergy, Seminarians, and Teachers

- Homily Helps—*lectionary resources for pastors, and RCIA leaders*
- Reference Works—*including a comprehensive Bible dictionary*
- *Letter & Spirit*—*journal of biblical theology*
- Scholarly Books and Dissertations—*on topics of Scripture, liturgy, and tradition*
- Studies in Biblical Theology and Spirituality—*reissues of classic works in the field*
- Seminars and Conferences—*including ecumenical dialogues and themes*

ST. PAUL CENTER
FOR BIBLICAL THEOLOGY

2228 Sunset Boulevard, Suite 2A
Steubenville, Ohio 43952-2204
(740)264-7908
www.SalvationHistory.com

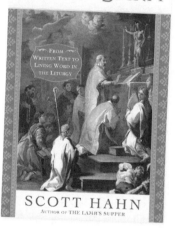